EIGHT EUROPEAN PLAYS

EIGHT EUROPEAN PLAYS

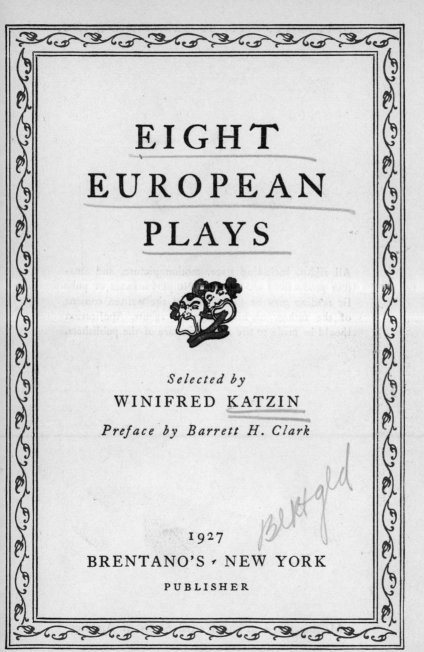

Selected by
WINIFRED KATZIN

Preface by Barrett H. Clark

1927
BRENTANO'S · NEW YORK
PUBLISHER

TO

BARRETT H. CLARK

Whose encouragement of foreign playwrights in
English translation is not the least of his
many services to the American drama.

412136

*Martine, Madame Legros, Glamour, Uncle's Been Dreaming,
The Fire in the Opera House, The Nüremberg Egg,* have been
translated by Winifred Katzin.

A Place in the World has been translated by Miss Katzin and
Barrett H. Clark.

PREFACE

This book needed a preface, and I have been asked to write it: fortunately, I think, for the cause of truth. As a critic of plays it is my duty to tell you honestly that the volume here offered for your delight is a misleading and fraudulent compilation. Just why I will tell you in a moment. As author of the preface I am going to blow my trumpet, of course, and tell you as emphatically as I can how good most of these plays are, but that isn't why Miss Katzin's octet needs a commentary.

The quality of the plays brought together within these covers is so exceptional that you are going to think the editor has struck a rich vein of ore in the contemporary drama of Europe, that all she has to do is to go on editing collections of masterpieces by new and comparatively unknown men, for the sake of us who are always delighted to find good things in the theater where we least suspected their existence.

But don't be deceived. This is not so. I don't know on just what basis Miss Katzin has made her selection, but she has managed to convey the impression that these plays are representative, presumably a few choice specimens of a far more extensive line of goods waiting only to be snatched up by enterprising producers. What she has actually done is to spot good plays wherever she has come across them, regardless of anything else, and she has searched in the most unlikely and unpromising places.

Who else, for instance, would think of reading Heinrich Mann's plays? Walter Harlan seemed so unlikely, and as for

Sternheim, it looks as though no one would have the courage or intelligence to offer his masterpiece to American readers after its twenty years' consecration in Middle Europe. And here is a young man who calls himself Bernard, a name beloved in France, for Tristan has delighted us since the days of the Spanish-American war. Jean-Jacques is his son, and how different he is in every respect from the author of *Le petit café!* Jean-Jacques must, as his countrymen would phrase it, give Papa furiously to think. How much he can do with just the shadow of a situation, a man and a woman! (Who was it who said that after all there are only two sexes?) *L'Invitation au voyage* is daintily spun out of what Bataille of Bernstein would have thrown into their waste-baskets as useless detail. We are given two of M. Bernard's plays, that we may realise that the man is not just a happy accident, for no one can be said to be a good dramatist until he has written at least two good plays. So for *Martine* we are grateful. Here the dramatist has captured something of the spirit of Eighteenth Century France; but how did he contrive to shake the dust of Paris from his characters?

Miss Katzin wisely lowers her curtain on the French exhibit after giving us the second of Jean-Jacques' plays. If anyone can find anything as good as these in the contemporary French theater it is surely the editor of this book.

Among the Germans she has had a wider field. I have already touched upon her choice of plays by men who stood preeminent as writers of fiction: *Madame Legros* and the Volmöller piece I am inclined to think exceptional among their authors' work, having something not quite of the theater still clinging to them. Yet this is a matter of small moment, for the Mann play possesses qualities that would have been lost if the writer had known more of the tricks of the trade than any artist ought to know.

Georg Kaiser is rather better known to us than the other

Germans in this collection, but it was wise to translate *The Fire in the Opera House,* in order to show us that the author of *From Morn to Midnight* has more than one string to his bow. I don't think either of these plays does full justice to the powerful if limited talent of Herr Kaiser, but Miss Katzin may be inspired some day to translate the entire *Gas* trilogy, if only to prevent producers from trying to make sense of the fragments when done independently.

The best play in the book is Sternheim's *Place in the World.* (Too bad the original title, *Der Snob,* had to be dropped.) This alone is worth more than the price of the volume. Here is a masterpiece. Ever since I saw it done at the *Kammerspiele* in Berlin in 1913, I have been trying to induce actors and managers to buy it. The truth of the matter is they couldn't understand it: Herr Sternheim writes a strange staccato stenographic style; he is as coldly bitter as La Rochefoucauld. Molière is his master, and humanity the butt of his shafts. *A Place in the World* is the most devastating satire I have ever seen. Who will act it? Have we a cast of players in America to do justice to it? I should like to see it tried out, anyway.

If the editor were here concerned with countries and movements and geographical limitations, we should ask her why she puts in an Italian play? Why indeed mix up France, Germany, and Italy? Well, she is concerned with plays, and nothing else. She selects what appeals to her. Why not? The San Secondo piece is new, brilliant, and good of its kind.

There is no further need, I think, in commenting on the contents of this collection. It is not an educational text-book; it doesn't show us the typical or representative work of any one national school of playwriting, and it is, as I have already pointed out, a deceptive thing. It is, on the other hand, an anthology unique among its kind, composed entirely of good plays, selected on the basis of personal predilection. I rather imagine that in accepting this play and rejecting that, Miss Katzin said to herself: "This is corking, and that is bunk!" Do you know a better method of procedure?

BARRETT H. CLARK

September, 1927.

CONTENTS

CONTENTS

GLAMOUR

by

JEAN-JACQUES BERNARD

CAST OF CHARACTERS

Marie Louise
Olivier, *her husband*
Jacqueline, *her sister*
Monsieur Landreau, *her father*
Gérard, *her son*

GLAMOUR

ACT I

*A semi-circular room, with windows almost all the way round, through
which a pine-forest can be seen extending in all directions.*
*In the foreground, right and left, a narrow section of the wall is pan-
elled to the ceiling. In the right-hand panel a door, in the one facing it on the left, a great stove of Sarreguemines faïence. Three low
armchairs round the stove.*
*The rest of the wall consists of very high windows, with a window-
seat all the way round.*
*On the left, facing the audience, a massive flat-topped desk. Chair to
match. On the right, a grand piano, the keyboard towards the background.*
*A small table. A small bookcase. Papers strewn about the desk. Flowers
on the piano and table. It is less the interior arrangement of the
room that gives its atmosphere than the pine-forest outside, gloomy
and overwhelming.*
*The windows are wide open. The rosy light of a fine September
afternoon is upon everything.*
LOUISE, *twenty-six years of age, is at the piano, playing a Chopin nocturne. After a moment, a clock outside strikes six. It is followed by
the shriek of a factory siren which lasts several seconds.* JACQUELINE,
who is twenty, appears at a window, and leans into the room.

JACQUELINE. Are you alone, Marie Louise?

MARIE LOUISE. [*Who has stopped playing.*] As you see, Jacqueline.

JACQUELINE. Have they changed the hours at the factory?

MARIE LOUISE. Yes; they come out at six now.

JACQUELINE. What were you doing?

MARIE LOUISE. [*Getting up.*] I'd just sat down at the piano.

JACQUELINE. Chopin nocturne!

MARIE LOUISE. Just for distraction. . . . Aren't you coming in?

JACQUELINE. Of course I am. [*She leaves the window and comes in
at the door.*] Were you in need of distraction?

3

MARIE LOUISE. I was bored with hearing about shoe-nails for an hour on end. I was with father and Olivier and the boy when some man came to go over the works. Olivier was busy and vanished. But father—you know how he adores doing that—asked me to go the rounds with them. The whole thing—factory, house, orchard, green-houses, garage, tennis-court—oh Lord! I should have gone with them to serve him wine in the drawing-room, but I honestly couldn't. I thought you and mother could do it.

JACQUELINE. I've not seen anyone. Who was it?

MARIE LOUISE. I don't even remember his name. Some manufacturer from Roubaix making a tour of the Vosges. Some kind of a cousin of Philippe Valbeille's I believe.

JACQUELINE. There's a man who doesn't believe in spoiling his friends with news of him, that Philippe Valbeille.

MARIE LOUISE. It's barely a month since he left.

JACQUELINE. It doesn't seem long to you, I notice.

MARIE LOUISE. Why on earth should it? The boy came here—we entertained him as well as we could. Then he went away, and we needn't think of him any more.

JACQUELINE. He might have written you a word of thanks. You and Olivier treated him absolutely like one of the family for three months.

MARIE LOUISE. That's nothing. He was the son of one of Father's business friends. If Father had a son to send to look over another factory, don't you think they'd do as much for him? You either do what you ought to, Jacqueline, or you don't. You'll understand that when you're married.

JACQUELINE. And in the meantime, dutiful soul, you allowed our dear father to hand out the wine himself to an important visitor. . . .

MARIE LOUISE. Oh well! There *are* times, you know . . . Besides Olivier doesn't care about that sort of thing one way or the other—thank Heaven!

JACQUELINE. But what about Father?

MARIE LOUISE. Oh! Father saw I'd rather not, so he didn't insist. If we had to go dispensing pleasant smiles every time a hardware merchant comes to see him, we'd have enough to do!

JACQUELINE. But he's so proud of us, and all that.

MARIE LOUISE. I know. He showed me off to that friend of his just now—"my daughter" . . . in the same way that he said "my house," "my garage," "my orchard." Do you know what we are? We're the factory accessories.

JACQUELINE. You're certainly at the end of your nerves. It's Father. . . .

MARIE LOUISE. Perhaps I am, rather.

JACQUELINE. You're not mad at Olivier for anything?

MARIE LOUISE. Olivier! Heavens, no! What on earth gave you that idea?

JACQUELINE. Then nothing else matters specially . . .

MARIE LOUISE. Or at all, Jacqueline. Isn't Olivier my own self?

JACQUELINE. You talk like a newly-wed. It's delightful.

MARIE LOUISE. I am still a 'newly-wed,' surely!

JACQUELINE. Eight years . . .

MARIE LOUISE. They've gone by so quickly. . . .

JACQUELINE. What an example your happiness is to me!

MARIE LOUISE. The credit is all due to Olivier. You see, there's more than mere love in my feeling for him—there's respect and admiration as well. Why do you smile?

JACQUELINE. I'm not.

MARIE LOUISE. Look at what he's done for the factory in these eight years. I don't say it to belittle Father. Still he *is* getting old now, and without Olivier . . . And look how highly thought of he is, all over the district.

JACQUELINE. Yes you have everything to make you happy; a good husband, a lovely child . . . I can't see *what* you have to complain of.

MARIE LOUISE. But I've not been complaining, Jacqueline. . . .

[*She goes towards the windows up-stage and stands dreamily staring out at the forest.*]

JACQUELINE. What are you looking at?

MARIE LOUISE. Those trees. . . .

JACQUELINE. What's the matter with them?

MARIE LOUISE. Nothing—I was just thinking. Hasn't it ever occurred to you that instead of these trees that never change their colour, we might have other kinds that would shed their leaves in autumn and grow fresh ones every spring?

JACQUELINE. If they gave us other kinds, you'd only want these back again. . . .

MARIE LOUISE. Possibly. Just now, father said to that man: "You can walk for an hour and a half in any direction from here, and you'll see nothing but pines, and pines, and pines . . . [*As if to herself.*] and pines . . . and pines. . . .

JACQUELINE. Why do you say that?

MARIE LOUISE. I don't know. Nothing. [*Comes back.*]

JACQUELINE. We get a lot of visitors though, luckily.

MARIE LOUISE. But what visitors! I'd just as soon see nobody.

JACQUELINE. You make up your mind about people too quickly. One gesture, one look, and they're marvellous or awful. What an imagination you must have!

MARIE LOUISE. I see more accurately than you think. But you know, all these people that come here one minute and are gone the next, give me a strange impression—of a window opening on the world outside and shutting again immediately. And what we've caught a glimpse of through it, is not for us.

JACQUELINE. You seem to wish it were. . . .

MARIE LOUISE. I? Heavens, no! They bore me to death, all of them.

JACQUELINE. Since Philippe Valbeille they've certainly not been particularly fascinating.

MARIE LOUISE. Oh, do stop talking about your Philippe. He was no more entertaining than any of the others.

JACQUELINE. There you go! If he'd been anything but the son of one of our customers, you'd have thought him perfectly charming.

MARIE LOUISE. He had hardware written all over him.

JACQUELINE. That was no fault of his.

MARIE LOUISE. He couldn't get rid of it even playing tennis. He had a way of hitting the balls that was exactly like the movement of that machine that flattens the nails on top.

JACQUELINE. I never noticed that.

MARIE LOUISE. Well, I did. There was something lacking in him— I don't know exactly what—anyway, something that you can't just pick up. . . . And as for when he recited poetry! I never could help hearing the buzz of the saw-mills. [*She laughs.*]

JACQUELINE. In other words, he got on your nerves.

MARIE LOUISE. Not even that. I admitted the nice things about him. Those fans he gave us, for instance—I thought that quite sweet of him. [*She picks up a fan from the piano, and smiles.*] Mine, of course—inlaid ivory—cherubs—as for *taste*, well . . . And that Baudelaire he brought me back from Epinal . . . [*She takes a book from the table.*] Naturally he wasn't to guess that my favourite poet was Chénier. I don't get much out of Baudelaire. Too obscure and complicated . . . [*Puts the book down.*] But anyhow, he meant well.

JACQUELINE. Olivier made more allowances for him than you.

MARIE LOUISE. Have you ever once heard Olivier speak ill of anyone? The trouble with him is that he doesn't know how to protect himself. Philippe used to come back here with us sometimes after dinner. That's where he used to sit. [*She indicates the three armchairs round the stove.*] Yes, the whole evening on that chair between us. Well, do you think Olivier ever tried to get rid of him? Nothing of the sort. They babbled together for hours on end. I was the one who had to shriek for mercy. One evening I fell asleep listening to them. He's such a child! But you can see how jolly it was for me!

JACQUELINE. You could have said something. . . .

MARIE LOUISE. Was it worth while for the few evenings Philippe had to spend here? As a matter of fact, I'm only too glad that Olivier is so easy-going. We don't let little annoyances bother us.

JACQUELINE. You've something to help you there—you're in love with each other.

MARIE LOUISE. Good Heavens, Jacqueline—you don't suppose I'm unhappy, do you?

JACQUELINE. How I wish I could find an Olivier. . . .

MARIE LOUISE. There can't be another just like him.

JACQUELINE. No—there can't be another woman just like you.

MARIE LOUISE. I'm as he has made me. [*The door opens.*] Here he is now.

[OLIVIER, *a man of thirty-five, enters.*]

JACQUELINE. We were in the midst of slandering you, Olivier.

OLIVIER. Really? May I hear?

MARIE LOUISE. You wouldn't like to. . . . [*Clinging to him.*] Good-evening, big one.

OLIVIER. Good-evening, little one.

JACQUELINE. Well, I'll leave you to it—you blessed love-birds!

OLIVIER. No, don't go, Jacqueline. I've got to be off again in a minute.

MARIE LOUISE. What an idea!

OLIVIER. A Monsieur Galais has been here . . .

MARIE LOUISE. I saw him. You ran away.

OLIVIER. With some scheme he wanted to submit to your father. I must go and look it over a minute.

MARIE LOUISE. Very well, look it over here while we talk. . . .

OLIVIER. [*Smiling.*] I wish I could, but your father's waiting. . . . [*He goes to his desk and takes some papers.*]

MARIE LOUISE. I was surprised at your staying down at the works so long. In another minute or two, I'd have been worried.

OLIVIER. [*Coming back to her, the papers in his hand.*] Well then, shuddering wife, listen to this: as I came across the factory yard, I met your son, all by himself!

MARIE LOUISE. Gérard, by himself?

OLIVIER. By himself, in the main yard. And do you know what he was doing?

MARIE LOUISE. No—no, tell me. . . .

OLIVIER. Unscrewing a hose. You will admit that for a child of seven, it was a curious occupation. . . . And guess what he was looking for—the pressure!

MARIE LOUISE. Oh!

JACQUELINE. [*Laughing.*] The pressure, indeed! And who told him about that?

OLIVIER. Apparently, Philippe. . . .

MARIE LOUISE. What business was it of Philippe's . . .

OLIVIER. Oh—it's nothing to make a fuss about—it's even very nice, I think. . . . By the way, I just had a letter from him. He's left Paris.

JACQUELINE. Philippe has?

MARIE LOUISE. *Bon voyage!*

OLIVIER. But where do you think the letter was from? Dakar. A sudden decision. He sailed a fortnight ago for America.

MARIE LOUISE. [*Surprised.*] America . . .

OLIVIER. Yes—on a big deal he'd spoken to me about—in the Argentine. It's been hanging fire for several months. He's in luck!

MARIE LOUISE. [*In quite a different voice.*] In the Argentine . . .

OLIVIER. Yes. Buenos Ayres and the other large cities. I'll tell you all about it tonight.

MARIE LOUISE. But . . . for long?

OLIVIER. How do you mean, for long?

MARIE LOUISE. Will it mean his staying down there?

OLIVIER. Certainly.

MARIE LOUISE. But how long?

OLIVIER. There's no telling. All his life, maybe—if things turn out well. In any case, there's a tremendous lot that needs to be done in all those countries. You can imagine . . .

JACQUELINE. That's what Father said the other day when we were talking about it.

MARIE LOUISE. Why—did you know?

JACQUELINE. Yes—I'd heard them discussing it.

OLIVIER. I say, let's get out some maps and encyclopædias if it would amuse you—it'll be a good way to spend a few evenings. [*He laughs.*] Well, good-bye—I'll not be long. [*He goes out.*]

JACQUELINE. If I were in Philippe's place, it would worry me rather to go off to the other side of the ocean, with the thought that there might be a chance of never coming back. Oh, but of course it must have cost him something! Although, for a single man . . . [*Noticing that Marie Louise is not listening.*] What's the matter?

MARIE LOUISE. The Argentine . . . How funny. . . .

JACQUELINE. Why funny?

MARIE LOUISE. I don't know. It doesn't seem to go with him. The Argentine . . . Well, he's very lucky.

JACQUELINE. That's all according.

MARIE LOUISE. The Argentine . . . Yes, it is funny talking about it when one's all walled in oneself.

JACQUELINE. How do you mean?

[*Marie Louise does not answer. She has gone back to the windows and stands looking at the forest.*]

JACQUELINE. [*Suddenly.*] Oh, that reminds me. . . . Just a minute; I'll be back. [*She opens the door.*] Oh, hullo, Father. . . .

[LANDREAU, *a man about sixty years old, enters.*]

LANDREAU. Olivier not here?

JACQUELINE. He's looking for you. I'll send him along if I see him.

[*She goes out.* MARIE LOUISE *has come downstage and stands beside the piano.* LANDREAU *sits down at the desk.*]

LANDREAU. I was to go over a scheme with that husband of yours. He must have forgotten.

MARIE LOUISE. [*Absently.*] Yes . . . no; he didn't forget. . . .

LANDREAU. While we were going over my place just now with that man who was here, a few changes occurred to me. Did you hear what I said?

MARIE LOUISE. Yes.

LANDREAU. Oh, you did. Well, don't you think my garage would be better in the new place I suggested?

MARIE LOUISE. Where was that, Father?

LANDREAU. At the back of the house, on the left coming from the works. We've got it now in what used to be the stables in your grandfather's time. But one must move with the age. What was practical for a stable is not so for a garage. Don't you agree?

MARIE LOUISE. Yes, Father.

LANDREAU. I shall make a big shed in the stables. One more will come in handy. Your mother won't have any objection—she's been complaining every winter for years that she's got nowhere to store her wood. But there's another thing that will interest you more than that.

MARIE LOUISE. What is it, Daddy?

LANDREAU. This little summer-house . . . [*Olivier comes in.*] Here comes Olivier. He'll give us his opinion too. Olivier, I was just beginning to discuss a plan I've got for this little summer-house. . . .

OLIVIER. [*Warningly.*] Now then . . .

LANDREAU. Don't worry—I've no idea of touching the interior. It's too charming to lay a finger on, with your desk here and Marie Louise's piano. Besides, it was part of your wedding present and it's yours to do as you like with. Still, I can't help thinking that in winter the few yards between it and the house are rather unpleasant to walk in the open, so I thought of having a corridor made for you. How about it?

OLIVIER. [*To* MARIE LOUISE.] What do *you* think?

MARIE LOUISE. I?

LANDREAU. No more rain, no more snow, no more wind. . . .

MARIE LOUISE. It's awfully nice of you, Daddy, but let's keep the rain and snow and wind, won't you? If the summer-house were connected with the house . . . it wouldn't be the summer-house any more, really.

LANDREAU. Oh! [*To* OLIVIER.] Is that *your* opinion too?

OLIVIER. Since it's hers.

LANDREAU. All right, don't let's talk about it any more. . . . Come and sit down, Olivier, and let's go over those Roubaix folks' proposition. [OLIVIER *sits down beside* LANDREAU. MARIE LOUISE *again turns back to her contemplation of the forest.*] They manufacture small stuff, you know, and have more orders than they can fill. But they're not ready to run the risk of enlarging their plant, just at this moment. . . .

OLIVIER. That's a mistake. It isn't as though they were just starting out.

LANDREAU. Well after all, that's their affair. They'd rather not give

out sub-contracts to other manufacturers in their line—so what's
their plan? Where do we come in?

OLIVIER. They want us to go in for small stuff, I suppose. We've never
done it, though.

LANDREAU. We could. . . .

OLIVIER. It's an idea, anyway. . . . What do they offer us?

LANDREAU. Three experts at their expense; a third share in the cost
of installing new machines. But chiefly, new clients for our own
specialty.

OLIVIER. Did you tell him we've already got more orders ourselves than
we can fill?

LANDREAU. His answer to that is that with the extra hands we'll
need to take on for them, we'll be able to manage whatever comes
in.

OLIVIER. But nearly all the men in Ambrosay are our employees already. . . . There are the other villages near by, of course. . . .
Well anyhow—what do you think of it?

LANDREAU. We might have considered it, if we hadn't our army contract. But with that covering two thirds of our entire output . . . I
can't see what we'd gain by switching over to anything new. Except
the English factories, we're the biggest shoe-nail plant in Europe.
What more do we want? Oh, if you've a mind to branch out later
on, you'll be perfectly at liberty to do so. But I doubt whether you'll
ever find any advantage in making anything but shoe-nails.

OLIVIER. I quite agree. . . .

LANDREAU. If you were to suggest anything but small stuff to these
Roubaix people, they wouldn't be interested, either.

OLIVIER. When must you give them an answer?

LANDREAU. Tomorrow morning; but I didn't hold out much hope.
[He gets up.]Ah! I'm glad we agree.

OLIVIER. I thought you seemed to be.

LANDREAU. I'll go now. . . . I'm sorry you don't like my idea for
a corridor. But young women have to be humoured! [Pats MARIE
LOUISE's cheek.] So long, my puss; I'll try and think of something
else. . . .

MARIE LOUISE. You're a darling, Daddy.

          [LANDREAU goes out.]

OLIVIER. He's awfully upset at your turning him down.

MARIE LOUISE. [Coming down-stage and sinking rather wearily into
a chair.] Didn't you understand?

OLIVIER. I understand these things very well, as you know. . . . What's on your mind?

MARIE LOUISE. On my . . . Oh, I was just thinking again of that letter . . . It's certainly odd . . .

OLIVIER. Letter?

MARIE LOUISE. From Philippe Valbeille. . . .

OLIVIER. Oh yes! Odd is certainly the word. I couldn't get over it, really. After spending a whole three months here and being treated like one of the family—then to vanish like that into thin air, and all of a sudden, four weeks later, a letter from Dakar! There's an excuse for him, of course—life in Paris provides little enough spare time. Besides our country quiet here, you know. . . . Well, this letter brings him back to grace! If I wanted to be spiteful, I could say he had another excuse besides—you were rather cool to him. . . .

MARIE LOUISE. I?

OLIVIER. I remember you wouldn't go to Epinal to see him off, because it bored you.

MARIE LOUISE. I never said so.

OLIVIER. Just as though you needed to. . . . However, that was the impression I got. And in the evening, when you mimicked the way he spoke and ate . . .

MARIE LOUISE. I don't remember . . . perhaps I did. . . .

OLIVIER. Unless you were only trying not to show you were upset. . . .

MARIE LOUISE. Upset? You're quite wrong, Olivier.

OLIVIER. Why shouldn't you have been? I'm that way too. When you come down to it, there's always something very distressing about people going away. . . . [Reflecting.] If that letter came from Dakar, he can't be very far from Buenos Ayres now. [A pause.] Don't you think so, too?

MARIE LOUISE. Think what?

OLIVIER. That it's distressing to see people go away?

MARIE LOUISE. Yes. . . . [Hastily.] Oh, but you exaggerate. . . .

OLIVIER. He wasn't a bad chap, Philippe. On the whole, we got used to him rather quickly. Not the sort one could make a great friend of, but pleasant to be with. Don't you think so?

MARIE LOUISE Yes. . . .

OLIVIER. It is rather funny to think that not a month ago, he was still sitting in that chair, joking with us, and now we'll most likely never see him again. . . .

MARIE LOUISE. [*Looking hard at the low armchair between the other two.*] Yes—in that very chair. How far away . . .

OLIVIER. No—not far away; that's just it. Oh well, I suppose it is, as something that will never be again. . . . Anyway . . . it's all a matter of impression, nothing else. . . . We'd hardly be giving Philippe another thought now, if he hadn't spent all those evenings with us together here; he was certainly entertaining company. Though I'm sure he'd have bored us in the long run, and it's just as well he left when he did. Still it is as though a page of our happiness had been turned. Do you see what I mean? That's of course what one means when one says that nobody ever does go away altogether.

MARIE LOUISE. Do you believe that? [*She looks about her and smiles somewhat painfully.*] Rather a terrifying idea, that is.

OLIVIER. [*Going to her.*] Yes—I do believe it has quite frightened you. . . . [*Laughing.*] Cheer up, impressionable one. Philippe Valbeille isn't the piano!

MARIE LOUISE. How do you mean?

OLIVIER. Where's your memory? The month they had your piano away, repairing it, you ceased to live. It made you quite ill to see its place empty.

MARIE LOUISE. Silly! [*She leans her head against him.*] Hold me very tight, Olivier . . .

OLIVIER. [*Holding her close.*] There, there! What is the matter with you?

MARIE LOUISE. . . . As if you meant to keep me and protect me. Like that, yes . . . I'm better now. [*She releases herself and moves away. Pause.*] Tell me . . . [*Hesitating.*] Are you working this evening?

OLIVIER. I may need your advice about a letter or two after dinner. Will you be free?

MARIE LOUISE. I'm always so glad when you need me for anything. I have the boy's homework to correct, but I'll have that done by then. [*A pause.*] Oh!

OLIVIER. What?

MARIE LOUISE. I wanted . . . to ask you something. . . .

OLIVIER. Ask away. . . .

MARIE LOUISE. It's still about . . . that . . . your talking of letters reminded me . . . have you any idea . . . in case you answer M. Valbeille . . . where to . . .

OLIVIER. I'll drop him a line in care of his father. They'll send it on. I'd not know how to go about addressing anything to him down there. . . .

MARIE LOUISE. To Buenos Ayres, do you mean?

OLIVIER. [*Smiling.*] Buenos Ayres . . . do you know that it's a city with a million inhabitants?

MARIE LOUISE. I know. . . . Don't laugh at me. . . . He might have told you in his letter where to . . .

OLIVIER. But he doesn't know himself where he's going to live.

MARIE LOUISE. Why, he'll go to a hotel, surely?

OLIVIER. He's cut out to make his career down there, that boy.

MARIE LOUISE. Yes. Did he . . . tell you in detail about his business?

OLIVIER. Nothing very much. See for yourself—I've got the letter somewhere.

MARIE LOUISE. Very well. . . . [*She goes up-stage again, opens a window, turns round and sees him watching her.*] It's rather sultry. . . .

OLIVIER. What are you doing now?

MARIE LOUISE. Now . . .

OLIVIER. I shan't do any more work till dinner. Would you like to go for a walk?

MARIE LOUISE. We might do that. . . . No—I don't want to. . . .

OLIVIER. All right, if you'd rather not. . . .

[*Knock at the door.* JACQUELINE *appears.*]

JACQUELINE. May one come in?

OLIVIER. You can always come in, Jacqueline.

JACQUELINE. Sorry if I disturbed you.

MARIE LOUISE. Don't be an idiot, Jacqueline.

JACQUELINE. She's in a bad temper, your wife. What have you been doing to her?

OLIVIER. Nothing serious. We went on talking a bit about Philippe Valbeille. So you see . . .

JACQUELINE. Oh yes—I see! If ever anyone got on her nerves, it was our handsome Philippe!

OLIVIER. [*To* MARIE LOUISE.] I'm not the only one, you see!

JACQUELINE. The thing that surprises me is that she hasn't put this fan into a drawer or something, now that he's safely out of the way. [*She takes the fan from the piano, and opens and shuts it as she talks.*]

MARIE LOUISE. Do let that fan alone, Jacqueline! [JACQUELINE *looks at her in astonishment.*] There's no point in breaking a thing that might have cost a good deal. Is there, Olivier?

OLIVIER. There's not much point in breaking anything, that I can see.

JACQUELINE. Oh, my Lord! [*Puts the fan down with great care.*] I say, you know . . . Philippe's letter reminded me that I had a photograph of him. Inside a book he left behind. . . .

OLIVIER. How funny, just as we thought we hadn't any reminder of him at all. . . .

[JACQUELINE *is about to sit down in the middle armchair in front of the stove.*]

MARIE LOUISE. [*Sharply.*] Don't! . . . [*With a forced smile.*] Please sit over there. . . .

[*She indicates at random the corner where the desk is.* JAC-QUELINE *takes the chair, while* OLIVIER *goes towards her. All three look at the photograph.*]

JACQUELINE. What do you think of it? Does it remind you of the way he hit the balls like the machine for crushing the nail-heads? [MARIE LOUISE *does not answer.*] And recited poetry like a saw-mill—do you remember. . . . [*She laughs.*]

OLIVIER. It's funny.

MARIE LOUISE. What's funny about it?

JACQUELINE. It makes him quite good looking, doesn't it?

OLIVIER. A very good likeness, I think.

JACQUELINE. Very.

MARIE LOUISE. I don't think it is, at all.

OLIVIER. Still, it's perfectly recognisable.

JACQUELINE. It's Philippe to the life.

MARIE LOUISE. Hardly! I think it's a wretched photograph.

OLIVIER. Oh no, indeed it isn't, really.

JACQUELINE. No question about it.

MARIE LOUISE. [*Dreamily—looking at it.*] Very well.

OLIVIER. Now, here's a curious thing. It's less than a month since the man was here, and already we can't agree about his likeness in a photograph. One of us three has decidedly too much imagination.

MARIE LOUISE. [*Moving away, with a shade of annoyance.*] Say it's I, and let's stop talking about it.

OLIVIER. Not at all; it simply goes to show that we haven't all the same eyes. Which is right and natural. [*Looking at the photograph.*] Of course when we saw him here, chatting with us in front of this stove in the evenings, his features seemed a bit finer-drawn than they are in this, but the lens is always less lenient than the eye. Here, look at it nearer. . . . [*He hands it to* MARIE LOUISE.]

MARIE LOUISE. [*Takes it without looking at it.*] I saw it quite well, thanks.

JACQUELINE. In a day or two, he'll have arrived at the Argentine.

OLIVIER. He may be there already.

JACQUELINE. That's a voyage I'd love to make, wouldn't you, Olivier?

OLIVIER. All voyages are tempting—especially when one can't make them. [*He laughs.*] Aren't they, Marie Louise?

MARIE LOUISE. Don't laugh like that.

OLIVIER. [*Surprised for a moment.*] I wasn't thinking . . .

MARIE LOUISE. [*Rushing to him.*] Don't! I'm being perfectly hateful . . . please go away and leave me alone. You'd much better . . .

OLIVIER. It's all right, stupidhead; you're not so very hateful. . . . Smile? . . . Admit that it's a good likeness, though.

MARIE LOUISE. [*With a forced smile.*] Do go, darling. . . . I've been talking nonsense. I'll see you at dinner. . . .

OLIVIER. She's throwing me out. And I'm going. I've no self-respect. So long, Jacqueline. [*In the doorway, he throws a kiss to* MARIE LOUISE.] There!

MARIE LOUISE. [*Returning it.*] There! (*But he has hardly left the room when her hand falls limply. For a moment she stands looking at the doorway, then goes back to her contemplation of the forest.*)

JACQUELINE. [*Softly humming.*]

> 'Neath the blue sky of the Argentine,
> All the women are divine . . .

MARIE LOUISE. [*Turning, exasperated.*] Jacqueline!

JACQUELINE. Yes?

MARIE LOUISE. You *are* annoying!

JACQUELINE. You mean my singing annoys you? I happened to be thinking of the Argentine, so . . . Don't you remember, all the soldiers were singing that tune in Epinal?

> 'Neath the blue sky . . .

MARIE LOUISE. Oh, do stop! [JACQUELINE *looks at her in astonishment.*] Oh well, sing if it amuses you. Why should I care?

JACQUELINE. Certainly I shall sing, but somewhere else. You don't seem very sprightly today.

MARIE LOUISE. Please yourself.

JACQUELINE. [*Looks at her, shakes her head and murmurs.*] Well,
well! [*She goes out, singing.*]

'Neath the blue sky of the Argentine . . .

[MARIE LOUISE *makes another movement of exasperation.*
Left alone, she stands very still, examining PHILIPPE'S *portrait.*
Then suddenly she tears it to pieces, and watches the fragments
as they scatter to the floor.]

CURTAIN

ACT II

*A year and a half later. Late afternoon in March. Nothing is changed
in the room; the three low armchairs are still before the stove,
and the fan still lies on the piano.*

MARIE LOUISE *is alone on the window-seat, reading.* OLIVIER *comes
in. She is engrossed in her book and does not hear him. He stands
watching her for a moment, then comes further into the room.*

OLIVIER. What are you reading?

MARIE LOUISE. [*Turns and springs to her feet, startled.*] You here,
Olivier?

OLIVIER. Did I frighten you?

MARIE LOUISE. It doesn't matter. . . .

OLIVIER. What were you reading?

MARIE LOUISE. Baudelaire . . . one of Baudelaire's poems. [*She
puts the book hastily down on the small table.*]

OLIVIER. Well—your tastes have changed.

MARIE LOUISE. What?

[OLIVIER *tidies some papers on his desk.* MARIE LOUISE *takes
up some sewing and works at it absent-mindedly.* OLIVIER *comes
back to her.*]

OLIVIER. What is that you're working on? You don't seem very keen
on doing it.

MARIE LOUISE. Well, it was *your* suggestion, my going in for needle-
work—I'm afraid it's not much in my line, though.

OLIVIER. I don't want you to do anything that bores you.

MARIE LOUISE. You are very kind.

OLIVIER. Don't make fun of me, Marie Louise.

MARIE LOUISE. I'm not making fun of you—I mean it. It is appalling
how kind you are.

OLIVIER. What do you mean, appalling?

MARIE LOUISE. [*After a pause.*] You haven't told me yet what you
want me to say to your tailor.

OLIVIER. Just tell him not to bother; I don't need anything. Next
month, say . . . It's nice of you to do these things for me.

MARIE LOUISE. Isn't that what I'm here for?

18

OLIVIER. Oh, I suppose so. . . .

MARIE LOUISE. [*Getting up.*] I'm going for a walk in the forest. . . .

OLIVIER. I say, Marie Louise . . .

MARIE LOUISE. Yes?

OLIVIER. You've not forgotten our arrangement with Lise and Arthur, have you?

MARIE LOUISE. No—we said we'd spend the last of the afternoon with them. [*She sits down again.*] Well, we shall. Just like yesterday and the day before yesterday.

OLIVIER. [*After a pause.*] That wasn't very nice.

MARIE LOUISE. No, Olivier; it wasn't at all nice. I'm sorry.

OLIVIER. They're only here for a week.

MARIE LOUISE. Yes, I know. It was disgusting of me. There—I've apologized.

OLIVIER. After all, it isn't as though we see so much of them. I'm awfully fond of them, you know—not because she's my sister . . . and their marriage always seems to me so much like our own. . . .

MARIE LOUISE. Do you think so?

OLIVIER. Yes—their eleven years, and our nine and a half have been . . . but you know.

MARIE LOUISE. Who should know better than I?

OLIVIER. [*Gently.*] So you please me very much when you are nice to them.

MARIE LOUISE. Am I ever not nice to them?

OLIVIER. I know you will be, for these last few days.

MARIE LOUISE. I'll promise that—to please you. Because, you know . . . I don't think quite as much of them as you do.

OLIVIER. You used to endure them more graciously, then.

MARIE LOUISE. One can't help one's feelings, Olivier. However, you shall have nothing more to complain of. . . . When you ask me so sweetly, I . . .

OLIVIER. You're always saying that, Marie Louise. But every now and then you forget again. The fact is, your nerves are all unstrung these days, and the moment anything begins to grate on you . . .

MARIE LOUISE. Don't exaggerate, Olivier.

OLIVIER. I'll say this though—when we *do* have a crowd, I hate to bother you with entertaining them, but when it can't be avoided, I try to be as tactful with you as possible.

MARIE LOUISE. I know you do, Olivier. I'm not finding fault; truly I'm not.

OLIVIER. So you can see, I've good reason to feel pretty worried about you. . . .

MARIE LOUISE. Worried? Why? . . .

OLIVIER. Because I don't seem able to understand you any more. You are sad, and . . .

MARIE LOUISE. Sad? I? Nervous? Sad? What else, I wonder. I assure you, Olivier, you're entirely mistaken. Look at me—I'm perfectly calm.

OLIVIER. At this moment, yes. That's why I'm talking to you while there's a chance. You are going to say there's nothing whatever the matter with you. . . . I wish I knew what it was . . .

MARIE LOUISE. But honestly, Olivier—nothing *is* the matter with me. I think I could be called an extremely happy woman, don't you?

OLIVIER. If you knew how you hurt me, Marie Louise.

MARIE LOUISE. Why? Because I tell you I'm happy?

OLIVIER. I dare say other men would be satisfied with what you give me—yes—you're faithful; you're honest with me; you keep my house beautifully. A man without a certain ideal would find that ample, no doubt . . . I can't explain, but you know what I'm trying to say. . . .

MARIE LOUISE. [*Weakly.*] No—I don't . . .

OLIVIER. [*Takes her hand between both of his, and smiles down at her.*] You queer little thing!

MARIE LOUISE. Why do you say that?

OLIVIER. [*Gravely.*] And how terribly serious you have grown.

MARIE LOUISE. Serious?

OLIVIER. Let's see—how long is it, now, since I first began to notice it? [*Pause.*] More than a year, yes. Has life begun to mellow you, darling—has my little girl actually grown up? And what a very grave person she has become! What were you when we married? Nothing but a child. And we were so happy that you simply remained a child all those years. Those pretty eyes never knew the shadow of sorrow. But it's all different now . . . [*He touches her forehead.*] What are you hiding in there? So many thoughts . . . I can feel them . . . but so deep down . . . so far away. . . .

MARIE LOUISE. No, Olivier—no! What makes you talk like this?

OLIVIER. I used to believe I knew you, but I don't know any more whether I do or not. . . .

MARIE LOUISE. You shouldn't upset yourself over nothing at all,

Olivier. It's foolish. You know me better than you think. Reconcile yourself to the idea that it's the way I'm made, and don't waste another thought on it.

OLIVIER. When you talk this way, I'm tempted to believe you—but how can I be certain that you mean it?

MARIE LOUISE. But of course I mean it, dearest. [*She stands beside him, leaning against him affectionately. She looks up at him and smiles.*] You can feel that I do.

OLIVIER. [*Hesitantly.*] Are you—disappointed in me?

MARIE LOUISE. Olivier!

OLIVIER. Do you mean that, too?

MARIE LOUISE. Darling—what a question! Where on earth can you get such ideas!

OLIVIER. I've had a feeling that something has been . . . in a way, eluding me . . . and I've wondered whether it wasn't perhaps my own fault that I . . .

MARIE LOUISE. You're not to say such things, Olivier—I won't have it, do you hear? [*She is behind him now—and covers his face with her two hands. But her own eyes are filled with tears.*]

OLIVIER. [*After a moment, takes her hands away.*] Ah, little witch! You are always unanswerable . . . and I'm a lout and an awkward fool. . . .

MARIE LOUISE. You are nothing of the sort. [*She has dried her eyes hastily, and now avoids looking him in the face.*]

OLIVIER. I don't know what to do to make you happy.

MARIE LOUISE. What more can you want to do than you have done already?

OLIVIER. A thousand things! Satisfy all your wishes—give you . . . I don't know . . . more jewels, more frocks . . . Would you like that?

MARIE LOUISE. If it would please *you*. . . .

OLIVIER. A car . . . a two-seater, all to yourself . . .

MARIE LOUISE. [*Indifferently.*] Very well. . . .

OLIVIER. A host of new friends . . . parties . . .

MARIE LOUISE. Yes . . .

OLIVIER. Books, perhaps. You're really fond of books. Or a few odds and ends of antiques . . . no? Or pictures . . . ?

MARIE LOUISE. Yes, Olivier.

OLIVIER. Or if you're a little tired of Ambrosay, what would you say to a trip to Paris? Yes, that's it—let's have a week in Paris. It's the season now, and there'll be theatres and races. . . . Would you enjoy that?

MARIE LOUISE. Yes . . .

OLIVIER. And not a single one of all the things I've said, would be the thing you're longing for.

MARIE LOUISE. Don't rack your brains over it then, dear. The best you can give me is in yourself—you know that.

OLIVIER. A charming little speech! Is it to point the lesson that happiness can only be within? Is that what you mean?

MARIE LOUISE. [*Her thoughts elsewhere.*] Yes . . . I suppose so. What time is it?

OLIVIER. Ten to six.

MARIE LOUISE. When are we to see Lise?

OLIVIER. At six.

MARIE LOUISE. [*Resignedly.*] We'll be there. Tell me, Olivier, have you ever been late in all your life?

OLIVIER. Not very often.

MARIE LOUISE. Do you know . . . what Jacqueline called you the other day . . . just in fun of course?

OLIVIER. No, what?

MARIE LOUISE. The chronometer.

OLIVIER. [*Laughs.*] That's one on me, isn't it?

MARIE LOUISE. [*Dreamily.*] Chronometer [*Pause.*]

OLIVIER. Are you ready? We ought to be going.

MARIE LOUISE. What is the time by you?

OLIVIER. Are you being spiteful, Marie Louise?

MARIE LOUISE. Oh no—I didn't mean it. I was only joking. Aren't they with Jacqueline, though?

OLIVIER. I'm sure they must be. They've become inseparable, those three.

MARIE LOUISE. She's going back with them to Epinal for a week. It is very plain to me that Arthur's young brother stands an excellent chance of becoming my brother-in-law.

OLIVIER. Would you be pleased?

MARIE LOUISE. If he made Jacqueline happy—that would be the main thing. But she'll be all right. She'll never have a wish that her husband won't be able to satisfy. She'll have her home, and her good peaceful bourgeois life, plenty of funds, children, Paris twice a year, friends of their own kind, little celebrations. . . . Jacqueline is not troubled with—dreams. . . .

[*An embarrassed silence falls between them.* MARIE LOUISE *stands gazing at the forest through the windows at the back.*]

OLIVIER. Come, let's go. [*A boy of nine appears outside the window.*]

GÉRARD. Hoo! Hoo!

MARIE LOUISE. [*Startled.*] Gérard! How you startled me!

GÉRARD. Sorry, mums! Please may I sit here, and do my lessons?

OLIVIER. Yes, if you like.

GÉRARD. I'll stay over here then, under the window. I'll be quiet.

[*He settles himself, with his back turned to the room—only his head is visible.* MARIE LOUISE *leans out a little way to see the book he is studying, but comes in again immediately, visibly agitated.*]

MARIE LOUISE. [*To Olivier.*] Please, Olivier, go by yourself. Tell them I've a headache and have gone to lie down. . . .

OLIVIER. Do you really think you'd . . .

MARIE LOUISE. I'd rather stay with Gérard.

OLIVIER. Very well . . . I'll make your apologies.

MARIE LOUISE. Good-bye then. [*Olivier goes out. For a moment,* MARIE LOUISE *stands very still. Outside* GÉRARD'S *head is seen, bent over his book.* MARIE LOUISE *goes to the window, and calls to him softly.*] Gérard . . . [*The boy does not hear, so she tries again, louder.*] Gérard!

GÉRARD. Yes, mums?

MARIE LOUISE. What are you working at there? Better come inside— I can't talk to you out of the window like this. Come, jump through. [*The child looks at her in surprise.*] Yes, you may, just this once. Get up on the chair. [*She helps him onto the chair, and from there to the window-sill.*] Goodness—what a weight you are, for eight years old!

GÉRARD. I'm nine.

MARIE LOUISE. [*Holding him on the window-sill.*] Of course you are! I beg your pardon, darling. So he is, my little man—he's nine years old! [*Gérard jumps into the room.*] Well done! That was a splendid jump! Wait though—you're forgetting your book. You'll not have your lesson learnt, and it will be all my fault, and Mlle. André will be very cross.

GÉRARD. Oh, I know it already.

MARIE LOUISE. [*Taking the book in her hand.*] Is it stiff?

GÉRARD. No, only review. That's what she makes you do in the Easter holidays.

MARIE LOUISE. Quite right too. Shall I hear you?

GÉRARD. Oh yes, mums—please. Won't she be surprised!

MARIE LOUISE. Why?

GÉRARD. Because I'll know it ten times better if I can go over it with you.

MARIE LOUISE. [*Turning over the pages.*] Aren't you very good at geography?

GÉRARD. Hm . . . middling . . .

MARIE LOUISE. Where are you up to? What was it I saw you studying just now?

GÉRARD. America.

MARIE LOUISE. North?

GÉRARD. Both—it's review.

[*While* MARIE LOUISE *is looking for the right page, he plays with the Baudelaire on the small table.*]

MARIE LOUISE. [*Agitated.*] Put down that book, Gérard. [*She looks round the room.*] Come, let's not stay over this side; the light has all gone. We'll be better here. Ready?

[*The light has in fact, begun to fade. She comes down-stage and lights a small lamp.* GÉRARD *stands beside her.*]

GÉRARD. [*Looking at the book in her hand, begins to laugh.*] You're holding it upside down, Mother!

MARIE LOUISE. [*Turning it the right way.*] There now—go ahead . . .

GÉRARD. Oh—aren't you going to ask me?

MARIE LOUISE. Very well, if you'd rather. What are the principal states of South America?

GÉRARD. South? That's over the page.

MARIE LOUISE. I know. Well?

GÉRARD. The principal states of South America? [*Reels off the lesson in a monotone.*] The principal states of South America are Brazil, Chile, the Argentine Republic, Columbia, er . . . er . . . Bolivia, Peru . . .

MARIE LOUISE. No, no, Gérard, that won't do. That's repeating your lesson exactly like a parrot. You don't sound as though you understand a word you're saying. I doubt whether you even know where those countries are.

GÉRARD. Of course I do, Mums.

MARIE LOUISE. Tell me, then; where is . . . let me see . . . yes, where is the Argentine?

GÉRARD. Don't know . . . [*Hastily bethinking himself.*] In America!

MARIE LOUISE. Really, darling, there's no use whatever in learning lessons this way. If no one's going to explain things to you, you might just as well put all your books away for good. You've been reeling off a string of names, but you don't seem to have the faintest idea that they stand for enormous countries, with fields and forests and rivers and great big cities full of houses and people and trains and noise and trees. Do you understand?

GÉRARD. Are they bigger than Epinal, the cities?

MARIE LOUISE. Some of them—oh Heavens, yes. Much, much bigger.

GÉRARD. Which, that you know?

MARIE LOUISE. I don't *know* any of them, but I've heard people who do, talk about them. It's all a very long way from here, you know dear . . . ever so far away—as far away as a fairy-tale. . . .

GÉRARD. Shall we be going there, ever?

[*A long pause. The dusk falls deeper.*]

MARIE LOUISE. No—not we. You know that is impossible.

GÉRARD. Not even when I'm grown up?

MARIE LOUISE. [*Looking hard at him.*] Yes, *you* might—one of these days.

GÉRARD. What about the rivers, mums? Tell me about them.

MARIE LOUISE. The rivers?

GÉRARD. Can the people see them?

MARIE LOUISE. See them? Why, they're the most important thing in the whole land. If it weren't for the rivers—that flow so slowly under the weight of their great burden of legends—if it weren't for the rivers . . . I wonder if it would have the same . . . [*She stops.*]

GÉRARD. The same what, Mother?

MARIE LOUISE. I'll come to that later on.

GÉRARD. Then will you tell me about the rivers now?

MARIE LOUISE. What shall I tell you about them, Gérard?

GÉRARD. Everything.

MARIE LOUISE. That's hard to do when you've never seen them.

GÉRARD. Are they the biggest in the whole world?

MARIE LOUISE. That I don't know. But they are certainly the most beautiful. I read somewhere that everything in those parts is more extraordinary than anywhere else. The flowers and all the other plants are fabulous—ten times the size of ours.

GÉRARD. Ten times—I say!

MARIE LOUISE. Yes; the trees too. They are so immense that many people holding hands can't reach round their trunks. And the wild animals are huge—there's nothing like them to be seen in France. So you can imagine what the forests and mountains and waterfalls must be like. Some of the rivers are so wide that you can't see the opposite bank at all. And they say . . . I don't know where I read that, though . . . that they are continually changing colour.

GÉRARD. How do you mean, mums?

MARIE LOUISE. [*Goes on talking, as if lost in space.*] Sometimes— that must be in the morning, just at sunrise—they are all pink, like roses—imagine! And on the very finest days, they are as blue as blue can be. Then there are times when a kind of fog lies very low on the surface of the water and makes it look as though it had been changed into milk. And when the sky is overcast and stormy, they turn grey and metallic, like rivers of lead.

[*A pause. She remains very still.*]

GÉRARD. [*Timidly.*] What else, mums?

MARIE LOUISE. [*With a violent start, as though recalled abruptly out of a dream.*] What else? [*She looks long at the child and suddenly takes his head between her hands.*] Ah, why shouldn't *you* understand? . . . No, no . . . what am I saying?

[*She releases him and rises, trembling. He stands watching her with wide eyes, as she goes to the piano. She sinks onto the stool and sits for a moment, dreaming silently at the keyboard. Very softly she begins to play Duparc's "L'Invitation au Voyage." She sings:*]

> Mon enfant, ma sœur,
> Songe à la douceur
> D'aller la-bas vivre ensemble;
> Aimer à loisir,
> Aimer et mourir
> Au pays qui te ressemble . . .

[OLIVIER *has come in as she sings the closing lines, and stands in the doorway watching her. It is now almost dark. The music weakens and seems to die under her fingers.* MARIE LOUISE *falls into a silent reverie.*

[OLIVIER *touches a switch and bright light suddenly fills the room.* MARIE LOUISE *rises abruptly and shuts the piano. She stands supporting herself against the instrument, completely unnerved, as though caught in a guilty action.*]

OLIVIER. *L'Invitation au Voyage.* . . . This passion for Baudelaire is really . . .

MARIE LOUISE. [*Trying hard to summon a smile.*] On the contrary . . . I've . . . I've been putting Gérard through some homework.

OLIVIER. Homework?

GÉRARD. Yes, daddy—we've been going over my geography review. South America.

[*A long look passes between* OLIVIER *and* MARIE LOUISE.]

OLIVIER. [*In a dead voice.*] All right, sonny—you can run along, now.

[GÉRARD *goes out. Silence. They stand facing each other.* OLIVIER'S *eyes are fastened upon his wife's face, and she meets them without faltering. Obviously he is waiting for her to speak, but she says nothing. She remains for a moment poised in doubt, then suddenly her head droops. She crosses the room and goes out without a word.* OLIVIER *watches her, completely bewildered. He hastens after her to the door and calls.*]

Marie Louise! Marie Louise!

[*She reappears almost immediately. He takes her hand, and leads her trembling, towards the middle of the room.*]

Marie Louise, I want to . . . I'm . . . I'm so . . . worried . . .

[MARIE LOUISE *almost inaudibly repeats his word.*]

OLIVIER. Isn't there something . . . you'd like to tell me?

MARIE LOUISE. [*Hanging her head.*] Tell you?

OLIVIER. Isn't there? Really?

MARIE LOUISE. No, Olivier. There's nothing.

OLIVIER. I thought you . . .

MARIE LOUISE. What?

OLIVIER. I don't know. . . .

MARIE LOUISE. Is that all you called me for? [*She is about to leave the room again, when a bell rings outside. They stand listening, then exchange another long look. Pause. She goes to him.*] There's the dinner bell . . . calling us . . . today, tomorrow, for ever and ever . . . and ever. . . .

[*She puts her hand on his shoulder and pushes him gently towards the door. Behind him, furtively, she brushes away her tears.*]

CURTAIN

ACT III

*The same scene. The windows are shut. Snow outside. The stage is
empty for a moment, then* MARIE LOUISE *and* JACQUELINE *come
in. Eight months later. December.*

MARIE LOUISE. At last we can have a moment's peace.

JACQUELINE. Are you sure Mother won't be hurt at my running away
from her as soon as I arrive?

MARIE LOUISE. You can go back presently. She knows we like to have
a little time to ourselves when you come over. We've been making
polite conversation for three quarters of an hour, so I think we've
earned this.

JACQUELINE. [*Smiling.*] I don't call that very flattering to one's
parents and husband.

MARIE LOUISE. Our parents have never been very exacting, and as
for Olivier, he couldn't be angry with me if he tried. In any case,
he's busy today. And you know, Jacqueline, even *you* can't be sorry
to get away from your husband for an hour or so occasionally, even
though you are desperately in love.

JACQUELINE. I don't find myself hunting for opportunities! In fact,
I only came away from Epinal today for these few hours because
he had to be off somewhere for the whole afternoon.

MARIE LOUISE. Yes . . . you're a good wife.

JACQUELINE. So are you, for that matter.

MARIE LOUISE. [*After a pause.*] . . . so am I . . . of course.

JACQUELINE. Well, aren't you going to ask me my news?

MARIE LOUISE. Have you any?

JACQUELINE. Oh yes—very special.

MARIE LOUISE. Hurry up and tell me, then. Yours first and mine after.
You come so seldom any more.

JACQUELINE. I'm afraid my doings don't interest you much.

MARIE LOUISE. You've changed your cook . . . you've had the Pre-
fect to dinner . . . you've . . .

JACQUELINE. You're a detestable person, Marie Louise! If that were all, I shouldn't have kept it until we were alone. No . . . I have something really amusing that I've been looking forward to telling just to you.

MARIE LOUISE. The suspense is more than I can bear!

JACQUELINE. All right . . . Philippe Valbeille is in Epinal. . . . *Now* what's the matter?

MARIE LOUISE. What did you say, Jacqueline?

JACQUELINE. That Philippe Valbeille was in Epinal.

MARIE LOUISE. How do you know?

JACQUELINE. I saw him.

MARIE LOUISE. Where? When?

JACQUELINE. Yesterday.

MARIE LOUISE. What did he have to say?

JACQUELINE. I didn't see him to speak to, but I shall soon, because he's there for two days and the Chaulieux have asked him to dinner this evening. We're going too, so I'll certainly have a chance to talk to him awhile.

MARIE LOUISE. But where did you see him? What was he doing? How did he look?

JACQUELINE. I was with Berthe Chaulieux. He was just coming out of the Post Office. I said: "Good Heavens, there goes Philippe Valbeille," or something to that effect, and Berthe said—"Oh, do you know him?" While we were still talking about it, he had disappeared round the corner without seeing us.

MARIE LOUISE. [*Overcome.*] Oh God! Oh God!

JACQUELINE. Marie Louise—what a state you're in! If I'd known . . .

MARIE LOUISE. Oh, Jacqueline—to think that this, of all things, was your news.

JACQUELINE. I can't see what's so stupefying about it. He's supposed to be in America, and he isn't. He's in France; in Epinal at that. Well, what about it?

MARIE LOUISE. [*Distraught.*] What shall I do?

JACQUELINE. Do?

MARIE LOUISE. With him in Epinal—oh no, I can't stand it.

JACQUELINE. What do you mean? What difference does it make to you?

MARIE LOUISE. It . . . it's a feeling. Nothing *you* could understand . . . no, not you, Jacqueline.

JACQUELINE. Thanks!

MARIE LOUISE. Don't mind what I say, please. But we always have looked at things differently . . . more so than ever, since you're married.

JACQUELINE. I have more understanding than you think, Marie Louise. I am not blind. I know how the Argentine has filled your dreams, night and day.

MARIE LOUISE. It's not true, and I don't know what you're talking about.

JACQUELINE. Not that I ever shared the dreams—no indeed! But is it likely that I should have brought you here, away from the others, to hear my news alone, if I hadn't had good reason to think you'd do something funny?

MARIE LOUISE. You've an odd idea of a joke.

JACQUELINE. No more odd than this crush of yours!

MARIE LOUISE. What do you mean by that idiotic word?

JACQUELINE. Do you expect me to treat it as anything else?

MARIE LOUISE. Ah, you don't understand . . . you don't begin to understand.

JACQUELINE. Then tell me.

MARIE LOUISE. What do you want me to tell you?

JACQUELINE. Don't look at me like that, Marie Louise. It frightens me.

MARIE LOUISE. It's you that . . .

JACQUELINE. That what? [*She takes her sister's hand.*] Darling, listen. . . . I didn't mean to upset you. . . . You love your little sister, don't you?

MARIE LOUISE. But you talk to me so . . . so . . .

JACQUELINE. It's only because I do so terribly want to understand you.

MARIE LOUISE. Do you really mean that, Jacqueline?

JACQUELINE. If I ever meant anything in my life.

MARIE LOUISE. [*With tears in her eyes.*] I do wish we could have a good, quiet talk together, Jacqueline. We have let ourselves drift very far apart, but all the same, I've no one in the world but you. . . .

JACQUELINE. I never dreamt it would cause you all this agitation to hear that Philippe was back again. . . .

MARIE LOUISE. If you only knew . . .

JACQUELINE. Tell me. . . .

MARIE LOUISE. It's a far more serious thing for me than you imagine. . . .

JACQUELINE. Than I imagine . . . well, we won't go into that.

MARIE LOUISE. You don't know that my whole . . . yes . . . that my whole life hangs on it.

JACQUELINE. Your whole life? Whatever do you mean?

MARIE LOUISE. I mean the one real chance of happiness, thrown away . . . deliberately . . .

JACQUELINE. I haven't understood a word so far.

MARIE LOUISE. . . . allowed to pass me by, because of a word that was never spoken. A simple answer was all he needed . . . and I didn't dare . . .

JACQUELINE. But *what* answer? He never asked you for anything.

MARIE LOUISE. Ah!

JACQUELINE. What *was* it, then?

MARIE LOUISE. As though it matters any more! It's all over now, and done with. There are some questions you know, Jacqueline, that stand right on the brink of speech. It was for me to decide whether or not they should be spoken.

JACQUELINE. What are these fancies, Marie Louise?

MARIE LOUISE. Memories, dear, not fancies. Words there could be no mistaking; looks, handshakes—a certain way of passing me things at table, of returning me the balls when we played tennis together. . . . Oh, and so much more that you can have no idea of.

JACQUELINE. For instance?

MARIE LOUISE. How can I put them into words? Trifles . . . so slight, so intangible . . . it is only today that I grasp their meaning myself. Well, don't let's think about them any more. . . . [*She looks about her.*] I have no right. But what hurts most of all, is the thought of his being so near . . . and already on the point of going away again . . . back to the Argentine perhaps—who knows? . . . Oh, if I could only once have . . .

JACQUELINE. Seen him again? If that's the worst of your trouble, it's easily mended. Come home with me and stay over until tomorrow.

MARIE LOUISE. [*Distractedly.*] What?

JACQUELINE. Why certainly, I shall take you back with me. It won't be the first time you'll have stayed in Epinal overnight. You'll come with us to dinner at the Chaulieux, and he'll be there for you to talk to. He'll say "I've quite settled down now," and you'll say

"I'm very glad." And you'll part good friends, at peace with each other, and happy.

MARIE LOUISE. You arrange it all very simply, Jacqueline. Of course, you would . . . how could you understand?

JACQUELINE. Then you don't want to come?

MARIE LOUISE. It is out of the question.

JACQUELINE. But why? Would you rather spend the rest of your life regretting a talk you never had? I begin to know you at last, Marie Louise, and I am quite positive it will do you no good not to see him. There's not the slightest danger in it for either of you. I know for a fact that he means to go straight back to the Argentine. Besides, even if you were once . . . in love with him . . .

MARIE LOUISE. Jacqueline!

JACQUELINE. Yes, if you ever were, you're not any more, are you? . . . It would be hard on poor Olivier. . . .

MARIE LOUISE. [Echoing her tone.] Poor Olivier. . . .

JACQUELINE. [After a pause.] You're not so sure of yourself after all, then.

MARIE LOUISE. No, I'm not. Now do you understand?

JACQUELINE. Yes; now I do. And I think we had better leave it as though nothing had been said, and you'll stay here.

MARIE LOUISE. [Sits still, thinking. She emerges from her revery, suddenly decisive.] No . . . your first plan was the right one. . . . I'm going with you.

JACQUELINE. Wait, Marie Louise. It's my turn to be unsure now. I begin to have my doubts about it. Perhaps it wouldn't be best now to . . .

MARIE LOUISE. No, Jacqueline—I'm going. I know I'm doing a frightful thing, but I must go through with it. If you love me, you will not stand in my way.

JACQUELINE. Now what have I done!

MARIE LOUISE. Olivier must still be in the drawing-room. Go at once and tell him you're taking me home with you tonight. It's to be your idea, not mine, do you hear? And whatever you do, be sure not to let him suspect that . . . he is there.

JACQUELINE. I believe that if you were to go openly and . . .

MARIE LOUISE. I know; but it's not possible this time. Things have not been quite as they were between Olivier and me since a certain evening . . . an account of this same thing, and we've let it in a way just remain like that, because we could somehow never discuss it frankly and without reservations. So that you see, if he were to know . . . Please go now . . . hurry . . . I'll wait for you here. [*She pushes Jacqueline towards the door.*]

JACQUELINE. What a will you have, Marie Louise, when once you *do* make up your mind.

[*She goes out, leaving* MARIE LOUISE *a prey to agitation and anxiety. She drifts unsteadily over to the small table, and stands beside it, turning over the pages of the Baudelaire, aimlessly, with one hand. There is silence. Then suddenly, hearing sounds outside, she shuts the book and moves away from the table, with an indifferent air.* JACQUELINE *comes in with* OLIVIER.]

OLIVIER. [*Crossing to the desk to find some papers.*] Going over to Epinal, I hear?

MARIE LOUISE. [*In a toneless voice.*] Yes . . . yes, Olivier.

OLIVIER. [*Still searching through papers.*] What's the idea?

MARIE LOUISE. Didn't Jacqueline . . . [*She implores* JACQUELINE *with her eyes.*]

JACQUELINE. I told you, Olivier. We thought it would be such a good chance to see a little more of each other. We're becoming absolute strangers. But Marie Louise was afraid you might mind. . . .

OLIVIER. Nonsense. That's a thing I can understand without trying. I'm always happy to see you two girls together—here or elsewhere. Shall you be leaving soon?

JACQUELINE. In half an hour.

OLIVIER. [*To* MARIE LOUISE.] And you'll be back tomorrow morning?

MARIE LOUISE. Yes, Olivier. . . . Yes, I suppose so.

OLIVIER. All right—that's splendid. I don't know if I'll be seeing you before you go.

MARIE LOUISE. Of course you will, Olivier. I'll come in when we're ready, and kiss you good-bye.

OLIVIER. But don't you remember I've got to go with Father in a minute to look at those trees they've been cutting down? It might take rather a time . . .

MARIE LOUISE. Then I'll . . .

OLIVIER. Then you may kiss me good-bye now. [*He crosses to her and takes her head between his hands, smiling down at her.*] Have a good time, little quitter!

MARIE LOUISE. [*Springing up.*] Olivier!

OLIVIER. [*Laughing.*] Look at that, will you? There's no joking with that girl any more! Remember me to your husband, Jacqueline, and mind you come again soon. [*He looks long and intently at* MARIE LOUISE.] Till tomorrow, then. [*She smiles back at him, but it costs her an effort.*] Good-bye. [*He goes out.*]

MARIE LOUISE. [*In anguish.*] Oh! [*Uncertainly.*] Jacqueline . . .

JACQUELINE. Yes?

MARIE LOUISE. What . . . what can Olivier be thinking?

JACQUELINE. What do you think he's thinking? I told him I was taking you with me; he thought it perfectly normal, I'm sure. . . .

MARIE LOUISE. Wasn't he surprised? Not at all?

JACQUELINE. At your wanting to stay overnight with your own sister? Such a great event! Now, my lamb, if you still have the faintest doubt in your mind, I have only one thing to say to you—stay where you are. Don't go. . . .

MARIE LOUISE. [*After a pause.*] What would he think then?

JACQUELINE. That you had changed your mind.

MARIE LOUISE. No . . . I don't mean Olivier . . .

JACQUELINE. What?

MARIE LOUISE. I mean . . . him . . .

JACQUELINE. Who—Philippe?

MARIE LOUISE. Yes.

JACQUELINE. He'll never know you had any intention of going.

MARIE LOUISE. Do you think not—really?

JACQUELINE. Well, he certainly won't hear of it from me.

MARIE LOUISE. It isn't a matter of telling him in so many words . . .

JACQUELINE. What then?

MARIE LOUISE. Suppose he were expecting me . . .

JACQUELINE. Expecting? You? Philippe?

MARIE LOUISE. Why not?

JACQUELINE. If he'd wanted to see you, he'd have come over . . .

MARIE LOUISE. No . . . not he.

JACQUELINE. Of course he would have.

MARIE LOUISE. You don't know him.

JACQUELINE. As well as you do, I should say.

MARIE LOUISE. You are mistaken.

JACQUELINE. So you imagine that he is . . .

MARIE LOUISE. I imagine nothing—it's perfectly clear to reason. Come here? Why most certainly he ought to have come here. The most elementary politeness demanded it. Didn't he spend months in this house? But he has made no attempt to see us.

JACQUELINE. Which signifies . . . ?

MARIE LOUISE. That he expects to see me in Epinal, Jacqueline. I know that absolutely.

JACQUELINE. If that were so, he would have managed some way to give you a sign.

MARIE LOUISE. He has . . . in this abnormal silence.

JACQUELINE. How can you imagine any such thing, Marie Louise! To keep away just because he wanted so much to come! Why, you might easily have gone on forever and never known that he'd come to Epinal at all.

MARIE LOUISE. News travels fast. He knows that. He must also have heard that you live there. It is quite probable he even contrived that chance encounter of yours. You say he didn't see you. What if he only pretended not to?

JACQUELINE. This is all very complicated.

MARIE LOUISE. Life is always more complicated than we think.

JACQUELINE. But I can't see any reason for so much mystery.

MARIE LOUISE. Suppose it's a test?

JACQUELINE. A test?

MARIE LOUISE. Couldn't he have said: "She'll know I'm here, but I'll not make a single move towards her. She shall come or not come, as she thinks best."

JACQUELINE. That theory won't hold for a minute, Marie Louise. Even if he had thought of such a scheme, where was the sense in setting all the chances purposely against himself?

MARIE LOUISE. There's the true gambler! And if I'm right, you'll admit that he has courage. . . . It is inconceivable that I should stay calmly behind, while he . . . [She walks about the room, in deep agitation.]

JACQUELINE. [Watches her intently for a moment.] Keep yourself in hand, my dear girl, or you'll drive me crazy too. We've got to keep our heads, you know. You're not going to stir out of this house, Marie Louise. Take my advice and don't go.

MARIE LOUISE. Absolutely not, Jacqueline. How can I let him go back without a word? What would he think of me?

JACQUELINE. But what do you mean to do?

MARIE LOUISE. Can't you realise that this is a crisis in my life?

JACQUELINE. No . . . what I do realise is that in this whole thing, you're making a mountain out of . . .

MARIE LOUISE. Stop, Jacqueline.

JACQUELINE. The way you've been talking is utterly insane.

MARIE LOUISE. Very possibly. I feel insane . . . unless it is that I have been insane until this moment, and have only now come to my senses.

JACQUELINE. Later on we'll . . . Listen, Marie Louise. Let's try and talk it over sensibly.

MARIE LOUISE. Talk it over . . . talk it over! Haven't I been "talking it over" all my life long? If you can give the name of life to an existence like mine. Look at me—exactly where I was at ten years old . . . I've not gone one step further. The prison has changed warders, that's all . . . Father first, Olivier afterwards.

JACQUELINE. You've had nothing to complain of, that I can see.

MARIE LOUISE. You don't realise that that is what makes it all the worse.

JACQUELINE. Don't go, Marie Louise. . . . I beg you not to go.

MARIE LOUISE. You're asking an impossibility then. I'll go alone if I must. . . . I'll walk. I *will* see him, Jacqueline. I will.

JACQUELINE. No . . . no. . . .

MARIE LOUISE. What do you mean, no? This man has come to me— yes, come to me—from the very ends of the earth, and you want me to let him go away again without a word. It would be monstrous.

JACQUELINE. It would be a great deal more monstrous to . . .

MARIE LOUISE. For once in my life, I'm not going to be a coward. He is expecting me.

JACQUELINE. He is not.

MARIE LOUISE. Well, I shall at least have seen him. I shall not have been afraid to do that.

JACQUELINE. You are courting disappointment.

MARIE LOUISE. That is not true.

JACQUELINE. He has settled down, I tell you, Marie Louise. You never considered that possibility, did you?

MARIE LOUISE. Because it is not a possibility.

JACQUELINE. You talk of him as if he were in love with you.

MARIE LOUISE. I have no reason to believe he is not.

JACQUELINE. Still . . .

MARIE LOUISE. And I shall find that out, too.

JACQUELINE. Oh, how could I have been such a fool as to have said a word about him! I feel I have it all to answer for, now. . . .

MARIE LOUISE. You have nothing to answer for. Only don't take my courage from me—that is all I ask.

JACQUELINE. Yes. You will need all you possess not to give in to the thing that is drawing you to Epinal.

MARIE LOUISE. I don't mean that.

JACQUELINE. Do you realise what is in store for you there?

MARIE LOUISE. Do you think I care?

JACQUELINE. You persist in refusing to think the thing over, Marie Louise.

MARIE LOUISE. What is the use?

JACQUELINE. There's every use.

MARIE LOUISE. I've done far too much thinking over, as it is.

JACQUELINE. Marie Louise, look about you.

MARIE LOUISE. Won't you spare me anything, Jacqueline?

JACQUELINE. Think of your home, and mine, and our people's . . . and our peaceful and happy lives. . . .

MARIE LOUISE. Don't . . . don't, Jacqueline.

JACQUELINE. Are you ready to ruin so much, all for an act of sheer recklessness?

MARIE LOUISE. Don't.

JACQUELINE. You were born in this house. It has known you in all the happy days of your life . . . as a bride . . .

MARIE LOUISE. Jacqueline, please don't.

JACQUELINE. And as a mother.

MARIE LOUISE. [Stopping her ears.] Jacqueline!

JACQUELINE. Surely *he* is not strong enough to fight against all that. . . .

MARIE LOUISE. Jacqueline, don't say any more! Don't talk to me like this! It's not fair or kind. I have been stifling in this house for years. You've known it. You ought to understand. I can't stand it any longer! I can't stand it any longer, I tell you! [*She breaks down, and sobs bitterly.*]

JACQUELINE. [*After a pause.*] Sh! Listen! [*The sound of voices is heard coming nearer, and soon* OLIVIER *and* LANDREAU *come into view outside.* JACQUELINE *whispers imploringly.*] Marie Louise, look . . . look. . . .

[*The two men pass by the closed windows, walking slowly, and talking as they go. Their voices die away in a confused murmur.* MARIE LOUISE *looks after them for a moment, then turns her head sharply away and leaves the room precipitately.*]

CURTAIN

ACT III

SCENE II

Scene:—The curtain rises again immediately. It is the next morning. Olivier and Landreau are at the desk bent over some papers they are examining together.

OLIVIER. November stands well ahead of October you see, and December promises better still. All our customers' orders are on the increase. We can manage as we are for a few months yet, but it would be wise to consider buying two new machines for next July.

LANDREAU. My dear Olivier, it's perfectly splendid. There's not been a single year that the factory hasn't gone forward, ever since you became my son-in-law and partner.

OLIVIER. It's only moving along on the impetus you gave it.

LANDREAU. Don't run yourself down, my dear boy. Haven't I seen you at work? I feel that I can go now with a quiet mind . . . not just yet, I hope, still it is a great thing to know that this place that has been handed down to me through so many generations will be left in such good hands.

OLIVIER. You give me more credit than I deserve.

LANDREAU. If you'd let me have one more grandson, or two, I shouldn't have another thing left to wish for.

OLIVIER. But isn't . . .

LANDREAU. Oh, I'm not reproaching you! You've done well so far, with our little Gérard. By the way, when is that rascally wife of yours coming home?

OLIVIER. I don't know . . . any minute.

LANDREAU. Whatever possessed her to go off to Epinal?

OLIVIER. It was Jacqueline's idea.

LANDREAU. I dare say. Well, it's no use trying to understand women. Especially when they're like your Marie Louise. I'm her father, and I've never really known what was going on in her mind. Not that it matters, however. She's the right stuff at heart, and that's the main thing. . . .

38

OLIVIER. [*After a pause.*] What does that mean?

LANDREAU. Nothing—nothing at all. You think I'm keeping something at the back of my head, eh? If I were, I should hardly be so foolish as to talk of her to you. No—you know as well as I do that Marie Louise is a dreamer and romantic. That's all. She's her grandmother over again—my late mother-in-law I mean—only thank Heaven, Marie Louise is not so flighty as *she* was. At the age of eighteen her grandmother fell head over ears in love with an acrobat—imagine it!

OLIVIER. [*Uncomfortably.*] That's a good joke.

LANDREAU. Oh, it was all *most* respectable, you may be sure! And very temporary. I merely mentioned it to show that when it comes to imagination, Marie Louise comes by her share honestly! My wife was always more staid and level-headed than her mother—Jacqueline takes after her. Oh, there's nothing to frown about. You're the better off, believe me. Anything else you want me to see?

OLIVIER. No thanks, nothing—I only wanted to show you we had a satisfactory balance sheet. Now, if you're ready, we'll get on with the mail.

LANDREAU. I'll leave that to you—you've made me lazy, you know. Never mind, when you get to my age, you'll be taking a rest too— I think I've more or less earned mine, don't you?

OLIVIER. You have indeed. [*He opens the letters, placing them under a paper-weight as he takes them out of the envelope.*] Nothing very interesting today that I can see.

LANDREAU. Why should you bother to open all this stuff? Can't you trust your typist?

OLIVIER. [*Still opening letters.*] I could, but I'd rather see it all myself.

LANDREAU. Don't know why I should have asked you that—I used to be exactly the same myself. Before you came into the family, I had never entirely relied on a single soul. [*Olivier has just unfolded a letter which he reads anxiously, holding it in trembling fingers.*] What's the matter, Olivier?

OLIVIER. [*Controlling himself.*] Look—look at this. . . .

LANDREAU. [*Taking the letter and reading it.*] "Dear Sirs, I am in Epinal on a flying visit and regret very much that I shall not be able to call on you at Ambrosay. Should I, however . . ." [*He goes on reading to himself, then looks at* OLIVIER.] Well?

OLIVIER. Well?

LANDREAU. I knew he was there.

OLIVIER. You knew?

LANDREAU. Yes, Gustave told me yesterday over the phone. . . .

OLIVIER. [*In a stifled tone.*] Gustave told you?

LANDREAU. Yes, you know Gustave—Jacqueline's husband. He called me up yesterday about eleven, and among other things, he said young M. Valbeille was in Epinal. It must have gone clear out of my head.

OLIVIER. Out of your head——

LANDREAU. I've never thought we could do anything worth while with the Argentine. German competition's strong down there. He can only have come back here for small stuff and gold-headed nails, as he says; we're not interested in those lines. This letter confirms my old opinion. [OLIVIER *leaves the desk and begins to walk up and down the room.*] What's worrying you now?

OLIVIER. Worrying me . . . [*He looks at* LANDREAU, *goes back to the desk and sits down.*] Nothing.

LANDREAU. That's no answer.

OLIVIER. [*Trying to keep calm.*] So Gustave knew he was in Epinal —then Jacqueline must have known also.

LANDREAU. Very likely.

OLIVIER. And she must have told Marie Louise.

LANDREAU. What if she did? [*He looks at* OLIVIER.] You're surely not angry with her for not telling you!

OLIVIER. [*His thoughts elsewhere.*] Oh, no—no—of course not.

LANDREAU. [*After a pause.*] You surely don't attach any importance to trifles like this, my dear boy! Why, you must be out of your mind. . . . [*He remains an instant lost in thought and when he speaks again his voice betrays a note of anxiety.*] Absolutely out of your mind.

OLIVIER. [*Starting on the rest of the mail.*] Ah! Let's talk about something else. . . .

LANDREAU. Not before I've . . .

OLIVIER. [*Springs up and throws open the window on the right. After a moment he turns round.*] Didn't you hear something then?

LANDREAU. No.

OLIVIER. [*Closing the window again.*] I thought . . . [*Comes back to his chair, and absently opens another letter.*] An answer from the Forges Committee about our dispute with . . . that's nothing special. [*Opens another.*] From Huchart's. Something real this

time, I think—they're asking whether we can increase our de-
liveries twenty per cent. Yes, by all means—don't you think? [*He
sees that* LANDREAU'S *thoughts are far away and that he has not
heard. Leaning towards him.*] You agree, don't you—Huchart's
you know.

LANDREAU. [*Coming back to himself with a start.*] Huchart! Oh,
yes, yes! Very big people—old substantial house. What is it they
want of you? Increase? Oh, certainly, for Huchart, by all means.
     [*Now it is* OLIVIER *who has ceased to listen. He looks at his
     watch and winds it idly.*]

OLIVIER. What time do you make it?

LANDREAU. [*Pulling out his watch.*] Ten to eleven.

OLIVIER. Thanks. . . . [*Listens, with his hand raised for silence.*]
Listen. . . . [*A pause.*] No. . . .

LANDREAU. [*With his watch still in his hand, winds it as he talks.*]
I used to know old Huchart very well—the founder of the business. A very decent fellow he was, too. He had a place near Saint
Dié and he used to drop in from time to time when he was in the
neighbourhood. When he died, his children went in with the son-in-
law, Santerre his name was. Since then I've only known them in a
business way. [*Looks at* OLIVIER *as he puts his watch back into his
vest-pocket.*] There, I'm going now. You don't seem to be in the
mood for business or conversation either.

OLIVIER. [*Indicating the letters.*] I'll be done with this in a minute
or two.

LANDREAU. All right, there's nothing you need me for—they're none
of them urgent.
     [*The door is flung noisily open, and the two men swing sharply
     round. But it is only* GÉRARD *bursting into the room.*]

GÉRARD. [*Throwing himself upon* LANDREAU.] Hullo, Grandpa!

LANDREAU. Good-morning, my little man, how are you today?

GÉRARD. I say, Grandpa, guess what Daddy promised me.

LANDREAU. What did he promise you, eh?

GÉRARD. That he'd take me for a walk with him this morning.

LANDREAU. Well, you are in luck. [*Looking at* OLIVIER.] But . . .

GÉRARD. I say, Grandpa, will you hear my fable?

LANDREAU. Not just now, old chap, I've got to go. [*Detaching the
child's arms.*] Steady, there, steady——

OLIVIER. Gérard, stop bothering your grandpa.

LANDREAU. He isn't bothering me a bit. There! Well, Olivier, I'll

leave you now with this young fellow. You have a lot to say to
each other I know. [*But* OLIVIER, *his thoughts still far off, seems
not to have heard.*]

GÉRARD. [*Sotto voice, tugging at* LANDREAU's *sleeve.*] Grandpa . . .

LANDREAU. Yes?

GÉRARD. Please tell me a story.

LANDREAU. Oh, your daddy knows ever so many more stories than I
do, and much better ones.

GÉRARD. No, I want one about you—when you were little.

LANDREAU. Heavens! but that was ages and ages ago——

GÉRARD. Long before that day we went fishing, I bet.

LANDREAU. I should say it was!

GÉRARD. How long is it till you'll be a hundred, Grandpa?

LANDREAU. Just a minute while I count . . . Whew! Thirty-two
years and a half!

GÉRARD. I say, won't it be lovely when you are!

LANDREAU. Will it?

GÉRARD. If you only don't go and die before!

LANDREAU. Sh! [*He looks across at* OLIVIER, *still lost in his own
thoughts.*] You mustn't say such things. I ought to scold you. . . .

GÉRARD. [*Scared*] Good thing Daddy didn't hear, isn't it?

LANDREAU. Sh! Stupidhead, can't you be quiet!

GÉRARD. What's he thinking about, Grandpa?

LANDREAU. Lots of things I suppose—you, maybe——

GÉRARD. [*His eyes fixed on his father.*] But why does he look as if
he's crying?

LANDREAU. [*Quickly.*] Look here now—will you please—— [*He
coughs, and* OLIVIER *turns round. He goes over to him.*] Olivier
. . . Shall I . . . would you like me to do this for you—I could
easily take it off your hands for today. [OLIVIER *cannot restrain a
gesture of impatience.*] No? Very well. I'll go now. Sh! That's all
right—I know how it is. Good-bye, old man. [*He hurries out.*]

GÉRARD. Daddy—can we go out now?

OLIVIER. [*Starting out of himself.*] No, not this morning. Later on,
if you like.

GÉRARD. Can I ask you something, Daddy?

OLIVIER. What is it?

GÉRARD. Why don't you take me for a walk every day?

OLIVIER. [*Absently.*] Why? [*He looks at his watch, and goes again
to the window.*]

GÉRARD. Are you going away, Daddy?

OLIVIER. [*Coming back from the window.*] No, I'm not. [*Sits down.*] What were you saying? You want me to go for a walk with you every day? I couldn't possibly manage that, you know.

GÉRARD. But sometimes, will you?

OLIVIER. Sometimes—yes. Ask me tomorrow, then we'll see.

GÉRARD. Where shall we go?

OLIVIER. Where? [*Looks at watch again.*]

GÉRARD. Are you expecting someone?

OLIVIER. What makes you ask?

GÉRARD. Because you keep on looking at your watch.

OLIVIER. You are far too inquisitive, Gérard. [*The child hangs his head, and* OLIVIER *suffers a pang of remorse.*] I'm expecting your mother, dear.

GÉRARD. What did she go to Epinal for, Daddy?

OLIVIER. She'll be coming back.

GÉRARD. If she doesn't, will I have to bring *you* my homework to look over?

OLIVIER. [*Gets up, in a state of nervous agitation.*] Yes, yes—we'll see. Mlle. André doesn't come today, so there's no hurry. [*He again walks up and down the room with disordered strides, his hands deep in his pockets, anxiously watched by* GÉRARD. *Suddenly* OLIVIER *becomes aware of his presence. He sits down and draws the child to him.*] What is your homework, eh? Come over here and tell me all about it.

GÉRARD. It's arithmetic.

OLIVIER. Stiff?

GÉRARD. Rather!

OLIVIER. Very well, then—you try and work it out quietly by yourself, and when you've finished bring it to me.

GÉRARD. Yes, Daddy. Now, must I?

OLIVIER. [*Already preoccupied.*] What? Oh no, whenever you want to.

GÉRARD. Then will you hear my fable now?

OLIVIER. [*Far off.*] If you like.

GÉRARD. I've got it off pat, you'll see. Wait—The Grasshopper and the Ant—No—the Grasshopper and the Ant, a fable.—Are you listening, Daddy?

OLIVIER. Yes, yes, go on——

[MARIE LOUISE *enters, and stands in the doorway unnoticed, watching them.*]

GÉRARD. [*Continuing.*]

> Miss Grasshopper having sung—
> All through the summer,
> Found herself—found herself in sorry plight . . .
> When the wind began to bite.

[*Turns round and sees her.*] Oh, here's Mother!

OLIVIER. [*Springing up, completely upset.*] Marie Louise——

MARIE LOUISE. [*To* GÉRARD *without moving.*] Go on.

GÉRARD. Shall I?

OLIVIER. No. Go now— [GÉRARD *takes his books and walks reluctantly towards the door.*]

MARIE LOUISE. [*Sharply.*] No, you needn't, Gérard—stay where you are——

OLIVIER. Marie Louise——

MARIE LOUISE. Well?

OLIVIER. I'd like to—speak to you, please.

MARIE LOUISE. [*To* GÉRARD.] Go into your room for a moment, dear. [*As he passes her she seizes him suddenly in her arms, holding him closely to her for a long moment, then pushes him away.* GÉRARD *goes out. She begins to take off her gloves, without looking at* OLIVIER.] Was it—was it necessary to interrupt the child's lesson?

OLIVIER. I couldn't very well go on hearing his fable when you— Well never mind. You've come home, anyway. I think we have something to say to each other.

MARIE LOUISE. [*With an exclamation of half-ironical protest.*] As though anything were more important than Gérard's fable——

OLIVIER. What do you say?

MARIE LOUISE. You haven't even— [*She offers him her cheek to kiss.*]

OLIVIER. [*Taken aback.*] Why,— [*He comes over to her, kisses her without conviction and withdraws immediately.*]

MARIE LOUISE. [*Taking off her hat and coat with assumed carelessness, but refusing still to look at him.*] Am I late? I hope you weren't expecting me any earlier, but it's only half past eleven, you know. Jacqueline sent me back in the car—she wouldn't let me come by train. If she had, I'd have been later still. Any news? I saw Dad and Mother as I came in. [*Their eyes meet.*] Why do you look at me like that?

OLIVIER. You have really nothing to tell me?

MARIE LOUISE. Tell you? Oh, just that I'm glad to be home again. Is that what you mean?

OLIVIER. Nothing else?

MARIE LOUISE. What more *should* I have? After a whole day away, too!—Dreadful, isn't it?

OLIVIER. What did you—do there?

MARIE LOUISE. Do there! You know everything I possibly could have done. Dinner—lunch at Jacqueline's of course, just the three of us. Just ourselves. After dinner we all went out—and spent the evening with the Chaulieux. Berthe Chaulieux—you remember her —we didn't stay late. They had visitors—quite a crowd. I—oh I was quite forgetting—whom do you think I met there? Philippe Valbeille, of all people!

OLIVIER. Ah!

MARIE LOUISE. Yes, at the Chaulieux—I was there last night—I told you—with Jacqueline and Gustave.—You know, Gustave was really quite charming. We talked a lot about you, and he said he was *so* sorry he didn't get over here more often.

OLIVIER. Did you know—M. Valbeille was in Epinal?

MARIE LOUISE. Yes——

OLIVIER. Before you left here?

MARIE LOUISE. Oh yes—I think so.

OLIVIER. Don't say 'I think so.'

MARIE LOUISE. Well then yes, I did. Jacqueline—Jacqueline mentioned it to me.

OLIVIER. Why did you go to Epinal?

MARIE LOUISE. Why? [*They face each other now.*]

OLIVIER. So you saw M. Valbeille.

MARIE LOUISE. [*With a forced smile.*] Yes, I *saw* him, of course.

OLIVIER. [*Out of patience.*] Can't you answer me straight?

MARIE LOUISE. I *am* answering you. What else do you want to know?

OLIVIER. Tell me what happened. Tell me what he said to you.

MARIE LOUISE. Oh, it was nothing particularly interesting.

OLIVIER. Nothing interesting?

MARIE LOUISE. You know how it is—an acquaintance out of the past that you happen to meet again casually after a long time. But I recognised him at once, oh yes—at once. That's all.

OLIVIER. He was surely very glad to see you again. Considering how

long he stayed in our house. How did he greet you? What did you
talk about afterwards?

MARIE LOUISE. Do you want so much to know? Well it won't take
long to tell. He said he employed eight hundred people and that
he turned out six hundred thousand nails a day. And that he had a
partner named Dupont, and that their only real competitor was a
German firm, Beekman or Stockman—something or other ending
in 'man'—I don't exactly remember— He said he was Vice-
President of the Buenos Ayres Chamber of Commerce, and that
he'd organised some kind of workmen's disability fund. He said the
Buenos Ayres streets all run in a straight line, and that he never
went to the theatre— He said—he said that trade outside the Argentine—the Argentine Republic that is—was—oh, just things like
that, you know——

[*Her voice, clear and indifferent when she began, has become
gradually fainter, and trails off into a dreamy silence.*]

OLIVIER. And what else?

MARIE LOUISE. Nothing else. Just words, polite, stupid words. [*Re-
straining a sigh.*] As though it matters. Is it of any importance what
he said? A dead man——

OLIVIER. Dead?

MARIE LOUISE. [*As though to herself.*] Certainly he is dead, so far
as we're concerned. Do you understand? I felt so very far from
him. Was it really the same man? Yes—and no. But one thing I
realised very clearly, and that was how little he had meant to me
before . . . less than nothing——

[OLIVIER *watches her for a moment without moving; then
goes over and takes her by the hand. He sits down beside her and
when he speaks his voice is very gentle.*]

OLIVIER. Don't cry, Marie Louise——

MARIE LOUISE. [*Stiffening.*] I'm not cr——

OLIVIER. Sh! Tell me—when are you to see him again?

MARIE LOUISE. Never——

OLIVIER. No, no—not today. [*Containing his joy.*] Don't tell me
anything—today, Marie Louise. You're staring at me—because
I look happy, perhaps. But I can't be that while you are still sad.
You look surprised because I smiled. Don't mind that; it isn't that
I feel like smiling. Not—not for a few days yet—when I shall
have seen happiness come back to you.

MARIE LOUISE. [*With tears in her voice.*] But I am very happy, Olivier.

OLIVIER. No—no—not yet——

MARIE LOUISE. How good it is to hear you talk to me so nicely.

OLIVIER. Have I ever talked to you in any other way?

MARIE LOUISE. [*Bows her head and whispers.*] I need you so very much.

OLIVIER. Is that true?

MARIE LOUISE. Quite true.

OLIVIER. [*With a full heart.*] Marie Louise. Then will you—— [*He stops.*]

MARIE LOUISE. What?

[OLIVIER *says nothing. He is looking at the little table.* MARIE LOUISE *follows with her eyes the direction of his gaze. Suddenly she goes over and takes the Baudelaire which she puts into the bookcase. Then, picking up the fan from the piano, she puts it in the table drawer. Lastly, she pulls the small armchair far away from the stove. As she steps back, she finds herself next to* OLIVIER, *who has stood watching her, silently moved. They meet in a long embrace. It is* MARIE LOUISE *who first disengages herself. With a light step, she goes to the piano and begins the piece she was heard playing in the opening scene.*]

OLIVIER. [*In a stifled voice.*] That Nocturne—yes—that you used to be so fond of— [*He bends down and kisses her hair.*]

CURTAIN

MARTINE

by

JEAN-JACQUES BERNARD

CAST OF CHARACTERS

MARTINE
ALFRED
JULIEN MERVAN
MADAME MERVAN, *his grandmother*
JEANNE CHAILLAND, *his fiancée*

MARTINE

ACT I

SCENE I

Scene—A high-road flooded with sunlight. Mid-day in July. To the right a grassy slope shaded by a little apple tree.

The stage is empty for a moment. A young peasant girl then appears. She wears a light dress, and is carrying a basket in either hand. She puts down her load with a sigh and wipes the perspiration from her forehead. She catches sight of the knoll shaded by the apple tree, picks up her baskets and hastens to it, and flings herself down on the cool grass in an attitude of utter relaxation. Her head thrown back seems to drink in the coolness like a flower. For a few minutes she remains still, but suddenly sees something on the road to the left, which causes her to sit up straight, and rearrange herself with more propriety. She half rises, supporting herself on her doubled fists.

MARTINE. Who's that? [*Pause.*] A man. [*Hastily she pulls down her skirt, smooths her hair, removes bits of grass sticking to her blouse, and places her baskets symmetrically on either side of her.*] A young man. [*Continues to gaze down the road.*] Who can it be, I wonder, coming from Bateux this time of day? [*Looks more intently.*] Isn't he hot! [*With increasing curiosity.*] I've seen somebody like him, but I can't think where. [*Another pause.*] Here he comes. [*Turns her head sharply in the opposite direction.*] [*Enter* JULIEN.]

JULIEN. Excuse me, Mademoiselle, but is it still far to Grandchin?

MARTINE. [*Looking at him.*] Oh, no! No more than a few minutes' walk. You can't see the village from here, but you will right round this corner.

JULIEN. Well, it can wait. I don't care if it's only a step further. Nothing is going to prevent my resting here for a little while first. [*Hesitatingly.*] Is there a tiny bit of room for me too underneath this tree, do you think?

MARTINE. Certainly, Monsieur. [*She moves along slightly to make*

51

room for him. He sits down beside her, heaving an immense sigh of weariness. He smiles.]

JULIEN. I've never in my life been so hot.

MARTINE. No wonder! *Walking* along this road in the middle of the day!

JULIEN. I ought to be used to it, though. In the country I've just come from, the sun's even worse than it is here. Ever so far away, that is. You're laughing at this little bag and my straw hat, I see. But I may as well tell you I didn't come from there like this. I'm only in from Paris now. There didn't seem to be any point in dressing up like a traveller for such a short trip. I got awfully hot just the same—as you see. And of course there wasn't a single cab at Bateux station or anywhere near it when I came in. I know this place of old.

MARTINE. Well, what could you expect? When a person arrives at this time of day and doesn't say they're coming . . .

JULIEN. Well, I left my luggage down there anyway.

MARTINE. [*In surprise.*] Did you bring luggage with you?

JULIEN. Oh yes! And I expect I'll have to do this road all over again to fetch it.

MARTINE. My father'll be taking the cart into Bateux in the morning. He could bring your luggage back for you.

JULIEN. Could he really, do you think? That would be splendid. [*He turns to look at her, and as he does so puts his clothes to rights and straightens his tie.*] You're from Grandchin, I see. Now isn't that nice? What's your name?

MARTINE. Martine. Martine Gevin.

JULIEN. [*Repeating the name in various tones.*] Martine . . . Martine . . . Martine . . . Such a cool name. . . . It has a sweet scent . . . Martine . . . Mine's only Julien.

MARTINE. Julien. [*Ingenuously.*] I think I know that name.

JULIEN. [*Smiling.*] It's quite a common one. Where I've just come from, in our regiment alone we had—I was still a soldier three weeks ago, you know—we had a good half dozen Juliens and as many Jules. One Julot even . . . Martine . . . Martine . . . How *much* nicer that sounds. And where were you coming from with all this? [*Pointing to the baskets.*]

MARTINE. Bateux. I go in every two or three mornings to do the errands for the family and everybody.

JULIEN. Why, we're going the same way then.

MARTINE. Yes.

JULIEN. I don't mind so much about the cab now. [*Looking at her again.*] Great heavens, Martine, how golden your hair is!

MARTINE. Is it?

JULIEN. *Is* it! I didn't know there *could* be such hair. You made it out of the wheat, didn't you?

[MARTINE *lowers her eyes.*]

JULIEN. Do you know, the minute I saw your hair I suddenly stopped feeling hot. [*Very carefully with the tip of his finger, he touches the end of one golden curl.*]

[*Martine in her confusion hangs her head lower and lower.*]

JULIEN. [*Becomes aware of her embarrassment and moves a little away.*] What have you got in those baskets?

MARTINE. Nothing special. Look—eggs . . .

JULIEN. No eggs in Grandchin?

MARTINE. Not enough to go round. We've got enough for ourselves. But we keep our own fowls. These aren't for us, though, they're an errand. So's the butter.

JULIEN. You can make butter yourself, I suppose, can't you?

MARTINE. Yes, I can, but Mother does that.

JULIEN. You shall teach me.

MARTINE. Teach you to make butter? What for?

JULIEN. Not for the butter—but to have *you* teach me.

MARTINE. All right. If Mother'll let me.

JULIEN. Don't worry. I shan't do anything your mother would object to. If you knew me better . . .

MARTINE. Oh, it's not *me* she'd mind about—it's the milk you'd spoil.

JULIEN. I see. Now tell me—what do you do with yourself? Work about the house from morning till night? Yes? No?

MARTINE. Oh yes, there's a lot to do. Even if it was only the housework, and the farmyard and the kitchen-garden. My little sister, Nicole—she's thirteen—she helps me with that. But I work in the fields too. In the country there's always something wanting doing. When you've got the hay in, there's the potatoes to dig up. . . . Only the new ones . . . the big ones come on later. That'll take us till harvest. Then there's all the times I go in to Bateux. But I've told you about that.

JULIEN. I should say that's the hardest work of all in weather like this.

MARTINE. It isn't always so hot. And anyway, it's only the way back that's bad—because I always leave very early, about six.

JULIEN. Then you must be most frightfully hungry, poor Martine.

MARTINE. No, I'm not—I always get something to eat in Bateux to last me. I never get back as late as this. But today I had more to do, and what with the heat too—that makes you later still.

JULIEN. You know, I really wonder what would have become of us if it hadn't been for this tree. [*He looks at her again.*] Please let me put this curl right, will you? . . . Nothing seems to exist in the whole world beyond this patch of shade, does it?

MARTINE. It seems like it.

JULIEN. Everything's unbearably hot outside of it. Just look. Not a soul on the horizon. All the people in the world have gone into hiding to eat their dinner. We've gone into hiding too under this apple tree. [*He takes her hand and they sit for a while silently very close together.*]

MARTINE. [*Embarrassed.*] Wouldn't you . . . won't you . . .

JULIEN. Wouldn't I what?

MARTINE. Wouldn't you like to see what else I've got in my baskets?

JULIEN. I should, very much. . . .

MARTINE. Here's some thread.

JULIEN. I say! I've never seen such fine thread in all my life.

MARTINE. It's for one of the neighbours.

JULIEN. Oh! Perhaps it's not so very fine at that.

MARTINE. You can't get everything you want in Grandchin. There is one draper, but just the things you need she never seems to have in stock. It's a good thing there's always Bateux to go to.

JULIEN. Grandchin is certainly no ordinary place. But then I always knew that—I wonder if I did though. However, if I didn't I'm certain of it now I've met you. I need only look at you to know that Grandchin is a fairy place—the place apart. It's the moon.

MARTINE. No, it isn't the moon.

JULIEN. Oh yes, it is. But we haven't done turning out our baskets yet.

MARTINE. There's nothing very nice in that one. The other's better. Wait, I'll show you. [*She opens the second basket.*] It wasn't quite full so I picked some broom along the road for a lady. She's ever so fond of it.

JULIEN. Broom! Let's see. [*He thrusts his hand into the basket and pulls out the flowers in bunches.*] But, Martine, this is your very

own flower. . . . No—let me, please! [*He takes down her hair
and she does not resist him. The golden tresses fall all over her
shoulders and breast. As he speaks* JULIEN *fills her arms with the
flowers.*] Martine . . . Martine . . . Just look, just look at them
together. You can't tell where the hair ends and the flowers begin.
It's all youth and all springtime in one. Isn't it? Isn't it, Martine?
And your smile in the midst of it. [*She sits looking straight in front
of her, her face radiant, her arms full of the flowers and her own
golden curls mingled together. He backs away from her to get a
better view, and clasps his hands in rapture.*] What a vision! I've
met a fairy along the road. Oh, Martine, promise you'll come
back with me on a pilgrimage one day to pray to this little apple
tree.

MARTINE. If you like.

JULIEN. [*Half whispering.*] Fairy Martine . . . [*He lays his hands
on hers which makes her tremble a little, and some of the flowers
fall to the ground. For a moment they remain in this attitude. Suddenly a sharp exclamation escapes her.*] What's the matter?

MARTINE. [*Looking toward the right.*] There comes a man from
Grandchin.

JULIEN. All right. There's nothing to be afraid of. Tidy your hair.
Put your flowers back into the basket. Take your time. Seem not
to notice me.

MARTINE. [*Who has hastily put her hair in order, and is nervously
gathering the broom into her baskets again.*] But I know him . . .
I know him.

JULIEN. [*Putting on his hat and picking up his suitcase and walking
stick.*] Never mind. I promise it'll be all right. He's not looking
our way, anyhow. And even if he were the sun's too bright in his
eyes for him to see us. He's looking down, as it happens. Just you
sit where you are. Don't get up. You don't know me and I don't
know you. [*He backs a few steps along the road toward the left.*]
I've just come. See. And I'm going to ask him the way. It's perfectly simple. You watch. [*He begins walking slowly toward the
right.*]

[*Enter a peasant, about thirty years of age.* JULIEN *stops.*]

JULIEN. Excuse me, is it straight ahead to Grandchin?

ALFRED. [*Stopping.*] Yes, straight ahead. [*He catches sight of* MAR-
TINE.] She could have told you that.

JULIEN. [*To* MARTINE.] Oh, Mademoiselle, I hadn't seen you up there! Can you tell me if I'm on the right road to Grandchin?

MARTINE. Yes, Monsieur.

ALFRED. What're you doing there, Martine?

MARTINE. What you see, Alfred, coming back from Bateux. It was so hot.

ALFRED. It must have been. Like to go back with me now?

MARTINE. There's work to do at home.

ALFRED. [*To* JULIEN.] So you're for Grandchin, Monsieur?

JULIEN. As you see.

ALFRED. Might you be going to stay there? I see you've got a bag with you.

JULIEN. That's exactly what I am going to do. I'm on my way to my grandmother's, Madame Mervan.

MARTINE. [*Horrified.*] You're——

ALFRED. Well, well, *you're* that grandson of hers? Then I know all about you. Wasn't it you that's been a soldier in Syria?

JULIEN. And still was up to three weeks ago.

ALFRED. I know. [*He points to* MARTINE.] Martine there, she lives right next door to your grandmother. Go along with Monsieur Mervan, Martine, and show him the way. Your grandmother'll be very glad to see you, Monsieur.

JULIEN. It will be a bit of a surprise for her. I didn't say which day I was coming.

ALFRED. You'll find she's expecting you just the same. Isn't she Martine?

MARTINE. [*Breathlessly.*] Yes!

ALFRED. Well, I'll be blessed! It was me that helped her carry the furniture upstairs to your room. To think of meeting you like this. Well, Monsieur Mervan, I'll not keep you now.

JULIEN. [*Cordially.*] Good-bye. I shall be seeing you again, I'm sure.

ALFRED. Sure to. Every day. Grandchin's not so big. [JULIEN *holds out his hand.*] Glad to have met you, Monsieur Mervan.

JULIEN. Then this young lady is to show me the way?

ALFRED. I'll be over to see you tonight, Martine.

MARTINE. No.

ALFRED. Why?

MARTINE. Because . . .

ALFRED. Well, we'll see. [*He goes on his way.*]

JULIEN. So that's that.

MARTINE. You're Madame Mervan's grandson?

JULIEN. I say, Martine, that chap seems to like you pretty well. What's his name? Alfred . . . Well, with eyes like yours I suppose . . .

MARTINE. So you're Madame Mervan's grandson?

JULIEN. Certainly I am. I could have told you that before only it didn't occur to me.

MARTINE. Now I know why I thought I knew your name. Your grandmother's told me about you ever so often. She's always talking about her grandson who was a soldier in the east. . . . I kept wondering where I'd seen somebody that looked like you.

JULIEN. Grandmother of course. I'm supposed to be the image of her, as she was in her youth. I've even got her voice. Mine sounds different rather, because it isn't tired and old like hers yet. The family resemblance is there though.

MARTINE. Madame Mervan's grandson.

JULIEN. Can't get over it? What *did* you expect me to look like then?

MARTINE. I don't know. But think of your coming back just like any *poilu*—just like all the poor ones—walking along the highroad—not even driving.

JULIEN. [*With a smile.*] This isn't the age of carriages any more. And I'm glad of it—because otherwise I should never have stopped here with you, Martine.

[*Pause.* MARTINE's *head droops again, and* JULIEN *gazes intently at her white throat and arms.*]

So you live next door to my grandmother, do you?

MARTINE. Yes, our house is the one before hers. First, there's the gate into our yard; and a little further up the road comes your garden gate.

JULIEN. I only remember it all very dimly. I was here once before, you know— Oh, but you must have been very little in those days. It's fifteen years since my grandfather bought the house. My people didn't like it, so they never cared to come again. . . . I lost them both during the war. . . . But I suppose you know all about that.

MARTINE. [*Without raising her head.*] Yes.

JULIEN. So grandmother's all I've got left now. I expect to stay here for good if my work'll let me. I write for the newspapers— but I daresay you know that too? Paris is really quite near. But

I can't decide finally just yet—at least I couldn't until this moment. I have now though, and I believe I'm going to stay. [*He looks at her again.*] Yes, I believe I shall stay.

MARTINE. [*With an effort.*] Your grandmother . . . will be very glad you've come. She's been waiting for word from you from one day to another. . . . Everything's been ready.

JULIEN. I'm sure of it. She's the kindest soul on earth.

MARTINE. And . . . that's for August though . . . she's asked your . . . your fiancée.

JULIEN. What's that? Who? My fiancée? And who's that I'd like to know?

MARTINE. You know . . . Mademoiselle Chailland.

JULIEN. Oh, Jeanne Chailland! She's not my fiancée. We had some sort of vague before-the-war understanding, you know. Certainly nothing else. Why, good heavens—I've not seen her for over three years, not since I left for the East. That's so like families. Always in such a hurry. I thought she was in Brittany, anyway.

MARTINE. She said she'd come next month with her mother.

JULIEN. [*After a moment's reflection.*] Of course, grandmother meant well. Still she might have told me first. I know she's fond of me, the dear old soul, but the things she does to please me are often not the ones I'd have chosen if she'd asked the question. She never said a word about it in her letters. Pages and pages about all sorts of trifles, her household and her garden and whatnot— never a syllable about all the lovely things round her.

MARTINE. [*Ingenuously.*] What lovely things?

JULIEN. Why . . . [*For a moment he regards her with a shade of doubt, then suddenly says.*] My grandmother never once wrote me about Martine Gevin. Odd, isn't it?

MARTINE. I suppose she didn't think to. But she'd talked to me about you all the time.

JULIEN. Do you see her often?

MARTINE. Every day nearly. The broom's for her. So are the eggs.

JULIEN. I say, that *is* jolly. That's *my* supper omelet in your basket.

MARTINE. Yes.

JULIEN. I hereby invite you to share it, Martine.

MARTINE. [*Scandalised.*] I . . .

JULIEN. [*Unaware of her agitation.*] Dear old grandmother. It will be great to see her again. [*He remains for a moment pensively silent.*] Look at our shadows on the road. They've been getting longer and longer. Noon is passing. We don't need our apple tree so much now. [*Another pause.*] Tell me, does grandmother tell you everything?

MARTINE. [*Embarrassed.*] I . . . Madame Mervan is very kind to young people.

JULIEN. [*Dreamily.*] I wonder if I'll recognise the house again. I couldn't even tell you now if the roof's tiles or slate.

MARTINE. Tiles.

JULIEN. Oh, tiles. [*Pause.*] You go on ahead and prepare her.

MARTINE. The minute I tell her someone's come, she'll know it's you.

JULIEN. Right you are. Heads up! Here we go! This is the perfect welcome home—I adore Grandchin already. Give me your baskets.

MARTINE. No, no! You'll never manage—not with your bag to carry.

JULIEN. Please, Martine. Well, give me one anyway. Let me take the eggs, and you can keep the flowers. Oh yes, you must! Because if you hang on to them both, how will you be able to take my arm?

MARTINE. But . . .

JULIEN. Now look here, Martine, here I've come all this way from the East—I've simply got to have something to lean on. Absolutely! Look—a poor devil of a soldier home from the war all knocked to bits. [*Laughing, he doubles up and pretends to hobble down the road alone.*]

MARTINE. [*Laughing too.*] All right then. Here's my arm, if you want it.

[*They dispose the two baskets as best they can, together with the suitcase and walking stick, and start on their way, arm in arm.*]

JULIEN. Now *could* anything be better than this? On the way to Grandchin, Martine—like two lovers.

[MARTINE *comes to a sudden stop.*]

JULIEN. Well, what's the matter? . . . Come along!

END OF SCENE I

ACT I

A fortnight later. MME. MERVAN's *house at Grandchin. Country interior, simple and homelike. Door at left. Rear, large window and door opening onto verandah. Right, fireplace and door.*

MME. MERVAN, *spectacles on her nose, is in her armchair at the window sewing. She is an old woman of about seventy.* JULIEN *is standing beside her.*

MME. MERVAN. Why don't you sit down?

JULIEN. I will. [*He does so and almost immediately gets up again.*]

MME. MERVAN. You don't keep still for a minute, Julien. You're all on the qui vive. But you would be, of course.

JULIEN. Not at all. Why should I?

MME. MERVAN. *Why?* Isn't Jeanne coming? She'll be here any moment now.

JULIEN. Is this the first time you've seen me restless, grandmother, these two weeks I've been in Grandchin? Really I'm not impatient to see anybody. I'm only happy; enormously happy to be free again, and in France. And in Grandchin with you.

MME. MERVAN. With me—well . . .

JULIEN. Yes *you*, grandmother—you're part of it all. I'm not always as demonstrative as I'd like to be, I'm afraid. But I can't help that. It's the way I'm made. By the way I behave, I know you'd never think I cared a rap about the very things that mean most to me. And on the other hand, I'm always ready to burst into raptures over any insignificant little flower growing by the wayside.

MME. MERVAN. [*As if to herself.*] Poor Martine.

JULIEN. What did you say, grandmother?

MME. MERVAN. Jeanne can't be long now, I think.

JULIEN. She's not likely to get here at all today, if she and her mother only got into Paris last night from Dinard. They'll be sure to spend the day there.

MME. MERVAN. Not when it's so near by. Jeanne's father has hired a car for the summer.

JULIEN. All right. Let them come for a few days, if they like. I promise I'll be perfectly nice to them both. But you're not to go trying to discover anything between Jeanne and me beyond the merest friendship, mind. The sort of friendship we have is one of those delightful things which families usually manage to make altogether impossible. And whatever you do, please don't discuss it with Jeanne, will you, grandmother? Her ideas happen to be the same as mine on that subject.

MME. MERVAN. Are they?

JULIEN. Yes. I have a great regard for Jeanne, and nothing else.

MME. MERVAN. Poor Jeanne.

JULIEN. By all means poor Jeanne, if she has anything else in mind in coming down here. But I know she hasn't. When I went away we promised not to forget each other, and to remain good friends always, and that's all.

MME. MERVAN. [*Not quite sure of her ground.*] But . . . Do you never think of getting married, my dear?

JULIEN. Oh, there's loads of time for that. Let me enjoy my life for a little while first.

MME. MERVAN. Jeanne Chailland is a very fine match.

JULIEN. Grandmother, please!

MME. MERVAN. You're *so* impulsive, Julien. I'm so afraid that . . .

JULIEN. That . . .

MME. MERVAN. The Grandchin girls are very lovely.

JULIEN. And Martine Gevin is the loveliest of them all—is that it? And all these remarks are inspired by the fact that you've had her to dinner three times to please me, and that I've gone for walks with her once or twice. . . .

MME. MERVAN. Don't say once or twice, dear—every day. . . . And often in the evenings, too.

JULIEN. Ah, Jeanne, my girl—you little know how much the fear of what the neighbours will say has helped your cause with this grandmother of mine.

MME. MERVAN. It's not Jeanne I'm thinking of, but little Martine. What do you want with her, Julien?

JULIEN. Oh grandmother, do I know what I want? Are you asking me my intentions? Or my plans? I made too many plans when there was not a chance of realising any of them. Now I just take things as they come.

MME. MERVAN. Julien, I'm very fond of that child's parents. The Gevins are good and decent people. What would happen if . . .

JULIEN. What am I to say, grandmother? Don't you know me any better than this? Haven't I inherited at least the basis of honesty from you? It's done me out of pleasure enough as it is, heaven knows. . . . Worse luck.

MME. MERVAN. What then?

JULIEN. Well, isn't that enough to set your mind at rest? God knows it's sufficiently humiliating to have to own up to such a thing— but I hope you won't go telling it all over the village.

MME. MERVAN. My dear boy, what things you do say!

JULIEN. It would make a pretty story—which might be prettier . . . or less pretty . . . It's all according. However, it doesn't matter. What's that work you're doing?

MME. MERVAN. This? Oh, just a bit of sewing, as usual.

JULIEN. It's very nice. Do show me how it's done.

MME. MERVAN. That *would* be wasting my time.

JULIEN. I suppose you think I'm afraid of manual labour. Well, you ought to have seen me reaping the other day.

MME. MERVAN. That's altogether different. And a fine state you came home in, I must say. I had to send you up three lots of hot water; perhaps you remember that?

JULIEN. Yes, it's hot work, but I did awfully well. I had the Gevins gaping at me open-mouthed. How wonderful it was going one behind the other without saying a word. It made you feel you were part of the earth itself.

MME. MERVAN. I've told those Gevins to buy a reaping machine till I'm sick and tired of dinning it into their ears.

JULIEN. A machine could never give you the same feeling.

MME. MERVAN. Did Martine teach you?

JULIEN. Yes. [*As* MME. MERVAN *lays down her sewing.*] Oh, you've not stopped, have you?

MME. MERVAN. Yes. I must go down to the kitchen now and see what the girl's up to.

JULIEN. Why?

MME. MERVAN. Now don't you start finding fault with me for giving our Simone a hand. If I left you at the mercy of *her* cooking, well . . . ! Not going out?

JULIEN. I haven't decided. I don't think I shall.

MME. MERVAN. When you first came to Grandchin your walks were your greatest joy.

JULIEN. [*Going toward the window.*] I know. The first contact with this peaceful countryside . . .

MME. MERVAN. Well, please yourself dear. [*She goes out through the door right.*]

[*JULIEN stands at the window a moment, then turns and contemplates the room.*]

JULIEN. Jeanne . . . [*He turns back to the window.*] Will she feel this too, I wonder? [*For a long moment more, he stands looking out, then suddenly catches sight of someone in the road below.*] Why, there's . . . yes, it's Martine. [*He leans out.*] Hey, Martine! Martine! What? Not coming up? . . . [*She blushes . . . and comes.*] She's coming . . . she is . . . she is! [*He runs excitedly to the door, rear, and flings it open. MARTINE appears, smiling and shy. He takes her hand, closes the door behind her and draws her into the centre of the room.*] Come in, Martine, and bring light into this room. It was so dark before. Where were you going to?

MARTINE. I've been—over to Roupre Mill Farm to pay for a rooster, and on the way back I meant to go in and see if the cow at Benoit's had calved yet. But I came straight home instead, because my ankle's so bad, where I fell the other day.

JULIEN. Does it hurt you still? Show me. . . .

MARTINE. What? . . . Oh, I . . . .

JULIEN. But I know of a fine cure.

MARTINE [*Sitting down.*] It's nothing really. Only when I hurry. . . . [*She pulls her feet in, under her chair.*] What's your cure?

JULIEN. [*On one knee beside her.*] I kiss it better. [*He takes the foot in his hand, then changes his mind.*] No, not like this, Martine. You'll have to take your stocking off.

MARTINE. [*Springing up in alarm.*] My stocking off? Here?

JULIEN. It would do this room too much honour! But don't if you'd rather not, Martine—I wouldn't distress you for all the world. Meet me tonight instead, down by the old bridge. Come barefoot—then I'll cure your ankle for you.

MARTINE. Yes, if you say I'm to.

JULIEN. It will be moonlight. Another magic evening, like the other day. Do you remember? We'll sit on the parapet again, with our backs to the road and our feet dangling over the water. How clear and beautiful that little brook is. And that great, dark tree will be beside us, and the moon over our heads. . . .

MARTINE. Not the moon; it won't be up.

JULIEN. Very well—no moon. It won't be up.

MARTINE. You'll have a whole month to wait before you see it again the way it was the other night. And then it mightn't be such nice weather.

JULIEN. I needn't wait a month—I needn't wait a minute. All I have to do is to shut my eyes, and there it is again, this very minute—now—just as it was then. Can't you see it too, Martine?

MARTINE. Where?

JULIEN. [*Touching his forehead.*] In here. [MARTINE *laughs, not understanding.* JULIEN, *embarrassed, leaves her side.*] It really is, you know. But perhaps I don't make it very clear to you. [*He comes back to her, though it obviously costs him an effort.*] You see, Martine, it's like this. When I see a thing that makes a deep impression on me, I keep it in my mind for ever and ever. And every time I think of it afterwards, I see it again exactly as though I were still looking at it with my eyes.

MARTINE. So do I. Like you, coming down the road a few weeks back, that day I was sitting under the apple tree and saw you. I'll never forget that . . . never.

JULIEN. Nor shall I. Neither of us will ever forget that. There's nothing like memories, Martine, for keeping people together. How big it was, that tiny apple tree! And then the harvest—I shall always see you as you stopped to rest on that little knoll, standing against the blue sky with your scythe over your shoulder. That is another of my beautiful memories.

[MARTINE *looks at him, a little bewildered. He turns again to the window. She follows him with her eyes. He stands there for a long while and at last begins to repeat, in a low voice, the verse of Chénier's.*]

The fork and crooked scythe then shall I wield;
From out my path the grass and fallen yield
Will come to fill your barn in the sweet day. . . .

MARTINE. What's that you said?

JULIEN. It's a poem. . . .

MARTINE. Poem?

JULIEN. Yes—a verse of André Chénier's—he was a great poet. [*Suddenly goes to her.*] I must teach you to love that too, Martine. It's not your fault you don't now. It's just that nobody ever tried to make you care for it. [*He takes her hands.*] Come here, while I show you what it was that made me suddenly want to say those lines aloud. That field over there . . . Look.

MARTINE. Which? That one?

JULIEN. Yes. There's something about that uncut field of wheat that stirs your heart. I never noticed it until today because the other fields were all round it; but they've all been mown now, so you can see that one's real shape at last. It has a symbolic form, Martine. Do you see? It's like a horn of plenty.

MARTINE. [*Laughing.*] A horn?

JULIEN. [*Dropping her hands.*] Yes. [*He moves away from her. She hangs her head. Soon he turns to her again.*] What's the matter?

MARTINE. I don't know. . . . I don't know. [*She falls into his arms, all her strength gone from her.*]

[*Pause.*]

JULIEN. Tell me, Martine.

MARTINE. It's nothing. I think too much. . . . I think too much.

JULIEN. How do you mean?

[*The bell of the garden gate is heard. They are startled into immobility. Then* MARTINE, *without speaking—for she has no strength to speak, points toward the window.* JULIEN *takes a step back, and looks at her, disturbed. . . .*]

MARTINE. [*With immense effort.*] Aren't you going to see . . . who it is?

JULIEN. [*Not moving.*] What do I care who it is?

MARTINE. [*Dully.*] You don't care . . . you don't care . . .

JULIEN. No.

[*They remain so for a moment, without speaking; then there is a sound outside and* MME. MERVAN *enters through the door, rear.*]

MME. MERVAN. Julien, Jeanne's come. She drove over. I thought she would. Her mother won't be here till this evening's train. Oh, here's Martine—good afternoon, dear.

MARTINE. Good afternoon, Madame Mervan.

[JULIEN *hesitates a moment.*]

JULIEN. I'll go down.

MME. MERVAN. Don't. Jeanne came upstairs with me. Here she is.

[JEANNE *comes. She is about 20, and dark. She is dressed for motoring. She stands in the doorway, and* JULIEN *looking at her seems to be struggling with some inner conflict. Suddenly he comes to a decision, and goes to her.]*

JULIEN. Jeanne.

JEANNE. [*Smiles and holds out her hand.*] Julien. [*They shake hands, and find no more to say.*]

MME. MERVAN. Let's go, Martine, and leave them to themselves. [*But* MARTINE *seems unable to stir from her place.* MME. MERVAN *goes out, left.*]

JULIEN. Jeanne—how are you?

JEANNE. And how are *you* after all these years?

MME. MERVAN. [*Reappearing.*] Well, Martine?

JEANNE. Oh, Madame Mervan, please don't go away.

MME. MERVAN. I must, my dears. I've all sorts of things to do downstairs. I shall see you again in a minute or two. Martine?

MARTINE. Yes, ma'am— [*Her head still drooping, she follows* MME. MERVAN *out.*]

JEANNE. [*Apparently seeing* MARTINE *for the first time, as she leaves the room.*] Good afternoon. [*But* MARTINE *has gone, without hearing her.* JEANNE *looks at* JULIEN.] Is that the maid?

JULIEN. No—oh no. [*Shuts the door.*] A little neighbour—Martine Gevin. I didn't introduce you. I'm sorry. . . .

JEANNE. Rather charming, isn't she? A passing fancy?

JULIEN. What do you mean by that? Well yes, if you like, I suppose she is. At Grandchin, you know . . .

JEANNE. Oh, don't apologise. . . . I wasn't finding fault. Well, Julien—aren't you surprised to see me turn up so early?

JULIEN. I'm very glad you did, Jeanne.

JEANNE. Mother and Dad put me into the car without asking me whether or no, and I let them. I wasn't a bit keen on doing a day's shopping in town with Mother. Besides, I thought it would be fun to see you again. Why do you stare at me so?

JULIEN. Very strange. . . . If anyone had told me ten minutes ago, I'd have . . . Jeanne, the more I look at you, the more I seem to have been very lonely so far away from you.

JEANNE. I'd have thought it not very nice of you to be as surprised as that, if I didn't feel just the same way myself. As a matter of fact, I was afraid to see you again. I wondered whether you wouldn't have changed awfully; I didn't know but that I'd find an altogether different Julien in the old one's place.

JULIEN. My own thoughts exactly. I dreaded this moment too. One's never oneself in letters. But the moment you came into this room, something seemed to shock me back to consciousness. Something came back to me. I know what it was—I'm three years younger, now.

JEANNE. Yes; we've found each other again quite easily. Because we were in no great hurry to, I dare say.

JULIEN. That's cruel. . . .

JEANNE. It's true, though. If you'd been my husband or my fiancé, we could never have met again so spontaneously. We'd have been hunting for each other—and been very clumsy about it. It would have taken us half an hour at least before we'd have even begun to feel natural. And we'd have been a lot more ridiculous than we have. [Smiles.]

JULIEN. I see you've not lost your pretty trick of self-analysis. It amuses me so much to see you at it again—I'd quite lost the habit of expecting it in you.

JEANNE. You don't dislike it?

JULIEN. On the contrary. I begin to feel I'm coming back into an atmosphere I was almost forgetting. A pleasant atmosphere, too. . . .

JEANNE. You poor dear—after what you've been through, whatever you found when you came back must have seemed good to you.

JULIEN. Certain things have a perfume of the past about them, and it goes to the head. The way you came into this room, for instance. And although you know they're the same as they were before, they're new too, and mean more.

JEANNE. I know—I understand what you're trying to say.

[A moment's silence. Both are occupied with their own thoughts.]

JULIEN. We were very close friends, really.

JEANNE. Had you forgotten that?

JULIEN. No—not forgotten. But . . .

JEANNE. Don't go on. You'll not be able to explain . . .

JULIEN. Your intuition is awfully touching, Jeanne.

JEANNE. What has intuition to do with it?

JULIEN. You couldn't know, of course.

JEANNE. Well, I dare say you've not been spoiled in that respect lately.

JULIEN. I've been talking a foreign language, Jeanne. And now I've found someone who speaks mine, and uses the same words and understands at once whatever I say. So that I needn't explain it all.

You know—the language of inexplicable things. . . . [*He looks at her.*] There are so many of them, aren't there, that have to be understood . . . just that way . . . aren't there?

JEANNE. [*Looking down.*] Yes.

JULIEN. [*As if to dissipate a feeling of awkwardness.*] It's strange to see you here. [*Looks dreamily out of the window.*] Jeanne, do you like this landscape?

JEANNE. I don't know. I confess I've never paid any great attention to it.

JULIEN. There's no reason why you should. It's just ordinary, every-day French countryside—the soft hills and the little symmetrical fields. But see how warm and smiling it is. I've been far and wide you know. I've seen some magnificent landscapes in the East. But the only real "country" is right here at our feet, at the very gates of Paris. Only one has to have eyes to see it with, and that is more difficult than to travel to the ends of the earth.

JEANNE. Now, here's a thing I'd never have expected to find! Julien turned bucolic! But I understand perfectly what you mean. . . .

JULIEN. [*With animation.*] Of course you do. Look at that uncut field over there. See how its mass of grain has formed itself so clearly into a design—it's a horn of plenty.

JEANNE. You're right. It *is* rather wonderful. . . .

JULIEN. It is indeed. I was looking at it a little while ago, and suddenly found myself reciting Chénier without knowing what it was that had put the lines into my head . . .

> The fork and crooked scythe then shall I wield;
> And from my path the grass and fallen yield
> Will come to fill your barn in the sweet day . . .

JEANNE. [*Stops him with a gesture and to his pleasure, slowly continues the verse.*]

> . . . So that no soul within your house shall say . . .

CURTAIN

ACT I

SCENE III

A few weeks later. Same as Scene I, the road and the little apple tree dominating the slope. But it is October now, and the tree is almost bare. It is the end of the day.

MARTINE, *silent and dejected, is sitting under the tree. For a long moment, she remains motionless, staring straight in front of her with such intentness that she does not hear* ALFRED *as he arrives from the right. He stands watching her before he speaks.*

ALFRED. Hey, Martine—what are you doing there? [MARTINE *starts to her feet in wild alarm; she looks at him with actual terror in her eyes.*] Scared you, did I? Didn't you hear me coming? What's out there to stare so hard at, eh?

MARTINE. What do you want, following me about like this?

ALFRED. First place, I'm not following you about. How was I to know you'd be here on the high-road? Not that I wouldn't have come all the same, if I'd known. And you know why without me telling you.

MARTINE. Go away.

ALFRED. Now, you look here, Martine, my girl. I can't go hanging on like this till kingdom come. Here's a whole year you've kept me waiting on your good pleasure. And now there's one thing I'm going to ask you straight, and I want you to answer me straight.

MARTINE. And it's "no." I've told you that already.

ALFRED. I've not told you yet what I'm going to ask you, and it wasn't that anyhow. What I'm wanting to know is *when* you're going to tell me "yes."

MARTINE. Never. I'll never tell you "yes."

ALFRED. The last time I asked you—that night—you didn't give me any answer at all. You only hung your head down, so I took that for "yes." You remember when I mean—at the dancing for Monsieur Julien's engagement party. . . .

MARTINE. It's not true! I didn't. . . .

ALFRED. Well, whether it is or not, we'll be married for sure. It's sooner or later. You know it as well as I do. You're not going to die an old maid. It's not as if you was in love with somebody else,

69

so why shouldn't it be me as soon as any other fellow? I've got a bit of land—your father's got nothing against me. Far from it. You're bound to come to it in the end, so why don't you now? . . . I know Monsieur Julien made a bit of love to you in the summer, but . . .

MARTINE. He didn't. . . . He didn't. . . . Stop, I tell you!

ALFRED. What of it? It's nothing to be ashamed of. I have no call to be jealous of him any more. Besides you only went with him to make me wild, though I don't see why you need have done it. I never did you a bit of harm; I only loved you all this time. It was the same thing over again as last Christmas, when you *would* keep dancing with that little Lucas.

MARTINE. You're jealous, that's what you are. And this Christmas I'll dance with somebody else—you see if I don't. I'll dance with *all* the boys and not one single time with you—not once, so there!

ALFRED. What have I ever done to you, Martine?

MARTINE. Nothing.

ALFRED. Maybe it's something you don't like to say, but I know you'd not treat me this way without you had some reason. Why are you angry with me?

MARTINE. I don't want to have anything to do with you. Isn't that enough?

ALFRED. All last year long you kept saying: "We'll see—we'll see." Well, you were in no hurry to get married—I could understand that. But you never said a thing like you didn't want to have nothing more to do with me. Everyone thought we was engaged. They still do, Martine.

MARTINE. Why can't they stop plaguing me to get married? Why can't they let me alone?

ALFRED. You don't want to stay an old maid all your life, do you?

MARTINE. I will if I've a mind to. . . .

ALFRED. And run the farm by yourself when your father gets old, eh? With your brother gone in the war—there's got to be *some* man in the house when the old man goes.

MARTINE. There's Nicole—she'll be married by then.

ALFRED. Nicole's thirteen. She's not thinking of marrying yet awhile.

MARTINE. What if I was to go away from here for good? They'd get along. . . .

ALFRED. Where to would you go? I'd like to see you!

MARTINE. You'd best not say that again.

ALFRED. No? Well, let's see. Go on, Martine—*go away.* You're on the high-road already—it's easy! [*She springs up to go. He seizes her by the wrist.*]

MARTINE. [*Struggling to get free.*] Let me be! Don't you touch me! Let me *be,* Alfred. . . .

ALFRED. Now, Martine, you listen to me, my girl. I want you—I can't go on without you. We're going to be man and wife because we were made to be that. You'd never be happy with any man but myself, I know it. We were made for that—I for you; you for me. Living together in the same house . . .

MARTINE. Alfred, stop!

ALFRED. . . . eating at the same table, and resting in the same chairs. Working in the same fields. And you cooking my supper for me to come home to at night.

MARTINE. Alfred, stop!

ALFRED. And you're going to have your children with me, and I'll sit by you while you nurse them at your breasts. We're to be one, Martine, you and I, you the mother and I the father.

MARTINE. Stop, Alfred—stop when I tell you!

ALFRED. Say yes—say it'll be so. Then I'll stop.

MARTINE. No—no—no!

ALFRED. Then what *do* you want?

MARTINE. Let me be—that's all I want. You're hurting—let go my arm. Go away and leave me alone.

ALFRED. That I'll never do.

JEANNE. [*Comes along the road.*] Oh here you are, Martine. Hullo, Alfred.

ALFRED. Good-day, Mademoiselle Jeanne.

JEANNE. Taking a walk? I expect you're making the most of the fine days while they last.

ALFRED. [*Reluctantly.*] Hm . . . yes. I was . . . I was on my way to Bateux; I've got some business there.

JEANNE. You too, Martine?

MARTINE. No. I was here when he came along. I was going home.
          [*Pause.*]

JEANNE. Is this weather going to last, Alfred?

ALFRED. Maybe yes; maybe no. It will if the wind keeps in the east, but it's new moon tomorrow, so there's no telling. [*Another pause.*] I'll say good-day to you now, Mademoiselle Jeanne. [*He begins to move away toward the right.*]

JEANNE. As you're going into Bateux, Alfred, will you take this letter for me?

ALFRED. Certainly, Mademoiselle Jeanne.

JEANNE. I needn't say, "Please be very careful not to forget it."

ALFRED. Don't you fear. If Monsieur Julien goes without his news of you, it won't be through any fault of mine. Is he gone for long this time, Mademoiselle Jeanne?

JEANNE. A few days.

ALFRED. That's no great matter. [*He takes the letter and starts to go.*] I'll keep it in my hand all the way, Mademoiselle Jeanne—don't you worry.

JEANNE. Thanks very much, Alfred.

[*He goes off left.* JEANNE *looks after him for a moment, then at* MARTINE *as she stands with downcast eyes in the middle of the high-road.*]

I'm sorry if I came at the wrong moment. Please forgive me.

MARTINE. You didn't . . . really.

JEANNE. Sure?

MARTINE. Oh yes, Mademoiselle Jeanne. . . . I'm very glad you came. . . .

JEANNE. What now, Martine? Must you go home, or could you stay here with me for a bit, instead? Unless you're in a hurry to get back?

MARTINE. I'd like to stay with you.

JEANNE. Let's sit down here then. This little slope looks as though it's just waiting for us, doesn't it? [*She sits down under the tree and waits for* MARTINE *to join her.*] What's the matter? Aren't you coming up too, Martine?

MARTINE. Yes. [*She joins* JEANNE, *but embarrassment makes her awkward and she goes unsteadily.*]

JEANNE. It's two days since I've seen you at the house. I wish you'd come more often——I enjoy talking to you so much.

MARTINE. I do come, Mademoiselle Jeanne——I'm always there. I was over this morning, talking to Mme. Mervan, but you were busy writing letters.

JEANNE. I know——but that's not what I mean. You only drop in on your way somewhere else——but never for a real visit. When I'm not downstairs you can always come up to my room, you know.

MARTINE. I didn't like to, without you asking me. But next time I will. Thank you.

JEANNE. Don't thank me, Martine. I know I'm selfish to want you all to myself—it isn't that I'm not awfully fond of grandmother, because I am. But we all need to be with people our own age. When you talk about the future to old people, however much they love you, they're only half interested in what you're talking about. But when *you* come into our house, you bring youth and freshness into it. You understand what I mean, don't you? Of course I do see you at your place, but it's not quite the same there—we can't have any quiet times there together, as we can at mine.

MARTINE. I know. Mother's all over a person with her questions always—and Father—he doesn't know how to talk to ladies. It's not his fault, though. But you ought to like Nicole—she's ever so nice.

JEANNE. I see exactly what you mean. I do understand you all, so much better than you think I do, especially as grandmother has told me all about your family. Does that make you laugh? Well she has—and Julien and I talk about you often. Did I tell you he's always asking after you, and sending you nice messages?

MARTINE. You never said . . . Monsieur Julien . . .

JEANNE. He never writes without sending his love to all of you. He certainly adores this place and his friends here. You especially, Martine. When I see your hair and eyes—I think I could easily be quite jealous of you. . . .

MARTINE. Oh, Mademoiselle Jeanne . . .

JEANNE. Why, Martine—that was only my fun. I know Julien far too well to have any such doubts of him—or of you either, for that matter. Oh yes, I do—I know you very well indeed. And I wish you were as happy as you deserve to be. Why won't you take the happiness that is there for you, Martine? Tell me. I'd like to talk to you about it—I'm sure I could make you see that that nice Alfred of yours . . .

MARTINE. No, Mademoiselle Jeanne—you mustn't think I . . . he runs after me, but you mustn't think I . . .

JEANNE. Very well—we won't discuss it. Let's forget I ever mentioned it. It's true—there are certain things that oughtn't to be talked about. But don't be hasty, Martine. Are you quite, quite certain that . . .

MARTINE. I am—I am! I don't ever want to have a thing more to do with him. Never—never, as long as I live.

JEANNE. Never? Well, let me promise you now that I won't remind you of this when you become Madame Murieux. [MARTINE

winces.] Oh, my dear—I've hurt you now. But I was only joking
—honestly I didn't mean it!

MARTINE. [*Pleading*.] You didn't . . . you didn't . . . trūly?

JEANNE. Of course I didn't, Martine. I meant nothing at all—you
can believe that. I can't tell you how I detest the sort of people who
spend their lives trying to make others happy in *their* way. I give
you my word of honour that I'll never mention this again in any
way. But I do wish that if you are ever ūnhappy or in trouble, you
will come and confide in me without my having to ask you to. Will
you promise me that?

MARTINE. [*With tears in her voice*.] Oh, Mademoiselle Jeanne, my
troubles aren't interesting.

JEANNE. What's the matter, Martine? It helps so much to talk things
oūt, you know. I hate to see you cry—I can't bear it, really.

MARTINE. Don't mind about me, please.

JEANNE. I'm sorry. I must have said the wrong thing again. Perhaps
I'm keeping you when you have things to do at home.

MARTINE. No—I've nothing to do. I can stay.

JEANNE. Aren't you chilly? [*She takes a scarf from her neck*.] Do
put this round your shoulders, please.

MARTINE. Then you'll be without, Mademoiselle Jeanne . . . you
can't, in the night air.

JEANNE. I'm too warm as it is. This weather is too much for me.
This autumn atmosphere is too heavy—or rather this summer atmosphere which has lasted much too long. Or it may be that I jūst feel
a little upset. . . . You do look nice in that scarf, Martine. Let
me arrange it for you—it's funny to see you in it. [MARTINE *smiles*.]
Do you like it? You can have it to keep if you do.

MARTINE. Oh no. Mademoiselle Jeanne—I woūldn't want to take it
away from you.

JEANNE. But I'd love you to have it. I've got some others; besides, I
want to give it to you. It was a good idea of yours to come walking
on this road today. I've been in a perfectly hateful temper ever
since early this morning. But yoū've made me feel quite all right
again.

MARTINE [*Without hesitation*.] I'm glad I met you too, Mademoiselle
Jeanne.

JEANNE. [*Takes* MARTINE's *hand, and strokes it absently*.] Do you
know what it is we're always looking for in the things around us,
Martine? Echoes. You're an echo. Such a gentle one, too. You're

the only person in Grandchin I can talk to for five minutes without feeling tired out. At least in my present state of mind—ordinarily it isn't so at all. But this trip of Julien's is lasting so dreadfully long. . . .

MARTINE. Will he . . . is he coming back soon?

JEANNE. He'll be away another week yet—that will make three altogether. Three long weeks without one single day's break—imagine it! But of course, this must bore you very much. Let's talk about you instead.

MARTINE. No. Not about me. Another week, you said . . .

JEANNE. Yes—the time is really getting shorter now, at last.

MARTINE. Much shorter.

JEANNE. What a dear you are, Martine! . . . When he came home with the news of that offer to go and investigate conditions in Germany for his paper, I tried only to look at the advantages; you know—the marvellous impressions he'd bring back with him—and how much better his position would be on his paper afterwards. I honestly thought I had more courage. This sort of thing is so silly—it's only another week, after all—then all the fretting and worry will be over.

MARTINE. A week—that's no time!

JEANNE. I know. Say so again, though. It does me good to hear it.

MARTINE. Very well, Mademoiselle Jeanne. You mustn't . . . [*She can't go on.*]

JEANNE. I know. I'm all right now. But won't it be splendid to see him again? We'll celebrate his homecoming with illuminations!

MARTINE. [*Her voice once more under control.*] Oh yes!

JEANNE. And you shall come over for the dinner of welcome! What a dinner it's going to be. Then we'll be married in the little Grandchin church, and when that's over, we'll have no more to do until the Chamber meets again after the holidays. He'll have to go up to town every day then, of course. But I shan't mind so much, because, there'll always be happiness in store at the day's end. But how I shall look forward to seeing my friend Martine, when that time comes. I'll see you very often then, I hope.

MARTINE. Yes. I'll come very often. I promise.

JEANNE. We ought to live in Paris by rights—but we couldn't very well leave grandmother. Besides there are practical reasons against it—you know what I mean. At any rate, for the time being. No— Paris will have to wait. Not longer than a few months though, I hope. [MARTINE *shivers.*] What is it, Martine? Are you cold?

MARTINE. No . . . no . . .

JEANNE. However long we stay here, it will always be more or less temporary. Because the ideal thing is naturally to make a home of one's own, isn't it? With all your own things about the house, and your own family hearth, so to say. A place that actually belongs to the father and mother themselves—and their children. . . . Why, Martine, you *are* shivering. You're certainly freezing to death. It's almost dark, too. Come, let's go.

MARTINE. Yes.

JEANNE. You're unhappy, Martine. Here I go on, talking all the time about myself and quite forgetting you. You have a sorrow, Martine—won't you tell me about it? Did I hurt you just now, by what I said?

MARTINE. There's nothing the matter with me, Mademoiselle Jeanne. Truly there isn't. . . .

JEANNE. Very well—you'll tell me when you're ready to. Shall we take the footpaths home? It's the longer way round. Yes? No— you'd rather we kept to the high-road?

MARTINE. No. Let's go by the footpaths. And you tell me about . . . about . . . if . . . if it makes you feel better. . . .

CURTAIN

ACT I

MME. MERVAN'S *house. Same as Scene II. The window and verandah-door are closed. End of December. Morning.*
MME. MERVAN *is sewing by the fire.*

ALFRED. [*Entering, left.*] You sent for me, Madame Mervan?

MME. MERVAN. There was no hurry, Alfred. The end of the morning would have done just as well, when you'd finished your work.

ALFRED. That's all right, Madame Mervan. Work's slack just now.

MME. MERVAN. Here's what I want, then. It's five days to Christmas, you know . . .

ALFRED. And you want your turkey.

MME. MERVAN. Right first time!

ALFRED. I'd a notion that was it. I've kept you one.

MME. MERVAN. There's a good boy. Better kill it on Monday—is it a nice one?

ALFRED. You'll have no fault to find with it.

MME. MERVAN. If you're going into Batcux tomorrow, bring me back some chestnuts, will you? Bring plenty. Julien has an enormous appetite—and his little wife can do her share too.

ALFRED. Monsieur Julien will have his work cut out for him, to get through *my* turkey tomorrow.

MME. MERVAN. Don't be too sure! He eats me out of house and home with this running to and fro to Paris and back. Ever since the first of the month, he's had to attend the sessions five and six times a week, and often morning and evening both. Now and then he stays over at his mother-in-law's. That blessed budget! Quite often, the deputies themselves stay away, but those reporters have to be there all the time. They must have been at it till all hours last night, for Julien didn't come home again. It's getting on Jeanne's nerves—that's perfectly plain to see. You know how these young wives are. . . . But you must be tired standing here listening to my chatter, aren't you, Alfred?

ALFRED. Not a bit of it, Madame Mervan.

MME. MERVAN. So I'm very much afraid they'll be moving into Paris after the holidays. As things are now, it would mean a tremendous expense to start housekeeping there. But I should be the last one to blame them for risking it. On winter evenings, the company of one's grandmother is not very entertaining—young people ought to have young people about them.

ALFRED. Oh, Madame Mervan—you can be as young as the youngest of them when you've a mind to.

MME. MERVAN. I'd rather *be* young than play young, Alfred. However, that's neither here nor there. The main thing is . . . [JEANNE *comes in.*] What, ready so soon?

JEANNE. Yes. I reckoned it out that he could get here on the nine o'clock. 'Morning, Alfred—how are you today?

ALFRED. I'm well, thank you, Mademoiselle Jeanne.
    [JEANNE *goes to the window.*]

MME. MERVAN. [*Whispering.*] Bring me back some truffles, too. . . . But—ssh!

JEANNE. [*At the window, looking out.*] It's twenty past nine, grandmother.

MME. MERVAN. Well?

JEANNE. It doesn't take twenty minutes to come from Bateux by cab.

MME. MERVAN. These trains are always late.

JEANNE. Not at this time of day. [*Stands drumming on the pane without turning round.*]

ALFRED. Well Madame Mervan, I'll look after your errands. Wish you a very good day, Madame Mervan and Mademoiselle Jeanne.

JEANNE. [*Still at the window—without turning round.*] Good-bye, Alfred.
    [ALFRED *goes out.*]

MME. MERVAN. Oh, Alfred! [*She jumps up and hastens to the door.*]

JEANNE. [*Turning round.*] What are you doing, grandmother? Why couldn't you . . .

MME. MERVAN. [*Not listening.*] Alfred! [*She goes into the next room for a moment; then comes back.*] Don't be impatient, dear. Julien will be here by ten past twelve.

JEANNE. If he'd been coming this morning, he'd be here by now. Oh, it's Saturday, and of course he hasn't been able to find a substitute. [*She sits down.*] Well, I'm resigned now to not seeing him before tonight or tomorrow morning. [*She gets up.*]

MME. MERVAN. What an idea! It's only that the Chamber sat far into the night, and he woke up too late to catch the 8.20 at Monparnasse.

JEANNE. [*Sitting down again.*] Do you think so, grandmother?

MME. MERVAN. If I were you, I'd be better pleased to have him rest awhile longer—the kisses could wait an hour or so.

JEANNE. Yes—that *would* be the more sensible way. Still—he has so often done the un-sensible thing, just to please me. So I'm spoiled, I'm afraid. Is it very horrid, the way I go on, grandmother?

MME. MERVAN. Just have a little patience, child. It'll soon be the holidays.

JEANNE. None too soon for me. . . . What time is it now? [*She gets up.*]

MME. MERVAN. Ah—you want me to say "It's twenty minutes to Julien" or "It's ten minutes to Julien"—but I don't carry that watch, unfortunately!

JEANNE. Are you sure there always are cabs at Bateux?

MME. MERVAN. Always, if you know where to go for them. There's Foissy, facing the station, or Thivet. And Mauroux further along. Except the day he arrived, Julien's never walked home. [JEANNE *has ceased to listen.*] Let's see—I think I know what *you* need, and it's not an old woman's chatter, either.

JEANNE. Grandmother! How can you say such a thing! You know quite well how I love to talk with you.

MME. MERVAN. I know you're a dear, sweet girl.

[MARTINE *appears suddenly in the open doorway, left.*]

JEANNE. [*In joyful surprise.*] Ah! Here's Martine!

MARTINE. [*To* MADAME MERVAN.] Alfred said you wanted me, Mme. Mervan.

MME. MERVAN. So I do, child. Were you busy on the farm? Anything special, I mean?

MARTINE. No, Mme. Mervan, only . . .

MME. MERVAN. Well, I have to run over there for a minute or two to see your mother. I'll tell her she needn't worry about you. . . . [*Getting up.*] My eyes don't last me any more for all the sewing I have to do; just look at this great pile of mending waiting to be got through. Do be a good child and stay as long as you can to help me finish this basketful—will you?

JEANNE. But grandmother, couldn't I . . .

MME. MERVAN. What, in your state of mind? Oh, but why not?— a very good idea, if you really feel like it. Yes, that will be splendid —do it between you while I run along on my little errands. I'll settle it with your mother, Martine—don't worry.

[*She goes out, left. Jeanne and Martine, on either side of the basket, begin lifting out the contents. When they have chosen their work, they sew and talk. But gradually their work falls listlessly to their sides.*]

JEANNE. You know, Martine—there are no words to describe that old lady's kindness to me. I needn't ask why she sent for you—it was because she could see I'd got to the end of my nerves, and she knew you'd be better company for me than she would.

MARTINE. I thought you might be coming down—or else sending for me. But I didn't think Madame Mervan would—not for that.

JEANNE. She's subtle, grandmother. One of those old people you meet every now and then who have a genius for doing the right thing. How did you guess I wanted to see you this morning?

MARTINE. [*Embarrassed.*] I . . .

JEANNE. Don't sew, Martine. Sit down. [*They sit down, close together.*] Julien isn't home yet.

MARTINE. I know.

JEANNE. And I'm afraid he won't be coming today again. Grandmother declares he'll be here on the 10.12—but she really oughtn't to tell such fibs. The only consolation she can think of is to go away and leave you with me instead. Because you know, you . . .

MARTINE. I don't know . . .

JEANNE. Yes, you do—you know what I mean. You never try to put me off with foolish reasons that I know aren't true. And when I bore you with my fussing, you never show it.

MARTINE. You don't bore me.

JEANNE. Honestly, Martine—I can't imagine what I should have done in this place if it hadn't been for you. These long, long days alone with grandmother . . .

MARTINE. Don't you like Grandchin?

JEANNE. Yes, I like it—and then again, I don't. When Julien is here . . . After all, it isn't as though I was born here, is it? I think it's a sweet place, but I don't feel close to it. And it's hard to endure in winter. Without you, truly I . . .

MARTINE. [*Hanging her head.*] You are kind to say it. . . .

JEANNE. You are so nice, the way you let me talk on and on. . . [*She gets up.*] You must think me a fool. [*She comes back and takes* MARTINE's *two hands.*] It's not simply impatience, Martine. I'm nervous these days—I'm all on edge. I'll tell you why, if you promise not to tell a soul. [MARTINE *looks up at her in surprise.*

I've been nearly certain . . . for days now . . . that I'm going to have a baby.

MARTINE. [*All the tone gone from her voice.*] Oh . . .

JEANNE. That would explain why I've been behaving like this. Only Julien and grandmother know . . . and you, now. Don't tell anyone else just yet, will you?

[*The door on the left bursts open and* JULIEN *rushes in.*]

JULIEN. Hullo there! Here I am!

JEANNE. Julien! I didn't hear you come!

JULIEN. Mulin gave me a lift. He dropped me at the other end of the village. Hullo, Martine!

JEANNE. Oh, Julien! [*She falls into his arms, sobbing violently.* MARTINE *stands by the window.*]

JULIEN. Look here, Jeanne, what's it all about? What an infant the creature is!

JEANNE. [*Standing up.*] I'm such an idiot. I decided all to myself that you'd surely come on the nine o'clock, and when you didn't, I began to get all sorts of the wildest ideas. [*She laughs.*] What must you think of me? I'm ashamed of myself, Julien.

JULIEN. You might have known there was nothing whatever to be alarmed about.

JEANNE. I wasn't alarmed.

JULIEN. What were you then?

JEANNE. I can't explain.

JULIEN. They sat till past midnight yesterday. They're at it again tonight, but Mourron is taking my place. . . . Did I say hullo to you, Martine?

MARTINE. When you came in.

JEANNE. So Mourron is taking your place. Then couldn't he . . .

JULIEN. Keep it? That's the very thing I . . . [*He looks at* MARTINE. JEANNE *follows his glance and they stand together watching her as she remains at her post by the window, as though her feet are riveted to the floor.* JULIEN *lowers his voice.*] He threw out a hint to the editor—and *he* seemed quite willing. Instead of the political work, I'd do the literary supplement—three afternoons a week at the paper, and the rest of the time, I'd work here.

JEANNE. Ideal . . .

JULIEN. There's a good chance for it, but don't say anything about it. [*Looking at* MARTINE, *he raises his voice.*] Very obliging fellow, Mulin . . . Grandmother not in?

JEANNE. No—she went out a little while ago. It's my belief she's planning a surprise or something, [*She hesitates and lowers her voice.*] for Christmas. Between you and me . . .

JULIEN. Well anyway, here we are till Monday with nothing in the world to do. I'm not going to give Paris another thought. I'm here, and that's all I'm interested in.

> [*He sits down. Pause. Both watch* MARTINE *without seeming to do so.*]

JEANNE. [*Embarrassed.*] Wouldn't you like to . . . rest awhile?

JULIEN. Oh, no thanks. I only want to talk to you. [*Pause.*] All well at home, Martine?

MARTINE. Yes thank you, Monsieur Julien.

JULIEN. That's good. Any letters for me, Jeanne?

JEANNE. No, not a thing this morning.

JULIEN. I saw your people. They expect to come over next week.

JEANNE. Is Father all right? Not too tired?

JULIEN. No. [*He looks at* MARTINE. *Gets up.*]

JEANNE. Shall we go upstairs? Oh no—I forgot. Simone's doing the room.

JULIEN. Very well, let's stay here. [*Drums on the mantelpiece.*]

JEANNE. [*With an effort.*] Had you . . . had you . . . anything particular to tell me?

JULIEN. [*With a vague gesture.*] No—except that I'm so glad to see you again.

> [*Pause.*]

JEANNE. [*To whom the conversation is becoming more and more difficult.*] Martine and I were just talking about you when you came in. Martine was nice enough to . . . to interrupt her work for a moment, to . . .

JULIEN. Oh yes, Martine, if, if you've anything to do . . . don't mind us, you know. . . .

> [*During the latter part of their dialogue,* MARTINE *has been looking at them fixedly, still immovable at the window. She has been perfectly aware of her false position there, but something has robbed her of the power to move.* JULIEN *falls silent, and she tries to answer him, but the words will not come. Suddenly, without a word, she leaves the room.*]

JEANNE. Good heavens!

JULIEN. I thought she'd never go.

JEANNE. That poor little thing! Oh, Julien—I blame myself for this. . . . And yet it's a relief to me that she's gone.

JULIEN. What do you mean, blame yourself?

JEANNE. She is suffering torture, that child. . . .

JULIEN. Still that old idea . . .

JEANNE. Why shouldn't we be honest with each other? It is as clear as crystal to me now. We shall never know what that few days' flirtation which meant nothing to you, has done to that girl's simple soul. . . .

JULIEN. Now you're talking nonsense, my dear.

JEANNE. No, I'm not. There's a poor little secret wound hidden there. And still I let her come. I do worse—I run after her. When you're away, I can't do without her. So I do her harm for my own benefit . . . because I can't see her.

JULIEN. Why do you talk to her about me?

JEANNE. Every time I swear I won't. But everything about her forces me to. So I give way to the temptation every time. I don't make her come because I enjoy hurting her—no indeed. But the thing that draws me to her is the feeling of how the poor child unconsciously clings to the thing—and *I* am all that is left to her of you.

JULIEN. Then if you know all this, why can't you be more strong-minded about it?

JEANNE. I try to be. But it is stronger than I. Because you see, on my side, I find something of you in her.

JULIEN. Absurd! Something of me . . .

JEANNE. Yes, when you're not here. You have left a part of yourself in her, just as you leave a part of yourself in a book you have loved or in the little dog that has been your playmate for a day or two. By all the rules, I should be jealous, shouldn't I?

JULIEN. There's no reason why you should be.

JEANNE. No. Poor child—poor Martine, there *is* no reason why, and she knows that very well. But the cruellest part of all is that the moment you come home, she simply ceases to exist for me. In fact, it all but annoys me to have her about. And that is so terribly unjust of me, for how can she be expected to understand that in one little minute . . .

JULIEN. That's exactly the point. Anybody else *would* understand.

JEANNE. And you hold that against her. . . .

JULIEN. No—but I do think you magnify the whole thing.

JEANNE. If they give you a change of work, we'll be more together, and then I shan't be tempted to have her with me so much.

JULIEN. But we'll have her before our eyes every hour of the day then. Every time we pass their farm, we'll think we're being watched from behind a window.

JEANNE. You're exaggerating now. You know we don't intend to stay in Grandchin for ever.

JULIEN. Thank God we don't. By the way, that reminds me. I *have* something to ask you about—very special. If there were a chance of leaving this place, would you like to go?

JEANNE. Is there?

JULIEN. My friend Balut is leaving town and giving up his flat. Of course it's awfully small, but we could get it for a song, furnished and ready to live in.

JEANNE. If it depends on me, I welcome it with open arms. Let's go now, this minute! What do *you* think?

JULIEN. That we should accept with joy as you're so keen on it too.

JEANNE. I'll go in Monday or Tuesday and look it over. But I know in advance that I'll like it.

JULIEN. Sh! [MME. MERVAN *enters left.*]

MME. MERVAN. So he came after all! Well, what did I tell you?

JULIEN. Why all this violent activity, grandmother? Where have you been?

MME. MERVAN. Doing errands for the house. Which are of no interest to you men. Well, Julien—what news have you? Holidays begun?

JULIEN. Not yet, worse luck. It's a pity too, because these trips in and out are decidedly wearing. [*He looks at* JEANNE. *Pause.* MME. MERVAN *studies them both.*]

MME. MERVAN. Something's on your minds.

JULIEN. [*Embarrassed.*] Jeanne and I were just saying . . . no listen, grandmother. There's no point in our being hole-and-corner with you. But as I was saying, this business of rushing back and forth to town is . . . I meant to tell you . . .

MME. MERVAN. [*Sitting down in her armchair.*] That you're going away.

JULIEN. How did you guess?

MME. MERVAN. Why, you surely don't suppose I expected you to live this way a whole winter long? That's no way for young married people to do, my dear boy. So I've been quite prepared for this, you see. And whatever you do, don't hesitate on my account. You shall come down for the summer, if you think you'd enjoy it. . . .

JULIEN. But we're not planning to go just yet, grandmother. It was only that a chance cropped up to—a flat that we . . .

MME. MERVAN. Yes—after the New Year would be best. . . .

JULIEN. Which means until the 15th at least, and more likely until the end of the month. And I needn't tell you how often we'll still be coming over to Grandchin to see you.

MME. MERVAN. As often as you like, my dears. I shall always love to have you.

JEANNE. What *would* be nice—that is, if you'd care to—would be for you to come to town and stay with us.

MME. MERVAN. Oh dear no! That is altogether out of the question. But don't you worry about me; I'll be quite all right here. [A *knock on the door.*] Come in!

MARTINE. [*Enters.*] Madame Mervan, we found an egg this morning. I brought it over for you.

MME. MERVAN. Why, how wonderful, Martine! Imagine that— an egg at this time of year! Show me.

MARTINE. [*Comes to her.*] It's the first this week.

JULIEN. [*Ill at ease.*] If you'll excuse me, grandmother, I'll go and change.

MME. MERVAN. Certainly, dear.

JULIEN. Are you coming along, Jeanne?

[*They go out together, right.* MME. MERVAN *has* MARTINE'S *egg in her hand, and looks at it absently. Then her hands fall into her lap, and she sits silently, absorbed in her thoughts.*]

MARTINE. [*Shyly.*] Madame Mervan . . .

MME. MERVAN. [*Startled.*] Oh Martine, I'm sorry. . . . They've gone upstairs, haven't they?

MARTINE. Yes, ma'am.

MME. MERVAN. Thank you for the egg, Martine.

MARTINE. That's all right, Madame Mervan. [*She goes dejectedly towards the door.*]

MME. MERVAN. Come over here a minute, dear. You're not in a hurry, are you? Sit down. . . . [MARTINE *takes a low chair at the old lady's side.* MME. MERVAN *holds* MARTINE'S *hand in hers, and they remain for a moment in that attitude, silent.*] You know,

Martine—I knew all along it would happen, and now it has. It was much, much too good to last. They're going away. [MARTINE *draws her hand away.*] What is it, dear?

MARTINE. Nothing, Madame Mervan.

MME. MERVAN. I'm terribly sad about it, but I wouldn't have them know it for the world.

MARTINE. [*Suddenly buries her head in* MADAME MERVAN'S *skirts.*] Oh, Madame Mervan, but *I* love you very much. [*She is weeping bitterly now.*]

MME. MERVAN. Ah, Martine—mustn't I tell you my troubles any more? What is the matter? Tell me.

[MARTINE *does not answer, but cries on, as though her heart would break.*]

MME. MERVAN. There, there! Come, little one, you mustn't cry like this! [*Absently, her hand caresses the girl's head.*] No? And I thought you could tell me anything. Not this? Then let me guess, will you?

MARTINE. No! No, please, Madame Mervan . . . [*She raises her head, and dries the tears on her face.*]

MME. MERVAN. [*Regards her anxiously for a moment, then turns away.*] Never mind. I know what it is. It's nerves. I've been thinking about you, Martine, and I'm glad of a chance to talk to you. You ought to be happy, child, and you could be. Happiness is right here, waiting for you, if you'll only put out your hand to take it. There's a fine young man making himself extremely miserable for love of you. Why do you insist on having nothing to do with him? [MARTINE *remains silent, with lowered head.*] You won't tell me? Ah, Martine, what is it you *do* want?

MARTINE. [*In a sudden rush of emotion, clings to* MME. MERVAN'S *hand.*] Oh, Madame Mervan, you *will* let me come often to see you this winter; won't you, please?

MME. MERVAN. As often as ever you wish, child. You know that. I shall love to have someone young coming and going about the house—it will remind me of them. Come now, don't cry any more —don't, dear.

MARTINE. [*Fights back another onrush of tears.*] I'm not—I'm not now any more.

MME. MERVAN. You've asked me to do something for you, Martine. Now, I have something I want you to do for me. That's fair, isn't it? Don't say no any longer to that poor boy. I am only

thinking of *your* happiness—you can trust me. . . . What will
become of you if you don't marry him? Tell me, Martine, what is
there in life but marriage with a good man, and bringing his children and yours into the world? . . . You know I'm right, don't
you? Say yes . . . No? . . . Not a word? [MARTINE'S *head,
drooping lower and lower, sinks again into* MME. MERVAN'S *lap.*]
That means yes. . . . I knew it. Would you like me to speak to
him? Shall I? Let me, Martine. I know what's best. Just so long
as you don't tell me not to. . . . I promise you that everything
will turn out right for you, and without your knowing that it is
happening at all. Truly. And one of these fine days, you'll find
yourself a bride, and you'll have your old friend me to thank for
it. We shall have a lovely wedding, and I'll give you your wedding
dress. How would you like it made, dear? You shall choose the
lace for it yourself. . . . There, do you hear? You shall have a
lace dress—and good lace too, I promise you. . . . So it's all settled? . . . I am so very glad for you, child. For you—and for
myself also. [*But* MARTINE *only goes on weeping desperately.*
MADAME MERVAN *stops short, and when she speaks again, it is in
another tone.*] As bad as all that, is it, little Martine? [*As if to herself.*] As bad as all that. . . . [*Brusquely.*] Martine, lift up your
head. [*She takes the girl's head between her hands.*] Listen to me,
my child. I'm going to send for Alfred, do you hear? You go home
now, and wait there quietly, and when we come to you, you know
what you are to say. Will you promise me to say it?

MARTINE. [*Faintly.*] It's all the same. . . .

MME. MERVAN. Very well. Go now. Try and see that your mother
and father are there too. [MARTINE, *speechless and overwhelmed,
goes slowly to the door, left.*] And don't cry any more, darling—
please don't. We'll have a fine engagement party for you at Christmas, all of us together. [*Listless and resigned,* MARTINE *opens the
door.*] And thank you so much for the egg, dear.

CURTAIN

ACT I

A year later. ALFRED MURIEUX's *house. Well-to-do farm interior.*
Left, window and door on the street. Rear, sideboard, stove, grand-
father's clock. Door, right. Centre, a large deal table with a lamp
on it.
ALFRED *is alone. He is in shirtsleeves, mending a chair. He sings*
to himself as he works, breaking off now and then to look for a
nail and hammer it in. There is a knock on the street-door. Without
leaving his work, ALFRED *calls "Come in."*
JULIEN *enters. He is in mourning and wears an overcoat.*

ALFRED. [*Goes to meet him, wiping his hands.*] It's you, Monsieur
Julien. All ready to go?

JULIEN. Yes, Alfred, all ready. Foissy's cab is here. My wife and
the little maid have got the house put to rights, but we've still an
hour to wait.

ALFRED. Please take a seat, Monsieur Julien. So it's good-bye for good
this time?

JULIEN. [*Sitting down.*] Afraid so, Alfred. Grandchin would seem
too sad to us after this. Just now while I was watching Jeanne
close up all the cupboards, I felt I couldn't stand it another minute.
So I came away.

ALFRED. I know how it is.

JULIEN. I've felt it terribly, these two days. So has Jeanne. I'd rather
have spared her this, but she wouldn't let me come alone. Besides
the old place had to be put in order—we had to come to some decision about it. [*He looks out of the window.*] That huge, empty
house—look at it. Isn't it sad? I simply can't bear to see all those
closed shutters. Houses go into mourning too, don't they? Well, I
never want to live through another few days like these. You don't
know what it cost me to go into my grandmother's room with her
old armchair by the fireplace . . . empty, Alfred. . . . [*He
pauses, sunk in thought.*] Do you know it's already a whole month
since we took her to the graveyard.

ALFRED. And even now I can't get it into my mind that she's gone,

Monsieur Julien. The whole village has gone into mourning for her. Everybody loved her.

JULIEN. You don't know how sorry I am that we went away last year. It may have hastened her death—one never knows these things.

ALFRED. Don't you say that, Monsieur Julien. You were back again in the summer for three months. She got mighty tired along towards the end. She'd had a long life. The first cold weather carried her off—she couldn't stand against it.

JULIEN. My only consolation is that she lived to see me married and herself a grandmother.

ALFRED. Yes, the baby made her go a lot happier. She often talked to us about that. She was more pleased with the baby than anything. I've never thought to ask you—is he well, the little one? Excuse me for forgetting.

JULIEN. He's very well, thanks. He's getting very nice now. I believe he's beginning to know us. He laughed last week. Think of it! His nurse wouldn't believe it when we told her, but I'm certain he did. He's a funny little chap. You must come and see him, Alfred.

ALFRED. I'd be glad to visit you, Monsieur Julien. But it'll be a long time before I'll be going into Paris, I'm thinking. It's none too easy getting away. Thank you for telling me about yourself.

JULIEN. I hear you're soon to be a father too, Alfred.

ALFRED. Not just yet.

JULIEN. In a few months, though.

ALFRED. Pretty nearly six months. Around Easter we reckon.
    [Pause.]

JULIEN. [Not looking at Alfred.] Martine's not taking it too hard?

ALFRED. Martine's all right. She's good and solid. We countryfolk don't pay much attention till the time gets near.

JULIEN. You oughtn't to let her tire herself, though. Sooner or later she'll pay for it if she does.

ALFRED. That's what they say. I've always said there's no use making a lot of fuss over yourself.

JULIEN. That's all very well—but not the rough work, eh?

ALFRED. You can rest easy I won't let her make herself ill, Monsieur Julien. I won't have it come before its right time. She'd be sorry if that was to happen. Reckon I would, too. What's more, I'd never hear the end of it from the old folks.

JULIEN. If there's anything you need when the time comes, Alfred, be sure and let us know at once. We'll send whatever you want from town, or do anything you say.

ALFRED. Same to you, Monsieur Julien, any time. If I can do anything for you, you've only to say so.

JULIEN. I'll not forget, Alfred. You've always been very obliging. If it hadn't been for you, we'd never have got that big place in order. Don't think I didn't notice all the trouble you took with things while I was talking to those people this morning.

ALFRED. That's all right, Monsieur Julien. You said you'd be wanting me to see about some packages.

JULIEN. [*Getting up.*] Oh yes—we'd better go and get that done at once.

ALFRED. No, Monsieur Julien, you stay where you are. I'll get Foissy to help me. [*He opens the door, right.*] Hey, Martine! [*Comes back to* JULIEN.] You stay here by the fire, and drink a good glass of cherry brandy. That'll do you more good than going back to the house.

JULIEN. It's very good of you, Alfred, but I don't like leaving my wife to . . .

ALFRED. If she needs anyone to give her a hand, I'll do it. And if it's on account of her feeling bad in the house, it can't be anything like as hard on her as it is on you, Monsieur Julien. She not being of the family, as you might say. [JULIEN *sits down again.*]

JULIEN. You may be right. Women can stand more than we can, anyway.

[MARTINE *stands in the doorway. She does not immediately come into the room. Her face wears a graver expression than last year. Her hair, that used to curl over her head, is now drawn back, straight and smooth.*]

ALFRED. Here you are. Where were you, Martine?

MARTINE. Out looking after the hens. The big red one hasn't eaten a thing for two days.

[JULIEN'S *eyes have never left her. He continues to gaze at her in silence.*]

ALFRED. All right, if she won't eat, we'll eat her. [MARTINE *comes a step forward.*] Here's Monsieur Julien ready to go, Martine. He's all upset with closing up the house. Get out that bottle of old cherry brandy for him, while I go along and help Foissy get the packages into the cab. [MARTINE *goes to the side board.*]

MARTINE. Don't you want some?

ALFRED. When I get back. [*Opens the street door.*] Your health, Monsieur Julien.

JULIEN. [*Absently.*] Thanks, Alfred.

> [ALFRED *goes out.* MARTINE *takes two glasses out of the side-board with the wine, and puts them on the table.* JULIEN *still watches her.*]

MARTINE. You'll feel better after this, Monsieur Julien.

JULIEN. [*Abruptly.*] Why do you do your hair like that? [MARTINE *looks at him.*]

MARTINE. It's the way I do it. Shall I fill your glass full? [*She fills the glass.*]

JULIEN. But look here, Martine—your hair used to curl so beautifully all over your head. You never used to drag it back this way.

MARTINE. Well a person can't always keep their hair like when they were fifteen! Working over the stove with all the soot—it would look pretty, wouldn't it? [*She sets the glass of wine before him.*]

JULIEN. Didn't Alfred object? Didn't he notice?

MARTINE. Notice what?

JULIEN. And the others—what did Nicole and your mother say?

MARTINE. Mother?—She showed me how.

JULIEN. [*As if to himself. He does not look at her now.*] Of course she did. It's the way she wears her own.

MARTINE. So you're going away again now, Monsieur Julien. It must have been sad for you, coming back to your grandmother's house.

JULIEN. [*Eagerly.*] I might have known you'd understand, Martine. It upset me so horribly just now, that I had to rush out of the place. The last few minutes are always so awful. . . . Poor grandmother. And by tomorrow we'll all be caught up in our old lives again. The baby won't even remember her. We'll say "grandmother," and we'll be meaning "the past and bygone days." . . . Happiness is a cruel thing, Martine.

MARTINE. Why do you say that?

JULIEN. I shouldn't have, I know. Perhaps it would be a good thing after all if the past were to die completely. [*Pause. He looks at* MARTINE *again.*] But it never really does. Does it? Does it, Martine?

MARTINE. I don't know.

JULIEN. I wish I could make you understand. For me, grandmother was a part of . . . of so much gaiety . . . and freshness . . . and youth. I was a bit crazy too at that age. I shall be less so from now on. When I think of Grandchin, I think of laughter, Martine. It is . . . Oh, it stands for so many things to me.

MARTINE. You were engaged here.

JULIEN. I'd have done that elsewhere just as well. But in Grandchin I found one thing that is nowhere else in the whole world. [*He breaks off; then says suddenly.*] What am I saying, Martine?

MARTINE. I don't know, Monsieur Julien.

JULIEN. Martine, there's something I've *got* to ask you. It may be indiscreet, but I must know. [*Pause.*] Are you happy? [MARTINE *bows her head.*] You don't answer me. Won't you?

MARTINE. What do you want me to say?

JULIEN. Are you happy with Alfred?

MARTINE. Oh yes, Monsieur Julien.

JULIEN. Yes?

MARTINE. What do you look at me like that for? Did you want me to say "no"?

JULIEN. I wanted you to tell me the truth.

MARTINE. Why do you ask?

JULIEN. You are right. Why do I? [*Pause.*] You're going to be a mother, Martine. Are you glad?

MARTINE. I don't know.

JULIEN. When the little one's here, you will be happy to have him. You'll see.

MARTINE. That's what they say.

JULIEN. Will you have others too?

MARTINE. Must . . .

JULIEN. There's something else I want to know, Martine. I've often told you how I treasure my memories. I may seem fickle and forgetful, but that's only on the surface. If a thing once leaves a trace upon my mind, it remains for always. There was a time . . . when you and I were great friends. . . . Do you remember? [MARTINE, *very still, does not answer.*] *I* remember. I'll remember it all my life.
      [*Pause.*]

MARTINE. Don't you . . . don't you want your wine?

JULIEN. Yes. [*He takes a sip from the glass.*] What do you do all day, Martine?

MARTINE. I don't waste my time. What with the housework and the cooking and the farmyard. . . . The fields too, only there's not much to do there in winter.

JULIEN. With a baby you'll have a lot more to do still.

MARTINE. Oh my, yes.

JULIEN. Is Alfred . . . is Alfred good to you?

MARTINE. Good to me?

JULIEN. Of course he is—why shouldn't he be? I know he doesn't beat you—but that's not what I mean. Is he a good companion, I mean. Does he make your life cheerful and happy?

MARTINE. There isn't hardly time for that.

JULIEN. You found plenty of time to spare for grandmother.

MARTINE. I always managed somehow when it was for her.

JULIEN. So then . . . so then . . . you *are* happy?

MARTINE. Why do you keep asking me?

JULIEN. And you feel you have nothing to regret?

MARTINE. What would I have?

JULIEN. Has there never been a moment in your life that you think of more tenderly than this? [MARTINE's *head droops.*] There has, Martine. Say that you have kept a corner in your heart for that beautiful July when we met upon the high-road. . . . I shall never be able to think of it without something going through my heart.

MARTINE. [*Completely overcome.*] Why do you say it? Oh, why do you?

JULIEN. Because I thought you'd forgotten.

MARTINE. I never said anything to you, Monsieur Julien. . . . I thought you wanted me to forget. . . . Then, what *do* you want?

JULIEN. [*Hesitatingly.*] What do I want? . . . Only . . . only to know that you still think of . . . of . . .

MARTINE. What's the use?

JULIEN. Nothing.

MARTINE. Then if it's no use, why do you talk about it now? Aren't you satisfied yet with what you've done to me?

JULIEN. Done to you?

MARTINE. [*Afraid of what she has said.*] No—I didn't mean it. But you see . . . Oh, I don't know . . . I don't know. [*She supports herself against the table. She cannot hold back the tears now.*]

JULIEN. [*Deeply moved.*] What's this, Martine? Tears? Ah no—don't try to hide them, Martine. They are too kind, these tears. They tell me that you also know . . . how to remember. I swear I didn't mean to say these things to you when I came. What made me do it? You see now, Martine—nothing does die. Don't shudder

like that, Martine. It's not wicked, what I'm saying. We may all
live the past again for a moment, now and then—there's nothing
against that . . . [*His voice breaks.*] . . . for a moment. . . .
[*Involuntarily, he holds out his arms to her, begging her with his
eyes.* MARTINE, *trembling and frightened, gazes at him in helpless
terror.*] Don't, Martine . . . don't tremble like that. [*He starts
towards her. She makes a slight movement of shamed withdrawal,
but she is ready now to yield to him.*] Martine . . . Martine . . .
[*Then suddenly, he hesitates. His expression changes to anxiety.
Slowly his arms relax. Embarrassed and awkward, he takes her
hand in simple friendliness.*] Before I go . . . I want—I want
to wish you happiness, Martine. [*He moves away brusquely.* MAR-
TINE *remains standing by the table, her breast rising and falling
with suppressed sobs.* JULIEN *mutters between his teeth.*] What
made me do it? What have I said? . . .

    [*They remain so, without speaking.* JULIEN *gnaws his fingers
in profound chagrin.* JEANNE *comes in, left. She is in deep
mourning.*]

JEANNE. Everything's ready, Julien. Alfred has seen to the luggage.
We can go now.

JULIEN. Whenever you say . . . [*He goes to her and presses her
hand hard.*]

JEANNE. [*Looks at him in surprise. Then in a low voice.*] Poor
Julien—I know how you must be feeling. . . . Come, let's go at
once.

JULIEN. [*To* ALFRED, *who has just come in.*] Thanks again, Alfred.

ALFRED. Monsieur Julien, I reckon this won't be the last time we see
you at Grandchin—I just said the same to your lady.

JEANNE. Of course not, Alfred. And if ever you come to Paris, you
know you'll always be very welcome in our house,—both of you.

ALFRED. We'd be happy enough to come if we could, but it's easier
said than done. The animals can't go a whole day without looking
after. Not much chance of us both getting away together. Maybe
I'll be going into Paris on business though—if there's a machine to
buy or one of the customers to see.

    [JEANNE *and* JULIEN *listen without answering.*]

MARTINE. [*After a pause.*] Alfred'll go . . . [*Pause.*]

JEANNE. [*Suddenly.*] Very well, Alfred first, and later on, when the
spring comes, it will be Martine's turn. Is that a promise?

ALFRED. There'll be the kid then. And you know what it means, once children begin coming to a house. They've got to be fed. And while the first one's at the breast the next one's coming on close behind. [*He laughs.*] We don't shirk any of our work, do we, Martine, eh? [*He goes to* MARTINE, *and beats a light tattoo on her shoulder.*]

MARTINE. [*In a stifled voice.*] Don't do that. . . .

JEANNE. [*Gently.*] Don't be afraid to have children, Martine. That is where true happiness is.

ALFRED. [*Filling his pipe.*] There was six of us. Hard on the mother, I reckon, getting up before it was light, scouring and cleaning—and cooking the porridge for all of us. All the animals to look after too. You can't go forgetting your animals just because you've got kids as well. Still, she'd not have changed with anyone else that had none.

JULIEN. [*Painfully.*] Jeanne . . .

JEANNE. [*Taking* MARTINE'S *hand.*] I won't say good-bye, Martine. There's no reason why we shouldn't see each other again.

MARTINE. [*With an immense effort.*] I want to see you again—very much.

JEANNE. I've no doubt we shall come back to Grandchin—once a year at least—for grandmother. Shan't we, Julien? On All Souls' Day?

MARTINE. [*As if to herself.*] On All Souls' Day.

JULIEN. Yes, we'll be sure to come then. [*Goes to her.*] Good-bye, Martine. I shall see you again. [*He takes her hand.*]

MARTINE. You . . . you needn't worry about . . . I'll see to the flowers. . . . I'll go every week.

JULIEN. What flowers?

MARTINE. At the graveyard. . . . [*A pause.*]

JULIEN. Thank you, Martine. [*He keeps her hand in his for a moment, then turns sharply away.*] Good-bye, Alfred. Let me see you one of these days, old fellow. [*He goes out.* JEANNE *puts her arms round* MARTINE, *who, seeming unconscious of the embrace, submits. Then* JEANNE *follows* JULIEN *out of the house.*]

ALFRED. [*In the doorway.*] Well, a good journey to you. Thank you very much—for all you've done for us. [*He stands for a moment watching them drive away.*]

MARTINE. [*Stands where they left her, in the middle of the room.*] On All Souls' Day . . .

[ALFRED *comes back. He smokes in silence.* MARTINE *does not move. The bells of the cab send back a faint tinkle.*]

ALFRED. Now they've gone . . . [*They say no more until the sound of the bells has died away.*]

MARTINE. [*As though to herself.*] On All Souls' Day.

ALFRED. Well, that's over—there's other things to do now. [MARTINE *does not answer. She is looking out of the window.*] What're you looking at?

MARTINE. [*Painfully.*] Look there . . . look . . .

ALFRED. Yes—Madame Mervan's. [*Pause.*] Looks funny to you too, doesn't it, all shut up like that? Dare say you miss running over there to talk to the poor old lady. You got used to it. I've known you to stay there listening to her for two hours and more. [*Pause. He goes to the window and closes the shutters.*] Did I tell you they've sold it?

MARTINE. [*Not understanding.*] Sold what?

ALFRED. The house—this morning. To the Duboyers' new son-in-law. He's going to change it a lot. Build on a wing. He doesn't like the view from this side, so he's going to have all the windows boarded up. . . .

[*He has lighted the lamp on the table. He sits down facing* MARTINE. *The only sound in the room is the ticking of the clock. The curtain falls slowly.*]

THE END

THE STAIRS

by

ROSSO DI SAN SECONDO

CHARACTERS

TERPI

CLOTILDE

MANUEL BARRITOS

SBRANI

CARENGO

NINA

GIANFRANCHI

FIRST POOR RELATION

SECOND POOR RELATION

VITALBI

CONCETTINA VITALBI

MARTA VITALBI

RICCARDO VITALBI

SIGNORA DOMETTI

SIGNORA CORDELLA

THE COMMISSIONER OF POLICE

THE JANITOR

FIRST SCHOOLBOY

SECOND SCHOOLBOY

A PORTER

A MOTORCYCLIST

AN ERRAND-BOY

A BANK CLERK

FIRST MAID

SECOND MAID

THIRD MAID

A DOCTOR

TENANTS

TIME: The Present
Any busy city

THE STAIRS

ACT I

Scene—*The landing of a damp, drab staircase in a populous tenement of five or six stories. The staircase is of the type commonly found in the "walk-up" houses of an industrial city swarming with middle-class people. Three doors open onto the landing, one on the right and two on the left. The first is always open, but has a sort of glass partition, and every time it opens, a bell rings. The floor is covered with sawdust mixed with the mud that has been trampled into it by hundreds of wet shoes during the morning. The fog, the rain, the damp are all evident on the staircase, and the people, hurrying indoors, out of the cold, go up and down continuously. Every now and then street noises join with the sound of the pouring rain. The curtain rises on the first and second maids standing before the door at right and the second door at left respectively, cleaning the brass knobs.*

FIRST MAID. [*Stopping her work to lean over the railing.*] Damn that janitor! Damn these stairs! The wind blows all the way up to the fifth floor!

SECOND MAID. You might better be in the street! My hands are something awful. Damp, nasty, filthy place! And the draught enough to give you your death of pneumonia!

FIRST MAID. Janitor! Janitor! Will you or won't you close that door? Will you be so kind, yes or no, damn you?

JANITOR. [*From below.*] Come down and close it yourself, Your Royal Highness—*you* leave it open when you come in! I'm not paid to shut doors after *you*.

SECOND MAID. Really? What *are* you paid for? That's what I'd like to know.

JANITOR. When you come down, I'll whisper it in your ear, dearie. But till then, you'd best be careful how you talk to me and don't let's have so much of your "damns."

FIRST MAID. Oh, I see! So early in the morning and the gin's warmed you already!

JANITOR. If *you're* cold come on down. . . . I'll warm you! . . .

SECOND MAID. Let him alone. You can't do nothing with him. He's another of Terpi's friends!

FIRST MAID. I wish I was that Terpi's friend! Seems to me he's God Almighty round this place.

SECOND MAID. You bet he is! You're new yet. . . . I've seen a thing or two the ten months I've been with Signora Dometti!

FIRST MAID. D'you think he shut it? Not a bit of it! All the automobiles, and carts, and cars and carriages on the street sound like they're going through this house! You can't hear yourself speak! Just as though the cold's not enough, but you've got to have that racket on top of it. . . .

SECOND MAID. This is a awful house! . . . But let me tell you, she gets a fat rent out of them just the same, that old paralytic.

FIRST MAID. You mean the one that's dying?

SECOND MAID. She's always dying, but she never does!

FIRST MAID. Say, is the house hers or Terpi's?

SECOND MAID. It's hers, the old hag, but Terpi's her lawyer and he's boss round here! More than that too. He gives his orders and makes alterations and he does her right and left! He's a match for the old skinflint, believe me——

[GIANFRANCHI *enters, a little bespectacled man round-shouldered and bent. His downcast eyes look to one side only. He comes through the first entrance at left without hat or coat, and looks at the two maids with suspicion, rubbing his hands over his stomach as is his habit. He goes to the railing and looks up.*]

SECOND MAID. What are you looking at, Signor Gianfranchi?

GIANFRANCHI. [*Still suspicious.*] At . . . I am looking to see that everything is all right!

SECOND MAID. I know what you mean . . . you're trying to see if the fourth floor lot are getting on with their moving. . . . Don't worry. . . . I just saw a desk and a sofa being taken away. . . .

GIANFRANCHI. Ah, that's good! . . . That's good! . . . It's really much the best way . . . my word of honour! . . . It's really much the best way. . . . [*Is about to go back, still rubbing his hands.*]

SECOND MAID. Signor Gianfranchi!

GIANFRANCHI. What is it?

SECOND MAID. Is it true that Signora . . . the old woman . . .
is . . .

GIANFRANCHI. [*Signs to her to be quiet.*] Hush! . . . sssh . . . Be
quiet! [*Exit quite red in the face.*]

SECOND MAID. [*Laughing.*] He got all red . . . shaking all over.
. . . He makes me laugh! . . .

FIRST MAID. Signor Terpi's secretary, isn't he?

SECOND MAID. He's sold his soul to Terpi. . . . He's the old hag's
doormat . . . that's what he is. No one can get past him into her
room . . . no one can go and talk to her. . . . You ought to see
him when some of her nephews come . . . lot of poor wretches,
not a *centimo* to bless themselves with . . . so often they try and
sneak in to her, for only a crust of bread . . . the poor . . .
[*Stops as she hears someone climbing the stairs, and automatically
returns to her polishing.*]

[MANUEL BARRITOS, *slim and delicate, with feverish eyes. His
movements and gestures are abrupt. He has his overcoat buttoned
and the collar turned up. His umbrella is dripping, his shoes
are sodden and shapeless. He mounts rapidly, and betrays extreme
nervousness, as though he is bound upon some desperate mission.
When he sees the maids on the landing, he stops short, undecided
whether to go further.*]

SECOND MAID. Are you looking for anyone. . . .

MANUEL. [*Speaks with a Spanish accent.*] Yes . . . no . . . I mean
to say . . . I look for a gentleman . . . but I think I make mistake. . . .

SECOND MAID. If you'll tell me his name! . . .

MANUEL. Yes, I tell you . . . but he surely is not here. . . . I
make mistake. . . .

SECOND MAID. All right. . . .

[THIRD MAID *comes downstairs from the upper floor and
stops, seeing the stranger.*]

MANUEL. I mean . . . I look in ze ozzer houses by here; if I do
not find . . . I come back . . . make mistake surely. . . . [*Goes
rapidly downstairs and disappears.*]

FIRST MAID. Well he's a queer one! . . . Looked fishy to me. . . .
Maybe *he's* one of the nephews.

SECOND MAID. No, I know them. . . . Besides didn't you hear the
way he talked? He'd a foreign accent. . . .

THIRD MAID. [*Hunting in her pocket as though looking for some-*

thing.] Drat the thing! I've lost my list. I'll have to go back upstairs for it! No . . . here it is. . . . [*Pulls a piece of paper out of her pocket.*] What's that you were saying? . . . That chap . . . he was off when he saw me!

SECOND MAID. Do you know him?

THIRD MAID. Well . . . he's been snooping around . . . yesterday he had the nerve to stop me when I was coming back from my marketing. He asked me if a woman name of Vallini . . . or Valletti or something lived here. . . . I don't know anyone by that name. Do you? No, and no more do I! Today it's a gentleman he's after! See? . . . all fake. . . .

FIRST MAID. Well I never did! I wonder who he's really looking for?

THIRD MAID. Um. . . .

SECOND MAID. What do you bet he's after the . . . party on the third floor? . . .

THIRD MAID. That hussy! . . . You may be right. . . . Yes, I thought of that too! . . . Well ta-ta, girls. . . . [*Goes down the stairs.*]

[SIGNOR GIANFRANCHI *comes out of his room.*]

SECOND MAID. [*Slyly.*] Oh, Signor Gianfranchi, whatever do you think? There's been someone here looking for the scented lady on the third floor. . . .

GIANFRANCHI. [*Terrified.*] Who? . . . When? . . . Why? . . .

SECOND MAID. Now, a minute ago . . . I don't know what he wanted. . . . I'm just telling you because I know your boss is very much interested in the lady. . . .

GIANFRANCHI. [*With his usual gesture.*] Ssst . . . ssst. . . . Be quiet. . . . [*About to go inside again, stops in the doorway.*]

SECOND MAID. Ah! Ah! Don't go, Signor Gianfranchi!

SIGNORA DOMETTI. [*Very stout and very much the grand lady, appears in a peignoir at the second door at left. To* MAID.] Well have you been long enough polishing two brass knobs?

SECOND MAID. It takes time, Signora. . . . It's no treat, I can tell you, standing about in the draught on these stairs. . . . Even Signor Gianfranchi . . .

SIGNORA DOMETTI. [*Poking her head out.*] Signor Gianfranchi! . . . Oh, how do you do, Signor . . . [*Comes out on the landing and detains him.*]

GIANFRANCHI. [*Tries to elude her.*] I'm in a great hurry, . . . I'll be back directly. . . .

SIGNORA DOMETTI. Please . . . just one moment . . . *just one moment*, if it is no trouble. . . .

JANITOR. [*From below.*] Mail . . . Whoever wants their mail right away, can come on down and get it!

SIGNORA DOMETTI. [*To* MAID.] Go down and see if there's anything for us.

   [SECOND MAID *rushes down the stairs.*]

FIRST MAID. I'm coming too. . . . [*Descends the stairs.*]

VOICE. [*From upstairs.*] Any mail for Marinelli?

JANITOR. [*From below.*] Nothing for Marinelli!

SIGNORA DOMETTI. [*To* GIANFRANCHI, *holding him by his coat sleeve so that he cannot get away from her.*] This scandal must stop! . . . For scandal it is, and there are no two ways about it. The woman is a regular hussy . . . perhaps Mr. Terpi does not know it! . . . She receives men all night long! . . . I have a daughter. . . . Last night, three young titled gentlemen leaving my house . . . friends of ours, of course . . . ran into most peculiar-looking people . . . if you had only seen them! Typical roués . . . what must those three young gentlemen have thought . . . a nice thing! Three young titled gentlemen come to spend a musical evening with my daughter!

GIANFRANCHI. [*Red in the face, hangs his head, but at last plucks up nerve enough to say.*] Well, you receive at night yourself. . . .

SIGNORA DOMETTI. Signor Gianfranchi, you astonish me! We are decent, respectable people. . . . Because I am a widow with a daughter, is that any reason why I should not entertain? I must get my daughter settled! . . . The idea of drawing such comparisons! Why, why, my dear Signor Gianfranchi, I'm going to speak very frankly to you . . . she is a . . . yes . . . she makes a business of it. . . .

GIANFRANCHI. Oh! . . . Oh! . . . Oh! . . . [*Tries to get away from her.*]

SIGNORA DOMETTI. And now I'm on the subject let me tell you that Signor Terpi is doing far from the right thing in allowing her to live here. . . . And that's the truth. . . . He should put her out as he has the people on the fourth floor. And after all, they are guilty of nothing worse than being poor! . . . But this hussy, it's too much, too much . . . and he defends her! . . . Now don't deny it, he protects her! . . . And I've been asking to have my rooms papered for the past two months, and I might just as well talk to the wall. . . . And *that* woman has had her entire apartment done over from cellar to garret. . . . Now why? . . . Ah, you see . . . that's the point, why? . . . a mystery! Yes, Signor, who could help thinking evil? . . . with all due respect to Signor Terpi. . . .

GIANFRANCHI. Ssst! . . . Ssst! . . . Hush! . . . I don't want to hear any more! . . . Such talk. . . .

VOICE OF FIRST SCHOOLBOY. [*From below.*] Hurray for old Grappino! . . .

VOICE OF SECOND SCHOOLBOY. Red nose! Red Nose! Good old Grappino!

JANITOR. [*From below.*] Those devils of boys! . . . What are you doing back here this time of the morning?

VOICE OF FIRST SCHOOLBOY. Oh, Grappino! . . . Blow your nose, can't you?

[*The two boys start to climb the stairs slinging their books around with a great deal of noise. They cross the landing and then climb the next flight up, passing a porter with a large box on his shoulders.*]

PORTER. Look out there! . . . look out! . . .

FIRST SCHOOLBOY. I say! . . . Don't squash me with that thing!

SECOND SCHOOLBOY. I'm for a good time.

FIRST SCHOOLBOY. Hurray for poor old Grappino! . . .

SECOND SCHOOLBOY. How long'll he be laid up, do you think, five or six days?

[*They disappear from sight.*]

SECOND MAID. [*Coming upstairs. To* SIGNORA DOMETTI.] There's only a post card, Signora.

SIGNORA CORDELLA. [*Standing in doorway at right, to the* 1ST MAID *who has also come up.*] Where have you been, Giannina? . . .

FIRST MAID. The Janitor called up to say there was mail. It's a notice from the Gas Company. [*Hands it to* SIGNORA CORDELLA.]

SIGNORA DOMETTI. [*Still trying her best to detain* GIANFRANCHI.] Good morning, Mrs. Cordella . . . just come here a moment, will you? . . . I'm talking to Signor Gianfranchi about something which concerns all the tenants in the house——

SIGNORA CORDELLA. [*Afraid of the draught.*] But really, Signora Dometti, there's a terrible draught coming up these stairs! . . . And I am just convalescing, I suppose you know. . . . I know what you mean . . . and you are absolutely right—oh I do. . . . Mr. Terpi will certainly have to do something about it.

SIGNORA DOMETTI. [*Trying to drag* GIANFRANCHI *with her.*] Let us come over to Signora Cordella's a moment. . . .

GIANFRANCHI. [*Losing control of himself as shy people do when annoyed and exasperated.*] Now that's enough! . . . I know all about it. . . . I understand. . . . Please let me go. . . . [*Frees himself with a shove and goes back to his own apartment, stroking his stomach as usual.*]

    [SHOP BOY *with his basket comes whistling up the stairs, crosses the landing and continues up.*]

SIGNORA DOMETTI. [*To* SIGNORA CORDELLA.] Did you see that? You can't talk to him or to Signor Terpi either . . . while we, respectable people, have to tolerate a prostitute living practically on top of us . . . a regular prostitute. . . .

    [PORTER *comes upstairs again.*]

    [SIGNORA CORDELLA *tries to make* SIGNORA DOMETTI *stop.*]

SIGNORA DOMETTI. No, let me speak! I have come to the end of my tether! I must talk now, or burst. Perhaps you have reasons to be grateful to Signor Terpi, and that's why you keep quiet; but I haven't! . . .

SIGNORA CORDELLA. Nothing of the kind! Only I managed to get the fourth floor apartment for my sister; that's all. . . .

SIGNORA DOMETTI. The one Signor Vitalbi has been turned out of?

SIGNORA CORDELLA. Yes, poor soul. . . . But he's not feeling turned out on my sister's account.

SIGNORA DOMETTI. I did not insinuate any such thing, Signora Cordella . . . the idea never entered my head.

SIGNORA CORDELLA. It was no great favour on Terpi's part; still I do feel in a way obliged to him, so I can't be as indignant as you are over that er . . . that person on the third floor! But I think you're absolutely right . . . and if you can get her sent away, I'll be very grateful to you! . . . [*Pointing to a gentleman who has come up the stairs and rung the bell at the front door, left.*] Is that the doctor? . . .

SIGNORA DOMETTI. [*Turning to look at him, as he is admitted to the apartment.*] Yes, that's the doctor, and it looks as though the old lady has really come to her end this time! . . .

SIGNORA CORDELLA. [*Softly.*] If that's the case, my dear Signora

Dometti, how do you think you'll get that *cocotte* sent away, if it's true she's got hold of that awful lawyer who's the master even now when the old lady is still alive, and will be three times the master when she is dead? . . .

SIGNORA DOMETTI. I won't believe he's lost his head over her unless I see it with my own eyes! . . . Hard men like that don't go mad about women. . . .

SIGNORA CORDELLA. They are the very ones that do! I'd go very carefully, if I were you. Find out first what that woman is to Terpi . . . and if she *is* anything to him. . . .

VOICE OF TERPI. [*From below.*] What's that motorcycle doing here. . . . Janitor! . . . Janitor!

SIGNORA DOMETTI. There he is! . . . I'm going! . . .

SIGNORA CORDELLA. We have a right to chat on the landing if we like! . . .

SIGNORA DOMETTI. Certainly! But . . . I'm not dressed! That kind of man has a way of always making one feel at a disadvantage with him!

SIGNORA CORDELLA. You see? That's exactly why I advised you to watch your step with him.

VOICE OF TERPI. [*Below.*] How many times have I got to tell you I won't have motorcycles, carts and cars parked all over the place? Take the whole damn lot of them . . . let them take the whole damn lot of them to hell out of here. . . .

[GIANFRANCHI *comes out all excited from left, goes to the railing, looks down, rubs his hands and goes in again.*]

SIGNORA DOMETTI. The minute he comes into a place, everyone begins to quake.

[SHOP BOY *comes down whistling.*]

JANITOR. [*Beside* TERPI, *cap in his hand.*] Signor Terpi, you are the only one who can do anything about these motorcycles and the rest. . . . Those two boys on the third floor, they both have motorcycles! . . . I can't make them mind me! . . .

TERPI. [*Coming up the stairs.*] No? Well I'll settle that. . . . [*Bumping into the* SHOP BOY *who is still whistling.*] Who taught you to whistle on the stairs? Good-for-nothing!

[SHOP BOY *rushes down the stairs, scared.*]

TERPI. Well, well! The ladies are out gossiping already . . . so early in the morning. . . .

SIGNORA DOMETTI. I heard you coming up the stairs, so I waited for you . . . I never can see you otherwise. In the evening, for instance, I should so much like to have you call on us . . . for a little music!

TERPI. Yes . . . thanks . . . music . . . [*Turns away and speaks to the* JANITOR.] Is Vitalbi out yet?

JANITOR. [*Nervously.*] Yes, Signor . . . they are just taking the last of the furniture away. . . .

TERPI. So he finally decided to understand me when I talked. If he hadn't, it would have been the police for him. . . . [*To* SIGNORA CORDELLA.] Has your sister moved in yet?

SIGNORA CORDELLA. Not yet. I expect her any minute now . . . her furniture is upstairs already . . . but . . . I heard . . . I heard . . .

JANITOR. It's this way, Signor. . . . I heard Signor Vitalbi too . . . he said . . . he said . . . he couldn't send the beds away . . . because his family would have to sleep here to-night . . . he has nowhere else to go . . .

TERPI. Nowhere to go? Does he expect me to supply him with a place to sleep? Tell Mr. Vitalbi to stop his joking. . . . I'm in no mood for his nonsense . . . let him clear out at once . . . and the sooner he does it, the better for him. . . .

JANITOR. Very well, signor! It's your orders. . . . I . . . [*Goes upstairs.*]

GIANFRANCHI. [*Comes in followed by the doctor.*] Signor Terpi . . .

TERPI. Ah! Doctor . . . [*Takes doctor's arm and draws him aside.*]

PORTER. [*Comes down stairs with another piece of furniture.*] Gangway there! Look out. . . .

[*A motor horn is heard loudly, three times.*]

TERPI. [*Jumping.*] Those damned . . .

VOICE. [*From third floor.*] Coming . . . coming right down.

BANK CLERK. [*Comes up the stairs with his coat collar turned up.*] Signor Terpi . . .

TERPI. [*Motions to him to wait, continues speaking to the doctor who spreads his hands, as though to say the case is hopeless. They shake hands. The doctor goes down the stairs. To* CLERK.] What's the matter? I've hardly left the bank, and here you are pestering me again! What do you want?

CLERK. [*Taking some papers out of his pocket.*] Signor Masseri begged me . . . to get your signature on this or he won't be able to put it through before noon. . . . [*Hands* TERPI *a fountain pen.*]

TERPI. Let him come earlier the next time . . . he knows I'm not at the bank after ten. . . . [*Signs and hands paper to* CLERK.]

CLERK. [*Hands him another paper.*] I came on account of this too . . . you forgot it on your desk. . . .

TERPI. What is it? [*Sees what it is.*] Oh . . . God damn! [*Grinds his teeth and clenches his fists.*] I forgot it . . . forgot . . .

CLERK. It's not my fault, signor. . . .

TERPI. Did I say it was? Forgot . . . I'm getting to be a jackass too. . . . forgetting an important paper. . . .

CLERK. It was only an accident, signor . . . we all . . .

TERPI. Thanks! I didn't ask you to make excuses for me that I know of . . .

> [NINA, *a lady's maid, comes down the stairs. She is daintily dressed.*]

TERPI. [*To* CLERK *who hastily takes his departure.*] See you later. [*Almost bumping into* NINA.] Where are you going?

NINA. [*Very much agitated.*] I . . . I was just . . . going on an errand for Madame. . . .

TERPI. You don't say so. . . . Is your Madame not up yet? She is lucky to be able to sleep till noon. . . . Anyone can see she's a grand lady! How does she like the apartment? We had it all done over for her! . . . And thereby aroused the jealousy and envy of these ladies here . . . who also deserve . . .

SIGNORA DOMETTI. Excuse me, Signor, we prefer not to be compared with the lady you are speaking of! . . .

TERPI. You don't say so? Good for you, Signora! That's what I call commanding respect! That's what I call having spirit! [*To* NINA.] You tell your mistress of this! Tell her what the tenants think of her . . . tell her the tenants don't think she's much good. . . . [*Laughs ill-naturedly.*] Ha-ha-ha. . . . Go right up now and tell her.

NINA. [*Pale and frightened.*] Signor, I must go and do my errands!

TERPI. You have some letters to post, perhaps?

NINA. I must go. . . .

TERPI. Secrets, eh? . . . Ah, these mysterious ladies! Now, you ladies here are not a bit mysterious; you're respectable! . . . Ha! ha! Come along, Gianfranchi . . . we must run in and look at our invalid. [*Exit with* GIANFRANCHI.]

> [NINA *stands hesitating, looking angrily at the two ladies;*

then, instead of going downstairs, she turns back upstairs in a state.]

SIGNORA CORDELLA. Do you think that girl will tell her mistress what we said?

SIGNORA DOMETTI. I hope she does. Let her. What a funny man Signor Terpi is, isn't he? He got so excited when he saw Nina . . . asking her if she was going out to post letters . . . and the way he insulted the woman he brought into this house himself . . . with so much ceremony too. . . . There's someone coming down. . . . I'll have to go. Signora Cordella, we'll talk this over some other time.

[*Both ladies go back to their apartments and close their doors quickly.*]

A MOTORCYCLIST. [*Comes rushing wildly down the stairs shouting.*] Here I am . . . here I am! . . . [*Collides with* MANUEL BAR-RITOS *who is just coming up on tiptoes, looking about him nervously.*] Beg pardon! . . . Oh, damn! [*Disappears.*]

[MANUEL *listens, frightened, then resolutely starts to climb the next flight of stairs. He has hardly gone one step, when he turns hastily and goes down again, crosses the landing, too frightened to go on. He stops, seeing the* FIRST POOR RELATION *coming up, followed by the* SECOND POOR RELATION.]

FIRST POOR RELATION. [*Turning to* SECOND POOR RELATION.] Don't be frightened. Come along. If that horrible janitor isn't about, it's a sign the coast's clear. [*To* MANUEL, *who tries to slip by him.*] I beg your pardon, Signor, I suppose you've just come from my poor sick aunt's . . . you're the doctor maybe. . . . Please tell us how she is, poor old soul . . . Not the doctor? . . . The attendant perhaps? Please do us one favour . . . that crook of a lawyer . . . Terpi is his name . . . won't let us near her. . . .

SECOND POOR RELATION. Did you know, he runs all her affairs? . . . I'll bet he has a will in his favour right in his pocket. . . . But that's not what we've come for . . . we don't care about her money . . . let him have it all . . . we just want to see her. . . .

MANUEL. [*Trying in vain to tell them he has not come from the sick room.*] But . . . I do not . . . come from zere . . . I am in great haste . . .

FIRST POOR RELATION. Just one moment . . . tell us at least . . . is Signor Terpi in with her?

VOICE OF VITALBI. [*Off-stage, apparently from fourth floor. Very*

loud.] Where is that lawyer? Let me see him face to face. . . .
Taking advantage of honest folks this way! . . . I know his kind
. . . let's go down . . . he'll see me all right!

SECOND POOR RELATION. [*To* FIRST POOR RELATION.] What did I
tell you? Terpi is here! [*They take the stairs in a rush and disappear.*]

[MANUEL *halts a moment, and then rushes after them.*]

VOICE OF VITALBI. Give me my hat. My coat . . . my cane. Come on!
We'll get out . . . but I'll see that Terpi first!

VOICE OF MARTHA VITALBI. [*Also from above. Shouting.*] Michael,
are you trying to ruin us? At the last minute too . . . Michael,
think of your children. . . .

VOICE OF VITALBI. I want to see him face to face . . . downstairs
. . . downstairs . . . let's go downstairs!

VOICE OF CONCETTINA VITALBI. Father, for my sake. . . . Please,
for my sake!

VOICE OF VITALBI. I've always done everything for your sake! Now,
I'm going to see this lawyer! . . .

[*Doors are heard opening, and the tenants pour out to see what
the trouble is about. The* MAID *comes through* SIGNORA DOMET-
TI's *door.* SIGNORA CORDELLA *comes out too.*]

SECOND MAID. [*To* SIGNORA CORDELLA.] You'll see something this
time! Terpi is going to get an earful. . . . Old man Vitalbi's on
the warpath. . . . It's his family he minds for. . . .

SIGNORA CORDELLA. Heavens! I am sorry for them. . . .

VOICE OF VITALBI. You get away! . . . You can't hold me back, so
don't try. . . . You can't hold an honest man back! [*He appears.
He has a grey beard, carries a soft felt hat in his hand. Banging with
his gnarled walking-stick on every step as he descends. His wife,
daughter and son, do their best to stop him. So does the* JANITOR,
but he shouts at them, turning back.] Coming out? Let them come
out . . . all of them. Let them hear what I've got to say. Not one
of them can say they've not been insulted by this Terpi . . . and his
last insult was for me and you and all the tenants in the house.
. . . How dare he bring a harlot into a house where respectable
people live? . . . a harlot. Yes, I'll yell it at the top of my voice!
A harlot!

MARTHA VITALBI. [*Pleading with him.*] Michael! Michael! . . .
Please, Michael! [*Speaks to some tenants she knows.*] You talk to
him, Signora ——! You too, Signora ——. [*Some of the tenants*

are seen, not many. Their mingled voices sound through the house.]
Signora ——, stop him, for God's sake!

CONCETTINA VITALBI. Father! Father!

SIGNORA CORDELLA. Signor Vitalbi, I am sorry if I am partly responsible for . . .

MARTHA VITALBI. Signora Cordella, we know very well it's not your fault . . . you mean about your sister's taking our apartment. Someone had to take it. . . . It's all that Signor Terpi . . . it's all his fault . . . the scoundrel. . . .

RICHARD VITALBI. Now, mother . . . you too . . .

MARTHA VITALBI. Yes, my boy, I know . . . but it's too much . . . it's too much!

VITALBI. It *is* too much! We have been living here six years . . . and we've always paid punctually. This month we were only a little late, and he wouldn't . . .

TERPI. [*Opens partition door violently, enters followed by GIAN-FRANCHI who is as red as fire.*] What's the matter? . . . What's going on? . . . Signor Vitalbi, do you think we are in the street?

VITALBI. Do you think you can frighten me, springing out on me like that? Well you can't! Come out here. . . . I said I wanted to meet you face to face.

TERPI. Stop shouting. Stop shouting, I say . . . or the police will take care of you . . . and I mean it.

VITALBI. One of these days the police will have you in jail! I'm an honest man; no one can say a word against that.

TERPI. Stop shouting, you old devil! There's a dying woman in there!

VITALBI. A dying woman! Listen to him trying to make you believe he has a heart . . . after throwing a man and his family into the streets because they were late in paying their rent! He couldn't wait a day for his rent . . . and he's sorry for a dying woman!

TERPI. That's a lie, Vitalbi . . . you're trying to pick a fight with me, because you think it will help you, but let's talk sense instead. Are you or are you not two months behind with your rent? Deny it, go on.

VITALBI. I deny nothing. . . . I'll tell the whole world all about my private affairs . . . because I've nothing to hide. I'll tell you all here that I was put on a pension by the bank I'd been with all my life, and I needn't tell you my pension is a good deal less than my salary was. I told Signor Terpi this, and asked him to have patience until I got some other kind of work. I'm old, but not by any means done for. My daughter will graduate soon, and my son just got a position. I've always paid my rent promptly the seven years I've been living here, and I think he could have . . . waited. . . . His conscience should have told him to wait. If I were a crook . . . if I'd got rich dishonestly, everyone would honour and respect me in my old age. Signor Terpi, the rich house agent, broker, banker and lawyer, would take off his hat to me then, instead of turning me out. . . . I'm not sorry I am what I am . . . and I'd have no use for respect from a man like Terpi. . . . I'm an honest man, and my honour, and my family and my home always have come first with me.

TERPI. Well, well! . . . you are becoming interesting! Your home! The honour of your family. . . . What's that to do with anyone else?

VITALBI. Nothing with you, naturally. You wouldn't even understand lives like ours. But these things have everything to do with decent people. I know all about your career . . . even if the others here do not. . . . I know it well! . . .

TERPI. Shut up, and stop making a fool of yourself. What do you know about me? You ought to be ashamed at your age!

VITALBI. At my age one has learnt to size men up. One can weigh them in the palm of the hand. You're a dead weight! You'd be better out of the world altogether! How dare you even discuss my family! Why, your wife ran away to America . . . he has a daughter, and no one knows where he hides her! . . . He keeps women, and then expects decent people to respect him!

TERPI. Really, Signor Vitalbi . . . I didn't think you had it in you. You know all about me, don't you? I never built up a home, did I? Well, well! . . . It was my duty to live on a small salary, and I'd no business to keep a woman! You are right . . . I take my hat off to you. Ah! Ah! Ah! . . . who can this be coming down stairs now? [NINA *and* CLOTILDE *come down.*] Ah . . . my dear Signora . . . Signora . . . Clotilde . . . No, I mean Inez . . . your first name *is* Inez, is it not? Inez Lodoletti . . . such a charming professional name. Come here, my dear. You're just in time. All these people are furious with you . . . they think you're a *cocotte* . . . a real *cocotte*. Come, tell them you're no such thing . . . tell Signor Vitalbi that you know all about the home too, and the family . . . it's not really indispensable for a person to live on a small salary, in order to enjoy the intimacy . . . of a home! . . . I may not know much, because my wife is in America, Signor Vitalbi has told you that . . . but you, dear Inez Lodoletti, you who are an artist, a great singer . . . perhaps you can tell these people . . . teach them. . . .

CLOTILDE. [*Trembling from head to foot.*] Please let me pass . . . let me pass. . . . Oh, I have to go out!

TERPI. Go out? . . . Where can you be going to so early in the morning? Nonsense! Do go back upstairs . . . go back to the intimacy of your home. . . . Don't be foolish! [*Forces her.*] And now that Signor Vitalbi has said all he had to say, he can get out too . . . Let him take the intimacy of his home, and the honour of his family, and his children to the park benches or some fourth class hotel! . . . Ladies and gentlemen, you may now all go back to your apartments: the show is over . . . over! Don't stay here, Signora Inez Lodoletti. . . . I told you to go back upstairs! Go . . . go . . . go. . . . [CLOTILDE *goes, followed by* NINA.]

VITALBI. [*Very tired and old, turns to his family and says.*] It's useless to try and strike a face of brass. Let us go. [*With his family he goes down the stairs and disappears.*]

TERPI. [*To* SIGNORA DOMETTI *who has also come to her door during the hubbub.*] And Signora Dometti . . . keep on with your musical evenings . . . music . . . music. All the fine young fellows, in the intimacy of your home . . . But you don't need any tips from me as to that, do you? Nor you either, Signora Cordella. . . . Go back, dear ladies, to your household duties. . . . This whole thing was just an interlude . . . a musical interlude.

[*Both women say good-bye timidly, and follow their respective maids into their apartments. Silence.* TERPI *signs to the* JANITOR *to go. He obeys. He then looks about him to see if all is quiet, and convincing himself that the row is over, he precedes* GIANFRANCHI *out.*]

[MANUEL *reappears, coming up the stairs on tip-toes.*]

JANITOR. [*From below.*] Hey! Hey there! . . . This is the third time you've gone up those stairs! Who are you looking for?

[MANUEL *rushes downstairs again.*]

CURTAIN

ACT II

A drawing room in an apartment, which at first sight, is seen newly furnished and freshly papered. The furniture has not been bought with a view to having it last long. A door at right, a window at left. Another door rear which leads to the hall, and faces the exit; so that the audience through this door, which always remains open, sees the street door, and when this opens, the stairway. A divan at right, a wicker table left; other furniture. It is night.

The curtain rises as NINA *opens the door leading to the stairs and* TERPI, CARENGO *and* SBRANI *enter, all bundled up in their overcoats.*

CARENGO. Ah! How good it is to come into a nice, warm, comfortable apartment, after being out in the biting cold.

TERPI. You are right, my friend. . . . I see you're a man who knows the meaning of comfort. Take off your overcoat, as I'm going to do, and give it to Nina who as usual is waiting impatiently. Tell me, you who know men, why is Nina always so impatient with us?

CARENGO. [*Looking sideways at* NINA *through his glasses.*] How should I know! You've got to know a girl before you can find out what's in her mind.

SBRANI. Ah! Ah! he always wants to get to the bottom of things. . . .

CARENGO. I'll have to see if Nina will let me . . .

TERPI. It's up to you. . . .

CARENGO. Well, you're the master here, and if I have your permission . . . [*Stretches out his hand towards* NINA.]

NINA. [*Has the overcoats on her arm and is waiting for their hats.*] Let me alone. . . . I've other things to think of. . . .

TERPI. [*To* CARENGO.] You're out of luck! It's just as I said. Nina has no patience with us; can you tell me why?

CARENGO. If you don't know why, how should I? . . . But why do you say "with us." She's out of patience with me; with Sbrani with you, it's another matter. . . . You're master here!

TERPI. There you have the matter in a nutshell. After all, Nina always considers me master here, yes, but not quite a legitimat master!

114

NINA. [*To* CARENGO *who tries to detain her by not giving her his hat.*] Will you give me your hat, please?

CARENGO. I say, listen to him, and don't be disrespectful.

NINA. Only money is legitimate, Signor Terpi.

SBRANI. [*Laughs.*] She hit the nail on the head that time—eh?

CARENGO. Upon my word, it fits the Stock Exchange.

[NINA *snatches his hat and is about to go.*]

TERPI. [*Stretches himself out in an armchair, and calls* NINA *ironically, hissing through his lips.*] Pss . . . psss . . . I'm talking to you, dearie!

NINA. [*Stops.*] You seem very pleased with yourself tonight!

TERPI. [*Pretending surprise.*] Oh! Oh! Oh! Sarcasm? [*Pretending intense solemnity.*] There is a question that I *must* ask you. [NINA *again manifests impatience.*] Look at her! See how stubborn she is!

CARENGO. Mulish!

TERPI. Don't abuse her! [*To* NINA.] A moment ago, if I understood you right, you said that only money was legitimate, and if I am not mistaken, it is for money that you stay here, likewise the sweet lady, your mistress, and both of you live in this apartment for the sake of filthy lucre. Am I clear?

NINA. [*Imitating him.*] Perhaps you are very clear. . . . [*In a natural voice again.*] I'm going now! [*Exits rear with the coats and hats.*]

[CARENGO *and* SBRANI *guffaw.*]

TERPI. And now, my nocturnal friends, you can see how, if one likes, one can artificially create the domestic hearth. Tell me, is there a hearth more hearth than this one?

CARENGO. You are a funny beggar, I'll swear you are! The better I know you, the better I like you . . . and to think that when I met you five years ago, on the Stock Exchange, I couldn't stand the sight of you! . . . You'd been painted to me very black indeed!

TERPI. Well I never! . . . A lamb like me!

SBRANI. I'd hardly call you a lamb! You're a man, that's all!

TERPI. Oh, prince of friends!

SBRANI. As a trio, we're beginning to attract a lot of envious attention——

CARENGO. We are!

TERPI. To hell with them! I used to think a good deal about you two fellows. Between the Bank and the Stock Exchange, poor old Carengo certainly never had much fun. Nothing but work from morning till night, with only an occasional card game at the Club, and certainly not much home life with just that old sister of his and two wild boys who won't ever live at home— And as for that poor old devil of a Sbrani with his invalid wife, he's got nothing at all but the street and the office and his Club . . . I'd also arrived at middle age, more or less; and at that stage a man feels the need of a home. Well, I got one. At least, between ten thirty or eleven and one we're not hard up for a place to go to!

CARENGO. Terpi! You're a great man.

TERPI. Napoleon! And to think that this very morning, a fool of a tenant, an old fool who hadn't even the price of his rent,—by the way, I kicked him out—well, he had the nerve to try and come it over me that he'd come to where he was because he'd always put home life before money-making! . . . [Laughs.] . . . The damn fool!

CARENGO. Yes, damn fool's what I'd say too, to that.

TERPI. Well, there you are!

CARENGO. I wonder——

SBRANI. [To CARENGO.] Honestly, Carengo, you're a bit of an ass for your age! You know, Terpi, if this chap could bring himself to own up to it, he'd tell you that he's sorry he never got married, but spent his life money-grubbing instead. . . . It's a form of softening of the brain! If he *is* thinking seriously of looking for a wife, then he's in his dotage—that's all I can say! He doesn't know it's all rot, this marriage business, the poor old goat; he's not yet learnt that life is just one knock after another, and there's never a minute's peace or rest anywhere. . . .

TERPI. I see you know what you're talking about! . . . Knocks did you say? Yes and shoves . . . and fights. . . .

SBRANI. Absolutely! I've always said I'd enjoy hanging the person that said that home and family was the centre of the world!

TERPI. Never mind about the centre of the world! We'll call it the nest!

SBRANI. [Disgusted, ironical.] Oh, the nest! By all means!

TERPI. Well-feathered, warm, quiet, soft!

SBRANI. Screaming and howling from morning till night, squabbles, all kinds of troubles cropping up at every turn; no peace, no certainty of anything; and just as everything seems to be going swimmingly, some damn new thing comes along and knocks the bottom out of it—sickness, a run of ill-luck, something— Nest! You're home after a day's grind; you close your door. Now for the peace of home! So far so good! But the next minute you find it's worse than the bank and the Exchange put together! Give me the streets, any day!

TERPI. What about being shoved up against, and knocked about——

SBRANI. Well, at least, in the streets you get bumped and jostled by people whose name you don't even know, who owe you nothing, and whom you owe nothing to; but at home . . .

TERPI. . . . In the nest, strangers? Yes, you're right. In that case, strangers in the nest are worse than the ones you pass in the street, and on the stairs! . . . It's useless to close your door, if that's so.

SBRANI. [To CARENGO.] They're all strangers, my boy, take it from me! All strangers, wife . . . children . . . everyone! And do you know who really understands that? [Pointing to TERPI.] He! He pays the piper and calls the tune! When he gets tired, he makes a change and fires the members of his family! Ah! Ah! Let's stop talking about it, or I'll begin to foam at the mouth. Shall we have our game of poker?

TERPI. Let's wait for . . . the other member of the family! . . . Admit she treats you like guests of honour. At this moment, you may be sure she's making herself beautiful for you, which is after all her duty, of course.

SBRANI. And don't you even look in on her? . . . to help her dress . . . give her a helping hand . . . you know . . .

TERPI. Helping hand?

[CARENGO and SBRANI laugh.]

CARENGO. I never saw such a man. . . . He can actually keep her . . . keep her . . . without . . .

SBRANI. As man to man now . . . haven't you spent a single night with her, all this month you've been keeping her?

CARENGO. Look here, Sbrani, he doesn't have to tell you whether he has or not!

SBRANI. He leaves here every evening with us, if that's any indication.

CARENGO. Not always. Two or three times he stayed behind.

SBRANI. Two or three times! [To TERPI.] You might tell us . . . at least tell us where you picked her up! You never told us that, even!

TERPI. You're getting all warmed up about it, aren't you! Wait till she comes, then we shall satisfy your curiosity! Ring, Carengo, will you?

[CARENGO *rings.*]

NINA. [*Enters.*] Yes, Signor?

TERPI. We should be much obliged to know whether the mistress of the house intends to join us now or how much longer we are to go on waiting.

NINA. She won't be long now, I don't think.

[CARENGO *and* SBRANI *laugh.*]

TERPI. Then while we are waiting, may we please have our usual drink?

NINA. If you hadn't called me away, it would have been here now.

TERPI. I beg your pardon! Let us have it, at once, if you don't mind.

NINA. [*About to go.*] Certainly!

TERPI. Oh, one thing more. . . . [NINA *stops.*] With all the tact indispensable in our civilised society, which is most pestiferously inquisitive and malignant even as represented by so narrow a community as the tenants of an apartment house, will you kindly descend to the first floor and find out, discreetly, from that faithful spider of a Gianfranchi, how things are going down there!

NINA. You mean: go and see if the old woman's dead yet or if she's going to die!

TERPI. What do you mean "the old woman"! Say, the distinguished and noble Signora Devoti. Assure yourself, also, if the doctor i with her, and if the nurses are doing their duty. . . .

NINA. Of course! You want to know if the distinguished and noble Signora is passing in proper style. . . .

TERPI. Quite; she must want for nothing that is humanly procur able. . . .

[NINA *exits.*]

[*The door at right opens and* CLOTILDE *appears, overdressed made up as if for the stage. Her forced smile does not hide th inner nervousness which never leaves her, and which shows itsel now and then in a vacant expression of face, when she forget her rôle for a moment, and in her staring eyes which at time seem almost idiotic.*]

TERPI. That's right, Signora Inez Lodoletti. I see you deck yoursel out every evening with the graciousness due such friends as these always rejoicing us with new items out of your repertory. Friend kiss her hands, her arms too, kiss her wherever you like, *if* you like!

CARENGO. [*Kisses her hand.*] We do not presume . . .

SBRANI. [*Doing likewise.*] My dear, Terpi has this method of hiding his jealousy. The fact is, he has never left us alone with you for a single moment, although we have been here every evening for a whole month.

CARENGO. By Jove, that's true!

SBRANI. He's crazy about you; he wants you all to himself. And after all, who could blame him?

TERPI. [*To* CLOTILDE.] Well, say something, say something, Madame Inez Lodoletti, tell us what you're thinking about; open your heart to us; deny these base insinuations!

CLOTILDE. What am I to say? It all depends on you!

TERPI. [*Laughing sharply.*] Splendid! Depends on me, does it? Then I give you leave to speak quite freely. . . .

CARENGO. Now, Terpi, be decent; don't embarrass the Signora.

TERPI. I should think not! Only I don't like to seem . . . well . . . too stingy with my treasure. . . . My sweet Inez, I promised my friends a moment ago to be very frank with them, and I will do so. I admitted them into our nest without restrictions, so that if at any time a desire should possess your soul for one or the other of these fine specimens of manhood . . .

SBRANI. [*Pointing to* CARENGO, *laughing uproariously.*] There's a fine specimen for you. . . .

CARENGO. [*Retorting in kind.*] No, he . . .

TERPI [*Continues.*] . . . banish from your mind the idea that you might be betraying me if you yield, because you have my permission now, in advance, to conclude the love rite whenever the fancy strikes you. . . .

[NINA *enters and serves the drinks.*]

CARENGO. [*To* CLOTILDE.] Signora, don't listen to him. Terpi is in a risqué mood tonight.

SBRANI. Let's play poker. Don't mind him. He's only feeling a bit ardent!

CLOTILDE. [*Laughing stupidly, but trembling in every limb.*] Oh, I don't mind! . . . I'm not excited! . . . I'm only a little nervous . . . no reason at all! Please don't stop on my account . . . please go on . . . I like it . . . it livens me up. . . .

NINA. Signora, drink something to wash down Signor Terpi's jokes!

TERPI. That will do from you; get out, you chattering little clown!

NINA. Clown yourself! [*She rushes off rear, opening first the door of the room, then the outside one, and closing both carefully after her before she starts down the stairs.*]

TERPI. [*Seats himself with his friends, ready to play poker.*] Keep that maid of yours within bounds, my dear Signora, or I'll be reluctantly compelled to send her away, even if I do thereby deprive you of a faithful servant!

CLOTILDE. She is faithful to you, too.

TERPI. We won't discuss that! She has certain special errands to run for you it seems . . . she is in possession of certain secrets. . . .

CLOTILDE. [*Alarmed.*] It's not true . . . it's not true!

TERPI. Oh, that's all right. I'll close one eye to it . . . both if you like! . . . Boys, I'm going to bluff you magnificently this time——

SBRANI. [*To* CLOTILDE.] Signora Clotilde, here's a piece of information for you. If you wish to take advantage of it, do so: Terpi cleared ten thousand in the market today.

CARENGO. Terpi, you should have brought Signora Inez a piece of jewelry! . . .

TERPI. I never did have much respect for you two fellows but I've certainly lost what little I had. This treasure of a woman is the most modest, chaste and simple creature living . . . she despises the vanity of jewels. How is it you never noticed that? . . . How vulgar the world is after all . . . with its preconceived notions! A woman goes on the stage for love of art . . . the middle classes don't know this, and you can't convince them of it; they all think a woman who takes to the stage . . . is a prostitute . . . mad for diamonds, and loose living! . . . The pot is mine. Full house. Your deal, Carengo. . . . My darling, if I am not mistaken, my friends here get fonder of you day by day. They proved it too, a moment ago . . . they insisted on my telling them just how I met you . . . discovered you! They must know that we have known each other for years. Tell them, dearest Inez, you tell them the truth!

CLOTILDE. [*Trembling.*] Why, it . . . it was this way . . .

TERPI. She is always truthful . . . I've never known her to tell a lie . . . I should say not. . . . She's crossed the ocean innumerable times . . . to Paraguay, Uruguay, California, Mexico . . . etc. . . . and after nine years . . . back she came again. . . .

Didn't I find her one night, sitting in a café next door to the Trianon, waiting until it was time for her act? Why, said I to myself . . . there's little Inez, after nine whole years, still young, and looking as ardent as ever! . . . Neither Paraguay nor Uruguay hurt her: fate had allowed me to meet her again, and I'd have been a fool not to take advantage of fate! I said . . . come, you delightful Inez . . . come to our love nest; give me back the intimacy of our past days together! [*He laughs.* SBRANI *and* CARENGO *join in uproariously. A loud knocking is heard, evidently at the street door.*] The devil! One of the tenants must have forgotten the key . . . and is raising Cain. . . . He'll wake the whole house if he doesn't look out. . . .

CARENGO. He's certainly kicking up an awful racket!

SBRANI. Let's get on with the game.

CARENGO. I pass.

SBRANI. It's up to you, Signora. . . . I'll bet you have a good hand.

CLOTILDE. [*Is scarcely able to see her cards for the trembling of her hands.*] I don't know. . . .

SBRANI. What do yoū mean, you don't know? . . . Now, Terpi, you must really stop your everlasting jokes, or she won't be able to play at all.

TERPI. Did you ever stop to think what a queer thing love is?

NINA. [*Lets herself in with her latchkey from the outside. She is greatly excited.*] The police!

TERPI. Where?

NINA. Downstairs, at the old woman's. . . . The two nephews are with them. Mr. Vitalbi's there too as a witness.

CARENGO. What's wrong, Terpi?

TERPI. Nothing, nothing, old man, nothing to worry about. It's old Vitalbi trying to get even with me for chucking him out; he's probably got those two poor fools into a state about Signora Devoti's will. . . . I'll bet they think I've got it hidden somewhere . . . so as to get all her money. . . . I'll send the whole pack of them to jail for their pains! . . . I'm glad they came! . . . [*To* NINA.] Were the doctor and the nurses in her room?

NINA. Yes.

TERPI. Were they with her when the police arrived?

NINA. Yes . . . I think so. . . .

TERPI. Good! Wait here, boys; we'll finish the game when I get back. [*To* NINA.] You come with me!

[*Exit rear, running down the stairs followed by* NINA, *who closes the door carefully after them.*]

CLOTILDE. [*As soon as* TERPI *has gone, cries out desperately.*] Damn him! . . . Damn him! . . . Those stairs are his curse! He's up to the neck in intrigue for all his joking. He's money mad; his passion for money hounds him all the time. . . . [*To both men, who sit gazing at her in astonishment.*] You've sat here every night for a month, and played cards with me, but I've never been left alone with you before. Neither of you knows who I really am . . . he won't let me speak . . . he's paralyzed me with fear . . . I'm in his power. . . . His awful eyes are on me all the time. . . . He makes you both treat me like a prostitute! And I am one . . . now . . . I've become one in the past month . . . since he's been keeping me. . . . But, Signor Sbrani, Signor Carengo, I am his wife. . . . His wife. . . . My name is not Inez Lodoletti. I am Clotilde Terpi . . . yes . . . you think I've gone mad! But I haven't, I'm perfectly sane. . . . Don't look at me as though I were mad . . . for God's sake, believe me. . . . I'm sane . . . perfectly sane. . . . Tell me . . . tell me at once, quickly please —quickly . . . where is my child? Where has he hidden her? . . . Where? . . . He told me she was away at school . . . for God's sake, tell me where she is! . . . I came back on her account . . . after nine years . . . nine years! Because he promised me to let me see her . . . my child! . . . I only want to see her, that's all . . . just see her for a moment. . . . I'll die if I don't. . . . For God's sake . . . tell me where she is . . . tell me where she is. . . . [*Sobs.*]

SBRANI. Be calm, Signora, be calm . . . try and explain what you mean. . . .

CARENGO. We are your friends . . . try and tell us. . . .

CLOTILDE. My little girl . . . my little Maria . . . where is she?

SBRANI. But just a moment, Signora . . . this is so . . . so unexpected . . . so astounding. . . .

CARENGO. I've only known Terpi two years . . . about two years . . . that's all. . . .

SBRANI. That's about as long as I've known him too. He never spoke to us of a child . . . he never said he had a child. . . .

CARENGO. He never even told us he was married! . . .

SBRANI. I did hear it mentioned once or twice that his wife had run away to America. . . .

CLOTILDE. Yes . . . I ran away . . . it was I who ran away to America. . . . Nine years ago . . . [*Rushes over to the window.*] let me go . . . let me go . . . [CARENGO *and* SBRANI *have followed her.*] No, no . . . I'm not trying to kill myself. . . . I'd like to throw myself down those stairs. . . . I'd like to break every bone in my body . . . those damned stairs. . . . Don't worry! I'm not raving . . . I only want to look out . . . I've got to look out. . . . [*Looks out of the window.*] Yes, there it all is . . . all of it . . . the cause of everything. . . .

SBRANI. What?

CARENGO. What do you mean?

CLOTILDE. Never mind . . . I know . . . I'm not mad . . . believe me . . . but I soon shall be. . . . My child . . . Oh, try and think! . . . won't you just try and remember if that devil . . . ever said one word . . . one word even. . . . Surely he *mentioned* her to you . . . a clue is all I need . . . any clue . . . then I could find the school she is in!

SBRANI. No; he never said a word so far as I can remember. . . .

CARENGO. Nor to me either. . . .

CLOTILDE. Damn him . . . damn him. . . . He's got me in his power . . . he knows he's got the whip hand . . . and he'll keep me there as long as he wants to. He knows he can keep up this revenge for the rest of my life if he wants to . . . he's made me a prostitute! . . . He's made me a prostitute! . . . I did go on the stage . . . but I wasn't a prostitute! . . . I never loved him . . . never. . . . He wanted me, I never wanted him! . . . I used to live here in this house. That's why he's brought me back here now . . . I used to live here with my father and mother. . . . My father was cashier in a bank . . . like that old man Vitalbi. . . . Once he needed some money very badly so he took some. . . . He thought he could put it back in time. . . . He went to Terpi . . . thinking he would help him out. . . . Terpi was looking after the Devoti affairs then. He made me marry him . . . for the two thousand dollars. . . . And I would have been faithful to him . . . but he was eternally up and down those damned stairs . . . on the street . . . making money. He's the devil incarnate! And . . . then . . . the child . . . that was my sin . . . to have brought her into the world! And I thought I could live without her. I ran away with the man I loved . . . a foreigner. He gave me every luxury that money could buy. He drugged me with pleas-

ure . . . to try and make me forget the longing for my child. . . .
And I brought him to poverty. I ruined him with my longing!
. . . He took me all over the world, and at last . . . I went on
the stage . . . singing in cabarets. . . . I had to do it. . . . I
left him . . . I wanted my child. . . . I left the man I loved
and came back here. I got a job at the Trianon. *He* goes there . . .
I followed that man. . . . I followed him for months, to find out
where he had my child. . . . All the people I'd known had disappeared. . . . No one knew me . . . and everything had changed
. . . after nine years. . . . Then he found out who I was. He
recognised me . . . through my make-up . . . he knew me . . .
damn him . . . damn him! Ah! Ah! Ah! . . . "I'll take care
of you," he said. "I'll keep you." And I said, "Let me see my child."
. . . And he promised. . . .

CARENGO. Signora Terpi . . . is this true? Are you sure you are telling us the truth?

SBRANI. Do such things really happen?

CLOTILDE. Yes . . . yes . . . it's true. . . . Oh no . . . no it's
all a lie! . . . I'm mad . . . grief has driven me mad! I should
not have told you! Oh, why did I tell you? . . . Why? I've told
you, so that you might help me . . . help me to find my child . . .
my little Maria . . . my little Maria!

[*The door is flung violently open, and* NINA *enters. A confused hum of voices is heard.*]

CARENGO. What's the matter?

SBRANI. Is anything wrong?

CLOTILDE. [*Seeing* NINA *pale and nervous.*] Nina, what is it?

NINA. There's a crowd downstairs. . . . The tenants are all swarming out of their apartments . . . they're all over the stairs. The
police are in the house!

CLOTILDE. [*Rushes over to the window and looks out again.*] Then
. . . then . . .

NINA. Don't, Signora . . . there's nothing down there. . . .

CLOTILDE. Where then . . . where . . .

NINA. In the crowd on the stairs, I . . .

[MANUEL BARRITOS *appears in the doorway.*]

CLOTILDE. [*Shrieks.*] Manuel! . . . Manuel! . . . [*Rushes to him
and throws herself into his outstretched arms.*]

NINA. [*To* CARENGO *and* SBRANI.] Please . . . please go . . . go
downstairs to Signor Terpi . . . he might need you. . . . Leave

them alone! . . . He has just come from the Argentine . . . two days ago. . . . Leave them alone . . . say nothing. For God's sake don't say anything . . . have pity on them! . . . They'll kill themselves if you tell Signor Terpi . . . have pity on them! [*She hustles the two men unceremoniously into their coats, and pushes them out of the door.*]

CLOTILDE. [*Crying in Manuel's arms.*] Manuel! . . . Manuel! . . . My dear! My dear! . . . It is you! It's really you! . . . Oh, Manuel . . . darling!

MANUEL. Clotilde! . . . Clotilde! . . . I find you again! . . . You wished to kill me, no? . . . Why have you left me? . . . Why? Tell me!

CLOTILDE. Never mind, love! It's all over now . . . you've found me again!

MANUEL. I have come here with a show . . . I dance in it. . . . I would have danced for the devil to come here . . . Oh, Clotilde, I am no good wizout you—I die wizout you. Only to see you every day —let me do zat and I will work my fingers down to ze bone, Clotilde! Querida! Querida! Look at me! . . . Say you have not gone away from me to stay. You love me, you love me? Say yes, Clotilde! Come, we go away togezer. I must die if I must lose you again. I want to die wizout you.

CLOTILDE. I should die too, if I lost you again. I only want to see my child, and then we'll go away again! . . . We'll go back to the stage . . . to our dancing . . . anything . . . anything. But I must see my child . . . just once. That's all I'm waiting for. I'd be satisfied to see her from a distance. Then at least my mind will be at rest, and I'll be able to love you again as you deserve, my dear. My poor Manuel . . . who gave up everything for me . . . ruined himself, all for me . . . and in return I have only destroyed your peace of mind and ruined your life.

MANUEL. Nozing is ruin if you love me still . . . only come back to me, Clotilde. Only leave me never any more.

NINA. [*On guard at the door.*] You can't stay here . . . you must go now . . . go down the way you came. They'll think you're one of the crowd, and you'll get away before it thins out!

CLOTILDE. Yes go, Manuel . . . go now . . . quick, quick!

MANUEL. I cannot go like zis! Tell me when I can see you again . . . where I . . .

CLOTILDE. I shan't be able to meet you . . . I'll write . . .

MANUEL. I cannot leave you.

NINA. You must . . . go . . . oh, do hurry up!

CLOTILDE. Oh God . . . why do you torture me like this!

NINA. Go, please, please, Signor!

CLOTILDE. I'll send Nina to you . . . she'll bring you a message . . . Go . . . go!

NINA. [*Opens the door and looks out, and closes it at once.*] You can't now . . . it's too late. He's coming upstairs. He's here already. . . . [*Pushes* BARRITOS *into the room at right, as the bell rings.*] Hide yourself in there, in there! [*To* CLOTILDE, *who has fallen onto the divan near collapse and on the verge of fainting.*] Pull yourself together! You know you've got to be careful! I must open the door now!

    [NINA *goes to the door and opens it.* TERPI *enters followed by* SBRANI, CARENGO, *the* POLICE COMMISSIONER *and some of his men.*]

TERPI. [*To* POLICE COMMISSIONER.] Sit down, Captain . . . sit down. [*Turns to some of the inquisitive tenants who have followed them up, and still hang about on the stairs.*] Go back home, all of you! I haven't killed anyone, have I? You've seen for yourselves there's nothing wrong. I've committed no crime. Those fools tried to darken the last moments of our sainted Signora Devoti. But thanks to Divine Providence, she was taken into eternity before she heard the foul slander they tried to throw at me, for their own vile ends. She died peacefully. Go home . . . go home, all of you, and pray for the dead . . . for all the dead. . . . We're all of us ghosts with a bit of flesh on our skeletons. We may be live ghosts now, but we must all cast off the flesh when the time comes. . . . [*To* COMMISSIONER.] Take a seat, Captain. . . . Take a seat. . . .

CURTAIN

ACT III

Same scene as Act II. Immediately afterwards.

When the curtain rises, CLOTILDE *is seated near the door, right. She is almost hysterical, and her eyes look demented.* NINA *keeps watching the door, right, panic-stricken at the thought of* MANUEL BARRITOS *hidden behind it.*

TERPI, *having ushered in the men he has brought with him, is aware that something peculiar has happened in his absence. All the time he speaks, therefore, he never takes his eyes off* CLOTILDE *and* NINA.

TERPI. There, my dear Captain and good friends! you've seen how a man may laugh at his fellow men. I say laugh, because they arouse no anger in me, and no indignation. Not even any rancour! . . . They couldn't be really evil, even if they wanted to; they're far too small and pitiable for that! Stupid! . . . Stupid is the word for them . . . yes, stupid!

CAPTAIN. My dear Signor Terpi, you saw of course, that I was on to their game at once! I saw what they were up to. Spite, that's what it was, spite, and damned nonsense.

TERPI. Anyone with a grain of sense could have seen that . . . and you've a good deal more than a grain. . . . It doesn't take you more than one glance to see what fools some people—I might say *most* people, are. Not that I'm trying to establish my moral status with you! I'm merely letting off steam! It does no harm to do that once in a while. Just look what a fool that old Vitalbi made of himself. A man who was never able to save a dollar in his life or put by a little nest-egg against a rainy day to avoid being turned out of his home and put to shame . . . he preferred poverty to renouncing his domestic, no, I mean his *home* life, so he lets himself be carried away by spleen, and descends so far as to come here with two poor devils like those tonight after publicly insulting me in the morning! That's what he's come to in his old age. Doesn't he know I'll send him to jail for it?

CAPTAIN. He'll go to jail all right!

TERPI. Even though he is blinded by fury, hasn't he sense enough to see I'm not the type of man that coerces a woman on her deathbed into making a will in my favour? Haven't I been her business manager for twenty years? What was it but my own ability and hard work that turned her small capital into a fortune? But no— the poor man who couldn't bear to sacrifice his sacred "home life" even though it kept him poverty-stricken all his days,—has to end up by acting like a damn fool, as if he'd had no experience of men and things. Like a savage instead of a man of the world! How on earth can a man like Vitalbi be such an imbecile as to imagine that a man in my position would even need to do such a thing! I own three pieces of property and a bank—my word is law in the financial world; yet I wait for that marvellous woman to die and force her to make her will in my favour—and hasten the end by terrorising her, I believe that was part of it! He might have taken the trouble to inform himself that Signora Devoti made her will before she became ill and paralysed, and that it was deposited with a reputable lawyer while she was in perfect health and sanity.

POLICE COMMISSIONER. I knew it! Signor Terpi, I never for a moment placed the slightest value on the accusation; I hurried here to investigate rather for your sake than for those poor fools.

CARENGO. We were all there and saw how the old lady died.

CAPTAIN. The doctor was with her; so were the nurses. . . . She had every care. . . . I'll swear to that! Those three will get a few years . . . they'd better learn that they can't play such tricks like that on a gentleman.

TERPI. Tricks, Captain? You're right. The world is full of fools, it's like bedlam let loose sometimes. . . . Now you know me as a lawyer, as a man of importance, if I may say so. But you don't know me really. Come over some evening and have a game of cards with me, and my friends here. . . . Then you'll find out what sort of a fellow I am in private life. You'll like knowing me. . . .

CAPTAIN. Thank you, Signor Terpi . . . I shall be honoured. . . .

TERPI. Honoured . . . nonsense! We'll have an hour or so together some evening . . . and you can tell us about some of your cases. . . . It should be worth hearing what rotten things our foolish humanity does every day . . . and we'll laugh at it all over a glass of wine and a game of poker. . . . We have a gracious little lady here too, ready to hand out her smiles to us . . . she's had her experiences too, oh, yes, but she's still young and fresh looking. . . . Having perhaps committed her share of folly, it is to be hoped she won't go in for any more! It doesn't seem possible, does it my friend, that after years of living, men's passions should be just a game? Yet it is so, although they don't know it. Following one's illusions means ending up like old Vitalbi. . . . The important thing is to see these illusions coming out of the corner of your eye, and as soon as they are born crush them as you would the head of a viper! Perhaps you might answer me that a man who really ceases to believe in anything, who has no illusions, becomes hardened. . . . But I tell you that if he knows how to laugh, that doesn't happen. Let him know *how* to live, and look at reality in all its ugliness, accepting it for what it is, that's strength! The man who stops wanting things, my dear Captain, and who expects nothing sentimentally in any form, who works, and goes on living just for the sake of working, knowing that nothing is worth while, and that nothing counts—believe me, that man is the only kind that's worth a damn. . . . And it takes guts to be like that!

COMMISSIONER. Signor Terpi, I go away filled with admiration for you. You are right. I have known you as an important man, but I did not know until now what a personality you were! If I can be of service to you any time, please call upon me. . . .

TERPI. [*During his entire speech has kept his eyes on the two women, who behave as before.*] Just a moment. I should like to prove that you are right in believing in me. Perhaps I may help you to uncover another example of our pitiful human illusion. [*Glaring at* CLOTILDE.] Before you go, please examine this apartment; I want to show you this soft nest, in which you will always be cordially welcome . . . it will only take you a few minutes . . . the place is prettily furnished, though I do say so myself! You shall see. . . . [CLOTILDE *gets up, embarrassed.*]

NINA. Signor Terpi . . .

TERPI. [*With feigned surprise.*] What is the matter? . . . There's surely no harm in showing the Captain over the place, even its most intimate corners? There's nothing hidden here, is there? . . . Am I right, friends . . . am I right, Captain?

NINA. It's not that . . . but the rooms are all untidy. . . .

CLOTILDE. Yes; that's what she means . . . the rooms are all untidy. . . .

CAPTAIN. That's all right, Signor Terpi . . . I understand . . . I quite understand . . . please don't bother Signora. . . .

TERPI. Very well . . . another time! . . . when . . . [*With emphasis.*] when everything is tidy again! [*Shakes hands with the* COMMISSIONER.] [*To* NINA.] Go down to the door with the Captain . . . and on your way upstairs see if Gianfranchi has seen to the body. That's the way of the world . . . some die, others prepare their funerals, others gossip, gamble, suffer, quarrel . . . and the merry-go-round never stops! . . . Good-bye, my friend.

[CAPTAIN *bows to* CLOTILDE, *shakes hands with* SBRANI *and* CARENGO, *and again with* TERPI *and goes out, followed by* NINA *who closes the door after them.*]

TERPI. Carengo, Sbrani, I'm tired, friends. For days, my days have been æons instead of days. A thousand people to see, a thousand things to do, hold this one off, keep an eye open for that one because you know he's out to do you, cheat you, trap you, get you into a mess. When I think back in the evening over what happened in the morning, it seems a century ago. . . . Well, let's call it a day now. Our game didn't come off. And at last a night has come when I'll sleep here beside my sweet Inez Lodoletti . . . Signora Devoti is sleeping too downstairs. Don't think it's out of cynicism that I want to sleep in this house, tonight . . . if one were to remain awake every time someone dies, one would never sleep at all. That's a fact. . . . Maybe you think it will not be easy for me to lie so quietly beside the fragrant beauty of Inez Lodoletti, and sleep . . . and you are not wrong! Sometimes I ask myself, is it not an obligation one owes to the places left empty to fill them with love! Death destroys and life immediately creates! . . . What harm would there be if Signora Lodoletti and I, having seen death creep down the stairs, were to concern ourselves tonight with repairing its damages?

CLOTILDE. [*Up to this moment has remained shuddering, and staring before her, without a word. Now she interrupts sharply.*] Stop! Stop! I can't stand it any longer! I can't listen to him anymore! . . . I'll scream! I'll beat my head against the wall! . . . I'll grovel on the floor . . . but this torture must stop!

TERPI. Sbrani, Carengo, friends . . . you realise that Signora Lodoletti is hysterical tonight. . . .

SBRANI. Terpi, I say it as a friend . . . Come along with us . . . leave Signora in peace. . . .

CARENGO. I think Sbrani is right . . . the excitement of the evening has been too much for Signora . . . she needs rest. . . . Come away and leave her to sleep. . . .

TERPI. [*Sarcastically.*] Oh . . . oh . . . the situation is becoming hot, to speak vulgarly. . . . Your sympathy for my beloved Inez begins to look a trifle suspicious, I must confess. . . .

SBRANI. I speak out of the merest friendliness. . . .

CARENGO. Now, now . . . Terpi . . .

TERPI. So that's as far as friends are to be trusted! . . . Just leave them alone five minutes with the coveted beloved! [*Putting an end to the argument.*] Well, if you want to stay here and help Signora Lodoletti over her hysterics, for my part, do so. . . . I'm going to bed. . . . [*Both men instinctively take a step as though they were about to stop him.*] Yes . . . to bed. . . . [*Ironically.*] Even if the room is so terribly untidy! . . . I don't care . . . I'm not the Captain. . . . I'm in my own home. . . . [*About to enter right.*]

CARENGO. [*Stops him.*] Terpi . . . I say . . .

SBRANI. [*Steps between* TERPI *and the door right.*] Terpi, we're all friends here . . . we are true friends to you. . . .

TERPI. [*Laughs in their faces.*] The untidiness of that room seems to be a very serious matter!

CLOTILDE. [*As though she has gone suddenly mad.*] Let him go! . . . Let him! Let him beat me! . . . Let him kill me! . . . It will be better . . . it would be better. . . . Only let him do it!

TERPI. [*With a burst of laughter.*] My dear friends, don't you see how ridiculous you are! Imagining that there's a tragedy about to occur . . . as though the happiness of my married life were threatened; as though adultery were destroying my domestic peace. You've forgotten that all this is an artificial home, and has this advantage, therefore, that if it *is* to end up in tragedy, the tragedy will be artificial too. How is it that you both, right after the example given by Vitalbi, how is it that you both can make the same mistake? What do you mean by treating me as though you think I'm a fool? [*Hears a key in the lock.*] Here comes the faithful servant, the servant in intrigue. . . . [*To* NINA, *who enters.*] Nina, little Nina, where did you learn to be the perfect maid? What school did you go to?

NINA [*Turning white.*] I don't know what you mean!

TERPI. No? . . . Well, go on and do your work. Go in there and bring that scoundrel I saved from the police, out here. Go on; I want to talk to him! . . .

NINA. I . . . I don't understand. . . .

TERPI. [*Suddenly furious.*] If I break your neck and then send you in, will you understand then?

NINA. [*Seems to shrivel up with terror.*] No!! No!! . . .

TERPI. [*Controlling himself; turns his rage to laughter.*] So you're taking it seriously too, are you? [*To* NINA.] You fool, I only wanted to show you that, notwithstanding the thousand and one things which Terpi, attorney at law, has had to do the past few days, he has still had time to see what was going on . . . what you thought you were doing so secretly, like the professional go-between you are. You see, what I said a moment ago was true; while someone is dying, in the same house, someone else is plotting, and dancing, and quarreling, and loving, and cheating. . . . Take the dance seriously and they'll have your scalp! [*Solemn and determined.*] Good-night, Carengo . . . . good-night, Sbrani . . . see you tomorrow at the stock market! . . . Don't be afraid, I'll settle this affair with Signora Inez Lodoletti, in a few moments; she is not my wife of course, so that makes it easier . . . goodbye. . . .

[CARENGO *and* SBRANI *cowed and thoughtful, shake hands with* TERPI, *forced to do so under pressure of his stronger will.*]

CLOTILDE. [*Crying out again.*] No! No! . . . Please don't go! Please don't go! Don't leave me alone with that man! He'll hypnotise me! I'll never have the strength to fight against him! . . . I *am* his wife! I am! I swear it! I am his wife! What I told you was all true! May God strike me dead, this minute if it was not!

TERPI. So? They know the story? Splendid! Now they really are our bosom friends! This woman does not even think herself worthy of the respect I tried to show her, by trying to save her from this last gutter she has sunk to. I tried to save her dignity by making you believe she was a *cocotte*. Good for you, Signora Terpi, you have rewarded me nobly again, as you did nine years ago. You want my friends to go downtown tomorrow, whispering "Poor Terpi, his wife betrayed him," to everyone they meet.

CARENGO AND SBRANI. Terpi!

CLOTILDE. I don't care! I don't care about anything now! I only want to see my child, and then go away again with the man I love. Nothing else matters to me!

TERPI. Ah! Don't think I care any more than you do! Against the man Terpi, the whole world may snicker when it pleases; as it pleases; as much as it pleases. This old wolf has certain arguments which make your society at large crawl to him like lambs. It doesn't matter who knows, my dear gentlemen, that Terpi has a wife who is unfaithful to him, because Terpi the lawyer only has to shout "I have no wife," "I've not been betrayed" for all of them to shout "He has no wife! Whoever said he had!" It's a lie. . . . My dear girl, I need nobody but everyone who knows me, needs *me*. You may want to answer that down inside, I know what you've made me, and others know too! . . . But all that stuff about the inner self is a fable, my dear woman, believe me; a fairy-tale, like your love for that imbecile who is in there listening to me. What is publicly discussed is the only thing of value in the world! Now even if everyone knows I am this or that, but also knows they dare not admit that they know it, then it's the same as if I were not whatever it is. [*He laughs.*] We're all friends together now, so come on, little spitfire, call in your lover and let's enjoy the next episode of our story!

[MANUEL *enters from right, staggering like a drunkard.*]

MANUEL. I am here, Señor, I am here. Wiz me you may do as you will, but let zis poor woman see her child. Don't make her out of her mind. And after, let her go away. My career is ruined. All I have had, I have lost; but I want nozing but her. She is all to me. She is nozing to you. It is a coward who does what you do to her. You are so strong man, you cannot be so hard for two poor creatures. You must have enough revenge now.

TERPI. Carengo, Sbrani, tell the truth now, wasn't it worth while staying on for this farce!

CLOTILDE. Gentlemen, even if you despise me, have pity on me. . . . Ask him to let me see my child just once . . . then let me go! I'm nothing to him anymore . . . nothing but a rag, a dirty rag! Why should he go on cleaning his shoes with the rag . . . when there is still a man to whom that rag is his whole life? I beg you on my knees, gentlemen . . . I implore you . . . have pity on me!

CARENGO. Signora, please get up!

SBRANI. Please. . . .

CARENGO. Terpi . . . I don't know what to say. . . .

SBRANI. I wonder if I might . . .

TERPI. Might what? . . . What do you want to know? . . . Maybe you want to see me kick them both out, downstairs? Would you?

CLOTILDE. Yes . . . do it . . . do what you like! But let me see my child! Just for one minute! . . . I won't even ask to go near her. Gentlemen, it has been a tragedy. Terrible. To live without my child. Never seeing her, only being able to picture her as she was when she was little! . . . She's not a baby anymore! She's a grown-up girl . . . she is sixteen. . . . I long so to know what she is like now, that I have no desire for anything else in life. . . . If I can see her, just once . . . if I can photograph her on my brain! See how tall she has grown . . . how she carries herself; how she dresses . . . what she is like! . . . Then I shall be able to go on living . . . in poverty, the old life of the cabarets . . . the life of a gypsy . . . I will be able to stand it all again . . . and Signor Terpi shall never be bothered with me again! . . . I'll never trouble him any more. Judge for yourselves whether it is right to keep me here like a prostitute, and not let me see my child?

[SBRANI and CARENGO turn to TERPI.]

TERPI. [Furious, white as a sheet.] From afar! Just for one minute! You want to see her, do you? Really see her! . . . In the school I've got her in? With a garden and trees round it! Behind the gate playing with her schoolfellows! All right, you shall! And photograph her on your brain! There in the midst of all the greenery. Of course . . . of course . . . you loved your child! Still, you ran away; because I . . . didn't know how to create the intimacy of the home for you, because I was always out quarreling . . . on the stairs . . . on the street! [Raises his fist to her.] Imbecile! Believing such nonsense! Nothing exists! nothing! . . .

CLOTILDE. [Shrieks at him.] Where is Maria? Where is she?

TERPI. Where? She doesn't exist anymore either! She's dead!

[CLOTILDE utters a terrible cry, and falls to the floor. All stand stiffly as though paralysed. A moment of silent terror.]

TERPI. [Goes to the rear, opens the door, and looks at what seem shadows of people going down the stairs with lighted torches.] For Signora Devoti! . . . That's right! Go up and down with your torches! . . . The dance goes on among the ghosts! . . . [Steps out on the landing. SBRANI, CARENGO and NINA lift CLOTILDE off the floor. MANUEL, evading TERPI and the others, throws himself on CLOTILDE's inanimate form.]

MANUEL. Dear Clotilde, come we will go away togezer . . . at once! Life will be good again, you will see! The days will pass and the pain will not be so big . . . Don't lie so there! . . . Querida! . . . Don't stay one minute more in zis house. He will let us go. We have no ozer place, but we will find a corner to sit and cry togezer. Perhaps we die, but we die togezer, Clotilde . . . togezer . . . alone, you and I. . . .

CLOTILDE. Behind the gate! . . . Playing with her schoolfellows on the lawns. . . . And she was dead all the time! Gone. . . . She never . . . grew up! I shall never know how she looked! . . . Dead, all the time.

TERPI. [Comes back. Harshly.] And now, all of you! Gentlemen, be so good as to go at once please. You first, you poor devil . . . go on! Wait for her in the street. . . . Not another word, if you prefer the stairs to the window! Go! [Takes MANUEL by the shoulders and pushes him out of the door, rear.] Good-bye, Carengo! Goodbye, Sbrani. . . . See you tomorrow, tomorrow down-town. . . . No matter what happens at night, the day after we go down-town, if our legs can still carry us. . . . Good-bye . . . don't worry about this . . . everything is all right. . . . [Shoves both men out, and when they've gone, imperiously signs to NINA to go.] Downstairs with you; you're to watch by the body, all night! . . . [NINA goes down the stairs, terrified. After a pause, roughly to CLOTILDE.] Are you going, or are you not?

CLOTILDE. [As though coming out of a trance.] Where to?

TERPI. How do I know? With your song-singer . . . with your lover!

CLOTILDE. I've not the strength . . . anymore. . . .

TERPI. You haven't the strength! . . . Well I have, and I've never been without it!

CLOTILDE. I'm only a poor woman. . . . I was a mother once. . . .

TERPI. If I'm not mistaken, I was the father. . . .

CLOTILDE. Yes.

TERPI. Well then!

CLOTILDE. I thought she was grown up . . . and she was not.

TERPI. Naturally . . . that's how it is! Men dream, and fate gives them hell! Fate, my dear, can do nothing to me anymore, after what it has done already! Now I sleep when I must sleep, eat when I must eat, and I hit my fellow men who dream, and hit them hard! . . . Hurry up, now, I'm sleepy!

CLOTILDE. [*After a pause.*] No . . . I've not the strength anymore! So long as I believed she was alive I wanted to live! To love, and dream . . . but what shall I do now?

TERPI. The singer doesn't suit you anymore!

CLOTILDE. Go away, and leave me in some corner here, like a dog! Have a little pity. . . .

TERPI. No one ever had any pity for me! And I never asked for any either!

CLOTILDE. Just a place in some corner. . . .

TERPI. So you want to stay?

CLOTILDE. What for?

TERPI. Nothing, my dear, of course! There's nothing for you to do! . . . You could be the servant and prepare my coffee in the morning, and clean my clothes and take my beatings, and swallow poison when I'm ready to give it you. And so pay for your sins that way, if you like!

CLOTILDE. You'd keep me here out of revenge . . . still?

TERPI. Not at all! If that were the case, it would mean I still believed in something.

CLOTILDE. Then what?

TERPI. Then, get out!

CLOTILDE. Everything is over.

TERPI. Get out. . . .

CLOTILDE. All I can do is cry for her! . . . There is nothing left but that! It is the way of life. . . . I know now. . . .

TERPI. You see, there is still some kind of bond between us. . . .

CLOTILDE. Our dead child, you mean?

TERPI. Yes, the dead! That is our tie! And don't worry, for we are only two ghosts ourselves. . . .

CLOTILDE. It will be a life of hell again!

TERPI. It's enough to say "life"; that includes hell.

CLOTILDE. If you can reconcile yourself to it, and not throw me out, after having kept me here as a prostitute, for a joke . . .

TERPI. One doesn't keep a person even as a prostitute, if she has lost all interest for one!

CLOTILDE. Oh, I know, even when I was your wife, you only wanted me for the most degrading of all reasons. . . .

TERPI. Degrading? We are ghosts of flesh.

CLOTILDE. That's why I hate you! I knew you only wanted my body . . . that was all the feeling you had for me. . . .

TERPI. Ghosts of flesh! Ghosts of flesh! . . . [*Furious.*] And out of the flesh, shadows are born! We created one ourselves! She was flesh! and now . . .

CLOTILDE. [*Standing upright.*] Now a shadow! A shadow!

TERPI. [*Laughing horribly.*] Throw yourself out of the window . . . if you can . . .

[CLOTILDE *flings the window open, but cannot bring herself to obey him.*]

TERPI. You can't! Try the stairs, then, that'll be easier!

[CLOTILDE *rushes out to the railing, but cannot throw herself over it.*]

TERPI. Not even that, eh? [*He goes after her, drags her in, takes her by the wrists and throws her on the divan like a rag.*] You fool, don't you know there is no need of killing oneself? We are dead already! That is the bond between us!

CLOTILDE. Stop laughing! Stop laughing! Oh, have pity on me!

TERPI. Perhaps! Perhaps I will!

CURTAIN

THE FIRE IN THE OPERA HOUSE

A Nightpiece

by

GEORG KAISER

CAST OF CHARACTERS

Monsieur
Sylvette, *his wife*
The Opera Singer
An Old Gentleman
A Servant
A Coachman
A Priest
Lay Brothers
An Usher

In 1763 the Paris Opera House burned down.

THE FIRE IN THE OPERA HOUSE

ACT I

The scene is a lofty room.
[*Enter from the left an old gentleman. He leans on a stick and is supported by a servant. He points with his stick to an armchair to which the servant leads him, and sinks down into it considerably out of breath.*]
[*Exit* SERVANT.]
[MONSIEUR *enters from the right deeply engrossed in a book. Seeing the old gentleman he shuts the book in feigned astonishment.*]

MONSIEUR. So soon?

OLD GENTLEMAN. Yes. . . . The merry-go-round has made another turn. . . . Pennants flying, lacquered carriages . . . [*He laughs silently.*] . . . Society.

MONSIEUR. You've hit on a witty simile there.

OLD GENTLEMAN. Yes. . . . Well, so I open a door . . . no wider than is permitted! . . .

MONSIEUR. In which you are merely making use of a privilege stipulated when you sold the house.

OLD GENTLEMAN. But a privilege whose scope is limited to what your own kindness allows.

MONSIEUR. [*Eagerly.*] Then you do not hold me to it?

OLD GENTLEMAN. Pray don't, on any account, allow me to become obtrusive.

MONSIEUR. [*Seating himself.*] You opened a door then? . . .

OLD GENTLEMAN. Such a commotion! The nooks and screens were alive with giggling and kissing!

MONSIEUR. There's the merry-go-round of your anecdotes set moving again. . . . One after another they come, in endless rotation!

OLD GENTLEMAN. And every now and then tumble over each other and land on the ground in pairs.

MONSIEUR. Always the climax!

141

OLD GENTLEMAN. The point is indispensable! [*He laughs noiselessly and wipes the tears from his eyes.*]

MONSIEUR. Was it as amusing as all that?

OLD GENTLEMAN. I sat in the circular green closet today, and there I assisted at a most delicious episode. . . . Mademoiselle de . . .

MONSIEUR. *Names?*

OLD GENTLEMAN. Ah! You disapprove! *I* should consider myself fortunate to go down to posterity in a ribald story. If discretion were to do me out of my chance of immortality, I'd eschew discretion. However . . . the little lady was as fat as a grub and amorous as a corn-beetle. She'd fall into a state of ecstasy at the sight of a pair of legs. Her eyes meowed at 'em . . . literally. . . . She was out in pursuit of her innocence, as Madame de . . . [*Laying two fingers on his lip.*] once put it. But it was not to be caught! She would gladly have enlisted the help of Monsieur de . . . [*Fingers on lips.*] Quite the handsomest man there. Whenever *he* came into view, the meow rose to a veritable concerto! Only the gentleman didn't happen to be musical. A real calamity for the little woman. . . . We were alarmed for her reason, so we made up our minds to cure her. We had Monsieur de . . . write her a note, inviting her to meet him in the Green Closet while we should all be in the garden letting off fireworks. Everyone was in on it, of course. Monsieur de . . . hid behind a bush and at the appointed time, our friend vanished also . . . whisked into the house. I give you a guess who was in the closet waiting for her. . . . Monsieur's trained bulldog.

MONSIEUR. [*Quietly.*] And?

OLD GENTLEMAN. What—and?

MONSIEUR. The point of the jest?

OLD GENTLEMAN. Have you missed it?

MONSIEUR. Shall I finish the story for you?

OLD GENTLEMAN. I am curious to hear it . . .

MONSIEUR. So the love-sick little person went back into the garden where Monsieur de . . . was standing in the light of the fireworks, surrounded by all the rest of the company, and said to him: "Monsieur, I was not aware until this moment that you were a cur."

OLD GENTLEMAN. [*Laughing.*] That would have been equivocal, to say the least of it.

MONSIEUR. So are all animal stories.

OLD GENTLEMAN. With a single exception. . . . Which happened to

take place in this very room. The perpetrator of this one was that
skin-and-bone Madame de . . . [*Taps his mouth.*] May it glorify
her memory forever! . . . You might as well have looked for a
needle in a haystack as for charms of person in *that* one. You grazed
your fingers on her angles! Wherever she appeared it was a continuous bombardment of personal remarks. The moment she became visible from the wings, so to speak, everyone began to scratch!
But one night she planned an act of vengeance. She caught a huge
quantity of fleas . . . had them caught for her more likely. I'm
ready to yield that point, for the creatures would have bored to
small purpose in *her* hide. And kept the bloodthirsty little beasts
several days in a state of starvation. I had a good many people that
evening. . . . Crowds of men and pretty women. When the time
was right, Madame leaves her armchair and puts a small snuff-box
on the mantelpiece over there . . . which I pick up to see how the
springclasp works. She pleads sudden indisposition, which compels
her to retire early to bed . . . and is gone the next instant. [*He
shakes with inward laughter.*]

MONSIEUR. And with her, no doubt, went all your desire to ridicule
her further?

OLD GENTLEMAN. By no means! The very reverse occurred. . . .
Then symptoms of the invasion began to show themselves . . . first
in a slight general restlessness. Someone gave himself a sur-
reptitious scratch. . . . Someone else began rubbing his shoulder.
But the thing couldn't be hidden very long, and suspicion
turned into certainty when we found one of the lancers dead inside the snuff-box on the mantelpiece. Madame had given us fleas!
. . . Very soon the situation became absolutely intolerable. You
needed *ten* hands to relieve the itching . . . and before long you
were driven to beg for aid from your nearest neighbour, for the
most wickedly-placed bites were simply not to be reached! And so it
went on until you couldn't help *what* you did. The bites burnt like
fire. . . . It was scratch or die! . . . The lights were put out, and
then at last we could help one another without embarrassment. And
we all let ourselves be helped! . . . I did not have the rooms lit up
again that night.

[MONSIEUR *rises and moves away from the table.*]

OLD GENTLEMAN. We found ourselves the envy of all Paris! For
weeks this room was besieged by visitors to the scene of the flea
hunt. The wild night passed into legend, and for long afterwards,

whenever two lovers were seen together, somebody would be sure to say: "They're catching the fleas out of Madame de So-and-So's snuff box."

[MONSIEUR *comes back a step toward the table and turns away again. He goes over to the window and stands drumming upon the pane.*]

OLD GENTLEMAN. [*Laughs long and silently.*] Where do people meet nowadays? Is there a regular centre? I wish you'd tell me all the news. I've been on such short rations in my little forest castle.

MONSIEUR. The Opera is the rage of the moment.

OLD GENTLEMAN. Is the ballet very brilliant?

MONSIEUR. They're all in it . . . from the King down to the hairdresser.

OLD GENTLEMAN. What? Who? Dancing at the Opera? What sort of a freak is that?

MONSIEUR. His Majesty has lost his head over a dancer, so we are now under the rule of a merry pair of legs!

OLD GENTLEMAN. Is the King in love with her? Does she love him, too?

MONSIEUR. Precisely . . . him, too. . . .

OLD GENTLEMAN. Isn't this treading somewhat close on scandal? Are you implying that she has betrayed His Majesty already?

MONSIEUR. No worse than any of the others.

OLD GENTLEMAN. Is this common knowledge . . . or rumour merely?

MONSIEUR. Oh, it's everybody's secret.

OLD GENTLEMAN. And not deposed?

MONSIEUR. It is a charm the more! Imagine how much more furiously the fire of passion must burn when coarseness is added to the fuel! . . . At noon the King; at night the hairdresser.

OLD GENTLEMAN. And is the current ballad very spicy?

MONSIEUR. It is pitched no higher than the key set by the royal lover himself!

OLD GENTLEMAN. And what key is that?

MONSIEUR. He bestows upon the favourite a ring set with a cut jewel of such value that it may not even be mentioned. . . .

OLD GENTLEMAN. But is twittered nevertheless on every lip. . .

MONSIEUR. And stammered out by babes and sucklings!

OLD GENTLEMAN. An infallible proof . . .

MONSIEUR. . . . that by the ring you may know whose wench you are entertaining under your roof!

OLD GENTLEMAN. Amazing!

MONSIEUR. Well, does this surpass your bulldog and your fleas?

OLD GENTLEMAN. When is it they dance at the Opera?

MONSIEUR. Every Monday.

OLD GENTLEMAN. That means tonight! . . . How does the King contrive it? . . .

MONSIEUR. He has invented the costume ball!

OLD GENTLEMAN. What does one go as?

MONSIEUR. Tonight, Chinese.

OLD GENTLEMAN. Chinese. . . . Our ladies in those tight little skirts?

MONSIEUR. At a dancer's "command," legs are the order of the day!

OLD GENTLEMAN. *There* you trump our trick! Ah, to be young . . . now! But one would always come too late, even on the last day of the world. [*At the window.*] That huge Opera House—full of Chinese! Royalty rubbing elbows with the rabble! . . . Come over here and see. . . . I can tell you every building. . . . That broad black roof, sloping from the top like a coffin-lid . . . that is the Opera House! Sh! . . . Isn't that the music of the ball? . . . Do you hear those voices? That's women screaming. . . . The whole of Paris over there, gyrating in a ballet thousands strong! . . . A triumph! . . . A ball in the Opera House!

MONSIEUR. [*Moves toward left.*] Lights!

[*Enter* SERVANT *who lights the candles on the mantelpiece. Then he draws the heavy curtains over the windows and glass door in the rear.*]

OLD GENTLEMAN. Quite right. The curtain comes down upon the spectacle! . . . And a chilliness makes itself felt between us. . . . Utterly unintended on my part. . . . Well, the spectacle will be there for a while yet . . . then it, too, will fade into darkness. And in the end the worms will hold *their* ball in houses whose pillars are made of bones. A lecherous little breed!

MONSIEUR. [*Standing beside the table.*] Did I understand rightly that you are willing to release me from a certain obligation? I hope you will forgive my seeming discourtesy.

OLD GENTLEMAN. [*Coming back from the window.*] You will surely not lay me under the necessity to do so.

MONSIEUR. Since the suggestion emanated from yourself, I put all my scruples aside. You come here to Paris every two or three months . . . in order to revive old memories.

OLD GENTLEMAN. [*Looking up at him attentively, with an expression of amusement.*] That is the one condition in our bargain upon which I must insist.

MONSIEUR. [*Suddenly enraged.*] And it is the one which I most strenuously contest!

OLD GENTLEMAN. However, I shouldn't dream of imposing upon you because of it. [MONSIEUR *gazes at him fixedly. The* OLD GENTLEMAN *taps him on the arm.*] I find my merry-go-round the most excellent of diversions. . . . Now, won't you go and perform your metamorphosis into a Chinaman?

MONSIEUR. What do you mean by that?

OLD GENTLEMAN. That I do not presume upon a claim to your society . . . with a ball going on at the Opera House.

MONSIEUR. [*Ironically.*] You are too considerate!

OLD GENTLEMAN. And *you* are already a precious quarter of an hour late through my fault. A gentleman of our set can hardly afford to absent himself from a ball like this. You'll have all the ladies laughing at you: "Monsieur is late. . . . Can it be that he has a sweetheart in the suburbs? . . . Do we not detect about his person an odour of tousled sheets? . . ." You could not live down such gibes as those short of expiation upon a hundred sofas. And that, dear boy, is devilish strenuous atonement.

MONSIEUR. [*Keeping his temper in control.*] Then would you not rather prefer to avoid a house into which I have brought my sweetheart . . . from the suburbs?

OLD GENTLEMAN. For the time being, perhaps . . . until the rooms have been properly aired. I moved out temporarily once before . . . after the flea hunt.

MONSIEUR. And in the event of the sweetheart's remaining. . . . Then?

OLD GENTLEMAN. Are you making game of me?

MONSIEUR. Today, Monsieur, I am going to cap your ancient stories with a new one, and this time I hold you at a disadvantage, for *my* story is relevant to the circumstance. Did you ever hear about the salons of Madame de . . . ? No names from me, either!

OLD GENTLEMAN. I am sorry to say I only heard of certain highly original caprices which she . . .

MONSIEUR. They are worth putting into a book, indeed. One especially, more than all the rest.

OLD GENTLEMAN. You have my feeble patience on the rack. . . . Don't keep it there, I beg of you!

MONSIEUR. It was with a curiosity just as great as yours, that we looked forward to an entertainment she had bidden us to. Gentlemen only. Most painstakingly selected. The summons went out to none but the wildest of the bloods. We prepared for an evening of unprecedented debauch. To have it in prospect was alone enough to send our temperatures soaring, and by the day before the reception, we were already in a raging fever!

OLD GENTLEMAN. Were you one of the favoured?

MONSIEUR. Can you doubt it? My reputation was in flower of its prime! I counted amongst my admirers even members of my own species! [OLD GENTLEMAN *applauds softly*.] Picture us then, arriving at Madame's . . . or it would be truer to say . . . picture us charging down upon her, headlong, like a herd of mad bulls . . . to find ourselves confronted by a room full of girls . . . dressed all identically alike, and with the utmost demureness. "Gentlemen," says Madame most innocently making the introductions, "I have asked the girls from the orphanage to be our guests this evening. I leave their entertainment in your hands. Here is your chance to spread the fame of your admirable manners." And I give you my word, we all sat there in mortal embarrassment, crouched in our chairs like yokels. We stuttered and fumbled for words like a pack of raw schoolboys. For the first time in our lives, our innuendoes evoked no echo. . . . Nobody caught our double meanings, which to us are as natural as they are unsavoury. Our vulgarities simply did not take . . . so we shrivelled up like so much burnt-out ash! Not men, but corpses, were sitting there. . . . The sight of them struck me to the marrow! . . . Bottles . . . Skins . . . Bags . . . all emptied out. . . . Not living, breathing men sprung into life out of the miracle of birth! Livid masks! Nothing else. Twisted into grimaces in the likeness of men. An obscene travesty of living humankind.

OLD GENTLEMAN. Madame de . . . oversteps the limits of good taste.

MONSIEUR. Was it not rather that walls . . . ramparts . . . which had shut out the sight of the world until then . . . had fallen at last?

OLD GENTLEMAN. So did you shortly retire discomfited?

MONSIEUR. How should I know what happened to the corpses? In that moment *I* suffered a rebirth, and with each new day that followed, my life has taken on new strength and power . . . thanks to my wife. . . .

OLD GENTLEMAN. [*Dumbfounded.*] You are married?

MONSIEUR. I married practically overnight!

OLD GENTLEMAN. No such thing as this has ever been known to happen before. . . .

MONSIEUR. You could pay my marriage no higher compliment.

OLD GENTLEMAN. I am appalled!

MONSIEUR. The following morning, I drove to the orphanage. . . . Heaven knows where it is . . . and sent for the matron to come and speak to me in my carriage. I explained my errand to her as best I could. I told her to call the orphanage together and make certain inquiries amongst them. I waited, meanwhile, at the gates. In a few moments she came out with one of the girls. I literally pounced upon my prize and dashed back home with her beside me in the carriage.

OLD GENTLEMAN. Are all orphans divinely beautiful?

MONSIEUR. Why do you ask that?

OLD GENTLEMAN. Because you appear to have chosen . . . somewhat blindly!

MONSIEUR. They all are chaste.

OLD GENTLEMAN. That is a quality an orphanage would necessarily encourage.

MONSIEUR. Therefore, it devolves upon me to protect her now. And here my story becomes relevant to . . . you. This room has a new tenant—myself. I am an utterly different person from the one all of you have known. While apparently sailing with your tide, I have in reality been moving miles and miles away from you. And now I have put in at this island, where I intend that none of you shall follow me. It breathes a clean and wholesome air. . . . There are no currents of evil odours. This house is forbidden to you from now on. . . . It's doors are shut against you. . . . I have pushed you from its threshold.

OLD GENTLEMAN. Is it possible that I still have such power to devastate?

MONSIEUR. [*In a stifled voice.*] You come round, sitting in all the rooms . . . in the Green Closet . . . in this room here. . . . The moment you set foot in them, they teem with your trooping memories. . . . There isn't a silent corner or cranny left. . . . You arrive, and instantly the entire house begins to whisper and mutter. You recall to life things which I am determined shall *cease to be.*

OLD GENTLEMAN. So will you be turning me out . . . betimes, tomorrow?

MONSIEUR. No. . . . Tonight!

OLD GENTLEMAN. Have you told them to call your watch-dog? [*A shrill whistling is heard.*] He won't be waiting to attack me in the front garden, will he? [*He gets up, and pulls back the curtains over the glass door as far as they will go.*] Dark as the pit out there! [*Something catches his attention.* MONSIEUR *at left beckons, and a servant appears bringing the* OLD GENTLEMAN's *hat and cloak.*] Are they illuminating the Opera House? [*To* MONSIEUR.] Is that part of Monday's programme? . . . What is all that whistling about? . . . Now they are running in the streets. . . . [*He closes the curtains.*] Am I begrudged the honour of kissing her hand?

MONSIEUR. My wife is . . . asleep.

OLD GENTLEMAN. Have you slandered me quite dreadfully to her? [MONSIEUR *looks at him fixedly. Nodding his head.*] The merry-go-round . . . fluttering flags . . . lacquered carriages . . . society! [*He offers his hand to* MONSIEUR.] So you have achieved your future. . . . Peace and clean air! [*He has taken his hat and cloak. The* SERVANT *draws the curtains back to let him pass out through the glass door.*] Great heavens! . . . It's brighter than ever now. . . . [*A great tongue of fire shoots up into the sky, flares for an instant brilliantly, then dies. The shrill whistling continues.*] Why, it's a fire!

MONSIEUR. [*Indifferently.*] Indeed? Is there a fire in town?

OLD GENTLEMAN. One moment . . . I know every building from here. . . . [MONSIEUR *approaches.*] [*Excitedly.*] That flat tower on the left, the Church. . . . Those tall chimneys on the right . . . They are my infallible landmarks. . . . The wide patch of black between them, like a coffin-lid. . . . Did you say the ball was in the Opera House?

MONSIEUR. You must be making a mistake. . . . [*A sudden sharp blare of trumpets.*]

OLD GENTLEMAN. There goes the alarm. The Opera House is on fire . . . and thousands are dancing at the ball.

MONSIEUR. And unlooked-for finale.

OLD GENTLEMAN. Paris will give me a send-off. . . . A fireworks display to celebrate my last farewell! . . . And well she might!

MONSIEUR. Are you not assuming rather much?

OLD GENTLEMAN. Paris is not the one to leave her friends in the lurch. . . . Paris could never deliver me over to the vermin in a hotel bed on my last night. Come . . . let's be going. . . . My final entertainment has been provided for. . . . Now all the Chinamen are beginning to jump down onto the pavement.

[*The* SERVANT *accompanies him out.* MONSIEUR *stands watching the fire. Re-enter* SERVANT.]

MONSIEUR. See that the curtains are well drawn.

[*He goes to the table. The* SERVANT *closes the curtains over glass door.*]

A light here. . . .

[*The* SERVANT *brings a lighted candlestick which he sets upon the table.* MONSIEUR *points to the other on the mantelpiece.*]

Put that out.

[*The* SERVANT *does so and exits on the left.*]

[MONSIEUR *sits down and becomes once more engrossed in his book. The noise of the fire alarm becomes increasingly more violent.* . . . *Trumpets are sounding from all directions. Whistles screech incessantly. Soon drums are heard. They are followed by the clanging of bells.*]

MONSIEUR. [*Beckons toward the left.* SERVANT *comes.*] There is to be absolute quiet in the house. Anybody found showing curiosity, or tampering with the windows, will be instantly dismissed. Are any of you out tonight? [*The* SERVANT *shakes his head.*] Lock the front garden door, then.

[*The* SERVANT *pulls back the curtains from the glass door and goes out through it. Comes back again, pulls curtains close and goes out left.* MONSIEUR *returns to his book.*]

[*Thunderous knocking at the garden door.* MONSIEUR *rises. Enter* SERVANT *from left.*]

That must be someone rushing here with news of the fire. Let him knock. [*Exit* SERVANT.]

[*The knocking becomes louder and more furious.* MONSIEUR *rises. Enter* SERVANT *left.*]

He'll wake my wife. Send him away.

[SERVANT *draws curtains apart and hurries out.* MONSIEUR *stands astounded at the vast reflection of the fire against the night. He goes over and shuts the door which the* SERVANT *has left open behind him, and is about to return to the table when a man appears on the outside of the door. It is an usher from*

the opera, groping wildly for the handle. MONSIEUR *turns back and flings open the door.*]
Are you out of your mind?
[USHER *falls into the room. His sumptuous livery is in rags and shows where the water has stained it. He attempts to speak, but only wheezing sounds come from his throat. To* SERVANT, *who enters from the left.*]
If you wish to gossip with your relations, you may do so on the corner.

SERVANT. I do not know this man. . . .

USHER. I am . . . an usher . . . from the Opera House. . . .

MONSIEUR. What do you mean by dragging mud into my house in this manner?

USHER. The Chinese lanterns . . . They were paper. . . . They caught fire. . . . The flames ran down the streamers. . . .

MONSIEUR. And you're making capital out of the disaster by carrying the story for pay from house to house.

USHER. They said they'd pay me well . . . if I ran.

MONSIEUR. You haven't spared yourself, at any rate. Your idiotic finery is in a lamentable condition. . . . Only you have come to the wrong house. . . .

USHER. She is . . . alive! . . .

MONSIEUR. *I* have no sweetheart at the Chinese Ball!

USHER. All the others are burning to death in the boxes. . . . They broke down the doors first thing, and the fire turned right back on them. . . .

MONSIEUR. I am not the lover of your rescued harlot!

USHER. She kept the curtains drawn in *her* box. That's what held back the draught . . . and saved her. . . . I took her down by the actors' staircase. . . . When I got her to the street she collapsed. But she pulled herself together again. . . . She begged me . . . So I came here . . . rushed. . . . The place is a sea of flames, but your wife is safe. . . . She is coming. . . . She must be close behind.

MONSIEUR. Are you still drunk from the bottles you've been sampling, or still out of your mind with terror . . . which?

USHER. [*Looking out of the door.*] Merciful God! There's not a brick left standing . . . and the burnt-out parts are crumbling down like dust already. [*With his eyes still fixed on* MONSIEUR, *he goes out followed by the* SERVANT.]

[MONSIEUR *does not move. Re-enter* SERVANT.]

SERVANT. Shall I bolt the garden door? [MONSIEUR *does not answer.*]

[SERVANT *waits awhile, then goes out left.*]

[MONSIEUR *remains standing, taut and motionless at the glass door which has been left open. The fire alarms have now mingled in an immense uproar. The street is swarming with people rushing hither and thither, shouting to each other. Fire engines race thundering over the cobbled streets.*]

[*In her yellow Chinese costume, waving her arms wildly, so that she looks like a flickering tongue of flame out of the great fire itself,* SYLVETTE *appears in the doorway.*]

SYLVETTE. [*Shrieking in a tone of mingled horror and exultation.*] I . . . am alive!

[MONSIEUR *does not move.*]

Did he come . . . The usher . . . Did he run? He wouldn't go at first. . . . He said it was too far . . . but I begged him . . . I kissed his hands . . . I clung round his neck . . . I gave him my rings . . . because . . . I was alive! . . .

[MONSIEUR *has backed to the table. With his bare palm he puts out two of the lights.* SYLVETTE *totters toward him.*]

You didn't believe him . . . I know. . . . You thought he was just saying so. . . . You heard the words, but your mind couldn't take them in. . . . I am . . . alive! . . .

[*She flings her arms around him.* MONSIEUR *braces himself against the table.*]

Down in that ball-room they're all on fire . . . on the stage, too . . . in the boxes, too . . . the whole way round. They're packed so close in the corridors they can't even fall . . . the fire goes over them standing there . . . upright. . . . Their faces burst . . . their screams are burnt out of their mouths. . . . None of them will ever get out of that place again. Only *I* am alive.

[MONSIEUR *bends far back from her.*]

Where are your arms? . . . Are you afraid?

[*She is utterly unstrung.*]

Are there sparks in my hair? Where? . . . Is my back on fire? . . . Do you hear flames crackling on me? . . . Beat them out! Beat them out! The whole sky is raining blazing splinters. . . .

[*She turns, gives a loud cry, and rushing to the glass door shuts it securely. With difficulty she pulls the heavy curtains together over it.*]

Help me. . . . Where are the servants? These curtains are heavy.
. . . But thick . . . They won't let the fire through . . . nor
the screaming!

[*She holds to the curtains for support, breathing heavily.*]
Now it's quite quiet in here . . . and dark.

MONSIEUR. Who . . . ?

[SYLVETTE *looks at him with eager attention.*]
Who . . . ?

SYLVETTE. [*Beside him, covers his face with kisses.*] I escaped . . .
out of the heat . . . out of the fire. . . . I am alive!

MONSIEUR. [*Involuntarily.*] Who . . . ?

SYLVETTE. It caught them as they danced. It seized them two by two,
from their feet to their heads, and high over their heads. So many
frightful towers of fire, turning with the dancers, round and round.

MONSIEUR. Who . . . ?

SYLVETTE. The musicians kept on playing . . . till the flutes burnt
their lips and the violins exploded under their chins. Suddenly there
was only the fire roaring through silence. . . . It hadn't gone
further than the ball-room then.

MONSIEUR. Who . . . ?

SYLVETTE. We were not dancing when it broke out. We'd gone to
the box we'd reserved. We wanted to eat, and rest awhile. I had
grown tired; that's why we went upstairs. We drew the curtains
on the ball-room . . .

MONSIEUR. Who . . . ?

SYLVETTE. So the flames did not burst in on us at once. I screamed . . .
and the usher broke in the door. . . . He dragged me into the corridor and down the stairs. . . . I never once looked behind
me. . . .

MONSIEUR. . . . to see whether or no the other one was burning to
death in the box?

SYLVETTE. I was saved!

MONSIEUR. Who . . . took you?

[SYLVETTE *stares at him in utter astonishment.*]
Who took you . . . out of my house . . . to the Opera House
. . . to the ball . . . to the box. . . .

[SYLVETTE *continues to stare at him.*]
Who . . . Who . . . [*With a cry that all but strangles him.*]
. . . has been *using* you?

SYLVETTE. Do you ask me that . . . now?

MONSIEUR. I am not asking. . . . The words are torn out of my mouth!

SYLVETTE. I am alive . . . and you ask me that.

MONSIEUR. It gagged me. . . . It bulged my cheeks. . . . It hung onto my tongue and swung it lolling and swollen about in my mouth. But it has said itself now. . . . It has rolled out. . . . Now it goes clattering through the house. . . . The walls are answering it back! *I* do not want to ask. . . . I do not want to! I do not intend this question to people all these rooms! There they go . . . whispering again! . . . Listen, to the carpet tittering. . . . The sultry wind from that outside is blowing through the house! The intruder which destroys everything it breathes upon, has found its way back at last . . . though I fought to keep it out. . . . I closed the door against it. . . . So it slips in through the cracks and crevices . . . and rises to a tempest in the heart of the house! . . . [*He stands beside her very close.*]

SYLVETTE. My dearest . . . My love . . . I am alive. . . . Feel me. . . . Not a hair of my head is harmed. I have not even a scratch on my skin. . . . Look at me. . . . Nothing is changed!

MONSIEUR. [*Freeing himself from her embrace.*] Let me breathe.

SYLVETTE. Let us kiss. . . .

MONSIEUR. You are standing in the midst of the fumes. . . . You set the very air on fire. . . .

SYLVETTE. I have come out of the thick, biting smoke. . . .

MONSIEUR. It is reaching out for me also. . . .

SYLVETTE. All I know is that I am alive. . . .

[MONSIEUR *is silent.*]

Have I not leapt back to your arms, out of the fire that reached out after all of us? Thousands are perishing in that burning death. . . . Now. . . . This moment. . . . There they lie . . . charred . . . grotesque. . . . [*Exalted.*] I am famished for life. The blood is clamouring in my veins. . . . All those thousands of lives burning down there in the fire live now in me. . . . I am filled with them . . . and with the sum of all their furious desires for the life they should have had! . . . I have not lived till now . . . but in this hour my life has begun!

MONSIEUR. [*With sudden intensity.*] No!

[SYLVETTE *tries to hold him.*]

SYLVETTE. Your arms!

MONSIEUR. *NO!*

SYLVETTE. Ah. . . . Your hands on my throat!

MONSIEUR. They touch nothing. . . . They grasp the empty air.

SYLVETTE. Can you not see me where I am?

MONSIEUR. Nothing is there. . . . I put out my hands and close them. upon nothingness!

SYLVETTE. [*Her body against his.*] Look! . . . *Here* I am!

MONSIEUR. Where? . . . I go forward . . . through you. . . . There is no obstacle there. . . .

SYLVETTE. Your lips! . . .

MONSIEUR. They suck the air. . . . They taste nothing. . . .

SYLVETTE. My mouth shrieks for you!

MONSIEUR. There is no breath to make it audible. . . . Listen to the din of the alarms out there. . . . Ruin holds carnival in the Opera tonight! . . . Every dancer in that hell irrevocably lost! . . . There is no life left for us to save; let us go and salvage the dead! [*Rushes to the left, clapping his hands.*] Hola! . . . You there! Wake up! . . . How can you lie snoring while the world is being destroyed?

[*Enter* SERVANT.]

Are you a block of ice, man, that the fire has no power to heat you? . . . Hats . . . Cloaks . . . Quick or we'll be too late for anything but sifting the ashes! . . . [*He goes around the room pulling back the curtains from the windows and the glass door.*] Immense fireworks display! . . . Excellent views from here! . . . Humanity in full course deluged under rivers of flame! . . . Retribution by fire, meted out before the Day of Judgment . . . to the most profligate of all the world's thousands! . . .

SYLVETTE. [*Clutching at him frantically.*] They are dead. . . .

MONSIEUR. Yes! Incandescent in the flames and the heat. . . . Baptism by fire in the pool of the ball-room!

SYLVETTE. I am alive!

MONSIEUR. And whoever escapes with his life . . . shall lose more than his life. From that hell they must and shall be protected. . . .

SYLVETTE. . . . burnt to death . . . thousands of dancers . . .

MONSIEUR. Then I shall not have far to look in the fire. . . .

[*Enter* SERVANT *from the left, with hats and cloaks.*]

I shall want you with me. . . . Come . . . whistle for a carriage. . . . Settle a price with the driver in advance, that will

keep him from refusing the fare I am going to bring back on his
cushions . . . lest he should find it too ghastly. . . .

[*Both leave through centre door.*]

SYLVETTE. [*In doorway. Throws up her arms.*] I am alive!

[*The noise of the fire has now risen to a tremendous uproar.
The tumult of bells and other alarms clangs and booms through
the night. The room is filled with the din and brilliant with
the reflection of the fire.*]

CURTAIN

ACT II

SYLVETTE *is standing in the same position as at the end of Act I gazing through the door-panes at the fire. The radiance of the conflagration and the din of the alarm are unabated. A wagon rattles by. The gate bangs. Voices are heard.*

MONSIEUR. [*In the doorway. Speaks to someone off-stage.*] This way —over here—keep to the path or you'll be catching the coat on the thorn-bushes. You'd see a frightful sight if they should pull it off!

> [*The* SERVANT *and* COACHMAN *appear, carrying between them a burden the length of a human body, wrapped in* MON-SIEUR'S *coat.*]

Straight on . . . into the library . . . All solemn spirits brood over that twilight room. . . . Careful, there! It will fall to pieces if you stumble. . . . We have brought it to its destination at last.

> [*Enters the room on the right,* SERVANT *and* COACHMAN *follow.*]

On to the table—lift it up . . . now . . . slowly . . . down . . . so . . . there! It does not feel the hard wood, but lies there as on its bed. . . .

> [COACHMAN *returns in haste, and waits behind the door.* MONSIEUR *comes out of the room on the right.*]

Where's the driver? [*He sees him.*] Running off without your pay, fellow?

> [*The* COACHMAN *makes a tremulous gesture.*]

Shivering? Is that all your self-control? A man like you, strong as a lion? Have you never driven one of these in your cab before? A silent sweetheart, what?— And her lover, chattering frantically to her?

COACHMAN. Give me my money, and let me go.

MONSIEUR. Hold out your hand—there! [*The* COACHMAN *does so.*] . . . The other one . . . [*The* COACHMAN *obeys.*] And if you find ashes in your cushions, go and buy yourself new ones and I will pay for them . . . I replace what I damage. . . .

> [*Exit* COACHMAN.]

157

[*Enter* SERVANT *from the right. To the* SERVANT.]

Lights . . . Bring them here and set them on either side of it. [*Taking candlestick from the mantelpiece, he lights the candles at the others on the table. Then hands one candlestick to the* SERVANT.] Take this one. [*The* SERVANT *puts out his hand to take it, and almost drops it.* MONSIEUR *steadies it as it is about to fall.*] Do you want to set *this* place on fire, too? Is the blaze outside not bright enough for you?

SERVANT. You were within an ace of being burnt to death. . . .

MONSIEUR. When I ran into the witches' cauldron?

SERVANT. To us outside, the flames seemed to sweep you into their grasp. . . .

MONSIEUR. Are you suffering terror in retrospect? You need not— look at me. Not so much as a hair singed!

SERVANT. Beside me . . . Behind me . . . They were all shriek- ing. . . .

MONSIEUR. Yes—the whole gaping crowd set up a shout as I entered the building—I heard it rise behind me as I ran. . . .

SERVANT. They gave you up for lost.

MONSIEUR. But I came out. . . . Carrying my burden before me. . . .

SERVANT. We could not believe our own eyes.

MONSIEUR. Then a vast cry broke from a thousand throats. I had achieved a dramatic production. . . . And they were applauding it for its happy ending. But I had found what I went to find. . . . [*He lights another candle.*] Bring the other one, and come! [*They enter the room on the right. Their voices are heard from within.*] Set it on the left, beside the head. Or can you not tell which is the head and which the feet? I grant you, it is hard to distinguish. But I will help you. . . . Here, this end is the head! . . . Is it not strange how a head can shrink—wonderful, is it not? No bigger than an egg. . . . There it lies in state, as befits this dead. I have fulfilled my duty. [*Returning with the* SERVANT *from the inner room.*] Lovely, the wavering glimmer of those little flames! How they leap and flutter, always towards each other, play- ing their strange game of hide and seek, burning all the while to death.

SERVANT. [*Diffidently.*] Who is that?

MONSIEUR. Who is that? For whom would I have hurled myself into that sea of fire—with the walls and balconies crashing down on every side? To recover a button off my pocket, do you think? Or a dropped handkerchief? Can you doubt whose sake I did it for?

SERVANT. I—do not know.

MONSIEUR. I went to bring my wife—home—home to me—to safety —under the shelter of my roof. Whom else?

SERVANT. [*Glances hastily—at* SYLVETTE—*stammers.*] But she is . . .

MONSIEUR. Are you seeing ghosts? Has the sight of that immense conflagration deprived you of your senses too? Does the air still seem filled with flying sparks? Are you seeing double? Do you see something there?

SERVANT. [*With a vague gesture.*] Yes, there!

MONSIEUR. [*Brusquely wheeling round.*] Where?

SERVANT. But there . . . over there!

MONSIEUR. Rub your eyes, my man. Nothing is there! If it were, I should see it too—I, too, have eyes.

[SERVANT *backs in fear against the wall.*]

Your legs are giving way under you. Come, what is the matter? I will help you, and you shall see that you are only being afraid of shadows. See now—watch me as I go! [*Passes* SYLVETTE *by, where she stands not attempting to move. To* SERVANT.] What is here? [*Takes a chair and shakes it back and forth.*] Or here . . . ? No? Then here, perhaps . . . ? [SERVANT *shakes his head.*] Well what is it then, that's making a fool of you? No ghosts walk here, except when the old gentleman wanders through the house—but he wakes them, and their wanton little faces come crowding behind all the screens and tapestries. . . . Not now, though—it is as silent as the grave in here. . . . You had best go up to bed. Darken your room well. Go back to your pleasant snoring. I shall watch in there. . . . I shall not need you any more, tonight. . . . Ah, one moment! Close all the curtains—whatever more may happen outside is no concern of ours. . . .

[*The* SERVANT *pulls the door to, and draws the heavy curtains over door and windows. Exit left.*]

[MONSIEUR *walks deliberately to the table and begins to blow out the candles one by one.*]

SYLVETTE. [*At the table, snatches the candlestick away.*] No!

MONSIEUR. Is it my turn to be made a fool of by the ghost? . . . The candlestick moves about the table of itself! . . . Do I hear the blood humming in my ears? . . . The corpse shall protect me from myself! . . . [*He approaches the door right.*]

SYLVETTE. [*Stands before him face to face.*] I am alive! . . . You lie! . . . I am alive!

MONSIEUR. Still dancing before me, the yellow flames? . . . Are my eyes still dazzled with their unutterable brightness?

SYLVETTE. [*With frenzy.*] I ran away—once—ten times—a hundred times. I lied when I told you where I went. It was not to visit the other orphans, no—nor the matron, either—nor the orphanage. It was to meet my lover! Every day—every day—every day! To the remotest corner of my thoughts I have been false to you . . . you have had a harlot in your house, since the tenth, the fifth . . . the third day!

MONSIEUR. [*Breaks into loud laughter.*] The old gentleman's merry-go-round is turning with a vengeance now!

SYLVETTE. *Who* it was that took me from you—makes no matter. He was a man like you—one of your own brilliant milieu. He beckoned—as you had beckoned.—I went to him. . . . as I went with you that morning, when you sent the matron in to us with your message. It was all the same to you which one she brought out to you, waiting in your carriage. Merely another toy for you to play with—you—and any other who chose.

MONSIEUR. Society! There it goes—round and round and round!

SYLVETTE. How was I to know? You were a stranger to me—and I to myself. You brought me here to these rooms with their tall windows and their hangings—illuminated by day with the streaming sunshine and by night with the candles in the great chandeliers. Until then, I had only known being sent to bed by the matron, in the pitch dark. Here, night was bright as day! Your tables were set with burnished dishes—wine sparkled in shining glasses. Water in tin mugs was all I had ever seen before! My coarse dress had turned into silk—I had rings with white stones to put on my fingers. . . . Life was no longer life, but a dream that held me basking in its glow—understanding nothing.

MONSIEUR. Do I hear new ribaldries whispered behind the tapestries?

SYLVETTE. I did not know you loved me! . . . How could I learn everything at once? My eyes saw nothing but the splendour in which I stood bewildered. *You* were not there—only the enchantment surging over me. I had yet to learn—that you loved me!

MONSIEUR. [*Speaking over her head.*] Dead one between the watching candles—is that your dry mouth mumbling?

SYLVETTE. I did not know you loved me! Only now my life begins. . . . Only now I awake to life, through you. . . . The splendour dazzles me no longer—the tumult is hushed. . . . *You* have come to me! Me, you have chosen—out of all the world. I—and no other—am your own elect! I alone, out of all the multitude! You called me to you from their midst—I, whom alone you sought. . . . I am your life!

MONSIEUR. Dead one . . .

SYLVETTE. Until now, neither you nor I have been alive . . . not you, until I came—not I, until this miracle! Until that blazing fire out there, your life too had not begun!

MONSIEUR. The day for the raising of the dead is not yet—you are too early, dead one!

SYLVETTE. You are calling me. Oh, you are not dead. Your life is in *my* life—and in your life I mean to live! Speak to me, that I may hear your voice—your voice that rebukes and reviles me! And your words shall call me forth to you—radiant—to you, to life— to life that is long—and kind.

MONSIEUR. The day of resurrection is still far off!

SYLVETTE. You *shall* speak to me! You ran into the fire to bring me back—because I am your life! You are your own betrayer—there is no measure to your treachery. I will force your life upon you— for it is *my* life also. I will force your lips to cry out for me—I tear them asunder—see—I kindle you with my life!

MONSIEUR. [*Wrenching himself away.*] Does this room become at night a battle-ground for cats? Ah, they spring upon me! Away! —Be off! Or must I have you chased with whips, the pack of you? [*He moves towards the left—stands still.*] All quiet again? Or do I hear the scuffling feet of mice, out after the odour of burnt flesh? Surely they will not venture into the light of candles that protect it on either side? [*He goes towards the room on the right ignoring* SYLVETTE *as he passes her.*]

SYLVETTE. [*Across the doorway with arms outspread.*] I am not dead!

MONSIEUR. Dead one—I am coming to drive away the creatures that would gnaw you!

SYLVETTE. I am alive! . . . I *will* be alive! . . . And with you to-morrow and tomorrow and for ever!

MONSIEUR. They grow importunate, the vermin!

SYLVETTE. I was not alive yesterday—nor today until this hour. I was plunged in a vortex that tore me hither and thither . . . I did not know where. . . . But I have forgotten that past—it has gone from my mind. Now it is life that I want—life—life—life!

MONSIEUR. [*Rushes to the centre door and pulls the curtains back. He throws the door violently open.*] This way out!

SYLVETTE. Give me back my life—the life that you awakened—and destroyed again in the fire!

MONSIEUR. Out, vermin! . . . Out—out——!

SYLVETTE. [*Beside herself.*] Until with your own voice, you pull me back into your life—I will live!

MONSIEUR. The garden-gate is bolted—they want to go out into the street again—into the gutter! I go to clear the way back home for them! [*He rushes out.*]

[SYLVETTE *leans far forward, looking through the open door through which* MONSIEUR *has gone. Then avoiding it in her haste, she runs over to the left, and stands there in a waiting attitude. As voices approach from outside, she hides behind the door-post on the left.*]

MONSIEUR. [*Appearing in doorway centre.*] What is this the night-mist has brought to my net? . . . I cannot trust the evidence of my ears! Come into the light, please. Let me look at you, in order that I may realise the rare, the signal honour that is being done me by this visit from the ascendant star of the opera! And at this incredible hour of the night; I am lost in wonder! Forgive me if I lose my last shred of self-possession, and find myself bereft of words!

[*The* OPERA SINGER *in yellow Chinese costume follows him in.*]

Or do you come with reproaches, perhaps? I have neglected latterly to visit the opera. In the densely crowded circle of the boxes, my empty box must have made an unsightly gap—which must unquestionably have looked like a slight upon your genius. Is that the account you have come to settle?

[*The* OPERA SINGER *looks about the room—his gaze is riveted upon the room on the right.*]

MONSIEUR. I am more than willing to explain, you see. I owe you

that, at least. And afterwards, you may tell me your conditions.
Whatever they are, I accept them in advance.

OPERA SINGER. [*shaking his head violently.*] Not you . . .

MONSIEUR. In all candour then . . . I was in love . . . hopelessly,
helplessly infatuated. You will spare me the details, will you not?
Your imagination will easily understand how the exigencies of that
love monopolised my time, day and night. It seized upon me like
a fever, and I went down under it—completely. That I was doing
you a wrong—even that went by the board. You—the god of the
opera—whose claim upon the attention of all men waits upon
neither time nor circumstance. I have indeed rendered myself
culpable of the most heinous crime of omission—I am yours to
deal with as you will.

OPERA SINGER. No—let *me* explain to *you*.

MONSIEUR. I long to hear, even in common speech, this voice of
divinest gold!

OPERA SINGER. I was among the witnesses of your intrepid attempt
to force your way into the burning Opera House. Never had a man
risked his life with such unheard of odds against him. My heart
stopped beating! Then you emerged—safe—not through a miracle
. . . no miracle could have been great enough to save you. . . .
I interpret your rescue far otherwise—how you must have loved that
woman!

MONSIEUR. Ah! I begin to understand you now. So that is what impressed you? As the perfect scene—to be played through intact,
for the climax. . . . You have a genius for stage effects. . . .
Will you sing in here, or in there—beside the dead? Do you require an audience? An orchestra, perhaps? . . . You have only to
command—I will order whatever you wish. . . .

OPERA SINGER. By your mockery I see all too clearly that you are in
possession of the truth. I need hide it from you, then, no longer.

MONSIEUR. Of course! You sing unaccompanied—Your pardon! I am
so unfortunate as to insult you with everything I say!

OPERA SINGER. It is *I* who have insulted *you!* And I have come to
offer you your revenge.

MONSIEUR. What do you mean?

OPERA SINGER. My admiration for your exploit wrenches this confession from my lips! I am the lover!

    [MONSIEUR *gazes at him.*]

OPERA SINGER. The game has turned to earnest. An hour ago, you made your life a stake—I do not care to set a cheaper one!

MONSIEUR. [*Shakes his head. Leads him to an armchair and seats himself in another.*] What was she to you?

OPERA SINGER. Do not drive me insane!

MONSIEUR. So! An opera singer's sweetheart! A murmur in the thunder of the evening's ovation. . . . An infinitesimal drop in the ocean of light in which the theatre is submerged . . . a stray petal upon a stage covered with flowers for a fabulous triumph. . . . You may answer my question without exaggerating the truth.

OPERA SINGER. I was profoundly moved to see you enter that building where everything was in flames.

MONSIEUR. Is she a matter for so many words, then? You keep to the truth, I see. It is to your credit to do so. It inspires me with confidence—to give confidence to you!

OPERA SINGER. You have nothing for me but the cruellest contempt!

MONSIEUR. I shall convince you of my sincerity—in due course! I did not intend to expose you to the tedium of a recital with which you must already be infinitely familiar, in your intercourse with us—with the gentlemen who fill the boxes at the opera. Forgive me if I belittle your art, but I do so all too justly—there is not one of them that would not give every note of your voice for a single glimpse of the dancers' legs. It is a thing you have experienced in the past, and will doubtless continue to experience in the future. Your sensibilities are most likely jarred more painfully still every day, by other things which have eluded my observation, for I . . . Is anything disturbing you?

OPERA SINGER. [*Turning toward the left.*] Are we not alone?

MONSIEUR. It is nothing! [*He rises closes the centre door and closes the curtain over it.*] The draught makes the candles sputter. [*He turns back to the table.*] But I'll make myself more readily understood, I believe, if I add the force of simile to my confessions! You know what it feels like I am sure—I presume you also spend your summers at the seaside. Imagine then, a hot July day. You go bathing in the ocean. You receive the shock of the first plunge, and it is not only a delight to the skin—the icy blow of the water seems to penetrate to the centre of your being—you feel clean, through and through. And when you return to the shore it is as though you had been purified. Is it not so?

OPERA SINGER. You merely express in another form the feeling which overwhelmed me as I stood outside the opera house tonight, watching you.

MONSIEUR. The rest will not be very clear to you. . . . The knowledge of myself struck me as a flash of lightning on a certain night which brought me face to face with a young girl sitting enthroned amidst the most extraordinary surroundings. Where that was, need not detain us . . . Out of the clear and candid mirror of her countenance my haggard features grimaced back at me. I was filled with loathing as I recognised them for my own. Foulness lay deep in every furrow—grossness was written large in every line. It was the face of a leper—but of one whose leprosy, far viler than that of the body, was of the mind. I returned home to this house like a man in the throes of fever. My impatience drove the night hours before me into the morning, and when it was daylight, I set out after her, who, I knew, alone could heal me of my malady.

OPERA SINGER. And you were not deluded?

MONSIEUR. An angel came to me! The blessing of heaven rained down upon my life. I—most undeserving of all the earth's creatures, found myself raised to high heaven. I rose to richer estate—I had great possessions. All at once, I was transported to life in the midst of treasures; and I ceased to understand how I had so long endured the poverty of my past. My eyes saw! I was good! Here, within me, lay a heart as fair and clear as crystal! I had become like her —like that young, pure girl. Like her—a child. . . . She was that, was she not? You know, of course. A tiny creature—and gave herself so shyly! To the fullest, though—ah yes, to the utmost! Was she not ignorant of all their arts? Did she know the meaning of dissimulation? Was she not innocent of guile? And of seduction? Do not soften the truth—it is past—you may disenchant me now.

OPERA SINGER. I cannot bear to see what I have destroyed in you!

MONSIEUR. [*Highly astonished.*] Nothing whatever—since she is dead! What stain can still remain upon her now that she has been burnt in the fire? That she should have given herself to you, do you think? To you as well as to me? . . . What is that, now? Is not her body ashes? . . . How should it still arouse desire? Surely we would not commit the most hideous of crimes—upon a corpse?

OPERA SINGER. Your memories are poisoned because your faith in her has been destroyed.

MONSIEUR. No! That—that is the triumph of death, which endures
to the end of time. Do not attempt to overthrow the majesty of
death. For every slighting word against the dead shall be terribly
avenged. We shall become dogs, and choke on our own slaver . . .
what might is as mighty as the defencelessness of the dead? Do
they not turn aside our assaults with their disdainful immobility? Do we not bow our heads before the magnificent tyranny of
those silent ones? Are we not defeated in that our speech with
them evokes no answer? . . . Do not slander death. What life
attempts, death fulfills. . . . Look at me. Fulfillment lay, as I
believed, within my very grasp. Only now do I discern the abyss
that yawned between! [*He points to the right.*] Look at her! What
trace of evil is there left upon her—what taint? Where will you
find it? Death is so great! . . . It is like this polished table, upon
which you can detect no single grain of dust—though there are millions there! . . . Whenever, wherever you meet the dead, bow
low before them, for they are clothed in immeasurable pride . . .
the dead are indispensable. Some day to lie dead, is the one obligation no one may ever shirk! . . . I am happy with the dead one
here! I shut the house more securely—and invest the rooms with
the great vision of her death. No noise from you can force an
entrance here. No more. With this victory, I have acquired empire
over my house at last . . . so immaculate the threshold. . . . Are
not the dead almost more to be loved than the living? [*He touches
the singer's arm.*] Come with me! In the lofty presence of the
dead, let us put her power to its first test—we cannot be enemies
at her bier!

[*The* OPERA SINGER *makes little resistance as* MONSIEUR
leads him into the room on the right. SYLVETTE *comes out of her
hiding place on the left; her breath comes in gasps; her whole
body droops. She remains leaning against the door-post for support.*]

MONSIEUR. [*Appearing in the doorway right.*] Collect yourself! We
must. . . .

[*He sees* SYLVETTE. *Returning once more to the room on the
right, he comes out again with the* OPERA SINGER *whom he
installs in an armchair with his back to* SYLVETTE.]
Well, did I not do right? What prize is there of greater price than
that which lies stretched on that table? You will admit that it was
worth the most perilous enterprise to recover?

OPERA SINGER. Her image is effaced from my remembrance.

MONSIEUR. To death the victory, then! That which was mine comes back to me, to be my own once more. . . . Tomorrow, you shall sing a hymn to the glory of the dead—the heaped-up dead, who lie charred and blackened tonight in the smouldering ruins of the Opera House! . . . You are distressed! Can it be that the idea revolts you to the point of nausea? Do you not care to be the uplifter of hearts? Why?

OPERA SINGER. Because what was beautiful in your action is being made hideous by others.

MONSIEUR. Am I then the subject of jokes?

OPERA SINGER. Worse. . . . of imitation!

MONSIEUR. That should meet with your enthusiastic approval!

OPERA SINGER. It is money that is arousing them to self-sacrifice—on behalf of the most notorious wench in Paris! The King has offered a reward for the recovery of his mistress's body!

MONSIEUR. Is it not possible that true passion moves him, too?

OPERA SINGER. If it were so, then he would have dared the fire, as you did.

MONSIEUR. His searchers will not be rewarded! Only the eyes of love avail there—the dead are piled in heaps, I tell you . . . they cannot be distinguished one from the other . . . they are all quite black.

OPERA SINGER. But there is one sign they cannot mistake.

MONSIEUR. Infallible?

OPERA SINGER. Absolutely. The ring with the oddly-cut stone.

MONSIEUR. Blackened with soot—like all else that glittered there tonight!

OPERA SINGER. [Staring at him.] Then how did you know whom you were bringing?

MONSIEUR. Only the eyes of love can find the beloved.

OPERA SINGER. Are you not terrified by the possibility of having been mistaken?

MONSIEUR. You fail to inspire me with that terror.

OPERA SINGER. There can be many a blind mischance on a night like this!

MONSIEUR. And if I were mistaken—would that be so appalling?

OPERA SINGER. [Staring at him still more intently.] Then you do not revolt against so dreadful a thought?

MONSIEUR. The dead are pure!

OPERA SINGER. It does not move you to . . .

MONSIEUR. Are you then so unteachable?

OPERA SINGER. [*Rising.*] You pin your belief to what is probably a delusion. . . .

MONSIEUR. I have not the least misgiving.

OPERA SINGER. Your composure shall not catch me unawares! [*He turns toward the door, and sees* SYLVETTE, *who has advanced to the middle of the room.*]

MONSIEUR. [*Leaping to his feet.*] Leave this house!

[*The* OPERA SINGER *stands transfixed before* SYLVETTE.] Why do you hesitate? You cannot find the way out, perhaps? The curtains hide the door. Allow me to open it for you! [*He pulls back the curtains and throws open the door.*] There! Now run! Don't hold back from so tempting a morsel! Go and join the fight over the prize. You may bring off a triumph that will put even your phenomenal triumph as tenor into the shade, and lift you to the giddiest heights of the royal favour! Go and fetch his sweetheart for him out of the fire! It can be done—I have shown you that!

[OPERA SINGER *does not move.*]

I forgot—you will need a scarf, to protect your invaluable throat . . . do me the honour to accept one of mine. [*He exits on the left.*]

OPERA SINGER. [*Wearily.*] Did you come while he . . .

SYLVETTE. [*Slowly.*] I did not come to him . . .

OPERA SINGER. Did he not see you just now?

SYLVETTE. No.

OPERA SINGER. Perhaps the fire has disturbed his vision?

SYLVETTE. Was I burned to death? Was I?

OPERA SINGER. You are standing before me. . . .

SYLVETTE. Breathing? Laughing?

OPERA SINGER. You seem more lovely to me. . . .

SYLVETTE. Am I tempting, alive?

OPERA SINGER. More lovely than ever—in escape!

SYLVETTE. One more leap, and I shall be in the midst of life! You must help me!

MONSIEUR. [*Returning with a scarf.*] The colour clashes with your costume, unhappily! But I'm sure that with your skill in these matters, you will create out of this apparently impossible material still another dazzling effect!

SYLVETTE. [*Snatches the scarf out of his hand and winds it about the* OPERA SINGER'S *throat—leaning close to him as she does so.*] My friend . . . it is you! . . . This is your hair . . . these are your hands . . . and your mouth! Your beloved mouth can kiss me still! Did you come here looking for me? . . . Really for me? . . . And have you been searching for me everywhere—amongst the injured they had dragged out into the square—for me? . . . Me? Amongst all the living, fleeing through the streets? Did you rush after me—fearlessly into my house? . . . My friend . . . Did you have to know . . . that I was alive? Alive?

MONSIEUR. [*Stepping back.*] Ah—I see you are no longer alone!

SYLVETTE. You have come to me—you have thrown your life away for my life! . . . for my life!

MONSIEUR. I defer to the dictates of discretion—allow me to leave you.

OPERA SINGER. Do not go!

MONSIEUR. As onlooker of an idyll? . . . Well, as you wish. [*Smiling.*] I give you fair warning!

OPERA SINGER. Will you assure me that . . .

MONSIEUR. I shall not spoil the fun? By all means—I delight in love-making. Particularly after such an event as this. Reunion out of the very jaws of death. A ravishing occasion! Even where a mere harlot is in question, rushing after you and slipping in through an open door, while I was absent for a moment! My interest is not a whit diminished! You must have much to say to each other— and if you do not oblige me to close my ears, I shall have vast pleasure in listening to you. [*He settles himself in a chair.*]

SYLVETTE. [*Pulls the* OPERA SINGER *over to an armchair.*] You must sit down—you are tired— Rest! [*On his knees, swaying back and forth.*] No—I was cheating you—I'm not a bit sorry for you, really—all I wanted was to perch upon your knees. So that you may feel me better—and be certain that I am alive, and breathing . . . and laughing . . . and kissing!

OPERA SINGER. [*To* MONSIEUR.] Can't you say one word to . . .

MONSIEUR. No—don't interrupt her! . . . An ardent one! Congratulations!

SYLVETTE. It is all cheating! Everything I do. Am I not a marvellous liar? I am naturally inspired! Perhaps that doesn't matter, though! Not while the other one goes on believing and believing me, always? . . . Am I stupid? . . . Am I clever? . . . Am I lovely? . . . Am I white? . . . Am I sweet? . . .

OPERA SINGER. [*To* MONSIEUR.] Are you playing with me?

MONSIEUR. Don't prolong her suffering, poor little thing. She is snapping for you like a fish for the bait!

SYLVETTE. Let us forget the fire tonight! Not the least hair of our heads was singed—neither yours, nor mine! Were many burnt to death? Poor things! All lovers, too! But they did not love enough —that was why they had to die! Only fire is stronger than fire— only the fire of illimitable love! . . . Do you not believe me? After my thousand kisses and vows? . . . And that mad sur- render in the box—on the morning when you came to me when the rehearsal was over! Did I not leap towards you, naked—and pull you with me, down upon the sofa? . . . You, still glowing with your songs, I with the joy of joys to be! That box became our paradise!

OPERA SINGER. This is madness!

MONSIEUR. So, even at rehearsals, the singers are pampered! I did not know that.

SYLVETTE. The first light word exchanged, and we were in love! Will you ever forget how I stopped the carriage outside the Opera House, because I so longed to take just one peep inside that huge building! So I told my husband to stay in the carriage while I went in. You had heard, and turned to laugh at me as you mounted the steps—that immense flight of steps I could not look at without turning dizzy! What was it you called out? What was it? "Come in the mornings to rehearsal then, if you must sit virtuously at home at night!" Did I not come punctually next morning? [OPERA SINGER attempts to rise.]

MONSIEUR. Now the text, singer! I do not know the text; otherwise I should prompt you!

SYLVETTE. Then at last, it was "Alcestis." The hall seemed to soar to the sky upon the music of the orchestra. As in a bath of ecstasy, I stood at the rail of the box—naked and without shame . . . no one looked up to where I stood, waiting for you to come. Waiting an eternity for you to enter from the wings . . . and then it was not you who came but only your voice . . . the chorus sank almost to a whisper, as your solo arose . . . I was near to dying of bliss . . . like Alcestis, dying for Admet . . . how I envied the fate of Alcestis, rescuing Admet with her own life! Death seemed to me in that moment most sweet and desirable—I should have wel- comed him without a sigh . . . but then my Admet came to me in the box—rewarding me for having all but died of love for him.

He found his Alcestis waiting! Am I Alcestis—returned to life?

OPERA SINGER. [*Rises and pushes* SYLVETTE *from him. To* MONSIEUR.] You are in error, Monsieur. . . .

MONSIEUR. Ah! Have I unwittingly made some mistake? I am inconsolable!

OPERA SINGER. The fire has not robbed you. . . .

MONSIEUR. [*Pointing to the door on the right.*] I have rescued my portion!

OPERA SINGER. But do you not see . . . ?

MONSIEUR. I see a Chinese girl, yellow—as everything else is yellow tonight. . . . Are you not labouring under a delusion too obvious to need explanation? And, moreover, your finer perceptions are still bemused by the fumes of recent drinking. Your mind is filled with the picture of the courtesan with whom you shared your latest supper . . . and so you take each other one who runs after you, for her . . . a kaleidoscope of yellow Chinese girls—nothing more.

OPERA SINGER. [*Speechless.*] You sacrifice . . .

MONSIEUR. Myself only—which you censured, when I went into the fire. [*In the doorway, right.*] But do not exaggerate the sacrifice—it has been amply rewarded.

OPERA SINGER. I leave you to your better recollection! [*He moves towards the door centre.*]

SYLVETTE. [*Detaining him.*] Stay—stay! You shall not leave this house. . . . It is our house, now, since you have come to me—and will come, again and again. The box was so small—but here we can chase each other from room to room, and out into the garden, until we fall behind the bushes, exhausted! . . . Here we shall bring this night to its close! So gaily it began—with costumes and dancing, and supper in your box! . . . We pulled the curtains close, in a fever of longing—I lay upon your breast. My mouth beside yours, we drank together out of the same glass—wine and kisses mingling, melted upon our lips. . . . There was no slaking that thirst—we were drunk, and yet the thirst would not be stilled. . . . Then the wicked flames came to disturb us, tearing at the curtains—trying to betray us to the world. . . . Ah, but we would not let ourselves be caught . . . swiftly we tore ourselves apart . . . who saw us? . . . Who surprised our secret? . . . What great good fortune we have had! And now we are once more together. . . . Boundless joy is the lot of those who are avid of their love. . . . This is a house—these walls are of stone—no fire can find a way through them. We are in safety here—for the first time, quiet against the music and secure against the peril of our lives! Here we shall live—my dearest love—my life! Carry me to my bed. Take me out of this motley—let me be naked before you—[*Almost swooning.*] ravish Alcestis!

[OPERA SINGER *holds her against him—staring at* MONSIEUR *in bewilderment.*]

MONSIEUR. [*Stands stiffly against the door-post. So immense is his effort to control his voice, that when he speaks he can scarcely be heard.*] The fumes begin to overwhelm me . . . my senses fail. . . . Voices and phantoms hover before my sight. . . . Yellow forms flit through the air—the room is alive with the fluttering spawn of hell-fire! . . . Smoke is rising from the table on which the dead one is lying— Poison gases out of the burning. . . . [*Left, claps his hands.*] Hola! No sleep until the last services have been performed. You went too soon to your beds.

SERVANT. [*In the doorway.*] I was not asleep. . . .

MONSIEUR. You are all the sooner awake, then, for your errand. Run to the nearest place where a priest is to be found—and bring him back with you . . . tell him it is to speed a poor soul with blessings towards Heaven . . . and I, meanwhile, shall see to another urgent matter. On a night like this, there must be some good people who can be moved by entreaty or reward to do an act of mercy. But the dead that stench are not to be endured! [*He takes his hat and goes out through the centre door followed by the* SERVANT *who puts on his hat and cloak as he goes.*]

SYLVETTE. [*She has drawn away from the* OPERA SINGER *who attempts to approach her.* SYLVETTE *looks at him.*] Why are you standing there?

OPERA SINGER. You shall live. . . .

SYLVETTE. In your box? In that cage, where the air is sultrier than in a grave?

OPERA SINGER. We could be happy. . . .

SYLVETTE. We? . . . By what right do you associate yourself with me? . . . Because I forced myself upon you here?

OPERA SINGER. Your kisses were more than a girl's kisses. . . .

SYLVETTE. Did you remark that, too? Indeed I was at great pains to make it clear to you.

OPERA SINGER. You love me. . . .

SYLVETTE. You are absurdly presumptuous. Who are you, that I should have sat just now upon your knees? A lackey would have served the same purpose. Accident brought you into this house—you should have served me usefully—so that the other should have cried out, and called me by my name! But so little did you count, that he did not one cry out—not once!

OPERA SINGER. Now you have learned that never will he call to you, as I have done—and do again.

SYLVETTE. Because my ruse with you failed to take effect? That does not dismay me, where my life is in question.

OPERA SINGER. Yes, your life which has been extinguished—and which I will quicken again!

SYLVETTE. Can you take that raging fire out there in your two hands and whirl it over my head, that this room may become illuminated with its glare? No—the whole conflagration would not suffice for that! . . . Take your life—if life you call it—and go. As for me, I freeze in your boxes and under your lamps

OPERA SINGER. . . . What is it you wait for?

SYLVETTE. [With extreme emphasis.] . . . For myself!

[OPERA SINGER hesitates a moment then goes out.]

[SYLVETTE raises her hands slowly to her face, and turns her head deliberately until she is looking into the room on the right. Suddenly her gaze fastens, fascinated, upon an object she sees there. Cautiously, she approaches the door—the next instant, she has passed in. . . . After a while, she returns—her head bent low over her hands which are clenched upon something . . . and in a voice, heavy with sombre laughter, she speaks.]

SYLVETTE. . . . The Ring!

CURTAIN

ACT III

SYLVETTE *comes in from the room at the right, carrying a candle-stick, which she takes to the mantelpiece, and blows out the candles. She then returns to the room, and comes back with another candle-stick, with which she does likewise.*

The garden gate is heard to slam. MONSIEUR'S *voice sounds close by. Lights move about outside, and there is a clatter of digging implements.*

THE VOICE OF MONSIEUR. This way—show your lights here! [*The lights disappear towards the left.*] Uncover the spot, and mind how you lift off the top of it. Tomorrow the grass is to be growing over the place, as before. . . . Now, to work! You have been recommended to me—see that you deserve it. The shorter your time, the more your money . . . so—begin! A deep one, mind! You know how. . . .

  [*Enter* MONSIEUR, *hastily from the garden.*]

MONSIEUR. [*Looking around the room.*] The priest? Not here yet? [*He looks towards the dark room on the right.*] What is this? Thieves at the bier? . . . The candles cannot have burned down so soon—they should not be more than half gone by the end of the ceremony. [*He takes both candlesticks from the mantelpiece, and lights them.*]

SYLVETTE. [*Crosses the room to the centre door, and draws the curtains over it.*]

MONSIEUR. [*Turns and sees her.*] Who's there? Wench, were you also at the ball? . . . Costume complete, even to the yellow fez, eh? . . . Aping your mistress! Safely too, for in costume there's no telling which is the lady and which the maid! . . . Bestir yourself, now! Go and get some of the wine you servants drink, and take it outside to the men digging in the garden. . . . You'll find them a friendly crew, and it's dark enough behind the bushes!

SYLVETTE. [*Comes close to him, beside the table. Her voice is very quiet.*] You are a very rich man tonight, Monsieur.

MONSIEUR. Yes. I scatter treasures amongst those men out there, so that they may work with a will at this late hour.

SYLVETTE. You have gained more than you have spent.

MONSIEUR. Is there profit to be derived then, from a funeral?

SYLVETTE. From this funeral. The favour of the King.

[MONSIEUR *sets the candlesticks down.*]

I am happy to be able to tell you this. It might have escaped your attention, and your bravery might have been cheated of its due reward.

MONSIEUR. The favour of . . . ?

SYLVETTE. You must be helped, I see. I rejoice in this opportunity to diminish my great indebtedness to you. I owe you much—you will not find me niggardly in repaying. [*She takes the ring from her finger, and holds it out to him, on the palm of her hand.*] It cost me all my strength to get—it was a fearsome sight. And ghastly touching the—touching it. . . . You, who are brave will appreciate bravery—in me.

[MONSIEUR *stands gazing at her hand.*]

Look! The strangely cut stone! Do not doubt it—it is you who have done the King the greatest service he can ask tonight. You have brought back to him the thing he most desires to have. Make haste, or the desire may lose its ardour—kings have small patience in the matter of sweethearts and rewards. Those are moods which change almost before they come. Make the most of your chance while it is still good. Accept it at my hands! I am deeply in your debt. Run! So long as the fire is still at its height, so long will this pledge stand. The reward is tremendous! If you delay, no one will ever compensate you for all your expense; but now your losses will be repaid to you. The money awaits you—go and receive it! A fortune! Go!

[MONSIEUR *raises his eyes from her hand to her face, and remains looking at her deeply.*]

Ah, no! You are rich—money has no power to move you. You are all so rich—all of you, that you do not trouble to know your own wealth. But the King is richer still. He has the sun in his house. That will warm you, ice-bound that you are. The King's house is open to you now. I see you there—the sunlight streaming over you. You kneel, you are raised up and kissed on either cheek. Before the eyes of everyone. . . . Their gaze is fastened upon you—in envy and admiration. Go! Sun yourself in your ennoblement.

[MONSIEUR *attempts to speak, but cannot.*]

That does not please you either? I know you imagine your-self withdrawn from the world. You are not longer to be seen amongst your fellowmen. You have grown weary of society. It is with reluctance that you stir out of the house. . . . Why disturb oneself for the sake of fame? They will come and sing your ex-ploits under your windows, and carol them over the garden wall, and whistle them along the streets. . . . You shall live in a ballad that the people will have composed by tomorrow. . . . It won't be a bit like a hymn, but it will nevertheless be sung for ever and ever. The most abandoned of harlots and her intrepid deliverer! The two indissolubly coupled in a rhyme! . . .

[MONSIEUR *goes towards the centre door, turns round, hesi-tates.*]

You do not wish to go? You should not leave your patron too long in suspense, or you may find him out of humour. Even now, you will need to ask his pardon for having but this mo-ment discovered the ring. Take courage! You go to receive your just reward.

[MONSIEUR *grasps his head in both hands.*]

Inform them of the preparation being made here. That will be useful, for people will then understand how you contrived to spare the royal lover the task of himself disposing of the corpse, transformed by the fire from his sweetheart into a thing of hor-ror. The King will be graciously pleased to let the dead remain in your garden, and to bestow upon you the honour of caring for the grave. They will set up a conspicuous monument, which an unceasing stream of pilgrims will visit until the end of time.

[MONSIEUR *presses his clenched fists against his mouth.*]

Throw open your doors! You hold a reception tonight. The rooms will overflow with the multitude of guests! The King himself will attend, with all his friends and yours. Rarely has burial been solemnised with such magnificence! They will come as they are—no time to change their costumes! The priest is al-ready on the way. A houseful of Chinese! And the ball will rage the wilder for following upon terror at the graveside, as the earth is scraped over the corpse. More vehement than ever, joy shall force its way back into life. For those who still have life will live it now to the utmost. The last vestiges of modesty will be torn away. . . . These rooms are dedicated to laughter and the joy of life. You ca hear it—gasping for breath and falling behind the tapestries and screens!—You can see it, clinging to the couches! This house is burning in a fire of joy!

MONSIEUR. [*Stammering.*] The merry-go-round . . .

SYLVETTE. Will you now absolve me of my guilt? I will try to cancel the balance by never boasting of the past in which I was your wife. We leave the orphanage nameless. We can disappear into the by-ways of the city, nameless also. I promise you, you need have no fear that we should ever meet again, to your annoyance. What more have you to reproach me with?

[SYLVETTE *stands before him, breathing heavily.*]

MONSIEUR. [*Flinging up his arms. In a loud cry.*] Sylvette! [*Reeling against the table.*] Little Sylvette! . . . Sweet Sylvette! . . . Lovely Sylvette! . . . Darling Sylvette! . . .

[SYLVETTE *gazes at him, silently.*]

Miracles stream from you—they clothe you in light, Sylvette! You are like a burning flower of seduction, Sylvette! . . . Lay your hands in mine, Sylvette—in mine, that I may feel you are alive! . . . Fingers out—so—each against each of mine, that the pulse of your life may beat against mine. Come, unclench your hands, Sylvette.

SYLVETTE. Is this a ruse to snatch my find away from me?

MONSIEUR. Do you feel you need defend yourself against me? Tear yourself away from me? Or call out into the street for help, per-haps?

SYLVETTE. [*Excited.*] Shall I destroy the ring?

MONSIEUR. Look—I give you back your life! I am calling you— can you not hear? With a wild cry that goes leaping forth from my lips. You live—come, give me the ring in payment. It is worth a life, I assure you!

SYLVETTE. Am I to buy my life from you?

MONSIEUR. You are alive—and here! You are a power in this house! Your glances command; you tap your foot, and your servants are gone! And you shall be mine, for I am driven towards you now, with a desire more furious than ever before. . . . I love you—let me love you, Sylvette! I am a passionate and skillful lover, Sylvette! We shall have mad nights of love together! . . .

SYLVETTE. Have you forgotten the misdeed for which the dead one in there is my punishment?

MONSIEUR. That is wiped out! It is swept away in the overwhelming tempest you have aroused in me. . . . You slipped out of my grasp —once—well, that will be no great matter, by the time they have made my scurrilous fame as the deliverer of the most hawked-about wench in Paris.

SYLVETTE. But the day will come when you will remember it—and then you will throw me out of doors.

MONSIEUR. Then I should have to pursue you through all the streets, and go running after you like a dog, for as long as I knew you still alive—wherever it might be.

SYLVETTE. Yes—to cry my betrayal from the housetops?

MONSIEUR. For you hold me captive now! I am utterly and forever in your power! So that when you speak, I am forced to listen . . . a beggar before you . . . and call your name as often as you care to hear it called.

SYLVETTE. I do not care to exchange this ring for that life.

MONSIEUR. All the doors are bolted and barred. They cannot reach us with their prying eyes—only their fingers point us out, and their bawdy whispers follow us. But those looks are trustworthy enough; there's not a crack for them to come in by—and I am safe from the ballad that's being sung out there.

SYLVETTE. The thought of remaining locked in with you does not tempt me, however!

MONSIEUR. But you must not go—stay by me here, always, or I shall be afraid.

SYLVETTE. That is hardly persuasion enough! It is too slight a task you set me—merely to protect you from ridicule—ah no!

MONSIEUR. [*All but shrieking.*] Can you do more than that?

SYLVETTE. [*Slowly.*] What if I should free you of the ring—and of myself as well?

MONSIEUR. What will that leave?

SYLVETTE. It will leave Sylvette—the Sylvette who could live with you!

MONSIEUR. A new life appears before you, Sylvette! Wild, passionate Sylvette. It is your life—will you not invite me into it?

SYLVETTE. [*Puts the ring on her finger. Stretches out her hand.*] Am I not the King's harlot—by virtue of this strange jewel?

MONSIEUR. [*In bewilderment.*] You are Sylvette!

SYLVETTE. Do you presume to claim the royal favourite? I am afraid you overestimate your privileges, Monsieur.

MONSIEUR. You are you—no ring can alter that.

SYLVETTE. Strange powers are at work tonight. [*She points to the right.*] Already they have altered the King's sweetheart.

[MONSIEUR *stares at her.*]

You bound the spell—it is drawing me now away—out of the house.

MONSIEUR. [*Beside himself.*] Where to—where to, Sylvette?

SYLVETTE. To a friend—he lost so much!

MONSIEUR. [*Raging, he flings himself across the table.*] Do you expect to get the reward because you found that thing? Do you mean to become the royal favourite? Is it possible that your vanity can soar even to that pinnacle—it is a daring project. I am lost in admiration. The merry-go-round of love turns once more, and this time the triumph is to you. You—the centre of the whirling crowd —my Sylvette.

[SYLVETTE *smiles.*]

So—now I let you go—to consummate my triumph! Who ever had a sweetheart like mine—fawned upon by the Emperor and rejected by a mere nobleman? Great is your worth—you wonderful Sylvette!

[SYLVETTE *restrains her smile*]

Out of the depths of your embrace, I laugh and pour scorn upon all that is not love of love— For if a man would save himself —first he must lose himself irretrievably.

[SYLVETTE *as before.*]

It has all turned out splendidly—don't you agree? I call it the happiest stroke imaginable! The courtesan is dead—long live the courtesan. Paris is Paris again—with the King dancing—this time in my house! With the magic ring, you shall lure them all to me, Sylvette!

SYLVETTE. [*Quietly.*] Are you in earnest?

MONSIEUR. Let the fire go on burning! There is nothing more of moment for it to destroy. While the ring is safe . . . the favourite is too. Let the festivities go on—I am King—my harlot wears the stone—the talisman of joy is mine.—I too am saved, from the relentless hounding of my thoughts. I have outrun them all! I have no more breath—I am spent—but I am safe! I await my guests— go and bring them here—that I may warm my soul in the yellow envy of all those Chinamen.

[SYLVETTE *holds out her arms to him.*]

[*Seizing a candle.*] Lights! Candles! Light up the mirrors! Lights here, I say! [*He pushes the candle across to her. He busies himself with the second candle.*]

　　[SYLVETTE *takes the candle with a trembling hand—moves away from the table—hesitates for a moment, then carries it into the room on the right. She comes back.*]

Will it be lighter here soon? Will the whole place be filled with the splendour? It is to flow with fire! Waves of brilliance upon waves of dancing, blending in one vast fireworks display! [*Pushes candle away.*]

　　[SYLVETTE *takes it, and does with it as with the previous ones.*] [*He takes a candle out of the candlestick to light the others with.*]

Lights! I'll have that rabble know where to find me, since they are staring so hard! They shall see me gyrating with my sweetheart in the dance! This way—that way— There shall be no shame in our ardour!

　　[SYLVETTE *returns.*]

[*Standing straight.*] Where are the lights? With the dead? You have been in there. What for? [*Seizing her hand.*] You think to make a fool of me—eh—by putting the ring back on her hand? To cheat me of my reward?

SYLVETTE. [*Holds out her hand.*] I am wearing the ring.

MONSIEUR. I should have been immensely chagrined to have gone into the fire for nothing! And the Emperor will pay for that, you say! Well, he's a bungler at it. You are what I want—you, glowing, burning, living—you! [*Seizes her in a wild embrace.*] Kiss me—as no one else can kiss!

SYLVETTE. [*Kisses him.*] Am I alive—now?

MONSIEUR. No one can kiss like you, Sylvette. Kiss me!

SYLVETTE. Am I alive—for you?

MONSIEUR. Twine yourself about me, Sylvette—hold me fast!

SYLVETTE. Am I alive—do you feel it—now?

MONSIEUR. This is the clasp that holds— This is the hunger of love.

SYLVETTE. Now—at last—I hold your life with mine.

MONSIEUR. [*Pushes her away.*] Guests—let the guests come! I must have an audience. That was the rehearsal—now for the grand opening! I know all the parts!—Protagonist of the blood royal!—I am sure of my entrance—I'll have no stage fright on your account— [*With a sweeping gesture*]—or on mine.

[SYLVETTE *goes slowly away from him towards the centre door.*]
Go—run! You have the ring—and I the dead.

SYLVETTE. [*With a faint cry.*] I have the ring——

MONSIEUR. Keep it safe from thieves!

SYLVETTE. With my life.

MONSIEUR. And life is your particular desire—it is valid security.

[SYLVETTE—*through the glass-door exit.*]

[MONSIEUR *stands helplessly, staring at the door. Enter* SERVANT, *centre.*]

SERVANT. The priest——

MONSIEUR. Priest?

SERVANT. Is coming at once.

MONSIEUR. Twenty priests for the Litany.

SERVANT. The men have finished in the garden.

MONSIEUR. Then chase them out! And set a guard over the grave.
[*Exit* SERVANT—*then returns and stands in doorway.*] What are
you at out there—gossiping! Throw open all the rooms—put lights
everywhere. An army of guests will be here tonight—and of such
rank that the slightest negligence will bring a fatal punishment.
For so little as an ill-folded screen, I might forfeit all the favour
that is now mine. . . . I shall take charge of the illumination of
this room.

[*Exit* SERVANT *left.*]

[MONSIEUR *wrenches aside the curtains over the windows. The
fire blazes against the night, more monstrous than ever.* MONSIEUR *stands gazing at the immense glare, rooted to the spot.*]

[*The* OPERA SINGER *appears in the doorway.*]

MONSIEUR. What? Already the first guest arrives? Swift-footed herald
of the Bacchanalia, eh? Does the Emperor of China approach? The
son of the Sun whose god-head he dethroned with this great fire?

OPERA SINGER. [*Breathes heavily—looks about him.*] Are you alone?

MONSIEUR. Yes—only we Chinese; the reception is closed to the rest
of the public. His Majesty may give full rein to his impulses—no
rumour ever leaves this house.

OPERA SINGER. Do you not recognise me?

MONSIEUR. A question! Why, the whole of you is contained within the
space of half a syllable! Are you going to sing? You came ahead of
the others, no doubt in order to test the accoustics of the room?
Which aria will you choose? What is playing now? [*Leads the
singer to an armchair.*]

OPERA SINGER. Let me . . .

MONSIEUR. [*Seating himself likewise.*] One moment—I used to know. I have latterly neglected the opera, to my deep regret. . . . Something out of mythology, if I am not mistaken. One of those ancient subjects which are the eternal source of artists' inspiration. An arrogant breed, these artists—who can find nothing to inspire them in the events of every day. . . . I have it—"Alcestis!"

OPERA SINGER. Tell me . . .

MONSIEUR. A fascinating theme—and one that demands skillful handling. Is it a good libretto? Well worked out? It is no subject for an amateur! Admet, the vacillating seeker, must go in shadow—the full splendour and glory must fall upon the figure of Alcestis. When she suffers the death that was meant for Admet, and thereby attains life herself, for the first time, vicariously in him—that, my friend, is a symbol of overwhelming power! . . . Is your Alcestis able to convey it in its deepest significance?

OPERA SINGER. I cannot discuss opera with you at this moment.

MONSIEUR. Can you tolerate conversation on any other theme?

OPERA SINGER. The fire in the Opera House . . .

MONSIEUR. Of course, the opera again! I was sure of it!

OPERA SINGER. . . . Has made still another victim.

MONSIEUR. Insatiable passion! Look out there—it is blazing higher than ever. Can it be that fresh fuel is being added?

OPERA SINGER. I may have been mistaken—the smoke is blindingly dense—and amidst such terror, it is easy to suffer hallucinations. [*He asks the question roughly.*] Is your wife with you?

MONSIEUR. [*Smiling.*] You cannot allow that subject to rest, I see. Why must you revert to the little trick I practised on you? [*Points to the right.*] I had made a somewhat painful error, which I was not quite ready to admit. A deed of heroism for the sake of a harlot whom I had not even once enjoyed—I feared it would set me in a ridiculous light and I was extremely proud of my self-sacrifice. . . . The unclean remains of the stranger I rescued are about to be buried. My wife is alive.

OPERA SINGER. Is she in the house?

MONSIEUR. From today on, life returns to this house. This night is the gulf between what is past and what is to come. Over there, one centre of pleasure is burning down—here we shall re-establish it. Our projects are all-embracing. Nor are we actuated by an odious desire to glorify ourselves—it is a task to which we have clearly been called. Tell me yourself, where in Paris will you meet another woman like my wife? Admit her rise has been remarkable—to have soared in so paltry a space of time from an orphan-girl—no longer ago than yesterday, was it?—to the Lady in your Box—only yesterday, I believe?

OPERA SINGER. Are you determined to . . .

MONSIEUR. Estimate your charming adventure at its true value? By all means! It has made me realise for the first time what a possession I had! And I am going to savour my triumph. With what impatience I now await the guests whose presence will shed such lustre upon it.

OPERA SINGER. You receive tonight . . . ?

MONSIEUR. All who come. The invitations have not been limited. The yellow costume is credential enough. You, as I said before, are no doubt the herald of the rest?

OPERA SINGER. Whoever danced in the Opera House tonight—is in no mind for festivities.

MONSIEUR. Not even if the invitation should come from the most seductive lips of all?

OPERA SINGER. Who is to invite us?

MONSIEUR. Let me persuade you to be in at the start. You shall see the whole pack in full flight leave the Opera House—headed by His Majesty, hot on the trail of the sweetest yellow-girl there!

OPERA SINGER. And who may that be?

MONSIEUR. Do you mean to insult me? [*Leans forward in his chair.*] [OPERA SINGER *rises.*] The play begins—I assure you it is not to be missed. Its equal has never been seen. It must be reviewed in all the papers—posterity shall envy all who take part in it.

[OPERA SINGER *leans against the chair-back for support.*] You are agitated—what is it? Lest you come too late? At least you will meet the garish procession.

OPERA SINGER. A figure ran across the Opera Square—and was seen in the distance—standing all alone—for the space of a moment only —no longer. Then went on—without haste—and vanished into the fire! The others must have only fancied they saw—but I, and I only, understood!

MONSIEUR. Some madman. He had his reasons—there is a reward out for one of the dead.

OPERA SINGER. In yellow—a Chinese——

MONSIEUR. For a sufficient price? . . . [*He smiles.*] He will have nothing for his pains.

OPERA SINGER. A Chinese girl—that delicate figure—I could not fail to recognise it——

    [MONSIEUR *is struck dumb.*]

    . . . because I knew it!

MONSIEUR. [*After a long pause.*] What did you say? Into the fire? . . . I am forced to believe your story, for I have already seen you face the most dangerous confession a man can make. . . . What did you say? Across the Opera Square? . . . Is your recollection at all distinct? The figure—thin—yes? . . . Alone, you say, crossing the square . . . into the fire? [*He shrugs his shoulders.*] I must beg your help—I do not understand.

OPERA SINGER. My heart ceased to beat.

MONSIEUR. [*With a visible effort.*] But I do not understand. Absolutely, utterly not. Why should she have done that—there is no sense in it! [*He stops abruptly.*] Or is there? [*Grasping his brow.*] Perhaps I can find the purpose—but the most shameless of all.

OPERA SINGER. What do you suspect?

MONSIEUR. [*Takes the singer by the arm and urges him towards the right.*] I brought away a corpse. Do you know who it was? To-morrow you shall know. You shall hear it in a popular ballad. I am the hero of a street-song. You yourself, if I do not err, are humming the verses? The new lines rhyme with some old ones—and I am inventing the prelude myself.

OPERA SINGER. She perished deliberately in the flames, of their foul hatreds. Even their own lives they will sacrifice for the satisfaction.

MONSIEUR. In order that I might be cheated of my just rights. Now I am left to burn with passion unappeased—devoured in the flames of my desire. Has she not left me to perish too, of my longing for her that must reach out for ever into an eternal emptiness? What have I now but the corpse upon its bier—stiff—charred? . . . This is the revenge of harlots then, when we turn them out of doors! So wanton they are, only hatred can overcome their desire for life.

OPERA SINGER. [*Gazing at him.*] It drove her into the fire.

MONSIEUR. Let me hear your story to the end. Did she not first speak with the royal lover, who stood urging men into the fire like retriever dogs? Did she not first lay in his hand a shining object? Did you not catch sight of a filthy bauble passing from her hand into his hand? A hoop—a ring? . . . And did you not then hear His Majesty burst into an immense roar of laughter? That went rolling across the opera square, above the crash of falling balconies and roofs? Echoing through the streets—shaking the city? Is my name not being bandied from mouth to mouth? Taken up by the mobs? Whistled? Shrieked? What are they calling the new poem? Come, release your celebrated voice!

OPERA SINGER. It was still as the grave!

MONSIEUR. You must have missed the best of it then. Run—it's worth it, to get a laugh out of catastrophe like this! There's liberation in that laughter—it slackens the grip of terror. Go on—laugh! I offer you the laugh at my own expense—after all, I courted the adventure—on my head, then, the ridicule!

[OPERA SINGER *moves away, slowly and with uncertain steps. He goes out.*]

[*Enter* SERVANT *from the left.*]

SERVANT. The rooms are open and lighted up.

MONSIEUR. Bang the doors shut—overturn the candles. And if they burn this house down, let them. . . . The world could go no better to its ruin!

[SERVANT *exits.*]

[*Enter through the centre door, the* OLD GENTLEMAN.]

[*Eagerly.*] Was there an episode in which His Majesty figured?

[*The* OLD GENTLEMAN *looks fixedly at him.*]

Did the fire burn the silken raiment from his body so that his unapproachable dignity stood exposed to the view of all?

OLD GENTLEMAN. A mandarin to the last! That is how I have always pictured China in the days of her glory—the infallible jest, even with Death himself!

MONSIEUR. What was it then, that so diverted you?

OLD GENTLEMAN. I might call it the Ring Game—that would be perhaps the most telling title. I hope it will lose none of its delightful piquancy in my version! [*He proceeds to tell the story, emphasising each point with his stick.*] His Majesty, it seems, loved to distinguish his favourite with a ring set with a stone of the most curious design. It happened that at the Chinese ball which became so famous on account of its ending—The night, you will recall, when the Opera House was burnt to the ground—the favourite, the then possessor of the ring—perished in the fire. His Majesty knew that by no chance could she be found alive, nevertheless, he desired her corpse to be recovered. [*Smiling.*] In token of fidelity, no doubt. He announced a fantastic reward, and the task was open to all who cared to undertake it. The mad race which ensued was not without its element of comedy. It provided moreover, an opportunity for the most curious observations upon human bravery. Some of the candidates turned back as soon as they approached the zone of intense heat—others went so far as to singe their hair; but no farther. Each cowardly return to safety was greeted with jeers from the onlookers. A few actually penetrated into the building, and did not come back. After one or two such examples as this, there was a falling off of volunteers. The ardour had gone out of the business. The rush abated, and soon it looked as though we had seen the last of the fun. Then all of a sudden, a little man appeared—a hunchback, a pitiable-looking object. He stood for a moment in the middle of the square, laughing. "Well if my hump burns off, I'll feel just so much the lighter!" he said. And marched straight into the inferno. . . . And in a few minutes came out carrying a body. And the ring was—where the ring belonged!—He had picked her up in the very doorway. All his predecessors had stumbled over the corpse they went to find. Fortune was with that fellow, for a certainty—it must come once, even to a hunchback. He sleeps like a god tonight, the rascal! While the Chinese ladies fight one another for the satyr!— There's a story for laughter, eh? [*He laughs.*]

[MONSIEUR *draws himself up to his full height, stands taut and silent.*] Don't you—[*He sees* MONSIEUR, *and the words die on his lips.*]

[MONSIEUR *gazes immovably at the raging fire.*]

[*The* PRIEST *and* LAY-BROTHERS *appear in the doorway, centre. The* PRIEST *sees what is in the lighted room on the right, and goes in, followed by the* LAY-BROTHERS.]

[*The* OLD GENTLEMAN *wavers—opens his mouth to speak, but does not. Frowns—bows his head as the* PRIEST *and his attendants enter from the right carrying the corpse between them, and unlighted candles in their free hands. They pass through the centre door, into the garden.*]

[*The* OLD GENTLEMAN *follows then—leaning more heavily than ever upon his stick.*]

MONSIEUR. [*Staggers to the centre door. The fire has attained its height. The whole sky is aflame with the reflection of it. The room is loud with the clanging of bells. Flinging up his arms, he shrieks.*] Alcestis! !

THE NÜREMBERG EGG

A Drama in Four Acts

by

WALTER HARLAN

CAST OF CHARACTERS

PETER HENLEIN, *Sworn Master-Locksmith*
EV, *his wife*
CHARITAS, *his sister*
APFELBAUM, *his apprentice*
GÜLDENBECK, *salt-fish merchant*
SCHEDEL, *Doctor of Fine Arts and of the Art of Medicine*
BRATVOGEL, *Sworn Master-Surgeon and Barber*
BEHAIM, *the navigator*
FRAU BARBARA SCHWERTFEGERIN, *Güldenbeck's cook*
A TIPSY WOMAN
A CARNIVAL FIGURE

In addition, a Moor, a peasant-girl, three young artisans and a student, two carnival-figures disguised as ravens, a crowd of women and a swarm of children.

The action takes place in the year 1500, in Nüremberg, in the summer.

THE NÜREMBERG EGG

ACT I

*The workshop of a master-craftsman. Like an interior by Dürer.
Intimate, spotless, sober.*

*At the rear, left (from the audience), a very wide window paned
with circles of thick, opaque glass. The window is now closed. At
the rear, right, the entrance door, giving directly on the street, without steps. In the wall, right, hearth and chimney, with bellows and
fire-irons. In front of these, a stool. To the right, a door into the
kitchen. Next to this, a wall-shelf with shining pewter plates and
six turned-down mugs. At the rear, left, the lower flight of a
spiral staircase is seen, bending to a landing at the head of which
stands a door with a beautiful wrought-iron lock. In the foreground, left, a perpetual light burns before a crucifix, so high that
Charitas must stand on a step to reach it when she comes to re-
plenish the oil. Prie-dieu below it. A little window set high in the
wall. Between the lamp and the staircase, breast-high from the
ground, a hanging cupboard containing saws, hammers, and other
tools. On top of the cupboard shine a handsome brass mortar and
pestle. Toward the centre of the room, a trap-door, with banister
round it, leading down into the cellar. In the foreground, to the
left, a wide-legged table. To the right of the table an armchair,
behind and to the left of it, two straight chairs. In front of it, a
chest. A small table and chair stand under the window, where the
floor is raised a step higher. A lute hangs on the wall.*

*Between the window and entrance-door on the rear wall, stands a
clock, almost finished but still without hands. The door of its
case is propped against the side. Here and there about the room,
hammers, saws, tongs and other tools of the locksmith's trade,
bunches of keys, dialplates, weights, brass chains and cog-wheels,
and a few fine pieces of wrought-iron. The fire on the hearth is
dying down.*

Summer evening is beginning to fall.

Peter *is at the window, reading in a parchment volume. He is a
man of some thirty-five years. He wears a leather apron, but looks
more like a scholar than a locksmith. His fine, white shirt with*

turned-down collar, is open wide at the neck. As he reads, he laughs
critically, merrily, aloud.

EV. [*Brings in from the right a bunch of roses in an earthenware*
jug. She is a young woman of three and twenty; is in her best
dress, ready to go out.] See what I've bought! For but two-pence!
[*She sets the posy on the wide-legged table.*]

PETER. [*Rapping the book, still in laughing annoyance.*] At the
Antwerp gate of the city of Ghent in Flanders, there stands a
scale, so placed that every waggoner, whether he will or no, is
obliged to drive over it. And hanging at the window of the toll-
house is an indicator with numbers on which the toll-gatherer can
read how many pounds and ounces the waggon outside weighs. Yes,
that is what this book-writer has to tell. And what next? Well,
what I want to read next is how that scale is set up. Yes, and what
does he go on to tell? [*Angrily.*]—a merry tale of what took place
that day at the scale; a tale, forsooth! Ah, that is the blight on all
books; that they are written by book-writers!

[*Ev has gone behind him to the window, and now nestles*
against him and kisses him. In a moment she will take her lute
from where it hangs on the wall.]

[SCHEDEL, *also about thirty-five years old, comes in from the*
rear upon this tender scene, and has to make his presence known
by loudly clearing his throat. He looks like a man who earns
much and lives well. He wears a faun-like goatee, and a schol-
ar's high-collared cloak of black broadcloth reaching down be-
low the knees. His knee-breeches and cap are likewise black.
With the opening of the door, a little square comes into view, on
the far side of which rises a tall Gothic church-window.]

PETER. [*Springs up and his arms go out in a wide, spontaneous wel-*
come.] Schedel! Too rare a guest!

SCHEDEL. [*Always at great pains to talk as cynically as possible, yet*
with genuine envy.] A man who takes a wife can dispense with
his best friend. [*He sits down at the right of the table.*] However,
I bring you something—a rich prospect. Oh yes, so it can be—that
a man may fritter his good days away doing noble deeds for his
friend. Just such a one as that am I, just such a donkey.

EV. What is the rich prospect?

SCHEDEL. Well, this afternoon in the Town Hall, Martin Behaim
handed us round that potato of his. The whole Town Council gath-

ered to look at it, as curious as a flock of women. It took four men to carry that wooden ball. . . . Well, when the performance was over, we crowded round the old potato, and now, Henlein, prick up your ears . . . Behaim complained that clocks with weights—and pendulums—are good for nothing on a ship. They get sea-sick, he said. And he said that if there was a man alive who would invent him a clock that would go on board a ship, that man he would call a second Prometheus who had wrung a precious secret from the gods. Then I shouted: "If there be a man in this world who can make you that sea-faring clock, Peter Henlein, Sworn Master-Locksmith of Nüremberg, is he." And I stretched out my arm towards the library and said: "There stands a circle of planets, each with a ball of iron, conceived and set in motion by that same master!" A ship's clock, Henlein! There's a task for you!

PETER. [*Smiling.*] The world is full of tasks, of thousands upon thousands of wonderful tasks. This one too—it is one of them. If the weights get seasick, perhaps a little steed could be harnessed to the hands. But that would be to discover a motive power—that does not exist.

[*Three-quarters of the hour chimes from the church-tower outside.*]

PETER. [*Gaily, to* EV.] Time to go to your lesson.

SCHEDEL. Lesson?

EV. [*Holding up her lute, merrily.*] I'm learning the lute!

SCHEDEL. Need a woman who has made sure of her man, still learn the lute?

EV. [*Holds out her hand to* SCHEDEL.] I wish you good-day, Master Schedel. And should you see the navigator again one day, say to him that he should tell his wish himself, exactly, to Master Peter Henlein. [*Gives* PETER *her hand. Alluringly.*] Dear . . . you will wait supper for me? I have no longing to sup my porridge alone again! [*Points to the place at table where she stands.*] Here I am to be, [*points to another place*] and there, my husband. And in the centre of the table, these flaunting roses! [*She hastens out with her lute.*]

PETER. [*Looks after her with love.*] Yes, I made a jolly bargain with the cantor of the Church of St. Lórenz. He teaches my good wife to accompany her singing on the lute, and in return [*He points to the tall clock.*] I make him this plaything for his soul. It is a clock which will play an artful and pious prelude to the hours before they strike. My wife's father will surely come again with his—"Foolishness! Good-for-naught and a nuisance to boot!"

[BEHAIM, *a man of forty, now in the brilliant full dress of a Knight of Portugal, enters from the street. He has the ruddy complexion of a seafarer and a patrician's assurance of demeanour. His hair, parted down the centre, falls in curls over his collar; a very small moustache lends him a dashing air. A* MOOR *follows him, and remains standing in the doorway with folded arms. As these two enter, the shouts of children follow them from the street. "Behaim! The Moor! Martin Behaim! There goes Behaim!" So long as the door stands open, the children clamour round the threshold.*]

BEHAIM. [*As he notices* SCHEDEL.] Ah, the Town Councillor and Surgeon. So this is your good friend? The man who can make a ring of planets turn with fourteen-pound weights, eh? Not even fourteen-pounds; I weighed them afterwards! [*Grasping* PETER'S *two hands with whole-hearted respect.*] Oh, greetings to you, Master. Has our Town Councillor and Surgeon told you that I must have a clock that will go on board my ship?

PETER. Without weights nothing can go.

BEHAIM. [*Undismayed, and with the utmost emphasis.*] Do you know the Arabs' circle of Heaven, [*Pointing upwards*] which points upward to the zenith and [*pointing upward again, to the side*] to the centre of the moon, measuring distance? [*Describing a semicircle between the two heavenly points.*] . . . However, I spare you my learning. Only this much need you know: can I but have a clock up on the high seas, I shall know my longitude, shall know at all times where I am,—thus, with both the moon and a clock, I can sail whithersoever I will, and the world is mine!

PETER. [*Lights a pine-splinter at the peat-furnace, sticks it into a lantern and takes a wine-jug. With sadness.*] Without weights, nothing can go! [*Raising the cellar-door.*] Though surely: it would be no plaything, that ship's-clock, it would be a fine and serious work! [*Going down a step or two.*] I go to draw a measure of wine, in honour of Martin Behaim. . . .

EV. [*Still with her lute in her hand, has come in again from the street, flushed and breathless, with something most urgent to tell. But she has heard the last words, and is very happy and proud.*] Martin Behaim! [*Bows to him.*] The whole town is telling of

your [*gesture describing a great ball, a yard in diameter*] potato!
And still more of the black man whom you have run after you
for ornament. Oh, if I were Empress, I should have two black
men running behind me!

PETER. [*Frowning.*] Why are you not at your lesson?

EV. Indeed, yes! I turned back, because I had forgotten to say what I
say now: Doctor, you must look down his throat. He has not eaten
a bite since yesterday, except oatmeal-porridge, spinach and soft
eggs. Am I not right to have come back? Or has he told you himself
that he cannot swallow? Has he? Oh, I know what you have talked
about; you have talked all about that ship's clock, and then he
forgot his throat and his body and the whole wide world besides!
Prescribe a medicine to paint it with; for I feel the pain in my
own—in my own throat. A medicine to paint it with will help.
[*Goes towards the door.*]

SCHEDEL. [*Laughing loudly.*] You feel in your throat what's amiss
with his throat, do you? [*Goes to the window. The sky is alight with
the sunset.*]

PETER. [*With tender annoyance.*] Go to your lesson now! He is
laughing at you!

EV. [*With her head high, while her voice changes tone and becomes
more meaningful, with a solemnity rare in it.*] Let him laugh.
What does a mere bachelor know, even if he has studied in Padua?
What does a mere bachelor know of the miracles of married life!
[*Hurries out.*]

SCHEDEL. [*Still laughing.*] A doctor must practise his art wherever he
may be. Come here! And make haste! It is growing darker with
every breath you draw.
    [PETER *sets jug and lantern on the table, and comes to the
    window.*]

BEHAIM. [*As* PETER *goes to the window, in a tone of rough, masculine homesickness.*] It is well for the man who can have his
wife beside him! Five months since I've seen mine, or Carol, my
son.

SCHEDEL. [*Gaily.*] Come—let the tired beams of evening shine down
your beak! [*He looks into* PETER's *throat.*]

BEHAIM. [*Still complaining loudly.*] Oh, this travelling about the
earth has its bitter side! Its martyr's stake!
    [SCHEDEL *dismisses* PETER *with a gesture.*]

PETER. [*To* BEHAIM.] Homesickness? Does a navigator get homesick from seeing the goodwife in a locksmith's home, does he?

SCHEDEL. [*Who has taken a thoughtful step or two about the room, diplomatically.*] Galenus counsels "Ubi pus, ibi incide!" Which translated means: "Where'er the evil saps appear, only the knife avails there."

PETER. [*Grasping his throat in fear.*] Cut—in my throat? [*Bethinking himself.*] Will it hurt right badly?

SCHEDEL. Only blunt knives hurt.

PETER. [*With the deepest trust and friendliness.*] A doctor surely knows what my throat needs.

SCHEDEL. [*Interrupting.*] I'll come tomorrow at market-time. See to it that your wife is not in the way, nor your sister either. [*He sits down at the left of the table, sunk in earnest, yet self-confident meditation.*]

PETER. [*To* BEHAIM.] You see—that is how the world runs in its courses! Even though I were able to make a ship's clock—even though I were able, which I am not—you see, something would come between! Oh, the ship's clock will be invented, and many another thing as well—in a thousand years. [*Taking up his jug and lantern again.*] In a thousand years, somebody will have learnt to draw sunlight into bottles, and then he will go down into his cellar without lantern or pine-splinter,—in a thousand years, or in seven thousand,—ah, God has plenty of time! [*Goes down with his lantern and jug.*]

BEHAIM. [*Emphatically.*] And tomorrow I come again. If there be a man who will make the clock that will not be seasick, he is the one! And I will give him no peace!

SCHEDEL. [*Speaks in a subdued tone, with the self-confidence of a great surgeon, though almost carelessly.*] Tomorrow you must not come. It may be that in three weeks' time our Peter Henlein can be at his trade again as now. Yes. I mean, in three weeks. And in the meanwhile, you must let him have peace.

BEHAIM. [*Sits down facing him. In a low voice, genuinely shocked.*] Is it a grave sickness?

SCHEDEL. Not a dying matter. Most assuredly, he will not die. His sickness is in its first beginning, and he has me.

BEHAIM. Is it a grave sickness?

SCHEDEL. [*With professional geniality.*] Imagine a tiny starfish with all its five arms out, yet no bigger than would go on my thumbnail. Such a little star-fish looking creature sucking itself into the cavity of the throat, Galenus calls a "carcinoma" or "crab," although it is no animal. It is a growth. [*Wrathfully, as an undertone of friendship comes into his voice.*] Yet it is, after all . . . so to say, an animal. More poisonous than a viper, more ravenous than a wolf. Were I not to cut this evil growth right out, and the sound flesh round about it too—and without mercy—Master Peter would have to die. And were he to swallow one tiny drop of that accursed poison into his stomach, Master Peter would have to die. For into the stomach no knife can penetrate.

BEHAIM. [*Involuntarily clasping his hands.*] Then he stands upon the edge of the grave?

SCHEDEL. [*Gaily, and proud of his fearless friend.*] No. No mishap can befall him. None whatever. For he has me. And he'll hold still for me, that man will hold still! [*With almost savage enthusiasm.*] He knows little enough of the Greeks and the philosophers, but I never saw in my life such a stoic as he.

[GÜLDENBECK, *a pallid old man, enters from the rear. His unkempt hair sticks out grotesquely in all directions. It has been long uncut. It is pale, blond hair, streaked here and there with gray. A shabby, wrinkled cloak flaps round his thin legs. His face is sour, peevish and crabbed. A hostile determination now lurks in his eyes. The Negro terrifies and infuriates him.*]

SCHEDEL. [*Without rising. In high good-humour*]: Ah, Herr Güldenbeck. Look, navigator, how your Moor has annoyed Herr Güldenbeck. There's a man who sits on two houses and has an iron wall-press full of money; and yet keeps up a wail from morning till night—wails in winter and wails in May-time. He's a man of Nüremberg well worth pointing out to the travellers who come. Moreover he is the man who gave his lovely daughter to Peter Henlein in marriage. . . .

GÜLDENBECK. More's the pity! More's the pity! [*Sits on the stool beside the hearth. In a querulous tone and in the manner of a deeply-injured, rabid anti-Semite.*] Doctor, it is well for me that I meet you here, a Town-Councillor. For I sent a writing to the Council today on the subject of the Jew, Mesech. [*He takes joy in pronouncing this "ch" with the guttural emphasis of caricature.*] It is not yet a year since the Council gave him licence to trade in salt fish, and already he is selling herring at a penny the pound cheaper than I. And whether my price goes up or down, still he sells a penny cheaper than I!

SCHEDEL. [*With a gesture of dealing out one by one. Vastly diverted.*] I understand. Strews them about to the populace: Here's a herring for you! And for you! And for you!

GÜLDENBECK. [*Fuming.*] I say the trade for a Jew is old clothes . . . or, or moneylending. Let them keep out of our trades . . . out of ours, I say.

PETER. [*Bringing the full wine-jug, is about to put the lantern on the table. Seeing his father-in-law, he calls out in his gay mood.*] Ah, Father-in-law—then I need five cups. [*He puts out his lantern, puts it on the hearth and holds out his hand to* GULDENBECK.] A good-day to you, Father-in-law! [*He takes the mugs from the shelf on the wall, fills them and gives one to each, to the* MOOR *also.*]

GÜLDENBECK. [*Sullenly.*] None for me! I've come for a serious word with you later on, a right serious word. I've no mind for beer or wine either.

SCHEDEL. [*Has little taste for lingering in* GÜLDENBECK's *presence. He takes a full glass.*] Let's make short work of this! [*With ironical solemnity.*] Herr Güldenbeck has come for a serious talk. [*Drinks to* PETER, *then gives him his hand in farewell.*]

BEHAIM. [*To* PETER, *with amiable fatefulness.*] Master, your health! I drink from my heart! Your good health! And look you, this new thing is to come into being. Remember the man, somewhere on land or water, who needs this thing—who, too ignorant to create it for himself, came to Nüremberg, found the right craftsman, demanded the thing, demanded it and means to have it. [*Very slowly.*] And demands it not in his name only. [*Goes out with* SCHEDEL.]

[*The* MOOR *follows them.*]

GÜLDENBECK. [*With feeble, yet deeply suspicious interest.*] A client? What—what is his order?

PETER. [*Rather to himself than answering* GÜLDENBECK, *and filled with the inventor's longing to serve humanity.*] A clock without weights. And not in his name only does he demand it.

GÜLDENBECK. [*With scorn.*] Ay, ay! A grand thing for you! And you'll rejoice to potter away three years on your clock without weights, and earn ten gulden maybe for your housekeeping. Ten gulden! Perhaps!!!

PETER. [*Sits at the table. With blissful intensity.*] For those ten gulden, I would give more than three years of my life.

GÜLDENBECK. [*Running about the room, and in genuine, bitter pain.*]

Pp, pp, pp! My salt-fishery going down and down, and all through a Jew! . . . Now here: A baker . . . from outside the town, a good respectable man and able to pay, came to my shop yesterday and offered to take this house you occupy now, for a rent all but twice as high as the rent you pay—you owe—me. Do you think I mean to let you and [*with painful irony*] my good, sweet little daughter, lead me by the nose forever? Now here: Sunday will be the first day of July [*pressing his forefinger upon the table for emphasis.*] Pay me on Sunday the old rent you owe me and the new rent as well—pay me on Sunday the sum of four and eighty gold Rhenish gulden, or I will relieve you of dwelling and workshop both. That I will! How many hundred times have I said to you: Instead of your one [*contemptuously*] dreamy-eyed apprentice, take three apprentices! Seek customers in Regensburg also, in Münich also! Your clocks are good—make many clocks! But no! Here you sit, you and your dreamer—and potter. [*A very humorous recollection comes to him, and he goes on talking with a kind of light and sour merriment.*] Ah yes, and a short time since on the Fleischbrück! I met the paper merchant, Katzenwurz. In three weeks is his silver-wedding. He would present his good wife with a clock, and out of friendship to me, he comes for his clock to you here. But you, a clock-maker, you—have no clocks! Ha-ha-ha-ha! A clock-maker, without a clock in his shop! And pray, what would you say, if I had no herrings in my shop, or if a paper-merchant had no paper in his shop?! Oh, spare me your answer. I know you're mad for reasons—for reasons marvellous to hear! Yes, for the dreamers to hear! Yes, for everyone who has not his money in you to hear! [*Is about to go. Turns back.*] Circles of planets you're bound to invent! [*Flinging up his hands in a frenzy of scorn.*] It is such a pity that nobody in his right mind wishes to buy circles of planets! Only a pity that you're bound to make a gift of your celebrated circle of planets, ha-ha-ha, to your beloved native city! [*Opens the door. Turns back again.*] Ah, my good Herr son-in-law, this I have to say and hereby make answer to all your speeches and all your lifetime of pottering: If a man wish to be mad, if he wish to be diligently and purposely a lunatic and mad, he must first of all have the money for it and that he must! [*Goes.*]

CURTAIN

ACT II

The summer morning streams in, the roses are gone, the furnace is blazing merrily. APFELBAUM, PETER'S *apprentice, is putting the hands on the clock, with careful strokes of his little hammer. He is in his twenty-ninth year. He has a lovable, schoolmasterish appearance and his movements are precise and schoolmasterish too. When he speaks to* PETER *it is always in a tone of profound respect.*

PETER. [*Again in his leather apron, comes with firm, rapid steps down the stairs.*] Good! This toy must be finished today. And after that we put three clocks in hand, three at once, three everyday clocks! For I must have money now. [*He fetches bars of iron from a corner and lays them in the fire.*] Is my wife gone out? Marketing?

APFELBAUM. [*In the manner of a man who has something else of great importance on his mind.*] Had her basket with her.

PETER. [*Quite lightly, in humorous morning mood.*] Then listen: Schedel means to cut away the little lump that hinders me from doing full honour to my goodwife's cooking. Soon he will be here. And this deserving action he will perform [*pointing to the stairs*] up there, in the bedroom. You stay here then in the workshop, and should my wife come home before we are finished, Schedel and I, see to it—with lies and guile,—that we are not disturbed. Do you hear? With lies and guile. And now to our merchandise—merchandise—merchandise! For I need money now. But I will not cease to search and ponder. There are still holidays. And two and fifty Sundays in every year. And I mean to show God what a man is!

[*He works the bellows and the fire blazes high. As they talk, he takes the drawing of a clock-work out of the base on the table, also compasses, pencil and ruler, and sits down making alterations and diligently working.*]

APFELBAUM. [*Raises his forefinger.*] Yes, there are cases when lies and guile are no sin.

PETER. [*Points to the kitchen. Lowering his voice.*] My sister too is not to come upstairs. Let a woman hear that the lancing of a wart or the letting of a vein is toward, and she will either scream or pray. Both can but hinder the surgeon.

[CHARITAS, *carrying an oil can with a long spout, crosses the stage from the left. She is twenty-seven years old, dressed somewhat in the manner of the Nüremberg Madonna, in grey or black, and looks like a pretty young scholar. The melancholy of a sorrow endured but never healed, sounds almost always in her voice. She feeds the perpetual light.* APFELBAUM, *as she enters, sets the clock at eight and the hammers inside it play upon metal pipes a "pious prelude," followed by full and beautiful hour-chimes.* APFELBAUM *looks at* CHARITAS *in joyful suspense.* CHARITAS *looks at the clock in surprise, smiling faintly.*]

APFELBAUM. [*With suppressed entreaty.*] It's your brother's latest work. Surely it is worth raising that ever-bowed head of yours to look at. [*As he speaks, he takes the two metal-cased weights out of the clock, sits down facing his master, polishing them with chalk and shamois.*]

PETER. [*With painful self-contempt.*] A plaything, a Nüremberg bauble! Oh, a bauble for the soul is a bauble nevertheless! . . . Apprentice, a stranger came here last evening, and brought an order. . . . Apprentice, you were a fool to go to your Holy Mass last evening! . . . Help me to think. We have a clock to make, without pendulum and without weights! Help me search! Weights pull, wind and water pull—they are all useless here—now what can pull besides?

APFELBAUM. [*Smiles helplessly.*] Ah, Master, in Augsburg a teacher has laboured nine years in vain, trying to square the circle.

PETER. And in Mainz, Gutenberg fed seven thousand with seven loaves. If one man can perform miracles, so can another too. I must search in every place, day and night, night and day. What is the other thing that can pull?

CHARITAS. [*On the step, slowly and with upraised hand.*] Do what you can, and what you can not, that God will do.

APFELBAUM. Oh, blessed wisdom!

CHARITAS. [*Coming down, with a smile of humility.*] Not my wisdom, but Thomas à Kempis'. During these weeks, I have been making me a little book, a collection of his deepest thoughts. I can decipher Latin enough for that. Ah, but my learning is a poor and miserable thing. . . . [*In mild reproof*] Look, Peter, not even what is nearest to me do I know. I, a clockmaker's sister, know nothing of a clock. And must needs take a lesson last Sunday to learn how the two hands go, the big one creeping over the small one, like two snails—a lesson on that.

APFELBAUM. [*Proudly.*] From me.

PETER. [*In joyful astonishment.*] You? Charitas? A lesson on clocks?

CHARITAS. Oh, Jesus does not demand that we think of Him only. I ask you now seriously, Peter: You never taught me that—why not?

PETER. I am a locksmith and nothing more, but this apprentice of mine, as you see, is locksmith and schoolmaster both. Twice a man.

APFELBAUM. Ah, how poor is a man who can do only what his master has taught him! Do nothing but what his master has taught him how to do. Ah, if only I had become a schoolmaster! [*In happy reminiscence.*] My own mother's father was a schoolmaster, had a little garden with a plum-tree in it, was what he wished to be. [*With a deep sigh.*] And so was blessed!

CHARITAS. [*With true sympathy.*] Then why did you not become a schoolmaster too?

APFELBAUM. [*Frowning.*] The bread of schoolmasters is hard and scarce, said my father. And in that time I had not learnt that hard bread tastes like cake and pastry in the mouth of a man when he's happy. [*Shaking the weight in his fist.*] So I came into the wrong lane. Soon I shall have passed into my thirtieth year—I shall never get out of the wrong lane now, never! [*Polishes desperately.*]

CHARITAS. The wrong lane. That is a paltry grief. For in this vale of sorrow, it is but an outward and visible thing that a man have trade or office, a worldly and an outward thing.

PETER. [*In great anger.*] No!

APFELBAUM. [*Lifts his finger.*] Maiden, maiden! There dwells an error in your lofty mind.

CHARITAS. [*Smiling pityingly.*] The outward is not the true being; the true being is not the outward and visible. [*Stands behind the table. With a gesture towards them both.*] What should two clock-makers know of what is outward and what is being! [*An idea comes to her. To* APFELBAUM, *in the voice of a reformer, yet in an involuntarily warmer tone than before.*] Ah, Herr Apfelbaum! I will make you a gift of my little book with the extracts out of Thomas à Kempis. It may be that Jesus, the Light and the Redeemer, will illuminate and redeem you through this book, redeem you from the outward and visible and from all worldly covetousness, as He redeemed me through the Holy Scriptures, through St. Augustine and through St. Bernhard. I will go and fetch the book. [*She puts the oil-can on the table and goes upstairs. At the top, as she is about to turn the handle of her door, another idea comes to her. Mysteriously.*] Let me remind you, Peter, the handle of this door rattles in my hand—it is loose. Please put it right for me. A lock that our dear late father made, and in which he therefore still lives and his soul as well—that lock should be kept in good order and held in honour always. [*Goes inside.*] [PETER *goes and examines the loose handle.*]

APFELBAUM. [*In the tone of a man who has something different on his mind.*] So that is a lock made by your father's hand. . . .

PETER. [*Unscrewing the handle.*] When I married, I brought it with me to this house.

APFELBAUM. [*Still polishing.*] Master! I have something to ask of you—have had these many weeks. It is a request so bold that I need to go to it warily. I only beg of you when I have said it not to laugh in my face. But first I must tell you who I am, for you know nothing of me. For close on a year have I been in your service yet you have asked me no questions, therefore I say you know nothing of me.

PETER. [*Who has a bright suspicion of what is about to come.*] Do I know you! I know you down to your heart of hearts. You are— a schoolmaster.

APFELBAUM. I mean you do not know my worldly estate. My father was an innkeeper in Augsburg and from him my mother had more than two thousand golden gulden when he died, and I as well two thousand and more. Of these I put out five hundred to loan at interest to a cattle merchant. An honest man. And two hundred and eighty-four golden gulden I have in my room upstairs, the rest has gone during these years of my apprenticeship.

PETER. [*Frowning.*] You forget that I stand owing you your wage for seven months, my good apprentice, that is a shameful debt that smells foully in my nostrils.

APFELBAUM. Oh, Master, you call me your apprentice but I am in name only. I am your pupil and the longer I stay with you the more do I earn. To a pupil no wage is due. Let me continue——

PETER. [*Laughing, interrupts him.*] Stop, stop. I have guessed your wish, [*With the lock in his hand he takes the whole staircase at a jump.*] and my heart leaps for joy. You would take that poor dear sister of mine to wife. Ah, good! [*Becomes thoughtful.*] And you . . . would fare right well. For what does ail her, after all? Sheer melancholy which husband and children would mend, husband and children, and the happy cares of home.

APFELBAUM. [*Putting his work aside.*] Dear master, you are to carry my suit to her, since you are the eldest of your name.

PETER. And yet—what leads you to believe that she will have you? She has sent four suitors home in these ten years, since she fell into this dejection.

APFELBAUM. A year ago, when first I came to Nüremberg, your market-place and lanes looked gloomy and dark to me—in a word, I wished to go away. But since the day I saw your sister this same city of Nüremberg seems to me the bright and blessed Paradise itself.

PETER. [*Taking the lock apart, piece by piece.*] And is that your assurance? Apprentice, apprentice! Then I must tell you the story of the accursed mischance [*He waves his arm toward her door.*]— which struck that heart blind and deaf to this fair world. [*Darkly.*] Oh, I can tell it calmly now—my fury has died down in these ten years. Well, it was thus: my father had taken into his house a poet learned in Latin for my instruction in rhetoric and grammar. When my sister came to her seventeenth birthday she had the desire to study Latin also, and as together— [*In bitter recollection.*]—we pored over the *ablativus absolutus*, my sister lost heart and reason to that curly-headed rat-catcher. . . . About that time the Emperor came out of Burgundy, having been betrothed there, and bethought himself of a poet who should celebrate that gallant episode, and his choice fell upon our curly-pate whose nose now scraped the clouds. Many a fine speech my father and I held forth upon it—the poet is in the service of the Emperor and of the Muses and cannot therefore cling to home or woman's apron-strings. And so my poor dear sister must needs let her poet go—must needs, willy-nilly. And very soon she fell into this brooding habit, which has endured in her more than ten long years, and her soul flew away from earth—and meantime our poet has become the Emperor's privy councillor and secretary. [*He puts down the lock brusquely and bursts into a vast fury.*] A sneak, an oily scoundrel! A cur!

APFELBAUM. [*Delighted.*] Master, dear master, one unacquainted with suffering weighs but little in the scale. When I hear your

sister speak I seem to listen to the voice of one who is one of themselves with all the saints and God the Father.

PETER. [*Takes up the lock again and works on it. His voice has become calm.*] Listen, apprentice, I have better proof than you that you
may go in hope—that you may have a tiny feeble hope. When you
first came into our house in Autumn, my sister's piety was a gloomy
thing, as though she walked in night with sore trouble and fear.
But that same piety, have you not noticed it, has grown more cheerful now. Ah, the godly maiden—she must learn now how the big
hand creeps over the little hand! And I say it is you who have
wrought this in her, you. A schoolmaster can talk with her. Now
you shall have my sacred promise that if there glow in her heart
even the least spark of love, though she may not know herself that
it is there, that spark I will blow upon and quicken into a fire like
the fires of hell. [*With sudden energy.*] Oh, I have work to do.
[*Counting on his fingers.*] This lock to make right, clocks to build,
merchandise, merchandise! And go a-wooing for my apprentice
into the bargain; and have the little lump cut out of my throat
as well. [*He takes the steel spring out of the lock and tests the
mechanism with his tools.*] And this besides, I have another task
too. I have a clock to make that I cannot make—a power to find
which will pull a clock without weights. . . . [*He falls silent,
stands up and goes a few steps to the right. With his back to* APFEL-
BAUM *he examines the lock in his hand.*]

APFELBAUM. [*In an ecstasy of joy.*] Ah, Master, you must think I
have lost the power of speech. Ah, dear Master, *you* talk instead!
But let me keep still for today for I have nothing to say but that
one word of yours over and over—hope, blissful hope!

PETER. [*Staring at him, like a man whose mind is completely occupied
with something else so that no other thought now exists in it.*] What
are you talking about?

APFELBAUM. [*Smiling.*] Master! About the Jungfrau Charitas Henlein.

PETER. Yes, that was it. . . . You were saying you seemed to be
. . . , in love, [*Irritably.*]—oh, let me alone with that sweetstuff.
[*And now, in a most joyful turmoil, he thrusts the latch-spring at*
APFELBAUM's *nose.*] Apprentice, schoolmaster, look at this.

APFELBAUM. [*Somewhat offended.*] It's a spring, the spring from
your father's door lock which raises the latch every time the hand
presses it down. It is a spring.

PETER. But, listen, apprentice, a thing that can lift can also pull. [*He opens the chest hastily and takes out of it a pair of pincers, also a small and ancient sieve into which the latch spring fits exactly. The sieve looks like a tiny tambourine. He shows it to* APFELBAUM *at all angles. Triumphantly.*] Look at this. It is an old sieve which separates fine energy sand from coarse. However, that is not what I need it for now. Look at it. It is shaped like a drum—a little low drum, but I'm not going to play on it now. See here what I do. [*He lays the spring in the sieve.*] I fit this steel spiral into this drum and screw it fast, screw it fast to the edge from the inside. [*He takes the spring out of the sieve, holding one end tightly between his fingers and gripping the other end with the pincers against the edge of the sieve inside.*] Now I seize this spring right in its heart. [*He pulls it out.*] Then I let it go and it will curl back of its own accord into the old position where it was comfortable. Do you hear that, apprentice? Of its own accord.

APFELBAUM. [*Regards* PETER *with open-mouthed astonishment as if he were a magician. Interjecting.*] And screwed to the edge.

PETER. Well? Well? !

APFELBAUM. Well, it turns the drum. [*But now dismayed and in deep thoughtfulness.*] And yet how to attach the escapement to such a drum. Ah, you have not done yet. There is no clock here as yet.

PETER. [*Suddenly putting everything down.*] If I have found the hardest thing I shall find the many easier ones surely. [*Turns again to* APFELBAUM, *now in the manner of a keen thinker reciting a gay process in logic.*] Listen, apprentice, to what Behaim, the navigator, said. "With the moon and a clock as well I shall be master of the seas and the world is mine," and I added: Every captain on earth shall have a ship's clock. Even I, should I wish to learn navigation. You too, apprentice. For who is master over the seas? I answer: all the people on earth, the whole race of men. We shall be stronger than the sea, apprentice, hear that! We. [*He pauses, takes a few steps about the room, drunk with enthusiasm. Then he sinks his head on his hands, and collects himself. A happy memory comes to him.*] Last night as I took my supper a bunch of roses stood here on the table and my wife said that one day she would love to deck everything with roses, the cupboard, the door, the walls, the whole house—when the right time came. Go to the market, and have them bring roses now. Three great baskets full of roses.

APFELBAUM. [*Takes his cap. Full of enthusiasm.*] Master, dear Master, I go at once. Three paniers full of roses.

CHARITAS. [*Comes slowly down the stairs, holding out a little parchment volume for* APFELBAUM. *With quiet solemnity.*] This is to read in the early morning. They are words out of the heart of God, directly out of His heart.

APFELBAUM. [*Takes the book. In great confusion.*] Maiden, look at your brother, maiden. [*He is about to tell her, but changes his mind.*] No, it is not for me to rob him of the joy of telling this. [*Looks at the book in his hand.*] Maiden, for many a week, you said, for many a week, you have been writing in this book? And now you give it me? [*Full of inward tumult.*] I thank you, maiden. Oh, I have no words! For yet another joy is in here— [*With a gesture towards his heart.*] In the little room in here! There is no place in such a little room for two great joys, two such great joys. Maiden, look at your brother. Ah, the blue sky is ringing with bells.

CHARITAS. He is a devout man, Peter, more devout than you. But what ailed him? His thoughts seemed whirling in his head.

PETER. [*Now filled with the deep gaiety of beatitude.*] Ah, what I might say would be worth nothing. It would but concern my trade. An event in it—an outward and visible, a worldly matter! He has gone to buy me roses. I would make a gift of roses to my wife. [*A joyous idea occurs to him.*] Charitas, little sister! I have something [*Mysteriously.*]—for you too. See, it is because you stand before me now and I am in the mood to give and give. So I shall give you such happiness as you never knew before. Listen, so young are you still in form and countenance, so richly lovable, the day is come when you will give the word of consent to one who seeks your hand. [CHARITAS *recoils as though his words defile her.*] Oh, I know your speech in advance, yet still I say, a maiden in sevenfold armour is still a maiden. And when you come to your marriage I shall give you your linen and all else for your household. And all your wedding-gear.

CHARITAS. [*With an other-worldly smile of compassion.*] My brother, you have a good and simple heart. I thank you. . . . But a true and whole-hearted devotion to the service of God you will not understand. You cannot see that I became the bride of Christ although I entered no convent. [*She raises her head.*] For I am of those who need no convent walls. Some of us may so trust our own faith that we can keep our troth and sacred vow to the Heavenly Bridegroom without walls of stone or rules of convent orders. [*With pedantic humour.*] See, thus writes Paul to the Corinthians: "She that is unmarried careth for the things that belong to the Lord, but she that is married careth for the things of the world, how she may please her husband." And later St. Paul has spoken God's whole opinion of marriage, thus: "He that marrieth doeth well; he that marrieth not, doeth better."

EV. [*Comes busily in from the street, her face flushed. Rhubarb leaves and a pot-bellied earthen jug stick out from her over-flowing market basket. Her other arm embraces an earthen preserve jar, the tallest and fattest to be found. She begins talking in the doorway, proud and elated.*] I bring news.

PETER. [*Takes the jar from her. Joyfully.*] Oh, beautiful, marvellous pot! [*He puts it on the table.*]

EV. Yes, is it not a handsome one? But that is not my news. [*Lightly and with impatience.*] Yes, in this pot I shall make you some preserves you've never yet tasted.

PETER. [*Peers into the basket.*] Currants? Raspberries? Gooseberries? [*Lifts out the jug.*] And—a jug?

EV. Yes, but neither is that my news.

PETER. [*Still teasingly holding her off.*] What is in the jug?

EV. [*Impatiently.*] Rye brandy, ten years old, to be poured into my jar here over all these berries, and by autumn the whole pot will be full, full of berries and pears and brandy. That is an art my mother taught me.

PETER. And when is the time to eat so admirable a conserve? At Christmas after the fat roast goose?

EV. [*As she dries her temples and forehead. With the happy pride of an artist, and voluble as a waterfall.*] Ah, I will tell my news, whether or no. I am to sing a solo in the Church of St. Lórenz, all by myself in front of the organ. As I was going to market, the Cantor was standing at his window. He called to me and came down. This is how it is to be. In seven weeks time a great Vesper Service is to be sung. It is quite new. It has been brought from Holland. "Faith and Good Works" is its name. Two choirs in contest. The choir of St. Lórenz is to invite the choir of St. Sebald's. The whole of Nüremberg singing praises to the Lord. Thus, "Faith" stands to the right of the organ and sings in four-part—"Good Works" to the left of the organ and sings in four-part likewise.

Each choir would show itself the stronger before the Lord and outsing the other. But I—I am to stand right in the centre in front of the organ. [*Very proudly.*] On a step, above them all. A messenger from God Himself, sent to make peace between them, a holy seraph. [*She takes the jug and goes with it towards the cellar door, raising her head.*] The Cantor said he knew of no one to sing that part better than I, he knew of no one better.

PETER. [*Looks at* CHARITAS, *then back to* EV, *gaily comparing them.*] A real woman and wife is seraph or cherub; a cherub on a step, who yet can make conserves in brandy for her husband! Little sister, little sister, if only you would let this wisdom penetrate your seven armours. This is the word of Dr. Schedel: "A right man is a whole man." And here and today I add this: "A right woman is a whole woman."

EV. I shall take my jug down into the cellar so that it will not be broken. It cost me nineteen pence. Don't scold me, Peter, I shall buy three more such. Do you hear that, Peter? And you are not to scold me, not even this evening or tomorrow.

PETER. [*Slowly, as if savouring his happiness.*] I scold? Never again. For we've become rich since you went out to market. [*He holds the latch spring towards her.*] In this spring a thought has lain—lain here a hundred years. [*Solemnly.*] And this is what the thought in the spring was saying: That which can lift can also pull. It was a thought of the Lord God's.

EV. [*Puts the jug down again. With a glad cry.*] Peter! My Peter! Now you can make your ship's clock! ?

CHARITAS. [*More calmly, yet in deep gladness also.*] My brother, then He has chosen you to be the first to look upon this thought of His, a part of Himself.

PETER. [*With Promethean pride that rises rapidly.*] In iron and steel, in all things whatsoever, lie the thoughts of the Lord God. He who can draw them forth, possesses them.

CHARITAS. [*In fear, as if to ward off evil.*] May God keep us in His grace that we may remain humble. It was He who gave you your mathematician's brain. Of His bounty you received it. He, the Creator, created also the ship's clock. All glory is to God alone.

PETER. [*Gaily putting aside this intolerable idea.*] Only a priest can hold the Lord God so poor that He needs demand all honour and glory, even to decking Himself out in my feathers. [*Deliberately.*] For I and no other drew the thought out of that spiral: I am no other was the first to fit the spiral into this drum—[*With an upward gesture of pride.*]—and no other.

CHARITAS. [*Takes her oil can. As one whose wisdom is from heaven, yet with a hint of roguishness.*] My brother and lord, your words are arrogance; I run from this room lest the further sight of me prompt you to worse blasphemy still. For why should I lead my lord and brother into hell? [*She goes out right.*]

PETER. [*Confidentially.*] Ev, did you hear that new note in her voice? How gay it rang, and the mischief that played round her lips? I tell you, Ev, my sister is in love.

EV. [*Smiles incredulously and quickly changes the subject.*] Oh, dearest love, let us talk of Charitas later on, in three hours' time. First I must hear about your ship's clock. For now I am the wife of a most illustrious master and it will take a good three hours to be over my rejoicing—more than three hours, a whole life-time after that. Oh, my Peter! [*Throws her arms around his neck.*]

PETER. [*Disengages himself, and with a new joyful inspiration goes and sits down on the chest.*] I shall make a ship's timepiece for you also, to wear on a little chain about your neck.

EV. [*Coming over and sitting on his knee.*] Could it be so small and so light?

PETER. It will have no weights and no pendulum, then why should it be large? Why heavy? It need be no bigger than—[*Rapidly reflecting.*]—a hen's egg. So there, my wife, the first living egg will tick upon your bosom! What do you say to that? Is it not a jolly trinket? Then you will cross the market-place with this new diversion about your neck, and from that moment forth not a burgher or alderman of Nüremberg will know a moment's peace until his own goodwife has an egg ticking on her bosom too. And they can buy them only from me. So you and I now—we are richer folk now than I had thought before. Ev, I shall build you a house with a garden like Schedel's, with pillars for grape-vines to climb and twine about.

EV. [*Blissfully.*] And in a few weeks from today as I walk through the lanes at your side, all the people will point us out.

PETER. [*Pulls down her hand with the pointing finger and says very sceptically.*] And will that be a great joy, think you, the pointing? [*At the height of his joy.*] No, Ev, this day is the day. This day I have foretasted heaven. A man who can live to see such a day as this, when his mind gives birth to a new thing under the sun—

a thing that is needed by thousands of captains on the seas—a man
who can live to see such a day as this—[*In solemn joy.*]—is in
Paradise already! Strolling in Paradise! Oh, and will never leave
it again. And never again can he be called a potterer by any man.
Never in the world. Strolling in Paradise.

BRATVOGEL. [*A man of fifty with powerful arms and a low forehead, enters from the street, carrying a shabby little surgeon's bag.
His pinched and meagre features now radiate a kind of malicious
self-confidence. He opens his mouth and makes the sign of the Cross
before it. He bows low to* PETER.] Bonus dies. [*Then to* EV.]
Bonus dies.

PETER. [*Is obliged to laugh. Slyly.*] Who are you? Would you like to
buy a ship's clock?

BRATVOGEL. [*In astonishment. With great condescension.*] Are you
Master Henlein?

PETER. [*With a proud laugh.*] Yes, it is a name crowned with laurel.

BRATVOGEL. [*Again makes the sign of the Cross before his mouth. In
deep rebuke.*] You are he? And laughing?

PETER. And why not? What, Ev? But why do you make the sign
of the Cross before your mouth? Do you think the devil might leap
out of my mouth into yours?

BRATVOGEL. [*Repeating the gesture.*] This I think— [*Turning his eyes
up to heaven.*] Lord *Domine* above the clouds, how comes it that
a man who bears the living fungus in his throat still can laugh!

PETER. Be brief. I have much work to do. Who are you? [*With the
merriest irony.*] And what fungus?

BRATVOGEL. [*With the gesture as before.*] I am he who saves from
death. I am Christian Bratvogel, sworn master-surgeon, and— . . .
also, alas, to my shame I say it, sworn master-barber as well. For I
have a wife, six daughters too. Only for their sakes I must smear
soap upon the stubble of burghers and dirty peasants, tell them the
latest news, shave them. And before I forget, do you know the
latest news? On Sunday after the carnival, a splendid miracle is
to be shown on the Haller-meadow—a pig with quills.

EV. [*Highly amused.*] With bristles, you mean?

BRATVOGEL. I mean what I say—with quills as long as my arm. A
wondrous miracle of God. Two monks brought it with them from
the Isles of the Blessed.

PETER. [*To* BRATVOGEL.] But tell me, what is it, the fungus which
you say I bear in my throat?

BRATVOGEL. [*Makes the sign of the Cross three times before his mouth. His voice falling to a whisper, and in great fear.*] It is when the Devil comes into swellings and bad growths.

EV. [*Frightened.*] How do you know this? These few days past my husband has had a little growth inside his throat. How did you know it?

BRATVOGEL. [*Sits in the armchair. With spiteful sarcasm.*] The—world-famous surgeon did me last night the august honour of coming to my humble barber-shop. The great doctor Schedel bade me come here this morning at nine o'clock promptly, in order . . . in order to hold your head while he cuts.

EV. [*Crying out.*] Cuts! [*She sinks down on a stool near the anvil with her head in her hands.*]

BRATVOGEL. [*Bitterly.*] Yes, to hold poor patients' heads, he find me good enough for that. To hold their heads! His vice, that's what I am. That's all he thinks I'm good for.

PETER. [*Very angry.*] Clumsy Klaus! [*Pointing to* EV.]—You clumsy Klaus!

EV. [*To* PETER. *In violent and anguished reproach.*] While he cuts! And so terrible is this carving to be, so cruel that the surgeon must have a helper, a living vice! To hold the head!

PETER. [*Distrustfully.*] No, Ev. It is nonsense. Schedel is going to take a tiny piece out of my throat with his knife—no more than, no more than letting a vein, oh, much less than a blood-letting.

EV. [*Reflects for a little while. Then with very serious dignity.*] I—I will have no cutting. Oh, that Schedel! He has a rage for cutting, and his best friend is just good enough for him.

BRATVOGEL. [*Has meanwhile taken out of his bag an apothecary's square bottle, half full of water. With immense solemnity, slyly and mysteriously.*] And he need not cut. I came on purpose a half hour earlier than the renowned surgeon bade me come. For I can save you from his knives and shears. I, Christian Bratvogel! who never was a student at the Devil's school in Padua! A German surgeon! Now then: I thought over your sickness this morning, Master Henlein, and a thought came into my mind from heaven—from heaven. Look you here—this boil in your gullet is no natural sickness, as the famous surgeon declares. [*With greater mystery. With a gesture of drastic intensity.*] In that boil lurks the fungus. It is a Devil, smaller than a wasp, shaped like a bat, smaller than a

wasp! It is a Devil! But be comforted. Hear how I shall outwit
him. There squats the cancer in your gullet, so through your gullet
you must pour a medicine and the Devil will take flight before it.
What, am I not right? And this is what my medicine is called—
Baptismal Water, consecrated, holy, incorruptible.

EV. [*Fetching a pewter mug.*] And this I say, though the Holy Water
may not help, what harm can it do? What harm can it do? [*She
pours the water into the mug.*]

PETER. [*With immovable fortitude.*] Were I to drink this water, then
you would see a scientist of Nüremberg turn into an old peasant
wife. [*He takes the cup from Ev.*] Schedel shall cut. Oh, joyous
century that has taught how such cutting may be done! Oh, joyous
century! [*He pours the water into the fire.*] If there be in Nüremberg any Saviour of the body, Hartman Schedel is he.

BRATVOGEL. [*Makes the sign of the cross. In a new tone of supplica-
tion.*] Master Henlein, if for your own sake you will not drink this
water that surely cannot harm you, and likely might cure—well,
then—[*Naively.*]—drink for my sake. Should I with the Holy aid
of God, drive this growth out of you, [*Beating his breast.*]—then
I shall be an *excorcista*. Which means one who banishes Devils, a
miracle worker. [*In an agony of covetousness and envy.*] Yes, and
for the poor I should perform my miracles for charity; but for the
rich, why should I not make money from the rich? As much
money as the famous surgeon makes?

PETER. Aha, aha! It is a pity Hans Sachs could not hear this speech.
He might have woven it into his Lenten play, as the speech of the
poor man tortured by envy. You would have heard it—Master
Envy's speech.

BRATVOGEL. [*In a white rage.*] Master Envy? you dare to say Master
Envy? [*He takes a white surgeon's-apron out of his little bag and
ties it round him with trembling fingers.*] Good! Then I shall drive
your laughter out of you instead. Hark now, to what I would have
spared you. [*Slowly and with spiteful glee.*] The last man whose
fungus our famous surgeon cut, these seven or six weeks past—
he lies rotting now in a narrow box in the dark.

PETER. [*Only slightly afraid.*] Ah, that must have been a different
sickness, it was a different sickness certainly. [*With a grin of triumph.*] It was the cancer.

EV. [*Falling on her knees before her husband.*] Oh, Peter, Peter!

[SCHEDEL *hastens in, carrying an oblong box, and stands regarding this agitated scene with alarm. He is surprised to find* BRATVOGEL *there already.*]

PETER. [*With his back towards him so that he does not observe his entrance, strokes* EV's *head.*] Oh, be of good cheer. Do you believe the Lord could wish me to die before I have held the first ship's clock ticking in my hand?

SCHEDEL. [*At the word* "die," *casts a look full of suspicion at* BRATVOGEL *who retreats involuntarily toward the right. Furiously.*] How do you come here already? It is not near the hour. And what is that white apron you are wearing? That stupid white apron? [EV *has risen at* SCHEDEL's *first words and stands to the left of the table.*]

PETER. [*Almost completely comforted.*] Ah, Schedel, greetings. Ah, yes, the master-barber, the master-barber! It was too well with my soul this morning. Like a brook in the mountains—like a little mountain brook over the pebbles, so did my thoughts go dancing. Then came the master-barber and threw a bucket of dirty water into the happy little brook, yes, swill. We came to words, he and I, for he covets your fame. And then he let out of that envious, envious heart of his that the last man whose throat you cut into straightway died.

BRATVOGEL. [*With the insolence of a bad conscience.*] Did I not tell the truth? Is our Archivarius not dead, is he not dead?

SCHEDEL. [*Goes to* BRATVOGEL. *With profound contempt.*] I will talk to you later.

PETER. Now tell this good wife of mine that you are to make no more than a tiny cut into this boil, and that no man could die of.

SCHEDEL. [*In a tone of philosophic cynicism.*] Since when do I speak the truth? Since when does any man speak the truth? Only when he has come to an end of his lying. [*Simply and confidently.*] The name of your sickness is "the crab." Praise be to God, it is the little one in your larynx—I can cut it out for you.

PETER. [*Gets up. Troubled.*] Our Clerk of Archives, was it the little crab he died of?

SCHEDEL. Since I began the practice of my art I have operated four times for the little cancer on four patients. One—[*With uneasy conscience.*]—died. Three lived. And, look you, that very Clerk of Archives—look you, he was a thin and pale little man, and for many years before his sickness came upon him he had swallowed more of the dust off his tomes than wine and vegetables—yes, all his life long. In short the Clerk of Archives was a clerk of archives, a bad plum, ready to fall. And a lamp about to go out, as surely without as with his sickness.

BRATVOGEL. [*Fanatically.*] But he died! And of the cancer! Of our cutting out the cancer! Though had he taken an incorruptible medicine into his throat, instead of that knife of yours, I say that his goosequill would be scraping yet in our Town Hall.

SCHEDEL. One died, three live.

PETER. And died of the same sickness that you would cure me of today.

SCHEDEL. [*Gloomily—fighting a painful resolution.*] Of the same. But there I made a mistake, and instant death resulted. [*As if freed of a burden.*] So—now you have it all! And it is nothing. For look you, Peter Henlein—I do not make the same mistake twice.

PETER. Some other then. Ah, there are many mistakes that might be made in so young an art. Many thousand mistakes.

SCHEDEL. [*Resorting to roughness.*] Henlein, Henlein! Since when are you a coward?

PETER. This is not my day to be carved, Schedel. [*Pointing to the armchair.*] Sit down—I have great news for you. [SCHEDEL *sits down.*] The ship's clock which Behaim desired of me yesterday, is—so to say—is finished in my mind. And as the tiny lark in the egg—curled up inside its tiny egg—must lie awhile yet; as the unborn lark lies there longing to soar aloft and fill the whole wide sky with song, so lies the clock inside my brain, waiting to be born, longing to sing its song: tick-tock, tick-tock, tick-tock! And will, come what may. Therefore I must run no risk of death. [*His cheerful warmth returns.*] Listen, Schedel: a woman who goes in the good knowledge that soon she will add a little future tailor or shopkeeper to the race of men, is also "a coward." She may not . . . stumble over a door-sill, nor be frightened by lightning—first the little future tailor must lie safe in his cradle, finished, finished. Afterwards, let the lightning come! Thus I. Until I have—borne my child, I must be a coward, a thousand cowards. For of tailors there is never any lack, but if my child be not born, it is lost to the world. Lost! So then, this is my resolve: I need six weeks to make my ship's clock ready, six weeks or five—cut then to your heart's content, cut then! [*He sits down again on the chest.*]

SCHEDEL. [*Springs up from his chair and takes a few steps about the room. In deep sorrow.*] Ah, that Plato, that visionary, with his hoax of a world governed in its courses by reason—reason, "divine reason." Imbecile, addlepate chance—that is what governs the world! Fate in a barber's hand! [*Makes for* BRATVOGEL *again, but the barber clenches his fist and stares at him with insolence.*] Ah, what have you not done here! Be off! I shall find me another barber-surgeon! Blunderhead! Blunderhead! [BRATVOGEL *goes off in a rage, forgetting his bag behind him.*]

SCHEDEL. [*Sees it, picks it up, runs after* BRATVOGEL *and hurls it after him with the whole force of his arm. Then sits down on the chest facing* PETER. *Sadly.*] You bid me wait five weeks, and I answer: I cannot wait five days. Could I do so, most gladly would I, for this is a bad season to lie convalescent in your bed. It was said in Council yesterday that the Hohenzollern seeks a quarrel with Nüremberg once more, disputes us now the right to our free jurisdiction and what not besides. . . . It may be that in a few weeks hence, the city may be at war with him. Look you, Henlein, could I wait, I gladly would. But all the while there is mortal poison in your throat; if you should swallow the least drop of such poison as that into your stomach, you would have more boils, many more. [*Explosively.*] And into the stomach no knife can reach.

EV. [*Who has been wringing her hands in deepest misery.*] Doctor! Is his life in peril?

SCHEDEL. No! ! His life is in his own hands. He holds his life in his own two hands.

EV. [*To* PETER, *with brave and firm decision.*] Dear Peter, with all that I know now—and I pray God that I speak aright—I say: Let him cut.

SCHEDEL. [*In joyful astonishment.*] Listen! Listen! Even women turn sensible—when they must.

PETER. [*At last in fear of dying, yet with unfailing self-trust.*] You "can wait no longer than five days" . . . oh! . . . I shall find a way. Ah, I will not die! I must make not my ship's clock only—but many things more—many things the world has need of. Invent and make them, though today I do not know or guess what they may be. [*Confidently, with a new idea.*] Yes. I shall take a walk down to the Frauentor across the fields. How often in my work, when the right way would not come to me at once, I found it—in the fields, on the Pegnitz—many a time in the alleys and market-place as well, amongst all the people . . . [*He takes his cap and stick.*] See, Schedel—my brain is slow to move—I need to know even the minutest points; and then to consider the problem broad and whole, and calculate it out. [*He is about to leave, but turns again to* SCHEDEL.] Wait—this I need yet for my problem: Were you not to cut the little crab, neither today nor ever, then how long should I still have to live?

SCHEDEL. [*In a resounding fury.*] A useless question! Little time enough you would have—perhaps ten, perhaps but six weeks. . . . A fool's question.

PETER. [*Ice-calm.*] That shall stand in the problem as I lay it out and calculate it. In six weeks, the ship's clock will be finished, surely. [*With profound emotion.*] Which the captains wait upon. Which the whole race of men waits upon—not knowing that they do so, yet doing so nevertheless. [*Collecting himself. Smiles.*] Everything, that too, shall have its place in the problem. I give you good-day! I shall find a way out—in the fields. I shall come home for dinner.

APFELBAUM. [*In bacchanalian mood, rushes in from the rear with a great basket filled to the brim with roses. Two garlands of roses hang round his neck.*] Three baskets of roses! Three baskets of roses! [*A* PEASANT GIRL *sixteen years old and glowing with rosy health, comes in behind him, carrying one rose-filled basket on her back and another in her two hands. Two garlands hang round her neck also.*]

PETER. [*Disregarding the interruption.*] Oh, be of good cheer—I will not die. [*Takes one of* APFELBAUM's *garlands. In wild desire for life.*] And since the sun rises on this workshop of mine, and since I have accomplished that which will defend me from the name of "potterer" for ever and ever—since all this is so, then I may make a gift of roses to my wife. [*Ev sinks onto the chest. Her head falls on her hands. She sobs bitterly.*]

PETER. [*Looks at her in deep concern, and gives the garland back to* APFELBAUM. *In a frenzy of grief.*] And again I say; deck the doors and cupboards with these roses, and be of good hope. For I shall find a way! I will not die! Ah, every true master gives his life to his craft—every one does that! But see how—drop by drop he doles it out—charily—over fifty years—over sixty. Shall I give mine all at once? In six weeks from today, or ten? All at once? ! [*He rushes out.*]

CURTAIN

ACT III

[*Down a cross-lane the town pipers are marching to the meadow where the carnival is assembling. At that range it is a very gay and frolicsome music, and a great clapping and laughter go with it. The fire on the hearth has sunk to embers, the clock has gone. Window and door of the workshop stand wide open, and the square outside is bright with the sunshine of the summer afternoon. The green leaves of a creeper hang over the window.*]

CHILDREN. [*Running with the band, laughing and calling.*] The carnival! There goes the carnival! Hooray! I'm not to go, but I am going! Hooray! Hooray!

[*Ev very simply dressed in workaday clothes, her eyes filled with fear, comes from the kitchen with a small earthen dish on which are cloves and a stick of cinnamon. She sets this on the table and fetches the mortar from the cupboard. She looks, frowning, in the direction of the noise and the music, presses her hand to her heart and draws a long, deep breath. The music turns the corner and is gone.*]

A CARNIVAL FIGURE. [*Masked, with an enormous fool's cap on his head, pokes a great sausage through the window.*] Hey there! Fräulein! Sausage! Off to the Haller meadow! Will you come along? [*Ev in her armchair, sits with her back to the window and does not answer.*]

THE CARNIVAL FIGURE. [*Hopping about, and making merry sport of a sad singer.*]

> Through the lanes and gate we hie,
> To where the fields do verdant lie—Sausage!!

[*Ev takes the mortar between her knees, puts the cinnamon-stick and a few cloves into it, and begins to crush them, with sorrowful diligence.*]

SCHEDEL. [*Goes by the window from the left, and comes briskly in full of confidence.*] Well? Three days I have waited. Will he le me cut it now? It is time to take serious thought—high time.

EV. [*The instant she sees him, puts the mortar on the table, rises an*
216

holds out both her hands.] Oh, praise be to God that you have come!

SCHEDEL. Will he let me cut it?

EV. I cannot tell. I know nothing. He has but one answer: "It will be better presently." And that he says as a man will say it when he is in no mind to speak. And sits and ponders, takes his half-finished work to pieces for the tenth time—all its hundreds of little screws and wheels and bridges and oddments. [*She goes to the table on which stands a half-finished clock shaped somewhat like an egg, supported on a simple tripod.*] Look—he has put it together again.

SCHEDEL. [*Takes up the Egg with extreme care, lifts the lid and peers in with the embarrassed wonder of the technically ignorant.*] Ah, and all this a craftsman can do in three days . . .

EV. And nights! Today again, a good two hours before sunrise, he must needs slip from his bed and down the stairs. And there I hear him, hammering and singing, my invalid, his song merrily keeping time with the strokes. It is a merriment to shudder at.

SCHEDEL. [*Returns the clock cautiously to its stand.*] Well may it be that this fragile mechanism here is a precious jewel—a glorious achievement of the human brain . . . [*Recovering his habitual cynicism.*] And yet I say: Primum vivere! Which translated is to say: First live! And let immortal works come afterwards. First live! Listen— As I was walking in my garden last night, in my beloved garden close, I fell to composing verses. And composed a strong and ringing line or two to shake up and wake up that Peter Henlein's soul. A true dirge, a raven's croak! Today is carnival, so late last night I and two neighbours got poem and croak by heart, thinking to come and caw it at him—and let him see his death in effigy. But you should show him life instead, you, the master's wife. I come now with this counsel—show him life; show him what he is to lose. For example—put on a gayer dress. Use all your art and it to deck yourself for his delight. For example: here he is sitting, hammering in this workshop—do you then sit outside and sing a song that will call him out of his confusion, back to good sense and life. For look you, this is the doctor's strongest physic and sole witchcraft—that he can sometimes call his patients home to life, that he can sometimes set life dancing before his patients' eyes. Frau Peter Henlein, do you be the dancing life before his eyes, today, tomorrow and the day after tomorrow! Those whom the Greeks called Maenads danced with soul and feet both, with soul and feet.

[CHARITAS *comes with a firm tread down the stairs. The sight of* SCHEDEL *is painful to her as always, but she controls herself perforce.*]

SCHEDEL. [*With his irony.*] Your servant! [*A malicious inspiration seizes him.*] Maiden, I had a question of theology to put to you: What is the Lord God's purpose, when he smites the best of men with a venomous sickness, such a man as Master Peter?

CHARITAS. [*With a smile from the summit of her altitude.*] God were not God, if we two lowly children of men could understand His ways.

SCHEDEL. [*With a light access of rage.*] Ah, that "above reason!" Yes, when your priest can find no more to say, that always remains! —And I have another question, maiden—of theology likewise: Were your brother to declare that he died in order that the ship's clock might live, what would you say to that?

CHARITAS. This morning I applied myself for two hours and more to the meditation of that same question. And this is my answer: If a doctor have it in his power to heal a man, yet is repulsed by him, that man has dispossessed himself of his body by his own hand, and forfeits thereby his right to lie in Christian ground. He has destroyed his body which is of God, and which belongs to God.

EV. [*Rejoiced.*] Oh, dearest sister! Then you will help us! ? [*Embraces* CHARITAS *with kisses.*]

SCHEDEL. [*In cynical satisfaction.*] Good—we are three allies now. And there is a fourth besides. And the fourth is of more use than us three together. It is the good reason in Master Peter's mind— *ars logica! Ars logica* will speak to Peter Henlein. Ah, many a man who once shuddered before my good knife has come back to be cut —has begged and prayed of me to cut. Oh, my Germans! They all desire Heaven—even Master Peter, he desires Heaven too. But strange, strange—they are in no haste to get there. [*Goes out laughing and is seen passing the window.*]

CHARITAS. [*Filled with compassion.*] Even so are men made blind by science. . . . I came to find you, Ev. Let us sit here and talk awhile.

EV. [*Sits at the table, to the left.*] A new misfortune?

CHARITAS. [*Goes to her. With a deep sigh.*] Many thousand times worse than "misfortune" . . . a soul's salvation in eternity. Listen, Ev, more than nine years past, I made a lifelong, solemn vow to Him [*Pointing to the crucifix.*] that never would I be wife

to any mortal man whomsoever. He, and no other was my bridegroom. Do you hear? He has my plighted troth for ever. It was a
sacred pact, for life everlasting.

EV. Ah, Charitas! My heart is full of fear for Peter, but I shall tell
you, if you will, how your vow seems to me—it is a stupid vow!

CHARITAS. [*With her other-worldly smile.*] I did not ask you your
mind upon the matter, nor any answer, Ev. To tell it to another
person was all I wished—to say that that was what I swore. Last
night as I dreamt, Satan came whispering temptation at my ears—
he came with a music of flutes. To tell another of a vow, is to make
it doubly fast. [*In terror and agitation, she seizes Ev's hand.*] Ev!
If ever I should break my vow, you are to curse me! Do you hear?
You are to curse me!

EV. [*Smiling despite her own anguish.*] That I shall surely not! This
I say: if you should break that vow, I should bless you and bless
you nine times over. Now go! I must put on a gay dress—I am to
be a [*Groping for the word.*] a Maenad! And there is no time to
lose! One who dances with soul and feet both—life dancing before
my husband's eyes! [*With the seriousness of the good housewife.*]
Do me this favour, Charitas. I have cloves and cinnamon in that
mortar yonder. Do you pound them for me—and fine as flour,
mind. I shall bake our invalid a spice-loaf, a loaf of mildest spiced
bread. Soft and tempting! For he has eaten nothing through his
poor throat these four days but porridge, spinach and raw eggs!
[*She hastens upstairs.*]

CHARITAS. [*Looks after her, with knitted brows.*] She would bless
me. . . . [*Suddenly, she turns rebukingly toward the crucifix, for
all the world as a wife regards a husband who has grievously failed
her. She goes to the prie-dieu.*] My Lord and Bridegroom, I confess.
I confess the dream I dreamt last night. [*Very distinctly and with
unconscious warmth, though still with profound reproach.*] I was
standing in the forest—mosses and ferns growing all about me.
And out of the empty air, my brother's apprentice appeared. Out of
the gold-green light he came. And look you, look you—I did not
shrink before him. No. And he bent back my head—scarlet, flaming
sin did kiss my lips. And I did not shrink away. A myriad angels
flew among the pine-trees. Ah, well I know they were not angels
of Heaven. But Thou, why dost Thou suffer the spirits of evil to
tempt me, coming thus disguised as holy angels, blowing upon their
reeds and trumpets? [*Furiously.*] Bridegroom! Lord! How, lying

on my bed asleep, should I be mistress of my soul? By what means shall I hold it then, that it should go no more roaming in the forest with Joseph Apfelbaum? Why temptest Thou me with the hair of a mortal man, with his keen eyes? ! [*Awaiting the answer, she gazes at the crucifix. Suddenly, her face becomes transfigured. She stands listening, as though the crucifix were speaking to her. Gratitude and intense love overspread her.*] What? My vow had become too old a staff? A crumbling staff—too old to sustain me? I should make me a new one? A new vow, a staff of young, fresh wood? Strong and young? [*With a deep intensity of love, as though the Heavenly Bridegroom had made some jest.*] If it be that my love is yours—yours still, Oh Sweetest Lord on High? [*She flings herself upon her knees before the prie-dieu, her face in her hands, sobbing. Then in blissful ecstasy.*] Oh, Sweetest Lord on High! Lord of the Heavenly Choirs! I swear. I swear that I shall remain Thy handmaiden all the days of my life, Thine and no mortal man's, world without end, amen. By Thy five wounds I swear it. [*Raising her hand in the gesture of taking oath.*] By Thy five streaming wounds, Thy holy, holy wounds! [*Then she rises, smiling in the triumph of absolution and redemption. She returns to her task of pounding the cloves and cinnamon, and works thoroughly, carefully, smiling and happy. When it is done, she turns the fine spice-meal onto the dish, thriftily tapping the mortar with her open palm.*]

PETER. [*Now enters from the street, right, with resolute and cheerful steps. He clearly rejoices to find* CHARITAS *there alone for the nonce.*] Ah, Charitas! For three days now I have been waiting for a quiet hour with you. I have an . . . an important petition to lay before you, important for your whole life. But see first what I have bought. Something more important even than my petition. [*He pulls a tiny box out of his pocket, and takes out of it two pig-bristles, holding them up before* CHARITAS. *In his teasing, fond brotherly tone.*] What are these?

CHARITAS. [*In her aloof mood, not welcoming this disturbance.*] They are . . . two bristles out of a brush!

PETER. Wrong! They are two bristles that have never seen a brush— they are two bristles [*tickling her nose with them*]—out of a pig's back.

CHARITAS. The same thing!

PETER. Wrong! These are . . . fresh bristles! Their young strength still in them! [*Showing her.*] Look—I bend one, and at once it jumps straight again. There's strength in that! [*With impassioned eagerness, holding the mechanism of his ship's clock towards her.*] Look at the big wheel. [*Showing her the movement with his fingers.*] It is to balance—like a scale! Tick-tock, tick-tock, tick-tock! But a laziness sits in this scale. Now, look you, I put one of my two pig-bristles on either side of the scale and now so long as the spiral remains wound up there is no rest nor peace for the scale any more. It must go on, tick-tock, tick-tock, tick-tock, tick-tock.

CHARITAS. [*With genuine curiosity.*] Wind it up then, oh, wind it up.

PETER [*Smiling sadly.*] Ah, if I could do that! Alas, this is a task full of snare and delusion. Give me two weeks, and I shall wind the spring, and bring this brass body to joyous life . . . [*Gloomily.*] or seven weeks. [*He sets the tripod to the right on the wide-legged table, and replaces the Egg upon it.*]

CHARITAS. [*In her new-found thirst for knowledge.*] What laziness sits in the scale?

PETER. I have no time. Ask your teacher who is locksmith and schoolmaster both. [*Smiling and with intense significance.*] Ask your schoolmaster. For I—I am no hand at discussing mathematics with women folks, not even with you. See, that navigator understood at once what manner of laziness sat in that scale. When I showed him these bristles he flung his arms round my neck and embraced me. [*Casually.*] And gave me money in advance to boot, and laughed as he did so. [*Fetches a tightly filled bag from his pocket and holds it out to her.*] There's proof he understood. Look you, Charitas, this is the first day of July. Today my father-in-law demands his rent of me, the old rent and the new. [*Locks the bag in the tool cupboard. Chuckling in expectation.*] Now let him come running, my father-in-law, let him come—I'll not show him the bag at once. All in good time. He shall give me notice first and say all his say. I long to hear his speech, the whole of it for my diversion, his speech of money-fear.

CHARITAS. [*Moralizing.*] Ah, my brother, I am often displeased to observe in you this eagerness to laugh at the folly of others, at their sins and fears. It is a vulgar diversion.

PETER. [*Laughing.*] No, for what harm do his speeches do to him? No, this is an entertainment I must have. [*Then suddenly with a deep sigh and in a voice turned sorrowful.*] And in this world who shall know how much diversion he will live to see?

CHARITAS. [*Crying out.*] Peter, dear brother.

PETER. [*Quickly interrupting.*] Now for my errand with you. [*Very gently.*] Ah, I do not like your dejection, Charitas. I mean this nun's attire and all this gloom, and your most beautiful hair all hidden beneath this wimple—you have worn them long enough. Does the good Lord give you wonderful tresses in order that you should hide them? . . . Now to my errand, my important petition —from the locksmith and schoolmaster. On Thursday, in his schoolmaster's way, he told me all his worldly fortune with much beating round the bush—how many gulden in cash, how many loaned out at interest to a certain cattle dealer. . . . In short he is of the opinion that a man making suit for a maiden's hand should do according to the old custom, strictly according to usage.

CHARITAS. [*Unconsciously folding her hands. Then with calm and cheerful arrogance.*] His suit? Ay! He aspires to wed with a bride of God? Me? He is bold.

PETER. He begged me do his wooing for him and indeed I saw no reason to refuse. Should I have answered him, "My sister, Charitas, will have no man whomsoever? For she is possessed by a delusion? By piety and arrogance? By the Devil of arrogance?"

CHARITAS. [*Astonished and with deep reproach.*] Brother, I give you a brief decision. I love no mortal man, I love God.

PETER. [*Looking before him in blissful reminiscence, now speaks with cheerful prophecy.*] This I know and declare. Your love of God is a false love of God. God is master in His own workshop, has the whole world to create, in all eternity and in every place. Therefore has His hand all full and His head all full of seven thousand cares. Look you now; this is true love of God, that we help Him, the Master in His workshop, help Him create. An example? A while since as I crossed the Eischbach by the Krotenmühl, Albrecht Dürer's little old mother went hobbling past me with her hollow eyes and wrinkled face. Eighteen children she has borne—eighteen, and Albrecht among them, Albrecht, I say. Now who has better served the Lord God, you or she?

CHARITAS. [*Scornfully and with agitation.*] Ah, a new religion! Not to be found in any Father of Holy Church, not written in the Holy Scriptures, invented at Nüremberg by Peter Henlein! He wishes to mate his sister with a mortal man and presto, a new religion is invented! [*Holds out towards him her ringless right hand with outspread fingers. Furiously.*] For on his sister's hand he could not see the Bridegroom's ring whose brightness streams to Heaven, nor on

her head the snow-white crown of chastity. . . . Ah, my brother,
I mean to keep that crown.

PETER. [*Easily and with a smile of hope.*] Strange that you should
say all this in angry heat! We have a song, Sister, that goes like
this—

> Chastity's straw, and dry as tinder—
> One spark of love doth burn it to a cinder.

CHARITAS. [*Lifts her head with the angry gesture of an outraged ab-
bess.*] That is a song for bathing-house girls and harlots. [*She goes
in dudgeon into the kitchen.* PETER *looks after her, tenderly and a
little uncertain. At last he makes a gesture of angry resignation.*]
Sweetstuff! I have no time! [*He fetches a little piece of brass,
going hastily about it. Then sits down in the armchair and examines the mechanism of his ships clock through a watch-maker's
magnifying glass. He bends the piece of brass with two pincers.*]

  [A CROWD OF WOMEN, *in grotesque disguises, wearing false
  beards, run past the window, laughing, a standard-bearer in their
  midst.*]

A TIPSY WOMAN. [*With a flushed face, also wearing the false beard,
shakes her stick of bells in at the door.*] Hey, neighbour! Master,
do you not go to look at the pig with quills? Hey! [*She shakes her
bells again.*] And a calf's to be hatched—[*Again shaking her bells.*]
—out of a cheese. It's a prank of Hans Sach's! [*With a long loud
rattling of her bells, she runs out after the others, laughing boister-
ously.*]

  [PETER *measures one of the pig-bristles against the piece of
  brass, fetches a pair of scissors with eager haste and cuts the
  bristle with great care. He again fits the magnifying glass into
  his eye.*]

EV. [*Is heard singing to the accompaniment of her lute, out of sight
on the staircase. Her song is a passionate love-song.*]

> My every thought—my every thought,
>   Is of thee ever.
> Thou, the sweet solace of my heart,
> Oh leave me never!
> Love, love,
> Keep me within thy heart, and I,
> Each hair upon your darling head,
> Will cherish till I die!

[PETER *in torment, clutches his heart.*]

EV. [*Comes down the stairs with the lute in her hand. She might wear a dress of blue silk with a red silk tunic over it. She stands at the table facing* PETER. *As her conscience pricks her, she rebukes him.*] I cannot sing. Just as I was about to begin the second verse something seemed to choke me in my throat.

PETER. [*Regards her, full of astonishment and love.*] Every day I see more and more how your whole face sings even when your voice is silent. All of you sings. . . . [*Afraid.*] But I have no time. [*He again applies the lens to his eye and takes a little screw out of the works. Ev remains standing there with knitted brow.* PETER *lays the screw carefully on the table. Entreating her tenderly.*] Ah, my dear heart, though you only stand there so quietly, it does my work no good. It was not your way formerly to stand by me like this.

EV. [*Stands a moment longer brooding. Then suddenly full of pain and reproach, incapable of playing a part.*] Oh, I am choking. Look, Peter, look, it was all a ruse. That I should dress my hair more temptingly and uncover my bosom to you. I plotted it in secret with Doctor Schedel. I was to be a Maenad and drive your foolish thoughts out of your head. Oh, dearest dearest! Schedel said this: if you do not let him cut you will surely die.

PETER. [*As if convincing himself with difficulty.*] I put no faith in Schedel. You yourself said on Thursday that he had a rage for cutting and wanted to practise his art on me. He has made the same speech to hundreds; "If I may not cut, you are among the dead." Ha, ha! And one morning found this chalked upon his house: "Many die, many die not, with the knife or without it."

EV. [*Springs up. In fiery anger.*] Ah, yes, and how you used to praise and commend him. What was that fine name you placed like a wreath about his head the other day? "Saviour of the body," you called him. Yes, your own words those, Saviour of the body. And today, Husband, must I believe what you say today? Ah, no woman could lie as guilefully as you do in this moment, so deceitfully! Oh, shame!

[GÜLDENBECK *has entered at the rear upon these last words. At the evident dissension between the young couple he makes no attempt to conceal his joy.* THE COOK *a clean and corpulent old woman follows him in. Raising her eyebrows she follows her master's gaze with suspicious and self-confident merriment.*]

GÜLDENBECK. Ay, look you there, how you dissembled when I came to see you—one heart, one soul. Ay, and look you now. I come of a sudden through the door, and what do I hear? Railing and chiding. Thus go all marriages in the world, that they do—railing and chiding.

EV. [*In torture.*] Oh, Father, how should I answer you now before a stranger? [*She goes to the table in the rear and stands there silent with lifted head.*]

GÜLDENBECK. It is my cook. I brought her with me, for I need a witness of that which must now be done, alas. It is a law of the city that I have a witness. She is my new cook. [*He roars out each of the cook's names before her face as if each separate one were a separate crime.*] Ursel Barbara, the widow Sweep, born Folz. For even a woman and a virago at that can be a witness according to the laws of the town—is a *persona*—[*Humorously.*] is a person according to the law of the town, that she is. It is a sad and sorrowful event in my life to be obliged to give notice which I do hereby to my son-in-law, calling upon him to vacate dwelling and workshop—[*In honest and true parental grief.*]—and upon my own daughter likewise who, these six or seven weeks, has found not an evening, not an hour, to devote to the comforting of her grey-haired father in his lonely and forsaken estate.

PETER. [*In alarm and in need of peace and quiet.*] Stop, let me speak.

GÜLDENBECK. [*To Ev, without pausing.*] Ah, yes. In debt for eleven months rent, and yet runs to singing masters and takes lessons in the lute. Ah, little daughter, how you have forgotten that holy commandment, "Honour thy father and thy mother." No, you have chosen to fall instead about the neck of a potterer and good-for-nothing, and after him you run.

THE COOK. [*Very merrily, for she is about to give* GÜLDENBECK *notice whether or no.*] Master, had I been your daughter I'd have done the same, I'd have done the very same.

GÜLDENBECK. [*In an access of rage.*] Ah, foul-mouth. In the month you have been in my house with your insolent laughing you have tried my lamblike patience more than plenty, more than plenty, I say. And hereby . . . [*Collecting himself. Craftily.*] No, I have need of your ears, dragon, for a quarter of an hour yet. [*To* PETER. *In great pride of his assumed calm.*] Do you see? A man who allows anger to overcome him is no merchant. Mistakes are made in anger.

PETER. Fisher of salt fish, were you to know what I am about to say to you you would not give me notice for many a long day. Now, listen.

GÜLDENBECK. Silence! Long enough, often enough I have listened to your hopes and consolations and the rest of your divine riga-marole! Both of you, may both of you some day when I lie in my coffin in the grave—may both of you with your laughter open the iron chest where I hold all my debtors' notes and my whole life's harvest! It will be yours then, but while I still buy my salt fish and sell it and keep my books and my mind in order, no one shall bring me to ridicule, no one shall lead me by the nose, not even my own son-in-law. [*Again in a frenzy of fatherly grief.*] Not even my daughter whom I dearly love! Oh, I need only look at that turned up nose of yours to see how dearly you love your father. Have a care, girl, have a care. Lightning will strike your nose some day. [Ev *sits in the bow window and remains staring into the street until* GÜLDENBECK *departs.*] Now, widow of the chimney-sweep, open wide your ears in order that you may swear to what you have heard in case this matter should come to law. Son-in-law, I hereby give you warning that on the last day of September three months from this day you are to go from here, from workshop and dwelling, from this house which is mine, from this ground, these premises. And that you are. [*He sits down comfortably in the arm-chair.*]

PETER. A fine speech, father-in-law, a brave speech. Now mine. A thing of grave and serious moment is finished in my head—all but finished. It is a clock that will hold its movement against the move-ment of ships—without pendulum, without weights—and never get seasick. [*He fetches the bag.*]

GÜLDENBECK. Just as I said, all but complete, all but invented. In his head. Hahahaha! And if you had invented it there it would hang on your wall—"Without pendulum, without weights"—and with an invention like that you hope to pay your rent? Ay? And drink wine with your customers? And clothe and maintain your pious sister? Fiddle-faddle, fiddle-faddle. [*Has turned his back to the table.*]

PETER. [*At the table sets out his money in rows.*] Yes, a clock that will hold its movement against the rocking of a ship will go in your pocket too.—Twenty.—The knight riding in the forest need look for no church steeple—he carries the time in his pocket.—

Forty.—It may be that soon the entire race of men will come to buy these clocks of me and pay their tribute into this bag of mine. —sixty.

GÜLDENBECK. [*At the sound of the money has turned gradually towards the table.*] What is this money? My rent?

PETER. Eighty.—eighty-four.—[*Light-heartedly.*] The customer who ordered this clock for his ship—Martin Behaim, navigator and scientist,—he is of a mind that my invention is already worth as much as this today. He paid me this much in advance. [*Sits on the stool by the hearth.*]

GÜLDENBECK. [*Rises and walks about the room in great though sour enthusiasm.*] In advance. Martin Behaim. [*Rings a coin on the table to hear whether it is genuine. Reassured and astonished.*] Paid in advance, and what was that you said? The merchant in his lane need no longer seek the church tower for he carries the time in the pocket of his pantaloons? Ah, I'd buy me a clock like that, though it cost me ten gulden. That I would. And what did you say, all the people in the world? [*In high excitement.*] Ah, it is nonsense, arrant nonsense—thousands upon thousands of customers—arrant nonsense. A worldful of people—and each one obliged to pay ten gulden, thousands and thousands and tens of thousands—[*In a blissful dream.*]—thousands and tens of thousands! [*Struck by a terrible fear.*] But, hold, hold! I see a dire misfortune. I must avert it! Ah, thank your God that I am here, a merchant wise in his trade. [*He takes out his handkerchief and mops his face, wiping away the sweat of terror from neck and temples.*] And that you may! The day is loathly hot! All the way here I boiled in the sun! Son-in-law, son-in-law, beware of your apprentice! Would you have that Apfelbaum, that dreamer, would you have him open a workshop next year in Augsberg to make clocks like yours? Clocks for the pockets of pantaloons? [*With profound dislike.*] Ah, even a dreamy-eyed lout may steal the secrets of your craft, even such an oaf, even such a numbskull! Son-in-law, beware! Or every locksmith under the sun will have your secret of you. [*Again wiping his face.*] And what should we have then of the thousands and tens of thousands, and tens upon tens of thousands, what should we have then?

PETER. [*Very slowly.*] The ships would have their clocks.

GÜLDENBECK. Pp, Pp, Pp! [*Mopping his face.*] I am cold. The gooseflesh rises on my back. I'm cold, cold.

THE COOK. [*In gay scorn.*] Am I to hear and remember all this—[*Lifting her hand as if taking oath.*] in case the matter should come to law?

GÜLDENBECK. Oh, and I forgot you there. Be off with you! And don't stop gossiping at every door. Go back home to your room, sit there and put your thoughts on what I am to eat tomorrow. [*Mops his face again.*]

THE COOK. [*Advances slowly to the table.*] Now I'll say what I have to say. This noon you ate your well-roasted pigeon at your counter without a tablecloth—without a tablecloth on a Sunday. Reckoning figures in your great ledger, and every night sitting crouched over your soup, turning up your nose with a face that turns the beer sour in it . . . so I have something to say today and this is it: on this first day of July before two witnesses—they are people too "according to the law of the city"—come the first day of August I leave you. I leave you, for a good cook and one that understands her trade has no lack of places where to go. And to be cook for a cross-patch is work for a fool! [*Goes out with dignity at the rear right.*]

GÜLDENBECK. [*Runs to the door and screams after her, and means it.*] Delighted, delighted, delighted and rejoiced! [*Comes back again, rubbing his hands.*] A day of joys, a day of joys! Ah, and now I go to that Mesech who sells his herrings a penny cheaper than I and cuts my prices winter and summer—[*With vast malice, anticipating the happy event.*]—I go now to Mesech [*Taking out of his pocket a yellowed paper, printed on both sides and on the front page "NEWE GEZEITUNG" surrounded by a decoration.*]—see, Son-in-law, the newspaper published last Friday. Have you seen it? Ha! [*Striking the sheet.*] In Cologne on the Rhine there's a clever fellow, Pfefferkron his name, but baptised! And the baptism has taken well—very well, haha—so well that Pfefferkron has composed a petition and sent it to the Imperial Majesty of Germany —begging that the Talmud, the Kabala and all the other writings of the Jews be taken from them and burnt. Haha!

PETER. [*Reflecting.*] My ship's clock is a fruit of man's mind—and so are books—also the fruit of man's mind. To destroy them were a sin—mortal sin.

GÜLDENBECK. The inventor! Wiser than the theologians of Cologne. [*Waves his newspaper in PETER's face.*] See there—the petition, signed and approved by all the professors and all the doctors of the faculty in Cologne! To be confiscated—all the writings of the Jews— [*Waving his paper in triumph.*] So—I go now to that louse-bitten Mesech who cuts my prices, and poke this at him through his window. Hahahaha! [*He puts the eighty-four gulden into his purse and as he does so notices the clock unfinished on the tripod. He takes it in his hands with curiosity.*] Is it begun? Is this the pocket clock?

PETER. [*Frowning.*] Let it be. If you let it fall that would be a real misfortune.

GÜLDENBECK. [*Replacing it.*] A delicate fine thing, a pocket clock— Oh, people will open their eyes at this. [*Holds out his hand to* PETER.] Greetings, inventor. [*He is about to leave but turns back at the door. Raising his head.*] If a delicate fine thing's to invent, it is at Nüremberg that it will be invented, and that it is. There are none like us of Nüremberg, none like us. [*He goes out rear and as he passes the window, waves his hand, grinning benevolently.*]

PETER. [*Brooding.*] Had a bolt of lightning struck me last night during the storm I should never have lived to know whether or no the Emperor Max will cause the Jewish books to be burnt—nor whether or no my sister Charitas will take Joseph Apfelbaum. Surely it may be—it may be, that the dead look down from a window in Heaven. But it may be also that eyes, ears and thoughts die too in death, and sink into darkness.

EV. [*Who has now come to him.*] My dearest one! You must not die!

PETER. [*Springs up, and in a cry of intolerable desire for life.*] No —I must know whether the Emperor Max will have those writings burnt! Ah, so many questions has every man to ask as the world moves on—thousands of questions! [*He takes a few steps through the room, grasping his head in his hands, as one who seeks a way out, passionately striving. Suddenly, still deeply troubled.*] What? Ah, have I found the way? [*He continues to walk about the room, then in great and whole-hearted joy.*] Ev, dearest heart, I need not die. Look you, look you, I'll tell my invention to another! It is so nearly complete, today! Look you, Ev! Then should I bleed to death from Schedel's knife as our Clerk of Archives bled to death the other will bring my ship's clock to life.

EV. [*Overjoyed.*] Then will you tell your invention to another scientist? Ah, why did we not think of that at once! Dearest Peter! [*She embraces him.*]

PETER.]*Moves away and goes to sit in the armchair. Cheerfully.*]

Yet, to be sure, the scientists of Nüremberg are not locksmiths, and the locksmiths of Nüremberg are not scientists—the only one but me who could know how to make this clock of mine. His name is Joseph Apfelbaum. Thursday he helped me, Friday, yesterday and this morning—and with his brain.

EV. [*Rushes upstairs, opens the door and claps her hands loudly.*] Apprentice! Hey! Herr Apfelbaum! Dear Apprentice!

APFELBAUM. [*Unseen above. In the gruff voice of a man disturbed out of desperate thoughts.*] Yes, yes, I am coming.

PETER. Is he at home? On a Sunday afternoon? With the sunshine and the carnival?

EV. A while since as I was decking myself out for you I heard him in his room hammering. [*In joyful hope.*] Ah, now I shall go to Flanders! [*In gay persuasion.*] Imagine, sailing on the water! Down the Rhine—past Cologne City where my mother was born . . . ah, dearest!—and as our ship brings us within sight of the Cathedral's tall spire—as we catch the first glimpse of the Cathedral in the blue dawn—then—[*She sits suddenly at his feet and lets her head fall backwards on his knees.*]—then I'll sit at your feet on our ship and sing a song in memory of my mother, the song of God's Holy Blood and of the roses in the golden chalice. . . .

PETER. Without her dreams and fantasies a woman cannot love— You can love . . . ah, that you can. [*He strokes her brow.*] But, get up now. Since you have called Apfelbaum I must first tell him my sad news.

EV. [*Springs up. With quick and heart-felt sympathy.*] Is it Charitas? She will not?

APFELBAUM. [*Enters, frowning. In a voice of deep dejection.*] What do you wish of me, Mistress?

PETER. [*Goes to the apprentice and lays his hand on his shoulder.*] First I have foolish news to tell you—and take it like a man— my sister, Charitas, desires to remain the bride of Jesus.

APFELBAUM. [*Does not start but gazes sadly at nothing and sits down to the left of the table. With a deep sigh and with his touching preciseness.*] You do not take me unawares. Up there in my room even now, I said to myself—"Your request was over-bold." For who am I? [*He bites his underlip, his voice gruff with tears.*] Ah, master— that jest you made the other day was a jest that put me on the rack. You said I was locksmith and schoolmaster both, and therefore twice a man. Am I schoolmaster? Alas, then where is my school? And a man in the wrong lane is not twice a man!—[*In his two-fold pain.*] Ah, he is no man at all—no man at all! [*Pause.*]

PETER. And now I have something to ask of you—I of you, Apfelbaum. [*Sits at the table frowning.*] Yes, into the very midst of your sorrow in love I must come with my petition. For there is no time to lose—it will not endure delay.

APFELBAUM. Ah, Master, ask even my life—it is worth little enough.

PETER. Well then, this evening I wish to say to Schedel: try your art on my throat.

APFELBAUM. [*Rejoicing in his grief.*] Ah, dear Master, that is good! At last! At last! [*Is about to rise.*] So, I shall go at once to Dr. Schedel and fetch him here.

EV. [*Impatiently, pushes him back on his chair.*] Tell me, apprentice —in case, oh surely it will not happen so, but in case my husband . . . should bleed to death of the doctor's knife—[*Pointing to the Egg.*]—would you have the skill to complete his work, so nearly complete already? You are a locksmith, a master-locksmith soon. You know this craft of my husband's as no other knows it in the world.

APFELBAUM. [*With an anguished smile.*] Ah, Mistress, why should you ask me this most cruel question? Listen, I must tell you a story and a hopeless story it is. This morning my master had a new idea —concerning two pig-bristles still lacking in this egg and to be most carefully inserted in the right place. Then my soul cried out, "There is nothing more to find now that I could not find also," and my vanity cried out, "I can do it too." Then I went to my room and all day long I pondered and filed, pondered and bored, pondered and hammered and would begin to make a ship's clock of my own. [*In bitter self-contempt.*] Yes, that I meant to do. [*He takes* PETER'S *Egg in his hand with a deep sigh.*] Ah, Mistress! [*With an expert's enthusiasm.*] When I see the simple clarity of this, I know that in these wheels and rods there lives a spirit more quick than mine. It dreams but as it dreams it calculates. [*Folds his hands over the mechanism as though it were a sacred thing.*] Mistress, in this egg there dwells—a god in little. . . .

PETER. [*Who has listened frowning.*] Hold your mouth. If you must sing my praises wait till I am out of the room. [*Laying his hand on the table palm upwards.*] Now swear into my hand that you will do as I shall ask you and it is this: If I should leave my life in Schedel's hands do you make of this egg here a healthy, ticking clock—a ship's clock.

APFELBAUM. [*Terrified.*] Master, what are you asking? Oh, Master, whether your egg be finished by me or by another tomorrow Dr. Schedel must cut into your throat. [*With determination.*] Yes, now I will tell you what I have concealed until now. Master, the sickness my late father died of two years since, began with just such a gathering in his throat, the same as yours, and in four weeks he lay shrieking upon his bed, shrieking and shrieking.

PETER. [*Greatly frightened, holding out his hand towards him.*] Well, well, do you swear into my hand?

APFELBAUM. [*Jumps up and recoils a step.*] Master, no man may swear to invent a new thing. You yourself could not do that—for invention comes by grace of the Holy Ghost.

PETER. [*Unconsciously closing his hand about his Egg.*] Look you, Ev, what he says is good sense. It is good sense after his fashion. Now let me be. I beg you, Ev, leave me alone. I must make this ship's clock.

[THREE FIGURES DISGUISED IN BLACK *enter from the street. They wear black caps with bird's eyes in the conventional simulation of ravens, not comical but gruesome omens of death. Ev, shuddering, withdraws towards the staircase. The figure in the centre,—it is* SCHEDEL, *recites his lines with the extreme cruelty of a cynic philosopher—*

As o'er the church we ravens three—
Henlein—Henlein—
Soar up aloft, what's this we see?
In the churchyard sod a spade—
Where a grave is newly made,
In the churchyard sod a spade. . . .

ALL THREE. [*Flapping their wings.*] Caw, caw, caw!

In that grave, how dost thou fare,
Henlein—Henlein?
No singing voice doth reach thee there—
Thy wife's dear voice, so pure and clear,
Never, never dost thou hear,
In thy coffin dark and drear. . . .

PETER. [*Calmly interrupting.*] Ah, have done, Schedel. Your rhymes are all in vain and so are all your learned arguments. I say again:

he to whom the chance is given—the blessed chance to create a grave and serious thing—he may not run his life into danger. First I must make my clock.

EV. [*Steps to the rear of the table.*] And I? and I? [*She moves the Egg backward and forward and then as though turning some hostile plan in her mind and talking herself into courage and fury.*] Ah, this is it. No garden close that you promised me, no journey into Flanders down the Rhine—my journey shall be back to my father's house! In widow's weeds of black. There is no wife on earth who loves her lord and husband more than I, yet you go on forever with your filing and your hammering and soon the day will come when you will swallow the poison into you, because you have more love for the captains on the sea than for your wife— More for your workshop, more for your tools, than for me. [*Again moving the Egg about.*] What is it to you that I return to my father's house where I could never breathe again, never again? What is it to you that I live or die? Ah, that is the conceit and arrogance of a man! And now I tell you to your face what in your heart of hearts, your closed-up heart of hearts, you will not say aloud—that woman lives only for the man's sake, never man for the woman's, never the husband for the wife's sake. That is what your false heart says in its silence, in its eternal silence. [*She seems to come to a resolve. Slowly.*] And this I will answer, with my own two hands—and it is the answer of all the wives of all the world! [*She flings the Egg into the mortar and pounds it wildly into fragments.*]

PETER. [*Has sprung up with raised fist, but holds himself in check. He walks once round the table, then comes back and stands aside to the right. There is a brooding pause. Then shrugging his shoulders and with high calm.*] What I have once accomplished in three days I can accomplish again in one. The hundred untrodden ways through which the mind went groping in that first search—darkly —now I can take my straight course swiftly over them in the glad sunshine. Yes, it will be simpler now, and what grows simpler grows better.

SCHEDEL. [*Pulling off his raven's cap.*] Henlein, when do I come?

PETER. [*Strangely calm.*] I shall go myself to fetch you when I hold this ticking in my hand—in four weeks or in three.

SCHEDEL. Then for the second time I say it, and I will say it a hundred times over—in three week's time it will be too late.

PETER. I will finish the ship's clock.

SCHEDEL. Oh, will someone tell me the sense of that!

PETER. I must finish the ship's clock.

SCHEDEL. [*Furious.*] There is no sense under heaven.

PETER. [*Rises filled with calm self-confidence.*] When I fled from you last Thursday out into the fields the thoughts went crawling over one another in my mind, like eels, like eels in a tub, crawling furiously about, tangled together. But far off yonder by the Frauentor I stopped awhile on a path in the fields. To right and left and all about me, the yellow corn stood ripening, ripening in the quivering heat. [*As if baring the secret of his inmost joyous heart.*] And out of those thousand ears of grain a single voice was speaking: "The grain bears its fruit and dies—bears its fruit." And it was the Voice that once did speak to Moses on the Mountain of Sinai.

CURTAIN

ACT IV

[*On the wide-legged table, two finished Nüremberg Eggs stand in their neat frames. Another table has been added to the furniture of the room—visibly a new one. The mortar is back in its place. Window and door stand wide open. A bleak twilight is beginning to fall upon the square outside. The fire on the hearth is blazing brightly. At the tables, and everywhere in the workshop new young journeymen artisans are at work.* APFELBAUM, *at the fire, is showing the pupil-apprentice how to bend a metal bar, and the pupil works the bellows meanwhile.*]

GÜLDENBECK. [*Cloak flying, runs hither and tither about the room, like a great lord of industry grown nervous with the cares of his vast enterprise. He takes a half-finished clock out of an apprentice's hands, examines it through a magnifying lens, and wails.*] Why is the spiral not set inside the drum? You are standing still! You are all standing still! It is a bad day for a greyhaired man when his son-in-law falls ill, and can no longer direct his growing business. And that it is! Bad and bitter for a greyhaired man, to have two businesses to direct—one in salt-fish and one in clocks. Four weeks tomorrow I've had this pestiferous task to do. Four weeks tomorrow!

BEHAIM. [*Once more accompanied by a swarm of children, enters from the square, magnificent in armour and helmet, and followed by his* MOOR. *He is in the sprightly humour of one about to embark upon the voyage home, after roving the world over.*] What? Not time to stop work yet? [*With a great joy clear to see, he takes a watch out of each pocket of his pantaloons—snaps open the covers and compares them.*] A quarter to six, a quarter past six.—[*Replacing the watches.*]—six o'clock then! [*As he speaks, six o'clock strikes from the bell-tower of the Lórenz church. The* JOURNEYMEN *with a short "A good-evening to you," leave work and workshop, the pupil-apprentice likewise. Two carry the new table out, to the right. Two leave by the street door.*]

235

GÜLDENBECK. Oh, sloth! sloth! [*Gradually the fire dies down to a quiet glow.*]

BEHAIM. [*In his hearty manner, holds out his hand to* APFELBAUM, *ignoring the old cross-patch. With warm friendliness, yet ever with his patrician's tone.*] Greetings, Herr Apfelbaum!

APFELBAUM. [*Into whose voice has now come the note of one who loves without hope and has done with life.*] You have come for the tenth of your Nüremberg Eggs. Greetings to you! [*He has in the meantime been examining one of the two finished watches, and this he now takes and fits into a padded box.*]

BEHAIM. [*Laughing.*] There is a sigh in your voice. [*In sudden alarm.*] How . . . how fares it with our invalid? Does his improvement not continue?

APFELBAUM. [*Confident.*] The livelong day he pores over his book on Flanders, for he is to take his goodwife thither, and his mind is full of plans. Praise and thanks be to God! [*He gives* BEHAIM *the watch.*]

BEHAIM. I have a pleasure for him today. I will order one hundred more of his little eggs. For I'm rid of them in a trice at every port I touch. For who would not give twelve paltry gulden for so priceless a trinket as one of these?

GÜLDENBECK. [*With grandeur.*] The price is higher now. Forty gulden.

BEHAIM. What? Twelve becomes forty?

GÜLDENBECK. [*Shrewdly.*] If your Excellency finds the price of forty gulden too high for him, then rob us of no more time.

BEHAIM. [*Signing the order.*] Take your bit of paper—I must have my Nüremberg Eggs. [*Frowns at* GÜLDENBECK, *puts on his helmet and shakes hands with* APFELBAUM.] Fare you well, Herr Apfelbaum! It may be that we shall meet no more until we come to Heaven. [*He is about to leave when a merry thought comes to him. He looks at* GÜLDENBECK, *and addresses him at first in the ordinary tone of conversation. But the end of his speech is like a rapier-thrust, though clear of anger, in the manner of the true man of the world.*] Do you know, Herr Güldenbeck, that my wife and my little son live on an island seven hundred miles from us here? In the Atlantic Ocean? As far, almost, from this town of Nüremberg as Jambri Minor where men and women have tails behind like dogs? Oh, His Majesty the Emperor spoke no more than the truth when he said that Martin Behaim of Nüremberg had sailed farther over the seas than any other subject of the Holy Roman Empire.—Do you hear that, Herr Güldenbeck? Farther than any other. Yet not in Salzburg—nor in Venice—nor in Palermo—nor in Lisbon—nor in Arabia—nor in the Azores—did I ever meet with such a Jew as you are! [*He goes out at the rear, the* MOOR *behind him carrying the little box.*]

GÜLDENBECK. [*With his laugh of contempt for all men.*] Because I've spoiled his trade at Lisbon—knocked it on the head! Pirate! What would he liefer do than buy a hundred of our eggs in Nüremberg at twelve gulden apiece and sell them to the captains at Lisbon for fifty! Fury! Helpless fury! [*He runs hither and thither again, grasping his head in both hands.*]

    [APFELBAUM *in his neat and precise manner, begins to gather up the tools that bestrew the workshop and hang them up in the cupboard.*]

GÜLDENBECK. [*In his desperate fear which now for the first time finds voice.*] Even you, my dear young friend,—I must—I must take you to task—like a father. Again I must tell you of this dread which never leaves me—embitters my days and steals my sleep at night. You keep poor watch over our secret. Again a short time since, as the apprentice worked there with the bellows and you the while explained to him the whole matter of the escapement—oh, had I not at that very moment interrupted you, our secret would have been out already! How he hung on your words, that wily fellow! How his eyes shone! My entrails turned over with fear!

APFELBAUM. [*Smiling through his pain. With the true teacher's pride.*] A most excellent pupil! From Glashütte in Saxony! He listens with his soul in his ears!

GÜLDENBECK. And do you wish him to return to his Glashütte in Saxony, and set up shop there for himself with our pocket-clocks, waxing fat on what he has found out in this workshop of ours? On our secret? Dear, dear Apfelbaum—this is the way: a wheel to file for this one; bristles to adjust for that one—but never let an apprentice know how the parts fit each into each and make the whole—never let that secret flash upon his mind, or we are lost!

APFELBAUM. Ah, were I the Lord God, I should betray the secrets of my craftsmen's minds the moment they appeared—a thousand times, and over all the world.

    [*Lights shine through the church-windows on the far side of the square. For a few moments the organ is heard.*]

[APFELBAUM *fastens the tool-cupboard and sits down by the window.*]

GÜLDENBECK. [*Shutting the entrance door—with great caution.*] I must acquaint you with my plan—now. And lose no more time. Or else you will go on cutting and cutting into your own flesh. And that you will! Yesterday then, I said to the surgeon: "Is the poison now in my son-in-law's stomach?" He gave me a doctor's answer which is no answer at all. But my reason tells me this: Schedel is a surgeon famous throughout the world. He said: Were he not to cut, then the poison must pour down into my son-in-law's stomach. And cut he did not. Therefore, I say this now: My son-in-law will not see Christmas-tide this year.

APFELBAUM. [*With unyielding hope.*] And I say he'll see many a Christmas-tide yet—a good fifty. Has it escaped you how his bed irks him? Were you not here a while since, when he sent his goodwife to the church to vespers. Saying he would be waited upon and nursed no longer?

GÜLDENBECK. [*Stands on the hearth, points at the dying fire. Satanically and very slowly.*] Flames as they are about to go out flare up once more.

APFELBAUM. I would ask you a favour, Herr Güldenbeck. It was my hope to spend this free evening alone at the window here and let the vesper music sweep my soul clear again.

GÜLDENBECK. [*With a smile full of promises.*] When you know this plan of mine you'll not be concerned with your vespers. Look you, if I and Master Schedel be not in error—and should this flickering flame of life go out, then—you, you only on all the earth can make the Nüremberg Egg. And—I have no wish to flatter you—yet it is a thing of joy to see the cunning flawless work that leaves your hands. You are a clockmaker of clockmakers! [*With the enthusiasm of the hopeful merchant.*] But this I ask you: Would you have got forty gulden from that pirate Behaim? Forty times one hundred? Would you have done that? So look you then—would it not be a thing as serviceable and fine as our pocket-clock itself—that you and I, two masters together—should make and merchandise the Nüremberg Egg.

APFELBAUM. [*In deep disgust.*] Would you already inherit and divide the property of the living?

GÜLDENBECK. [*Smiling meanly.*] And look yoū, my friend—one point more. One more. You are a gentle and a courteous man, made

to please the heart of woman—well enough to look upon. You
might—try your fortune with the childless widow, and kindle her
heart again.

APFELBAUM. [*After many vain attempts to speak now leaps to his
feet.*] Oh, I will stop this foul tongue in your mouth. Now you
shall hear my plan—my plan! And not a jot of it shall change: this
day or tomorrow I shall ask my Master's leave to tell his secret to
another—the whole secret and minutely. In two hours the apprentice from Glashütte will possess it hand and brain. And having thus
instructed him I will go to the Town Hall— [*As he speaks he takes
out of the tool-cupboard a great sword in its sheath, shining new.*]
You know the Brandenburger is about to march on Nüremberg—
All who would lend their swords to help protect the free jurisdiction of Nüremberg are summoned to the Town Hall there to sign
their names and receive an earnest of their service. [*He pulls the
sword from its scabbard with a resolute hand. GÜLDENBECK
screams.*] This is my sword. I have bought it. God has made no
commandment that a man may not escape upon the battlefield from
a life that has grown dreary and full of emptiness.

GÜLDENBECK. [*Who has listened in an increasing anger now almost
bursting with fury.*] Ah! [*But his disgust for the dreamer chokes
him. He takes his cap, and in a low tired voice.*] There is no such
thing as a man of sense! 'Tis a world of dreamers and of men
possessed! [*Spits with contempt and goes out at the rear right. AP-
FELBAUM looks pityingly after him, then practices sword-thrusts at
the kitchen door, painstakingly as is his wont. CHARITAS on the landing with an earthenware bowl in her hand looks at him for a while
unseen. Her appearance has lately become most radiant. She has dis-
carded her wimple and charming curls cluster about her ears. Her
voice is full of joy and friendliness.*] Oh see, military exercises on
a free evening!

APFELBAUM. [*Gloomily.*] How is my master?

CHARITAS. [*With great confidence, showing the upturned bowl.*] He
has eaten every bit. Cleaned up the bowl as you see. [*She comes
downstairs.*] But you interrupted me. I rejoice to see you at this
military sport— Oh, if it could only send the blood coursing more
wholesomely through you— If only it could dispel from your poor
brow those clouds of melancholy.

APFELBAUM. [*In violent rage.*] I know a better remedy for that. [*He
is frightened at what he has said.*] I ask your pardon, pious and

learned maiden, that so vulgar and furious a sound should have escaped my lips.

CHARITAS. [*With unconscious roguery.*] Oh, I should be far from chiding a man whose heart—should overflow his tongue.

APFELBAUM. [*Looks at her timidly, hope faintly glimmering once more.*] Maiden, since you gave to him I sent a-wooing for me so sharp and short a "no," I have not troubled you with my words. . . . And yet— Oh, dearest maiden—[*Full of dark menace, shaking his sword towards her.*] But something's afoot! Of no importance to the world, only to my own most miserable life. And tomorrow it shall come to pass—[*Precise again.*] or maybe the day after tomorrow. [*Suddenly folds his hands over the sword hilt. Entreatingly.*] Ah, dearest maiden, I stand before you as before a saint. . . . But I will not lie—the Lord who breathed my soul into me—the same Lord poured [*Very proudly.*] hot blood into my veins. . . . CHARITAS *puts her hand to her heart in fear. Runs quickly by the table into the kitchen.* APFELBAUM *sinks down upon the chest with deep self-reproach and contempt.*] Ah, a beggar for love is a beggar none the less. There is no virtue in him. [*For a moment he remains in thought with staring, desperate eyes, then with heightened determination he grasps his sword again and continues the exercises with such energy that the sword whirrs in the air.*]

CHARITAS. [*In great agitation comes back, polishing the bowl with a linen cloth.*] Like a hideous bat a thought has just flitted through my mind, a new question! It frightened me. Herr Apfelbaum, the Hohenzollern is approaching Nüremberg. Something important in your life is afoot you say—Herr Apfelbaum, is it in your mind to test this sword in war?

APFELBAUM. I do what my manhood demands of me. I think that in a day or two the work here will no longer need me—and then I mean to march against the Margrave of Brandenburg in the cause of free tolls and jurisdiction for our town of Nüremberg.

CHARITAS. [*Utters a cry.*] To war! You must not go to war!

APFELBAUM. [*Hope reviving.*] I do not understand you, dearest maiden. [*Comes a step nearer.*]

CHARITAS. [*Warns him from her with a frown and a gesture of entreaty—retreating from him as far as the room will allow.*] You are to sit on that side of the table. [APFELBAUM *obeys.*] My brother and lord lying sick at this hour and in great pain of body—it would

not be becoming in his sister—[*She sits on the stool at the hearth.*]
—that she discourse light-heartedly upon her separate wishes in this
house—that you and I should talk together of our hope of worldly
joy.

APFELBAUM. Dearest maiden. . . .

CHARITAS. Must I leave you again? Is your—hot blood—beyond your
power to tame? [APFELBAUM *sits down again.*] Herr Apfelbaum,
let me speak, and I pray you, sit still. When I gave my "no" to you
through my brother and lord—an honest "no"—he brought to my
mind's eye a picture of Albrecht Dürer's aged mother. Eighteen
children she has borne and Albrecht one of them. And my brother
said to me that she had served the Lord God better than I. My
brother said that the man of greatest piety was he who helped the
Creator to create—the most pious one he who brought forth fruit
according to his kind. And I laughed at him. For it came into my
mind: that is a new religion—not written in the Holy Scriptures.
But two days later, as I sat alone at evening in my bedchamber—
St. Matthew whispered of a sudden to my soul. "By their fruits
shall ye know them," he said. And I—I turned then to his gospel—
quickly, quickly—the seventh chapter, and there it stood written—
"Ye shall know them by their fruits. Do men gather grapes of
thorns, or figs of thistles? Ye shall know them by their fruits."

APFELBAUM. [*Leaps from his chair.*] Maiden!

CHARITAS. Unless you keep your chair—I cannot tell you further
what is in my heart. [APFELBAUM *obeys instantly.*] And when I read
this in the Holy Gospel, my heart leapt up, yes leapt up. But of a
sudden it stopped again, terrified. And mocked me saying, "Ah,
yield fruit? An excuse of the flesh, a brave excuse! Of the flesh that
desires the living man! An excuse out of the Gospel itself." And
then, Herr Apfelbaum, my thoughts ceased to dwell upon the mortal bridegroom—came back no more to him, neither by day nor in
my dreams at night. [*Very proudly.*] Nor in my dreams at night.

APFELBAUM. [*In bitter torment.*] And is this all your say?

CHARITAS. [*Quite frankly now and with great sweetness, though still
a little sad.*] In a moment. The last is still to come. And remember
—the last of a tale is not its tail but its head. Then came that
awesome glorious time with my brother and lord at work upon his
ship's clock—ready to die rather than fail in his task of adding the
Nüremberg Egg to God's Household. Doing now in his own person what he had preached a while since to me. It was only preach-

ing then. But in his example my brother rose three cubits in stature
before my eyes, three cubits higher than I, than any of us. Then
look you, Herr Apfelbaum, I became a convert to his new religion
and prayed a new prayer, "Ye shall know them by their fruits."
And now I prayed it with a free heart in happy fervour.

APFELBAUM. [*As if riveted to his chair, shakes the table.*] Maiden,
do you force me still to keep my chair?

CHARITAS. [*Rising, with fond severity.*] So long as my brother and
lord lies sick it is not seemly in a true sister—nor is it seemly for
an honourable and praiseworthy apprentice—to discuss their own concerns and desires—further than need be. It was your intention to
go off to the war—therefore I told you what needed to be told
before you went. [*With nunlike austerity.*] But I will not make
merry. I go now to look after my brother. [*Goes quickly up the
stairs.*]

PETER. [*In shirt and pantaloons, with a fur-collared house-robe over
them, comes down the stairs. He has grown thin and gaunt. His
skin is the colour of dried clay, a greyish yellow. But his spirit runs
high.*] Spare your feet. The time is past when two women must
needs nurse their brother and dear husband day and night as though
he were a great baby. [*He sits in the armchair.*] What was that
word of Schedel's? "I must cut—or Peter Henlein swallows the
poison down into his stomach." Oh, my good friend! Oh, surgeon!
Now I shall instruct you in a new article of a doctor's wisdom—
the stomach of man into which an omelet and also poison may slip,
has not an entrance only, it has an exit too. [*With a loud and joyous laugh.*]

APFELBAUM. [*Drunk with his own joy. Going to him.*] Dear master,
I bring a charge against your sister! Dear master—this is the way
of it, if I must tell it in its order—in order of time—This is how
the miracle has come to pass—Your sister is jealous of your Nüremberg Egg,—jealous of the fruit of your brain—jealous too of Albrecht Dürer's aged mother and her eighteen children—all fruits.
—Therefore, for the sake of children—that is, fruits—your sister
—praise be to God—desires to change her single state to the state of
marriage. And I—[*Blissfully.*] Oh, dear master—I am no more intolerable to her than another might be. And yet, master,—I must
complain of her to you, for she will not allow me to embrace
her. With the embrace of the betrothed, the true and honourably
betrothed! And her reason for so refusing me is that yoū are still

very sick—still a little sick. It is so fine-drawn a reason, master, that it is a foolish reason—a woman's reason.

PETER. [*With quiet joy.*] Yes, apprentice. Have a care. Fine-drawn she is, this bride of yours—a harp with cobweb strings. I shouldn't care to have her. Praise be to my own. But to you, oh, harp with cobweb strings, I say this: I am well and more than well. For a man who recovers from sickness feels better and merrier than a well man. If your heart be overflowing therefore—well then, let your mouth tell of it.

CHARITAS. [*With face upturned. In a last access of fear.*] Lord Jesus, but a few weeks ago I made a new vow to Thee—I know that. Lord Jesus, it may be—indeed I know it may be—that this new religion of mine is but an excuse of the flesh [*She looks at* APFELBAUM.] —that desires the man of flesh. [*She screams.*] Have mercy on me, Christ. [*The tempest within her drives her to* APFELBAUM. *She falls into his arms.*]

PETER. [*With true brotherly joy.*] A schoolmaster and a Godfearing woman! Ah, sister, sister! And did you think a sight like this would do me harm?

[*A posthorn is heard in the distance.*]

PETER. [*With a shuddering gesture in the direction from which the sound has come.*] Ah, do you hear that? It is the postillion from Regensburg. That is the only tune he knows—"Innsbruck, I must leave thee"! Last week as I listened to that horn of his it sounded in my mind as though the song were meant for me Innsbruck, this life that I love, my wife, and all my joys—that I must leave them.—Leave my good wife all alone, my poor, poor wife. And that, you see, the Good Lord had not the heart to do—he had not the heart to do it. [*But again suddenly he looks about him in great fear. A terrible access of pain seizes him unawares.*]

APFELBAUM. [*Rushing to him.*] Let us take you to your bed.

CHARITAS. Peter, dear Peter.

PETER. [*Waving them both away, gazing fixedly before him.*] It was but a last remainder of my sickness. It is over now. . . . Worse than last week, however. [*Bitterly.*] And Schedel will come again And ask me how it was. Thus it was: a hundred needles driving through my body, shot with gunpowder out of a cannon's mouth.

APFELBAUM. Let ūs take you to your bed, dear master. Shall I fetch Dr. Schedel?

PETER. [*Excited and angrily.*] No, I've had my belly-full of Schedel's twisting winding words. I'll tell you now—he knows nothing. It may be that a doctor comes hard by his knowledge of the stomach and heart, for when he cuts his dead bodies to see inside them, it is but corpses and not the living men that lie before him. [APFEL-BAUM *sits down timidly and frightened behind the table.*]

CHARITAS. [*Goes toward the street door.*] Had Ev but known that on this evening another attack of pain would seize you, she would' not have gone to her singing. I'll go for her.

PETER. [*With fond longing.*] Ev, yes, fetch her here. No, do not go. There is time enough for her to know that the sickness is still at its trial of strength with my hope of life. Why disturb her singing? That must be a joy almost as great as the joy of invention—though not quite, for the song that is sung is over and done with. [*He sits brooding for a moment, then with quick resolution.*] But I have meant these several days past, apprentice, to talk to you of my good wife. Suppose a roof-tile were to drop upon my head this year, or in another year or two— [*Very coolly and practically.*] You are to see to it that my Ev shall not want. And if any business is to do with that father of hers, the salt-fish dealer, you are to see that it is all set down in writing with the help of an honest lawyer who knows his trade. And listen, both of you, should such a tile fall upon my head, you are to give my wife this word from me: that she take another husband soon. Soon, I say! Before the first wrinkles come to mar her loveliness, her sweet loveliness. [*With joyous fervour.*] And you, apprentice, meanwhile, are to be my travelling schoolmaster—in Strassburg—in Antwerp—wheresoever you will! You are to show them how the Nüremberg Egg is made, and see that you are paid well for your instructions. Get all you can. [*Merrily.*] And thus, look you, your life's dream would come to pass. You would become a schoolmaster and wear the Nüremberg funnel on your coat of arms.

[*From the church the sound of many voices singing comes faintly into the workshop. They are singing the Magnificat Anima Mea Dominum, or some other joyous anthem of praise.*]

PETER. [*Continuing without a pause.*] This too I will say: wheresoever you go on your journeys hither and thither, take your good wife with you, for it is a true joy to have at your side the wife you love, a manifold joy. [*With ominous gloom.*] And may it be God's pleasure that I live to see it.

CHARITAS. [*Comes to him.*] Amen. Amen.

PETER. How well they sing. And when Ev comes home we shall sit about this table here, two wedded pairs—and celebrate this happiness of yours with a measure of Würzburg wine. A Godfearing woman and a schoolmaster. Ah, surely that is a pleasant thing! [*He falls to brooding and suddenly takes the finished Egg in his hand. With fervour.*] And yet, apprentice, though I sit here sick and wretched I would not change with you. If I were to be the whole of you and you the whole of me, still I would not change with you. [*Holding the clock to his ear.*] For when I listen to the song this clock is singing, my heart is warmer than the heart of a bridegroom.

CHARITAS. And see, Peter,—your soul has gone out into your fruit, and even though a thousand years be past, it shall still live, ticking in all men's pockets.

PETER. [*To* APPELBAUM *Eagerly, with a passionate gaiety.*] She is right. Look, apprentice. . . .

EV. [*Hurries in from the street, overjoyed and surprised.*] What, out of your bed? Oh, thanks be to God, thanks be to God!— What foolishness I sat in church imagining! Is he not in pain again, I thought. And could hardly sing for thinking so. My throat seemed strangled. [*In gay reproof.*] Oh, husband, my husband, how you worry me! [*Tenderly she throws herself down on her knees before* PETER.]

PETER. [*In great merriment. Laying his hand on her head.*] Look you —no sooner does she enter than she talks a whole waterfall! And never thinks to ask what serious matters,—what matters of great moment—we are discussing. I say, one thing at a time—one thing at a time. [*He looks at the Egg in his hand as if prophetically.*] Look you, apprentice—this is what I had still to tell you: My sister spoke truth. When the thought comes into my mind that some day my soul will go ticking in all those pockets as yet unstitched—then from the highest heaven a sevenfold sun glows within my heart— all my life long I have waited, freezing, for that sun to warm me. [*A new and sharper spasm of pain twists his body.*]

EV. [*Screaming in terror.*] Peter! Peter! [PETER *again rapidly presses his clock to his ear then falls unconscious. The Nüremberg Egg rolls across the floor and* PETER's *body slides heavily out of the chair.*]

EV. [*Takes his head in both of her hands.*] Peter, Peter!

APFELBAUM. [*Flings himself upon the body listening for the heart-beat. Then cries aloud in grief.*] Dead! It is not possible!

[CHARITAS *falls on her knees a little apart from the three, to the right. The anthem grows louder.*]

CURTAIN

MADAME LEGROS

by

HEINRICH MANN

CAST OF CHARACTERS

MADAME LEGROS
MADAME TOUCHE
THE COMTESSE D'ORCHAT
THE MARQUISE DE SCARCLE
QUEEN MARIE ANTOINETTE
MADAME CROZET
A YOUNG RELATIVE OF THE COUPLE LEGROS
TWO OLD WOMEN
A WOMAN
ANOTHER WOMAN
A NEIGHBOUR
FANCHON
LEGROS
VIGNON
CHEVALIER D'ANGELOT
LIEUTENANT RAMON
MONSIEUR COUSIN
A MEMBER OF THE ACADEMY
A YOUNG MAN
THE ABBÉ DE ZORANE
A LACKEY
A TALL GUARD
TWO FOOTMEN
FOUR CHILDREN

Populace, Neighbours, Soldiers

Paris, 1789

MADAME LEGROS

ACT I

Scene:—*The greater part of the stage is occupied by the shop belonging to the couple Legros. It is open at one side to show linen goods set out for display. There is another window on the narrow lane which runs between tall old houses (the finest of which is the Inn of the White Horse), and at the end is the Place de la Bastille. One tower of the prison closes the lane in the background.*

YOUNG RELATIVE. Such a pretty bonnet! The Comte de Coutras did well to take this one; it will become Mademoiselle Palmyre to perfection. Do you not think so, Mme. Legros?

MME. LEGROS. [*At the till, writing.*] The comte chose the bonnet he considered most suitable.

YOUNG RELATIVE. No such thing. I chose it, and I persuaded him to buy it. *That's* the one he would have taken, but it's not nearly handsome enough for Mlle. Palmyre. We're good friends, she and I.

MME. LEGROS. You are in our service, I believe. That should be reason enough for you to recommend our best.

YOUNG RELATIVE. It is. . . . I might take the bonnet over there at once.

MME. LEGROS. I have still to sew on the bows.

YOUNG RELATIVE. I could do that.

MME. LEGROS. And do you imagine the difference would not be noticed?

YOUNG RELATIVE. I've learned good taste since I came to Paris, Mme. Legros. I am no peasant. M. Legros is related to me; he will not thwart me so.

MME. LEGROS. The box of stockings has not been tidied away; a costly ruffle is left lying about on the floor—but Mademoiselle has no other thought in her head than running after a ballet girl at the opera and staring at the gallants from the wings.

YOUNG RELATIVE. No need to stare at them from there! You begrudge every one their pleasure, Mme. Legros. You think of nobody but yourself.

MME. LEGROS. I think of the interests of Monsieur Legros. I am his wife.

M. LEGROS. [*Enters.*] Good day.

MME. LEGROS. Good day, dear husband. Is all well in your workshop today? Are you pleased with the new apprentice?

M. LEGROS. He's an excellent fellow.

MME. LEGROS. But I can see by your face that something has put you out.

M. LEGROS. Maître Ambroise came about the money for his wool.

MME. LEGROS. It is not yet pay day.

M. LEGROS. Maître Ambroise was in need of the money. His wife has been ill this long while. Times are hard for him.

MME. LEGROS. Did you pay him?

M. LEGROS. They're hard for us too—and for everybody else these days. But I said to myself: we must help one another.

MME. LEGROS. Dear husband, whatever you do is right.

M. LEGROS. Still I don't know who will help *us* when our day comes.

MME. LEGROS. Oh, but it will not, husband. We have just sold our finest bonnet to the Comte de Coutras for four hundred livres.

YOUNG RELATIVE. It was *I* that talked him in to it.

M. LEGROS. That may be. It was Mme. Legros' handiwork, however.

MME. LEGROS. But praise and credit are due to her only—not to me, for you are my husband.

M. LEGROS. True.

MME. LEGROS. Soon we shall have no more laces. How much longer will they be coming from Alençon?

M. LEGROS. [*Uneasily.*] That is what I wonder, too. It is possible they may be here already, lying at the city customs. It occurs to me, Mme. Legros, that your kinsman, the customs officer, has not been to see us this long time. . . . What are you doing?

MME. LEGROS. I still have the bows to sew onto Mlle. Palmyre's bonnet.

M. LEGROS. You can do that later on. You will go now to your cousin at the customs and invite him to dinner on Sunday.

MME. LEGROS. At once?

M. LEGROS. I owe him that courtesy.

MME. LEGROS. Cannot Lisette go?

M. LEGROS. That would be lacking in courtesy, Mme. Legros.

MME. LEGROS. Dear husband, your wish is my command. [*She makes ready to go out.*]

M. LEGROS. And tell your cousin there will be a fine fat goose. . . . And be back in time for dinner.

MME. LEGROS. It is a long way but I shall make haste. [*She goes out.*]

M. LEGROS. Bring me the ladder. . . . What's this? Can it be that you are crying?

YOUNG RELATIVE. And no wonder. I sell the most costly bonnet in the place, and what is my reward? That I am not even allowed to go and see my own friend.

M. LEGROS. [*Consolingly.*] It is not like Mme. Legros to be hard. Why should she forbid you that little harmless enjoyment?

YOUNG RELATIVE. And what's more she does it in your name.

M. LEGROS. She believes she is doing right.

YOUNG RELATIVE. Oh, M. Legros, is there nothing you would teach a girl but these tiresome duties?

M. LEGROS. [*Coming closer.*] What else should I teach you?

YOUNG RELATIVE. If you don't know, well. . . . I need some one to look after me in the city. I could have wished for a man of serious character—still there is much to learn from my friend; Mlle. Palmyre, that is, of the opera ballet.

M. LEGROS. That is a friendship I cannot approve of.

YOUNG RELATIVE. And why not? Mlle. Palmyre is from our village. She likes me, and would gladly have me for her maid.

M. LEGROS. Maid to a low-born girl like that?

YOUNG RELATIVE. Whom the Comte de Coutras befriends. She is already rich.

M. LEGROS. And you would like to become so by the same means, eh? It has been done. You need to be watched—and Mme. Legros did well to keep you indoors.

YOUNG RELATIVE. So she went out instead—to her cousin, the customs officer's.

M. LEGROS. What do you mean? Guard your tongue, young woman.

YOUNG RELATIVE. Ha! See how angry you are now. And a moment ago so very nice that it's a good thing Mme. Legros didn't see you.

M. LEGROS. I know my duty to Mme. Legros—the truest and most blameless of wives.

YOUNG RELATIVE. Not so—blameless—as you.

M. LEGROS. And so honourable that you would do well to take an example from her.

YOUNG RELATIVE. Yes—so honourable that she goes to the customs, for all the world as though she doesn't know why.

M. LEGROS. She goes because I tell her to. And I told you to get me the ladder.

YOUNG RELATIVE. All in good time. Mme. Legros knows as well as we do that her laces will now come into the city duty-free. And for this she is to invite her cousin to a nice fat goose—and something else besides—who knows?

M. LEGROS. What are you saying! I'll throw you out of my house!

YOUNG RELATIVE. Do so—and I shall go straight to Mlle. Palmyre.

M. LEGROS. That's where you learn these things—*I* know. Mme. Legros' mind is as innocent of evil as my own. Her kinsman is always glad to see her; he is her godfather. And without a friend in the customs you pay till you're ruined.

YOUNG RELATIVE. I meant no harm. But take my word for it, M. Legros, with women it's six of one and half a dozen of another. [*She goes close to him.*] No man need have scruples about us.

M. LEGROS. And wenches like you are none too plentiful.

YOUNG RELATIVE. Get away! There comes Mme. Legros.

[MME. LEGROS *returns, after greeting her neighbours all along the lane, and at the foot of the tower picks up something from the ground. She takes the rest of the way running, and reaches the entrance of the shop, hiding a paper, terrified that the others are watching her.*]

M. LEGROS. Secrets?

MME. LEGROS. It was no fault of mine. All of a sudden it was in my hand. Oh . . .

[M. LEGROS *snatches the paper from her.*]
[YOUNG RELATIVE, *inquisitive, comes near.*]
[MME. LEGROS *hides her face.*]

M. LEGROS. What is this? Who gave it you?

MME. LEGROS. It dropped down from the tower.

M. LEGROS. What tower?

MME. LEGROS. The Bastille.

M. LEGROS. Before, you said some one put it in your hand.

MME. LEGROS. It is so terrible that when I'd read it, I felt that it was my crime too.

M. LEGROS. Yours?

MME. LEGROS. It is everybody's crime.

M. LEGROS. Written by some lunatic! And you waste your time over it.

MME. LEGROS. Lunatic? A man, innocent, who has been kept in that tower for three and forty years?

M. LEGROS. A practical joker, then. Worse perhaps. There are certain people only too eager to sow discontent against the King and his government. No doubt it was one of those who cast this slip of paper at random into the air.

MME. LEGROS. I saw it fluttering down. I looked up, and at the very top of the tower—right on the platform—there stood a man waving. But only for a second. And before I had really seen him, a soldier had dragged him back.

YOUNG RELATIVE. [Reads the letter, haltingly.] "Passer by, whosoever you be, it is an innocent man who here adjures you. Under the late régime, in the time of his Majesty, our gracious King Louis, I was flung into the Bastille in consequence of an indiscreet attempt to attract to myself the attention of Mme. la Marquise de Pompadour. Here I have lain for forty-three years, forgotten. Even my guards no longer know who I am. Oh, friend, to whose feet the wind or the breath of God has wafted this piece of paper, make known this to all men. Tell them this which no one now remembers, so many having since been born, and so many having since died: that my name is Latude, that I am innocent, and that I suffer!"

[MME. LEGROS has turned away, sighing heavily.]

YOUNG RELATIVE. It is horrible. And such beautiful words—as if the priest had told it.

LEGROS. [Painfully stirred.] There is a man to pity. But such things are not for us to meddle with. It would be imprudent. We must not mention it to anyone.

MME. LEGROS. No indeed, for nobody would believe us. They would think us wicked.

LEGROS. They would think us very stupid.

MME. LEGROS. Then what are we to do?

LEGROS. Keep it to ourselves, by God.

MME. LEGROS. What did you say?

YOUNG RELATIVE. I'll tell everyone! How curious they will be! I shall run at once to the Bastille and ask my friend the soldier Colas there if he knows anything about this prisoner.

[They are silent, moved.]

M. LEGROS. You will keep a bridle on your tongue or you will have me to reckon with.

MME. LEGROS. What does this mean?

M. LEGROS. It means that you are to put that paper in the fire, and without more ado. We are respectable people. The affairs of political criminals are none of our business.

MME. LEGROS. But he is innocent.

M. LEGROS. So *he* says. If the late King put him in the tower he must have had a very good reason for doing so.

MME. LEGROS. The King is dead. And it is all so long ago. Where are the people he wronged—if he *did* wrong them—where are they now—? Ah! What is the good of all this? You have heard what the man says. You have heard the truth, and so have I. We all have ears, one no different from another. It is clear to everyone.

M. LEGROS. Since you have ears then, have the kindness to listen now to me. I am your husband, and I command you to hold your tongue, Mme. Legros.

MME. LEGROS. [*Bows to him.*] You are my husband—but you are also kind. Are you testing me again, as you did that day soon after our marriage—before you had had time to know me well—when you neglected to enter the sale of a bonnet in the book, and went out leaving me alone in the shop to see whether I would take the money? Do you still need proof to convince you that I am honest? [*She leans against him.*]

M. LEGROS. You are a good wife. You have always worked for your husband's welfare. That is why you know very well how we should conduct ourselves in this matter.

MME. LEGROS. [*Ingratiatingly.*] Indeed, yes—like honest people. We shall not abet the world's injustice. No—worse than abet, for the rest do so in ignorance while we *know*. [*Reflecting.*] Dear husband, your name will be praised for this—you will be revered. Every honourable man would do likewise.

M. LEGROS. One might truly believe that the minds of women can never quite mature. You would have it that it is our duty to go to the authorities and declare that they are wrongfully holding prisoner a certain man. If anyone were to overhear you, he would believe us all out of our minds.

MME. LEGROS. [*Beseeching him.*] Husband! A man's life is at stake.

M. LEGROS. Quite apart from the fact that no one would ever deal at our shop again for fear of the Bastille to which we so recklessly expose ourselves, so that even if the authorities let us go unharmed we should be ruined just the same. . . .

MME. LEGROS. And if we keep silent the bread we eat will be the bread of dishonour.

M. LEGROS. Wife, take care. I am a burgher of Paris. I do not eat the bread of dishonour.

MME. LEGROS. You have never done so yet. You will henceforward. Look at the tower—an innocent man is there—he has lain there suffering so long that no one now remembers him. Look at the square and all the people. While their parents were still hurrying to and fro across that square, even then he lay in his chains. When their children shall be grown and walk across that square, what then? Shall he be there suffering still? Must unrighteousness flourish in the world forever? Now I understand what we mean when we tell the children of original sin.

M. LEGROS. It is true, this is a bad world, and bad it will always remain. It is well enough for the great ones, they give no thought to our oppression. What happens to our neighbours must not be our care—we must close our eyes to it or it will come upon ourselves.

MME. LEGROS. And if it should, do I stand calmly by while someone screams for help at my very door? Hidden in the shadows of this lane, I sit waiting for customers—I turn away those who come after our money—I eat, I chat, and at last close my shop for the night and go to sleep with my husband. And at the other end of this good and comfortable lane of mine, chains clatter and someone crawls—a skeleton weeping tears of despair—crawls and weeps forever through damp cellars. Will you try to make me believe that that is nothing? But I can hear it—he is screaming now. [*She holds her ears.*]

[M. LEGROS *signs to the* YOUNG RELATIVE *to shut the door.*]

MME. LEGROS. I hear it through the door.

M. LEGROS. It is you who are screaming—people will begin to notice.

MME. LEGROS. Let them—they shall come and hear. This is too much for me to know alone.

M. LEGROS. A child is what you need—you'd think no more then about other people's troubles.

MME. LEGROS. A child. I had one once. But it died before it came.

M. LEGROS. You shall get another.

MME. LEGROS. Yes—there could be another. And that tower over there could open too, and the man who is buried in it live again.

M. LEGROS. I will have no more of this!

MME. LEGROS. That is your stubbornness—and yours alone, poor man. But men and women desire the right—oh, I know they do! I need only call them here and talk to them, and at once, this very hour, they will go with me and lead that innocent man out of his prison.

M. LEGROS. She has gone mad.

MME. LEGROS. Your pardon, husband! I have always obeyed you without question. Now I obey you no longer. [*She flings open the door.*] Good neighbours! M. Vignon! Mme. Touche!

M. LEGROS. Merciful Heavens!

YOUNG RELATIVE. Now the fun begins!

MME. LEGROS. Injustice has been done.

VIGNON. What is your wish, Mme. Legros?

MME. LEGROS. An innocent man lies in the Bastille.

A NEIGHBOUR. Only one?

MME. TOUCHE. What did he do?

MME. LEGROS. No one knows any more—it is so long ago. He has written to me—we must help him.

A YOUNG MAN. I'll fetch my axe.

TWO OLD WOMEN. Come away, neighbour! We shouldn't be listening to this. [*They withdraw.*]

MME. LEGROS. Good people, you are Christian men.

VIGNON. I have philosophy, Madame.

MME. LEGROS. M. Vignon, think of the time that robber fell upon you at the corner—you shouted for help and the whole lane rushed to save you.

VIGNON. That is true, but the King is no robber.

A NEIGHBOUR. Often in his great kindness, the King pūts rogues in the tower in order to rid their families of them.

A WOMAN. M. de Talmont had committed no crime—yet they put him in.

ANOTHER. He came courting you, and that displeased his father.

MME. TOUCHE. [*Pointing to* MME. LEGROS.] The prisoner is her lover. Why else would she get so excited over him? [*The women laugh.*]

YOUNG RELATIVE. Do you hear that, M. Legros?

MME. LEGROS. You are wrong, Monsieur. You are wrong, all of you! It was the Marquise de Pompadour who had him imprisoned, and when she died he was forgotten.

VIGNON. The Marquise de Pompadour? Everything she did should be forgotten.

MME. LEGROS. We must make that good! Forty-three years.

FANCHON. My father died when he was forty-three.

MME. LEGROS. Look, Fanchon—suppose that on the day when your father was born a man named Latude disappeared and was never heard of again. Until today, when after forty-three years, his name is spoken again for the first time. For forty-three years your father went his way in the world. Think how many times he laughed— how many times he kissed you. And every time he did so another man in that tower there, groaned. Do not all those years look different to you now?

[FANCHON *weeps. There is an embarrassed silence.*]

VIGNON. If one had to think all day of how things were going with others, there would be an end of happiness.

A WOMAN. We need what we can have of that.

MME. TOUCHE. A tile fell from a roof and killed my husband, but he'd never done any wrong.

AN OLD WOMAN. Who knows? God does nothing without his reasons.

MME. TOUCHE. What's that? You old hag, are you insulting my husband? [*Makes for the old woman. The men separate them.*]

[*The* YOUNG MAN *who suggested fetching his axe, speaks to the* OLD WOMAN.]

YOUNG MAN. These are bad people, grandmother. Come away.

MME. LEGROS. Why need you hurt each other? We have already so much guilt upon us. We have connived at a grave injustice. Oh, come with me! You must see we must first atone for that.

VIGNON. Mme. Legros, be it permitted me to tell you in all neighbourly friendship: you begin to weary us. You, a quiet respectable burgher's wife, come here and set the people against one another. And what for? For the sake of some good-for-nothing who has been in a hole all his life and has never managed to get out of it.

A NEIGHBOUR. What has come over Mme. Legros? We've always known her for such a serious-minded shop-keeper.

MME. TOUCHE. I tell you there's some love business behind it. The rest is nothing but invention.

WOMEN. Look at Legros! Old fat Legros! Standing by while she carries on with her lovers behind his back.

YOUNG RELATIVE. Do you call yourself a man, M. Legros? I'll never be nice to you again.

M. LEGROS. [*Forcing his way through the crowd.*] Mme. Legros, have you brought scandal enough upon me now? Come into the house this instant.

FANCHON. She's in pain! Can't you see, M. Legros, your wife is ill? Such a good woman, too. [*She supports* MME. LEGROS, *who sways on her feet.*]

M. LEGROS. You're right, her illness has not left her yet. It's the baby being born dead that has made her like this. I ask your pardon, Messieurs.

MME. LEGROS. [*Freeing herself.*] Let me alone, Legros! See the sort of people these are! They know an innocent man is suffering, and yet they would go on with their lives as before—selling their rubbish, drinking their wine. I despise you all! The whole world can go to rack and ruin so long as nothing touches your alley! But I shall have it in ruins for you soon! Good people! Good people all! Come!

[CROWD *comes surging into the lane from the square.*]

[*The* NEIGHBOURS *scatter violently—they take refuge in their houses and bolt the dors.*]

MME. LEGROS. [*In the centre of the crowd.*] Help me, I beg of you!

VOICES. What's the matter? Who is that shouting?

MME. LEGROS. You don't know what hideous things are happening here! If it comes to your children's ears they will love you no longer.

VOICES. What does the woman want? Let her get up on the curb so that we can hear her.

MME. LEGROS. [*Pushed by the crowd gets up on the stone before the house opposite.*] You men and women of the people! A letter has been dropped from the tower by an innocent man imprisoned there. You must set him free.

VOICES. Go on, this is good! Trying to get yourself hanged, are you, mother? You're going the right way about it. Keep on! Where's the letter? Let's hear it.

MME. LEGROS. I don't know what has become of it. But can you not see in my eyes that read it how terrible it was? Look, these poor hands of mine that held it tremble yet.

VOICES. Something ought to be done to put this right.

A HOLLOW VOICE. One day when everybody was starving we had a bit of a to-do, and I was in it. I got a lump of lead in my arm from a soldier but not a crumb of bread.

MME. LEGROS. Yes, for a few days you went hungry and then began committing acts of violence. But in that tower there a man is lying who has not merely starved. He also freezes in the darkness, and for longer than most of you have been in the world he has not heard a human voice. What act of violence is great enough to avenge that!

VOICES. She is right. There are crimes the people know nothing about. The gentlemen up above do nothing but commit crimes all the time! They are murderers!

A WOMAN. They cut off my daughter's hair and sent her to America.

ANOTHER WOMAN. [*Scornfully.*] Is that the sort your daughter is? Well, she's plying her trade among the savages now.

ONE OF THE CROWD. [*Stealing some of the* LEGROS' *wares exposed for sale.*] And who's this wench showing herself off on the curbstone? Cut off *her* hair too.

M. LEGROS. [*Who has been forced inside his shop by the pressure of the crowd, now rushes out.*] Scoundrel, you've stolen my goods, and that is my wife! [*The thief slinks away.*]

VOICES. Your wife, is she? What does she want?

M. LEGROS. Now Mme. Legros, do you see what they're taking you for?

MME. LEGROS. Yes, for a harlot. And what if I were? My shame would be less than it is now. Men have been known to die for a harlot! But would a harlot shut an innocent man in a living grave? That is what I'm doing—and so are you—and you—and all of you! Set him free, else you are hyenas round his grave! More destitute of honour than those who hang upon the gibbet! A plague that smells to heaven!

VOICES. This is going too far. She is insulting the people. Pull her down! Cut off her hair! Down with her!

MME. LEGROS. [*Clinging to an iron ring in the wall.*] Drag me away if you can—I shall hold on! I have strength to stand against all of you. You shall see how I shall throw open the tower for the Innocent. Then the world will be beautiful again. Now the tower holds it in darkness. Can you see the sky at all? Can you ever laugh? I must break open the tower so that you may laugh again. It is for you that I do this, because of my love for you.

A WOMAN. How pretty she is! And she talks like an angel.

A MAN. How much difference would that make? We shall always suffer.

MME. LEGROS. How happy the Innocent will make you all! How he will reward you! Do you suppose he is not rich, and handsome? As only innocence can be? [*Leans toward a woman in the crowd.*] You will love him, you over there. [*To another woman.*] Not you! I see you already desiring him with your bold lips!

M. LEGROS. She is out of her mind! Messieurs—that you can see for yourselves.

VOICES. Is there money in the tower then? She is right. Let's go and set the prisoner free! Freedom for all!

A VOICE. [*Shrieking.*] The soldiers!

MME. LEGROS. [*Shouting.*] The soldiers! Don't let them in. They helped to put him in the tower. Chase them away.

[*There are sounds of scuffling in the rear.*]
Chase them away! Kill them! [*She jumps down into the midst of the mob.*] Fall back you there—we are marching on the Bastille! The Innocent shall be delivered. Let them all die—all the soldiers, all the insolent riders in the square, all the heartless ladies in their sedan chairs—murderers all!

CROWD. Down with the murderers! To the Bastille!

MME. LEGROS. The tower shall spurt blood! The blood of the Innocent shall drown them all! [*She struggles with a soldier.*]

[*The men at arms have pushed forward. The mob gives way, fleeing in all directions.*]

A SOLDIER. Here is the shrew, Lieutenant. I've got her fast.

LIEUTENANT. Be careful, she looks as though she is about to faint. Two of you take the prisoner between you and march!

YOUNG RELATIVE. [*Emerging from some hiding place.*] There, M. Legros, now see what she has done. Well, I had *my* fun out of it, indeed I did!

M. LEGROS. Lieutenant, I ask your pardon, but this poor sick woman here is my wife.

LIEUTENANT. Then you come with me too.

M. LEGROS. Lieutenant, I am a citizen of good repute. I own the shop which is known as "At the Sign of King René's Oak."

LIEUTENANT. A citizen of good repute whose wife incites the mob to violence, eh? I'd like to see one.

VIGNON. [*From the inn, opposite.*] I will bear witness to that, Lieutenant. You know this house of mine. It is the Inn of the White Horse. Mme. Legros has always been one of the most worthy shopkeepers of this quarter.

WOMEN. [*From various houses.*] Our neighbour taken by the soldiers? That would be a disgrace for all of us.

M. LEGROS. But when I tell you she is ill, Lieutenant! Her child was still-born, hardly a fortnight since. It has left her with a weakness of the brain.

FANCHON. Ah, Monsieur, have pity on her!

LIEUTENANT. What about the other prisoners? I cannot show favour to one.

[*Enter the* CHEVALIER.]

CHEVALIER. I have the honour to wish you good day, Lieutenant. I am the Chevalier d'Angelot.

LIEUTENANT. The honour is mine, Monsieur. My name is Ramon.

WOMEN. A gentleman from the Court.

VIGNON. He is a friend of the Queen's.

CHEVALIER. Mme. la Comtesse d'Orchat with some gentlemen has just witnessed the scene created by this person. They were in the square down there. Mme. la Comtesse is deeply interested. M. le Marquis de Launay was with us. Are you acquainted with him, M. Ramon?

LIEUTENANT. I have the honour to know the Governor of the Bastille. All these lords and ladies, including yourself, are also known to me, M. le Chevalier.

CHEVALIER. Then you will not hesitate to grant my request, and will set this woman free without delay. Certain reasons of state make it imperative that she be not arrested.

LIEUTENANT. I obey, Monsieur. [*To the soldiers.*] Fall in! Forward march! [*Exeunt.*]

[*The spectators gradually leave the lane.*]

M. LEGROS. How am I to thank you, M. Le Chevalier?

CHEVALIER. By granting me leave to bring my friends into your house. Mme. la Comtesse d'Orchat desires to meet your wife.

M. LEGROS. It is too great an honour. Mme. Legros, thank this gentleman.

CHEVALIER. [*Leading* MME. LEGROS *by the hand into the shop—in a low voice.*] Need I say, Madame, that it was chiefly *my* wish to see you?

MME. LEGROS. [*Gradually recovering her strength.*] The people did not understand. They are weak. And now the Innocent must go on suffering.

M. LEGROS. The Innocent! Is she not like a little child, whimpering for a toy it may not have? You will pardon me, Monsieur, customers have come.

CHEVALIER. It must be confessed, Madame, that your husband understands you still less than the people. Yet that should not be so difficult.

MME. LEGROS. Should it not, Monsieur?

CHEVALIER. It is enough to see your face, Mme. Legros. Rebellion becomes you.

[*Enter the* COMTESSE, *the* ABBÉ.]

ABBÉ. [*Standing in the doorway.*] Courage, Madame.

COMTESSE. A somewhat daring plan, to penetrate into the monster's very lair. Rather anything than ennui though, Monsieur.

M. LEGROS. Will your lordship and your ladyship graciously accept my humble services?

COMTESSE. Thank you, Monsieur. Are you the husband of this interesting woman?

M. LEGROS. I am the hosier Legros, at Your Highness' service.

ABBÉ. Mme. la Comtesse gives you permission to offer her a chair.

[M. LEGROS *takes a chair from the* COUSIN.]

M. LEGROS. Go and put the dinner on. [*The* COUSIN *exits.*]

ABBÉ. [*To* MME. LEGROS.] Mme. la Comtesse has been with us the witness of your very interesting performance, Madame.

M. LEGROS. I beg Mme. la Comtesse and Monsieur to accept my deep regrets.

ABBÉ. On the contrary, you should offer thanks. Mme. la Comtesse was diverted.

COMTESSE. Oh, more than that! I was filled with excitement—quite carried away. At last I have seen a revolt.

MME. LEGROS. Then you will help to deliver the Innocent? I was sure of it!

COMTESSE. [*Withdrawing.*] You are importunate.

ABBÉ. [*To* MME. LEGROS.] A little calmer, Madame. You have seen where violence leads.

MME. LEGROS. An innocent man's life is at stake.

CHEVALIER. We have only your word for it.

MME. LEGROS. His story is known to no one now—after three and forty years.

COMTESSE. Your pardon—I have it from M. de Launay himself.

CHEVALIER. The youth Latude had the insolence to love a lady who was too powerful.

ABBÉ. His example is a warning to you, Chevalier.

CHEVALIER. Against what? I am no Latude.

ABBÉ. The Queen could make one of you.

CHEVALIER. You fortunate ones have always the protection of your cloth.

ABBÉ. My cloth! Are you aware that I have my breviary read by my servant?

COMTESSE. Nevertheless, neither of you would send his lady love an infernal machine, as Latude did.

ABBÉ. [Sighs.] For love.

CHEVALIER. And in order to protect the lady from the danger to which she was exposed through him.

COMTESSE. The Marquise de Pompadour withstood his advances. She even had the swain himself thrown into the Bastille.

MME. LEGROS. She would not have punished him for his love, Madame.

ABBÉ [With a sigh.] What tells you that?

MME. LEGROS. She could never have cut him off in the flower of his youth! You would never destroy a whole life for the anger of a moment.

COMTESSE. [Moved.] I am not cruel. You touch me, Madame. [To the gentlemen.] To think I was afraid! She is far from terrifying. She is even well-educated.

ABBÉ. In the age of superstition they would nevertheless have expelled an evil spirit from her.

MME. LEGROS. This is against nature and as if God himself had died.

CHEVALIER. [Ironically.] We are all against nature, Madame.

ABBÉ. And it is all as if God had died.

CHEVALIER. [As before.] You forget, Madame, that we are living under an ancient régime, which has its rights, its prerogatives and its victims.

ABBÉ. She forgets everything.

MME. LEGROS. I remember the Innocent, whom all others should remember also.

M. LEGROS. Mme. Legros, you are annoying these gentlemen. Thank them for their kindness in explaining things to you.

ABBÉ. M. Legros, this wife of yours is a strange being.

CHEVALIER. If we were to open our eyes for the first time upon a virgin world, then perhaps we might see things as Mme. Legros sees them.

COMTESSE. [Sighs.] That would be so delightful. Monsieur, I shall

never be bored again. We have made a great discovery. We have
found an exquisite example of virtue. Do not fail, Chevalier, to inform the Queen of it.

ABBÉ. Since virtue is a subject upon which you and her Majesty so
happily discourse.

COMTESSE. Mme. Legros, I understand you, for I am no less sensitive than you are. Confide in me. Do you know this M. Latude?

MME. LEGROS. I heard of him today; how could I otherwise have
lived as I have until today?

COMTESSE. He writes to you. Where is his letter?

MME. LEGROS. I lost it in the crowd.

COMTESSE. You are jealous. None the less, I wish to help you. You
please me. I understand mistakes that are caused by sensibility.

MME. LEGROS. Reflect, Madame, upon that long life in wretchedness.
Consider the thick terrible walls in those damp cellars where he
has lain longing for some human heart to pity him.

COMTESSE. You are that heart. You must come and visit me. You
shall publish your cause to a company of sensitive listeners. Promise
that you will come.

MME. LEGROS. I do not feel worthy of that, Madame. It is a task
that I should fear.

COMTESSE. I pledge myself to find you a worthy audience who will
give your merit the attention which befits it.

MME. LEGROS. What do you expect of me, Madame? If you are
prepared to take this burden from me and deliver the Innocent,
I for myself have no other desire than to return to my quiet life.

ABBÉ. No such thing. You must be seen or they will cease to be interested.

COMTESSE. You must acquire the deportment of the *beau monde*.
Nothing can be won without art and the usages of gallantry. Monsieur Legros, make your wife listen to reason.

M. LEGROS. Mme. la Comtesse is being very gracious to you, Mme.
Legros.

MME. LEGROS. I was prepared to go to prison for the sake of the
Innocent. Yes, I would have died for him, but this I cannot do.

COMTESSE. [*Adjusting her lorgnette.*] Look at the little savage! Perhaps she will at least deign to give me her word to accept no other
invitation until she has seen me again.

M. LEGROS. I ask your pardon, Mme. la Comtesse, we are simple folk. But since it is your desire to entertain Mme. Legros at *your* house, may I venture to offer you the hospitality of ours?

COMTESSE. I am not as proud as Mme. Legros.

M. LEGROS. Will you then condescend to drink some wine which we have from a kinsman of mine—it is peasants' wine—for it is to the peasantry, Madame, that we bourgeois are kin.

COMTESSE. [*To her escort.*] How enchantingly naïve an invitation!

CHEVALIER. I do not know that the intention is as naïve as the words.

COMTESSE. Messieurs, we are to see a bourgeois interior. It is an idyll I have long dreamed of.

[COMTESSE, ABBÉ *exeunt with* LEGROS. MME. LEGROS *slowly follows.*]

CHEVALIER. [*Closes the door before her.*] Madame, I vow discretion if you will tell me now when you mean to become a guest in the house of the Comtesse d'Orchat.

MME. LEGROS. I have not yet said that I should ever be there, Monsieur.

CHEVALIER. I know you are too astute to accept at once, but you are also too astute by far to decline altogether.

MME. LEGROS. Why should you doubt my word?

CHEVALIER. I observe your actions. They are none too scrupulously inspired now. They will hardly be so in the future.

MME. LEGROS. It is true. In the face of events so overwhelming one does not seem to have the right to choose.

CHEVALIER. You realise it then.

MME. LEGROS. Others can do more than I; you, Monsieur, so very much more.

CHEVALIER. Nothing escapes you. Then I am to solicit the interest of the Queen in Mme. Legros?

MME. LEGROS. No, Monsieur, in an innocent man. I beseech you, you are young, how can you be not also generous?

CHEVALIER. Mme. Legros, you are not happy.

MME. LEGROS. I used to be. No, I am not happy anymore.

CHEVALIER. I understand that within these narrow walls the ambitions of a woman like you can find nothing to feed on—and one comes to hate the unattainable.

MME. LEGROS. I hate nothing—I love only the Innocent.

CHEVALIER. You are miraculous, Mme. Legros. I believe you capable of denying your hatreds, even to yourself, in order that you may stir the conscience of the rest of us and render us defenceless through our own virtue. Your tears shall break the earth which did not yield to your fury. We have no antagonist as clever as you, Mme. Legros. I myself feel moved to help you now, to make easier your ascent in the world, in order that some day I may myself defeat you and pull off your mask before all men.

MME. LEGROS. You would be but defeating innocence.

CHEVALIER. Defeat, did I say? That was not what I meant. It is seeing you at work, watching you grow like the peril which is my native element, like the passion that is in me! I walk through this city of blood as yet unshed—I inhale the air of your desire, the poison of your minds. Justice, reason, virtue—I do not believe in those things, and yet I hear them all in my deepest heart, I whom they are to overthrow. Every day there is the flare of a new revolt, and I, living through each hostile moment, am filled with joy. Think of me born into these times, how young and lost,—these days of revolution in which everything, myself not least, is bent upon my ruin. Nor would I have it otherwise. I love these times, this carnival of hatred. And never was this borne in upon me as today, here in this lane, when a woman cried out for blood. Was it not my own blood she was crying for? She shall have it. You are wild, you are danger—I love you and want you. [*He seizes her.*]

MME. LEGROS. [*Struggling free.*] Don't touch me! Who shall touch me so long as the Innocent lies in the tower! [*More calmly.*] You merit pity, Monsieur. It must be very hard to see goodness and desire it when one is as clever as you. But do so nevertheless. I can hear in your words that that is what you long for in your heart.

CHEVALIER. Hypocrite!

MME. LEGROS. You are wrong. I am merely humble. Help me.

CHEVALIER. You keep guard over yourself, remembering the Queen.

MME. LEGROS. Tell her, Monsieur, that an Innocent is suffering.

CHEVALIER. And that Mme. Legros is his deliverer.

MME. LEGROS. Do not tell her for my sake, but for her own. Free her of the fearful burden of having an Innocent suffering near her.

CHEVALIER. You are not easily convinced. What if I were to ask a price for doing this thing?

[MME. LEGROS *bows her head.*]

CHEVALIER. You would have to pay the price—some day you will. Your hatred will grow and grow until you will promise me your love.

MME. LEGROS. [*Looks at him.*] Then I will promise it you now.

CHEVALIER. Are you in earnest?

MME. LEGROS. Help me, and I will be yours, if you still want me then. For you will come to know that until then I belong only to the Innocent though I should die in the arms of another.

[*Re-enter* COMTESSE, ABBÉ, M. LEGROS, YOUNG RELATIVE.]

COMTESSE. I have seen a bourgeois home. The people sleep in real beds.

ABBÉ. The beds of straw disappear and, thanks be to God, religion with them.

COMTESSE. And they have veal broiling on the fire. Why should people who have veal broiling on the fire start uprisings?

ABBÉ. For philosophy, just as you play shepherdess while eating truffles.

CHEVALIER. [*To* MME. LEGROS.] But we turn the uprising into a pastoral hour.

COMTESSE. [*To* CHEVALIER.] Have you brought her round?

CHEVALIER. Mme. Legros now realises that the triumph of innocence is worth certain concessions.

COMTESSE. I shall now hasten to spread abroad the news of this curious discovery. Everything about you, my dear Legros, has captivated me —your Innocent. . . .

ABBÉ. Your broiled veal.

COMTESSE. Everything.

M. LEGROS. Be pleased to pardon us, Mme. la Comtesse, that there was so little. We were not expecting the honour of such a visit.

COMTESSE. Adieu. [*To the* CHEVALIER.] Did he mean *that* in the way he said it? [*Exit.*]

[CHEVALIER *and* ABBÉ *exit.*]

YOUNG RELATIVE. What courtesy! Only the lords and ladies of the court have such fine manners.

M. LEGROS. Courtesies of that kind make one long to cap them with a courtesy of another kind. [*He beats upon the table with his fist.*]

YOUNG RELATIVE. It is perfectly clear, M. Legros, that *you* have never been in the wings of the opera.

M. LEGROS. You had better put the soup on the table.

YOUNG RELATIVE. I suppose one may be allowed to *admire* the beau monde. [*Exits.*]

M. LEGROS. What do you say to all this, Mme. Legros?

MME. LEGROS. It is well that they came. I have learnt much.

M. LEGROS. You see that further effort cannot be made either through the nobility or through the people.

MME. LEGROS. That would seem to be true. They too, did not understand. None of them understands what has happened.

M. LEGROS. You should have trusted your husband.

MME. LEGROS. So great a guilt lies upon all of us—but *they* think only
of the entertainment it can afford them.

M. LEGROS. You have tortured yourself enough. Come now and eat.

MME. LEGROS. I have no time for that. Shall I ever have time again?
Dear husband, try to understand—I have learnt at last how much
is to be done and how long is the way. I must go now to everyone
throughout the city, great though it is, and beyond—and I must
show them what are the things that matter, I must enlighten and
cleanse by my words their minds that are now so filled with useless
things, until they learn what matters—until they know——

M. LEGROS. Your feet will hardly bear you now. A long way you say.
You cannot walk three steps. I will not let you go.

MME. LEGROS. [*In the doorway.*] You will let me go, for it must be
clear to you that I have no choice. I am not weak. In spite of all,
I know that men are waiting for the Innocent. The hearts of all
men are alike, and I need only draw away their vices and their dis-
dain as one would draw a curtain for them to recognise the Innocent
and in him themselves. [*She goes out.*]

CURTAIN

ACT II

Scene—La Comtesse d'Orchat's garden. Tall hedges, table and stools, an armchair. A wrought-iron gate with gilded spikes and coat of arms closes the garden in the background. Through it can be seen a meadow and groups of the populace stare through the grating at certain intervals during the scenes, clinging with their hands to the iron bars. A tall guard in gorgeous livery continually chases them off.

The Marquise in a wheel-chair under a tall shrub, a lackey behind her. The Comtesse is at the table with the Abbé. The Baron stands near by. Two footmen are serving lemonade.

COMTESSE. [*To the* BARON.] Just one glass of lemonade, my dear, and one moment of shade, and I'll have my revenge on you. . . . [*To the* MARQUISE.] Do you know, Mme. de Scarcle, there's not another ball-player like this M. de Clairvaux. He is of course not to be troubled by serious matters. The Innocent's cause finds him totally indifferent. But that is where my little d'Angelot is useful. He obtained me entré to the Bastille. I have seen the Innocent.

ABBÉ. Mme. d'Orchat is the first and only lady in Paris to have seen him.

MARQUISE. And what did you see?

COMTESSE. It smelt like a rabbit hutch.

MARQUISE. Which must have been not unfamiliar, since you are from time to time a shepherdess.

ABBÉ. It was indeed with admirable eloquence that Mme. d'Orchat made known her beautiful emotions to the Innocent.

BARON. To think of what an Innocent may see! One could positively envy him! And how did he look?

COMTESSE. Do not ask me that.

BARON. What did he say?

ARRÉ. You may gather, Clairvaux, that he does not receive countesses every day.

269

COMTESSE. He should be made presentable and tamed. What a dream it would be to have him here to a party. Only think of it, an Innocent in the flesh!

ABBÉ. It would be a triumph.

COMTESSE. But Monsieur de Launay, the governor of the Bastille, is far from gallant. He refuses to lend him to me.

MARQUISE. Nobody is so innocent that he should be celebrated for it.

ABBÉ. But the forty-three years of suffering, Marquise.

MARQUISE. Those belong to God. We have no right to touch them.

COMTESSE. You are severe, Madame, and may I be allowed to say that you no longer quite comprehend all that we feel.

MARQUISE. In my day, we were given to comprehend that suffering is a grace by which we are ranged among God's chosen.

COMTESSE. But it should be mitigated. You speak in the manner of the old school, Madame.

ABBÉ. [*In a low voice.*] One would never believe that once upon a time she too knew how to enjoy herself.

MARQUISE. Yes, I am old, but I have at least this advantage, that having lived as long as the one you call the Innocent, I therefore know him better, believe me, than you, who have but seen him.

ABBÉ. [*As before.*] She is beginning to wander. Shall we go back to our game?

COMTESSE. Madame, these gentlemen insist that I keep on playing ball.

MARQUISE. Do not mind leaving me alone.

COMTESSE. [*To the footman.*] I am to be called the moment Mme. Legros arrives. [*To the* MARQUISE.] That is the bourgeoise whom the Innocent wrote to. She goes about talking of nothing else.

ABBÉ. The one whom she least pleases with it is her husband.

BARON. I feel with him.

COMTESSE. She is so touching. She accosts strangers in the street, imploring their sympathy for the Innocent. She sits indefatigably in anterooms, waiting for audience. The other day did she not go so far as to stop the carriage of the Prince de Conti himself?

BARON. That is done by the chorus girls from the opera as well, probably to more purpose.

COMTESSE. She will come to good purpose here, she will be a sensation. The Chevalier d'Angelot is to bring her. I cannot have the Innocent but I have Mme. Legros.

ABBÉ. His prophetess.

MARQUISE. We too had actors come and play before us.

ABBÉ. She is not gracious, but that was how they were in the bygone days of piety.

COMTESSE. Au revoir, Madame. [*To the gentlemen.*] Messieurs. . . . [*They go out left.*]

MARQUISE. [*To one of the footmen.*] Baptiste, arrange my cushions for me, and push me further back into the shrubbery. In my day, gardens were not arranged with a view to providing a spectacle for the populace.

[*Enter* MME. LEGROS *and the* CHEVALIER.]

MME. LEGROS. I am tired. I have spoken to so many people that I have ceased to distinguish faces and scarcely hear my own voice. [*She sees the guard at the gates.*] Monsieur, my reason for coming here is no light one. I have come to see an immense wrong set right.

CHEVALIER. Madame, I implore you. You are wasting your time.

GUARD. Madame, M. le Chevalier, Mme. la Comtesse will be with you presently.

MME. LEGROS. Everyone must learn of it, for every one is guilty of having brought it about. [*To the guard.*] Monsieur, an innocent man has lain in prison for forty-three years.

GUARD. I regret to hear it, Madame.

MME. LEGROS. And through all that time he has suffered such great torture that we should think shame, Monsieur, to have lived and laughed during those years.

[CHEVALIER *slips a coin into the guard's hand.*]

GUARD. I am ashamed, Madame.

MME. LEGROS. [*To the two footmen.*] And you, Messieurs, you will not fail to do your part in repairing a wrong for which your children would hold you to account—an immense wrong, a crime generations old, a sin that has come down from father to son.

ONE OF THE FOOTMEN. Madame, you must intend this for Mme. la Comtesse. I will call her. [*Exit.*]

MME. LEGROS. [*To the* CHEVALIER.] But you, Monsieur, you at least will not be able to endure the disgrace which is brought upon the whole world by this so shameful suffering. Under our very feet here as we move can be heard the moans of one who lies buried alive, our victim. He is with us always, everywhere.

CHEVALIER. Mme. Legros, I am the Chevalier d' Angelot.

MME. LEGROS. Ah yes, I had forgotten.

CHEVALIER. You have forgotten that I know this all by heart. For weeks I have been hearing your recital in the salons and in the public places. I have very often wondered whether you will not come to believe it yourself by and by. Indeed for my part, I had almost done so.

MME. LEGROS. Listen to what your own heart says! Help me.

CHEVALIER. And then I remind myself that you are but pursuing with a persistence I am forced to admire ambitions so far-reaching that I can only surmise what they are.

MME. LEGROS. The salvation of an Innocent.

CHEVALIER. Where will you end? Had we a different monarch your destiny would be to become one of those mistresses who precipitate the greed and hatred of the populace into the royal bed itself together with their charming bodies.

MME. LEGROS. You insult me and yourself.

CHEVALIER. I will admit that you are greatly daring. Your home is in confusion—business, husband—you have left everything behind.

MME. LEGROS. Everything has left me since I realised the thing that was most important of all.

CHEVALIER. And from one day to another any of these uprisings you cause may send you to the gallows. This is no trifle for a person of such delicate charms as yours.

MME. LEGROS. I no longer fear anything.

CHEVALIER. Not even the condition under which I became your ally.

MME. LEGROS. Nothing.

CHEVALIER. When I look at you—this redoubtable enemy of mine, with the rosy glow in her cheeks and her lowered lashes—angel, devil—I do not know whether I want to embrace her knees or call the Provost.

MME. LEGROS. You will come to learn that this creature with all her mystery was nothing—nothing but the voice of the Innocent.

CHEVALIER. For my good fortune your Innocent shall be released from his tower, whether by achieving it I gain the grace of hell or heaven. You do not yet know what is to happen here today. A certain person is to be present, and upon her you are to bring your whole power to bear.

MME. LEGROS. Is she then so mighty?

CHEVALIER. To have brought that person here is as though I had embraced your knees.

MME. LEGROS. Monsieur, you have aided me in a task which when fulfilled will restore to mankind its vanished innocence. Yes, th

Innocent shall stand in our midst and the kingdom of heaven will have come.

MARQUISE. We too had actors come and play before us.

CHEVALIER. Your pardon, Madame, I had not seen you.

MARQUISE. My watching you will not put you out of countenance? I have seen these things so often.

CHEVALIER. It is little likely that you ever saw a Mme. Legros, Marquise. [*Exit left.*]

MME. LEGROS. Madame, I have come here to recall to your memory an innocent man. You have forgotten him. Every one has forgotten him. And yet the Bastille is so immense it is visible everywhere.

MARQUISE. In my day we chose for ourselves the piece we wished the actors to play before us.

MME. LEGROS. Madame!

MARQUISE. Be silent, you insolent actress! You parade your emotions as others do their bosoms. You have put your soul to school and can cause its voice to overflow the moment you find a place not altogether empty, even though it be occupied by one old woman only. An innocent man—forty-three years of torture in solitude—has that ever been your experience? For if it has, so much the worse to have abused it and turned it into a part that you play.

MME. LEGROS. [*Covering her face.*] How terrible this is! I am empty of word and thought. I am evil. Let them take me away from here. But there was a time when the Spirit filled me, and then the truth was there. That was a glorious moment! In the open sky I saw him—he spoke to me, and I told the people what he said and what I had seen. But they did not understand me. How few have understood me since. And yet there are thousands who need to know. . . . I too cannot at every moment feel so vast a thing, and therefore, what I speak sometimes becomes lies and empty chatter. But I must act if by acting the Innocent may be saved. Though through my own deeds it may be that I have become evil.

MARQUISE. [*More mildly.*] Have you ever reflected upon what it means to save a human being? This man, whom you call the Innocent, has grown old without your being aware of his existence, and now you wish to save him.

MME. LEGROS. Because I have been shown the horror of his life, and know that he did nothing to deserve them.

MARQUISE. Deserve is a word of vanity. Look at me. You know no more of me than of him. Would you insinuate that I deserve to have spent my lifetime behind walls? Yet that might well have been my fate, for of twin sisters one of us had to enter a convent because we were not rich enough to maintain our illustrious name. It did not fall upon me, but upon my sister who was better than I. And now when I think over the past, I know why—it was the wish of God to reward and shelter her.

MME. LEGROS. Have you then never known love?

MARQUISE. I counsel you to love God.

MME. LEGROS. God has no need of me. Whom has He need of? Like every one else He has forgotten the Innocent. But I am here, my heart beats for him, beats with such strength that it shall hammer down his walls be they never so strong.

[*Enter* COMTESSE, CHEVALIER, ABBÉ, BARON.]

COMTESSE. These gentlemen would not release me earlier from our game.

ABBÉ. The Innocent has waited long already.

COMTESSE. These things are no subject for jests.

CHEVALIER. Not in the presence of a bourgeoise, at least.

BARON. The Chevalier is afraid.

CHEVALIER. No—but he knows how to respect a passion.

COMTESSE. [*Embraces* MME. LEGROS *with kisses.*] Dear Legros, do let us be friends! Your Innocent enchants me beyond words. Ah, if only the Governor were more complaisant.

MME. LEGROS. I do not understand you, Madame.

COMTESSE. I am expecting guests. You will be nice to them, will you not? And tell them all your stories? I know that everything you do is inspired by true zeal for virtue. I too when I found myself face to face with the Innocent, had to cover my eyes.

ABBÉ. And your nose.

MME. LEGROS. But you cannot have seen him. The tower walls are of an immeasurable thickness and it is for me alone that the Innocent is waiting.

COMTESSE. Does he then know about you?

MME. LEGROS. I have been at work these many weeks. I have toiled to exhaustion. I lie, yes, I play the hypocrite—oh, what am I saying! —I am in torment, torment. I have not yet penetrated to where he lies. People stand between us, thousands and thousands of people—

all of them I must win over, touch their hearts and conquer them before I may reach the side of him who awaits me. And *you* say you have seen him. [*With a broken laugh.*]

COMTESSE. And so I have. You forget, my little Legros, that there are certain differences. One word to the Governor and I was conducted to where the prisoner lay. He fell at my feet, he kissed them, and the clanking of his chains at that moment was terrible and sweet to hear. And there and then the Innocent swore that to the end of his days he would never love nor worship another.

MME. LEGROS. You lie.

COMTESSE. You forget yourself.

MME. LEGROS. You lie and you are full of malice. You have not seen him, and you do not know that his face shines like the sun. Had you once but heard his voice you could no longer show yourself so petty and so spiteful. But I alone have heard it. He calls only to me. He loves only me. Understand, none but myself has any claim upon him.

COMTESSE. So naïvely jealous! Is it not diverting?

ABBÉ. One should not permit people of this kind to go too far.

[*A slight commotion in the crowd outside the garden gate.*]

MME. LEGROS. He is mine! I have given up everything for him— husband, home and peace. He warms me, he nourishes me; the whole of life, even you who are so unworthy, seems to me once more good when his eyes are upon me. Have a care, Madame, before you say that *you* have seen him.

COMTESSE. I grieve for you, my little Legros. But it is true.

MME. LEGROS. Hussy! [*Flies at her.*]

COMTESSE. My dear woman, why this agitation?

ABBÉ. You show great courage, Madame, but it is time this woman was removed from here.

CHEVALIER. [*To the* COMTESSE.] There is something I must inform you of later—some matter of importance.

BARON. I who understand nothing of affairs of state, should be glad to know when we are to go back to our game.

CHEVALIER. Affairs of state?

ABBÉ. That is his word for everything that is not tennis.

MARQUISE. You are wrong, Sylvaine. I was wrong also. This guest of ours is no actress. [*To* MME. LEGROS.] Give me your hand, child. I feel it quiver and tremble. It is as my sister's hand felt in mine on the day she took the veil. You are mistaken, child. You do not love a man in trouble. You love God.

MME. LEGROS. I love the man.

MARQUISE. [To the COMTESSE.] It seems to me, Sylvaine, that it is not you who have inherited our stormy hearts—I think they have passed over into the people. [To MME. LEGROS.] Let me look at you, my sister.

[MME. LEGROS kneels.]

COMTESSE. What is the matter with her?

ABBÉ. She is wandering again.

MARQUISE. I should like to be alone.

COMTESSE. Our guests will be arriving later. You would meet them in the house.

MARQUISE. Let me be taken to your chapel then.

[The COMTESSE accompanies the MARQUISE; CHEVALIER and ABBÉ follow. Populace leaves the gates.]

[The BARON furtively leaves the others as they go out and returns to MME. LEGROS.]

MME. LEGROS. [Startled, rises.] Monsieur.

BARON. [Earnestly.] I am the fanatical tennis player, just as you are the indefatigable altruist. You being willing, let us both unmask.

MME. LEGROS. I have no mask to take off, Monsieur.

BARON. Then keep it on. All that matters is that you understand me correctly. I have something agreeable to tell you, first of all. You are to meet the Queen here. . . . You did not understand me.

MME. LEGROS. I am glad of it, Monsieur.

BARON. Does it not frighten you?

MME. LEGROS. Once it would have frightened me very much, Monsieur. You must pardon me that now a Queen can frighten me no longer.

BARON. You are aware of the advantages you may derive from such an encounter?

MME. LEGROS. Ah, the Chevalier, that is his doing! How good he is. I knew it. It is only through error that people are not good.

BARON. The Chevalier may have his reasons for doing you a favour. But that has nothing to do with his true object in bringing the Queen here today. This is the rendezvous for a political meeting between the Chevalier and the Queen, which, as he is watched by us, he could have nowhere else.

MME. LEGROS. Who are you?

BARON. A messenger in the service of someone who mistrusts the Queen.

MME. LEGROS. But she is coming here. She wishes to see me! She will help me.

BARON. You will never realise that the attention of this world is not focussed upon you and your Innocent. You imagine that upon these lawns nothing else is discussed or thought about. It is as though I were to imagine that tennis is the only game worth playing.

MME. LEGROS. Then make it so, as I make all those whom I meet in byways and in palaces and in attics, from the gutter to the royal throne, see only this one thing, care and long for this alone.

BARON. I have no interest in hindering you if you will consent to do me a slight service in an unimportant matter—oh, I am not going to ask of you what the Chevalier has asked. There is a certain name I wish to know, merely a name that will be mentioned in the conversation between the Chevalier and the Queen. Nothing more.

MME, LEGROS. Why do you ask?

BARON. I am inquisitive, Madame! This name will pass between the Queen and the Chevalier. It is the name of an Austrian agent whom the Queen does not yet know, and whom she wishes to approach unobserved. We wish to prevent this, and what we expect of you, Mme. Legros, who will be the only witness present at their interview, is the name which the Queen is coming here to learn.

MME. LEGROS. But she is coming here because it has reached even her ears that an innocent man is suffering. Monsieur, you too will help me. You are no different from the Chevalier and the rest. You all believe that what you want is to satisfy your own wicked desires. But at last you learn that what your hearts truly long for is to be free from the burden of this great wrong.

BARON. You are all too persuasive. I confess that no scruples deter you. Observing you, one is tempted to believe that you know much, too much, of the vices of men and the chimeras by which they live.

MME. LEGROS. I was not so before I took up my task. Since then I have learned to know people a little. One cannot cast out vices, one can but cosset them until they turn into virtues. Men are ashamed of the good that is in them. They need to be seduced into the wantonness of being kind.

BARON. Mme. Legros, you are dangerous. You are a courtesan of virtue.

MME. LEGROS. Too well I know I am not worthy to be the instrument of such great events.

[COMTESSE and CHEVALIER enter at left. The CHEVALIER is

talking in a low voice, then lays his finger on his lips. COMTESSE *startled, bows involuntarily.*]

BARON. He is telling her now. You perceive that we have no time to lose. [*To the Chevalier.*] You are right, d'Angelot, this person is worthy of respect. She is not merely interesting. I hope she may even be useful. . . .

CHEVALIER. At tennis?

[COMTESSE *and* CHEVALIER *go out.*]

BARON. You will overhear the name, Mme. Legros. Do not fail to inform me of it.

MME. LEGROS. What name? Pray, Monsieur, do not ask me to do an injury to the Chevalier. He is so good.

BARON. Let us be brief, somebody is coming. Obey me or your Innocent is lost. Doubtless you will exercise all your artifice and all your charms of candour upon the Queen, but you will do so in vain. We have means to render ineffectual even the most beneficent orders of Her Majesty.

MME. LEGROS. That, Monsieur, you will not do. You will not prolong injustice. What other object could you pursue more urgent than the salvation of an Innocent?

BARON. It is superfluous to declaim. Will you tell me the name they mention?

MME. LEGROS. That would be treachery. How should I betray the Chevalier who has lent me his aid in the fulfillment of the task by which I am to rid my soul of its great guilt?

BARON. He could never know. He has no suspicion of my identity. Shall I have the name?

MME. LEGROS. I cannot. Would their revenge fall on him?

BARON. I will not hide from you the fact that his freedom is endangered. But you shall have the Innocent instead.

MME. LEGROS. I cannot do it.

BARON. Then your cause is lost.

MME. LEGROS. Already I have turned to lies. I have become an actress. I have promised my body as a price. Now I am to become a traitress.

BARON. Your word, Mme. Legros.

MME. LEGROS. I give it.

[COMTESSE, CHEVALIER, ABBÉ *come back.*]

COMTESSE. Nobody is to see. I am weary of the annoyances you cause me.

CHEVALIER. I am inconsolable, but it is the Queen's desire. She wishes to remain incognito, and talk only to Mme. Legros. I shall be present. You will see that your guests avoid the garden.

BARON. [*To the* COMTESSE.] This Mme. Legros is so strange to this world of ours here, that she truly believes that it contains none but evil and scheming people. Imagine that!

CHEVALIER. [*To* MME. LEGROS.] The person of whom I spoke will be here presently. She is a stranger but she has much influence.

MME. LEGROS. I am—[*She hesitates.*]—ready to face whatever may come, that I may win him.

CHEVALIER. Nobody here will receive her, and she will depart unaccompanied. Nobody will be allowed to follow her. If you should ever see her again you are to make no sign of recognition. Do you agree to these terms?

MME. LEGROS. To any.

[CHEVALIER *gives whispered instructions to a guard at the gate, and withdraws left.*]

[MME. LEGROS *is left standing alone, centre.*]

[*The* QUEEN, *in a hooded cloak of dark silk, emerges hastily from the shrubbery. She is accompanied by the* CHEVALIER *and* MME. CROZET, *who remains in the background. The* COMTESSE, ABBÉ, BARON *make deep obeisances and silently disappear.*]

QUEEN. [*Regards* MME. LEGROS *closely and with disfavour. She turns away.*] Chevalier, are you there?

CHEVALIER. [*Bowing slightly as he advances.*] Madame, I await your commands.

QUEEN. The person in whose behalf you spoke to me . . . ?

CHEVALIER. This is she, Madame.

QUEEN. [*Raises her lorgnette.*] Indeed, I should have noticed her standing there in the broad sunlight. Mme. Crozet, was I brought here to have this person's youth flaunted before me? [*She draws her hood far down.*]

CHEVALIER. [*Whispering to* MME. LEGROS.] Make haste and move into the shade.

[*The populace gathers at the gate.*]

QUEEN. She has moreover the flat nose so characteristic of the common people here. Even with such a nose, however, one is of course young once. [*Whispering to the* CHEVALIER.] The chief thing first. The name?

[CHEVALIER *whispers.*]

[BARON *appears behind a shrub and signals to* MME. LEGROS.]

[Mme. Legros *listens, starts, hears the* Chevalier *divulge the name and whispers it to the* Baron *round the corner of the shrubbery.* Baron *exit.*]

[*The* Queen *in some fear moves downstage.*]

QUEEN. Those crowds there at the gate—let them be chased away. What do these people want of me? I do not doubt, Chevalier, that this person whom you are to present to me has but some insolence in mind. Are you certain she does not know who I am?

CHEVALIER. Most certain, Madame. She is a simple woman and will touch you deeply, Madame, by the unworldliness of her innocence. It is as though one were to meet a being out of the morning of the world. She is proof of the original virtue of mankind.

QUEEN. That is a thing I have always believed in. It is only the long process of corruption down through the ages that has caused their minds to stray so that they deny us our rights. [*To* Mme. Legros.] I am a friend of virtue. You also are reputed to love it. That is why I have come.

MME. LEGROS. [*Standing with bowed head, starts.*] Madame, my guilt is great. I am a traitress.

QUEEN. A traitress?

CHEVALIER. She accuses herself of every crime because she believes that the suffering of an innocent man is at her door and at the doors of all of us. It is very strange.

MME. LEGROS. Yes, we must assume the burden of all crimes until the tower is forced open and innocence returns among us. Madame, fearful things are coming to pass in this country.

QUEEN. In this country? Why do you tell that to *me?*

MME. LEGROS. And in all the world, vast though it is. But the Bastille is here, and it is there that an Innocent has groaned unheard for three and forty years. So massive is the tower here, Madame.

QUEEN. [*To* Chevalier.] Is this all? Nothing but the usual excitable complaints about the so-called tyranny in the Bastille? Without the Bastille how would our rule be possible? As well ask for the end of the world. So this is the entertainment you promised me, Monsieur.

CHEVALIER. Madame, I am in despair that you have fared so badly. This person is *gauche.* She used to be more amusing. It may be that her talent is failing her. Besides, she has suffered a certain annoyance in this house, for the Comtesse d'Orchat was inspired to display too vivid an interest in the Innocent. That is comprehensible. He is all the fashion now.

QUEEN. That I cannot be said not to understand. [*To* MME. LEGROS.] Your name then is Madame . . .

CHEVALIER. [*Whispering.*] Legros.

QUEEN. Legros. And you are working in the interest of the prisoner . . .

CHEVALIER. [*As before.*] Latude.

QUEEN. Latude. It would appear that he is a very dangerous man. You are doing something that is strictly forbidden. However, I share your sensibility as all the others do. Madame Crozet, my handkerchief. [*She wipes her eyes.*] It moves me to hear of people whom life goes hard with, although—had they done their duty . . .

MME. LEGROS. Madame, of such tears as these I have seen too many by now, wet eyes and a dry heart.

CHEVALIER. [*In an undertone, to* MME. LEGROS.] What are you doing?

MME. LEGROS. Leave me. I have been invited here to bring tears to the eyes of people dying of ennui. I am weary of bringing great suffering to small hearts. I thought this was not as the others. When this lady entered, I felt as though I stood in the presence of goodness and majesty. New hope revived within me. Treacherous hope. Go, Madame, the Innocent cannot help you nor you him.

CHEVALIER. [*Whispering.*] This is astounding. She sensed the presence of the Queen.

QUEEN. What is there amazing in that? The reverse would have been. Besides her speech is bold, too bold by far.

CHEVALIER. That is what I meant. I am in despair, Madame, to have incurred your displeasure. [*He retires, and as he passes* MME. LEGROS, *whispers.*] Have a care.

MME. LEGROS. [*Breaking out.*] I have been careful long enough. Now they shall hear the truth. How I have flattered in order to turn duty into pleasure for all these people! I have penetrated the hearts of market women with the emotions of holy saints. In the houses of the common people I have spiced their food with noble thoughts. I have entered the carriages of grand ladies decked out in gay attire and they have invited me to drive with them so that they might be made to sigh just as they had used their little monkey pets to make them laugh. How deep has been my shame before him, the Innocent, watching me from his dungeon. How I have hated you all— the concerts in your mansions, where some light singer would first appear, then I! Hated—your cooing and flirting, your courtesy devoid of love, your passive benevolence, your beauty and your glamour—so paltry and insipid did you but know it, as know you would were the Innocent—the Innocent—once to set foot among you.

QUEEN. Ah! You confess it. She admits, Chevalier, that she hates us. I foresaw this. The people are false and insubordinate. I hate them too. I have always hated them, from the first day.

MME. LEGROS. But I have won you back, I have made you desire the good, sigh for it. Now you cover your ears when you hear the rattle of the chains which you have forged. You yourselves now throw your weight against that tower until it must give way—yes, I have bored my way through to you, working in my tunnel until it brought me to the highest lords of the land, to the foot of the very throne itself. I have been at Versailles.

QUEEN. You have been at Versailles?

MME. LEGROS. I had surmounted all the barriers of your society, the walls of all your hearts had fallen before me. Then when the Queen drove by . . .

QUEEN. You saw her?

MME. LEGROS. I had of her only the mud from the wheels of the carriage that bore her from one vain pleasure to the next. But as she passed by me then I knew—I had assumed too great a task, I had driven my strength beyond endurance. Oh! I should have dragged her from her seat, and spoken to her then in words that only three and forty years of innocent suffering could find. [*She advances menacingly.*]

QUEEN. [*Shrieks.*] Chevalier! [*Her cloak slips from her, and she stands revealed in a dress of vivid colour.*]

[CHEVALIER *springs to her assistance, grasps* MME. LEGROS *firmly, pulls her away.*]

MME. LEGROS. [*Breaks down.*] But they wrenched me back. I fell. I knew no more.

QUEEN. Yes, you fainted. And the Queen laughed, did she not? [*She laughs.*] Let her go, Chevalier, we would hear the rest of this story. This child interests me. She has made my heart beat a little faster. [*Raises her lorgnette and subjects* MME. LEGROS *to a long and minute scrutiny.*] She shall tell me how she became as we see her now. What has this Innocent to do with her? What is the origin of this impertinent concern in an affair of state which should occupy none of our common subjects?

[LEGROS *and the* YOUNG RELATIVE *appear among the crowd outside the gates.*]

MME. LEGROS. [*Hesitantly, puts her hand to her brow.*] How did it happen? A letter fell from the tower. I have greatly loved, Madame. So beautiful is he who wrote that letter. You too would love him. All, all are capable of loving. I have not judged you amiss. [*She stands erect.*] Men have a common heart, a great and glowing heart. Mine is but a little part of it, yet this love I have for the Innocent has given it much power. [*In vehement exhortation.*] Love him, all men, and you shall be invincible!

QUEEN. [*Trips mincingly before* MME. LEGROS.] Now she is boring me. [*To the* CHEVALIER.] Is this all she can do? I have naturally my own thoughts as to her relations with this M. Innocent. [*She laughs and whispers to the* CHEVALIER.]

M. LEGROS. I shall put an end to this.

YOUNG RELATIVE. Those are great lords and ladies in there.

M. LEGROS. And I am her husband. Who, if not I, should have compassion for her to see these people mistreat her so? At home, she hears no word of kindness and spends the nights upon a chair.

YOUNG RELATIVE. A harlot, ready for every noble lord that wants her—the byword and abomination of the whole quarter, carrying on some unnatural love affair with her loathsome Innocent wallowing in his dirt. Everybody knows it, even Colas, who is a soldier in the Bastille, and whom I shall marry when you bring this person back.

M. LEGROS. This is too much. I will make an end of it once for all. [*Tries to force his way through the gate.*]

GUARD. No admittance here.

M. LEGROS. I'll have no nonsense. That is my wife. [*Thrusts the guard aside. The crowd gathers.*]

QUEEN. What is this? [*She looks out.*]

CHEVALIER. [*To* M. LEGROS.] What do you want here?

M. LEGROS. Something that does not belong to you. I want my wife. I stand upon my rights. [*Seizes* MME. LEGROS.] Harlot! Get back to your home.

CHEVALIER. [*Releases* MME. LEGROS.] I must demand respect before these ladies. [*To the* QUEEN.] There is nothing to fear, Madame. It is only her husband. You will realise that their ménage has suffered some slight disturbance.

QUEEN. How amusing! What is he going to do?

M. LEGROS. [*Removing his hat.*] By your leave, Mesdames, I have always been a man of courtesy. It shall never be said that I fail in the regard due to ladies. But this is my wife, and her conduct is—I may not say what it is. [*To* MME. LEGROS.] Are you not ashamed, Mme. Legros? Your name is a byword. People point their fingers at you. You neglect your business and your home. Have you any complaint against your husband? Then why should you run away from him?

CHEVALIER. [*Indicating the* YOUNG RELATIVE.] M. Legros, you have not been without consolation. I congratulate you. You have taste.

YOUNG RELATIVE. [*Who has meanwhile entered.*] No one can say any slander of me.

QUEEN. A charming family. This is just as I imagined the people to be.

M. LEGROS. Though I may have erred, that is a matter which concerns none but Mme. Legros and myself—certainly not the lords and ladies who have turned my wife's head for their own amusement. There are those who say that the day will come when all accounts shall be brought to balance. A burgher of Paris is not to be laughed by any ridiculous, bedizened old woman like that one there.

CHEVALIER. [*Drawing his sword.*] Get out!

M. LEGROS. Less still by the young jackanapes whom she keeps. [*Strikes the sword out of the* CHEVALIER'*s hand.*]

[*The crowd behind the gate grows turbulent, trying to pass the guard.*]

MME. CROZET. Fly, Madame!

QUEEN. [*Moves a step forward.*] Down on your knees, fool! Do you not see who I am?

M. LEGROS. [*Kneels, terrified.*] I am lost!

VOICES IN THE CROWD. It is the Queen! Down with her!

[*Soldiers disperse the mob.*]

QUEEN. Get up—I do not wish to have a scene.

M. LEGROS. If your Majesty would only deign to consider a poor man's distress! My wife causes me much grief—it has become almost impossible to make a livelihood. The taxes on materials rise continually—nobody can afford to buy. These are hard times.

QUEEN. Only the people of Paris are greedy and insurgent. Why do you not live in the country? Shepherds are carefree and well content.

CHEVALIER. Her Majesty dismisses you.

[M. LEGROS *and the* YOUNG RELATIVE *bow and leave.*]

CHEVALIER. Will your Majesty not profit by this opportunity to leave under military protection?

QUEEN. Not yet. Our heroine only now becomes interesting—the heroine whose name you have so dinned into my ears. I now see that she displays the most piquant manners.

CHEVALIER. Then let us at least take shelter in the shrubbery.

[MME. CROZET *withdraws.*]

QUEEN. Yes, that will be more cosy. . . . Now let our heroine confirm certain suspicions of mine concerning her Innocent. [*She whispers, titters.*]

CHEVALIER. Mme. Legros.

[MME. LEGROS *rigid and withdrawn, starts.*]

CHEVALIER. Have your wits gone wool-gathering, or did you observe what has just happened here? There was noise enough.

MME. LEGROS. I am bewildered at the high honour of finding myself in the presence of the Queen of France. [*She bows.*] Madame, a great wrong has been committed. Your noble kingdom groans under it. You have it in your power to make all your subjects happy again.

QUEEN. Entertainment is what I desire above all things. Can you blame me for that?

CHEVALIER. [*Not without irony.*] That is what your subjects love you for.

MME. LEGROS. Madame, an Innocent . . .

QUEEN. Ah yes, come nearer, little one, tell me your story in all true honesty. If you do that, I shall be well inclined to help you. You know that I can . . . well, you may surely trust your Queen. Come now . . . come now.

CHEVALIER. Do you allow a Queen to entreat you, Mme. Legros?

MME. LEGROS. I do not know what the Queen wishes me to say. A letter fell from the tower.

QUEEN. Appointing a rendezvous.

MME. LEGROS. [*Recoiling.*] You would believe that? That is what only the most unworthy say.

QUEEN. No one said it to me. It was my own thought.

MME. LEGROS. Those who envy me say it, unclean minds that they have. It is the opinion of the gutters.

QUEEN. Come, confess now, how did you obtain entrance into the Bastille? By giving your favours to one of the guards? Is it not so? Or to several? Perhaps to many of them.

[MME. LEGROS *bows her head, with a low moan.*]

QUEEN. [*Reaches her hand backwards for the* CHEVALIER'S.] Do you see? It is as I thought.

CHEVALIER. So much the worse then, for the good burgher who had the temerity to disarm me a moment ago.

QUEEN. And how was it in the prisoner's cell, very dismal? It comes to one's ears that some of our subjects indulge in strange pastimes. The Comtesse d'Argilles spent a whole night in the vaults of her house with a corpse, so they say.

CHEVALIER. [*Erect.*] We have experienced until we are satiated— everything but death. That alone can still tempt us.

MME. LEGROS. I have loved him. Promise me his freedom and I will tell you all.

QUEEN. I promise.

MME. LEGROS. I have the Queen's word.

CHEVALIER. [*Leaning towards the* QUEEN.] You are to be envied.

QUEEN. Well, how was it in the tomb? Did he treat you brutally?

MME. LEGROS. He took me as if I were on the threshold of death. I felt him gaunt as Death himself. The odour of dissolution was in my nostrils as we kissed, sweeter than the perfume of flowers in the earth above. For the flowers lie—up here anguish and vulgarity alone exist. I wish to join him in his tomb again—to be dead—dead.

[*She staggers, sways, bows her head in her arms, and sobs.* QUEEN *stretches her limbs as if in the exhausted aftermath of passion.* CHEVALIER *kisses her upon the mouth. Pause.* QUEEN *sighs, rises.*]

CHEVALIER [*To* MME. LEGROS.] This is what I call sending for the Provost.

[MME. LEGROS *lifts her head and looks at the* QUEEN. QUEEN *drops her eyes.*]

CHEVALIER. Is it your Majesty's wish that your carriage be brought?

QUEEN. I am going. [*Formally.*] You have done well, Chevalier, in presenting this person to me. She well merits attention. [*To* MME. LEGROS.] You have pleased me. You may ask a boon.

MME. LEGROS. Your Majesty has promised to set free the Innocent now in the Bastille.

QUEEN. Oh yes—I had forgotten. But for yourself—what do you wish for yourself?

MME. LEGROS. [*Looks about, shrugging her shoulders.*] Here?

CHEVALIER. At court, her Majesty means—a pension—an office for your husband.

QUEEN. I am waiting.

MME. LEGROS. I have no other wish.

CHEVALIER. That is not possible.

QUEEN. You are lacking in manners, my good woman.

CHEVALIER. She is not yet quite herself. I refuse to believe she knows what she is saying.

QUEEN. Or can it be out of virtue? This is most touching. Mme. Crozet, my handkerchief.

CHEVALIER. That would be too much. I should indeed be embarrassed to have to believe it.

[MME. CROZET *hands the* QUEEN *her handkerchief.*]

QUEEN. It shall never be said that the Queen of France does not know how to reward virtue. We command that the prisoner be released from his remaining term of punishment. He shall be brought before our Academy together with the person who has so greatly interested herself in his behalf. And upon this person the Academy shall bestow the prize for virtue. This is our command. [*She goes towards the exit, turns, in haste.*] But the grounds for the bestowal of this prize shall not be made known. Chevalier, I forbid the Speaker of the Academy to say why this award has been made. [*Exit.*]

[*Re-enter* COMTESSE, ABBÉ, BARON *from the left. They talk in whispers as the* QUEEN *departs.*]

COMTESSE. This is unheard of. The Queen has given this woman audience for more than an hour. What can it mean?

[CHEVALIER *returns, bows low before* MME. LEGROS.]

ABBÉ. See how he treats her. We will be wise to go carefully.

COMTESSE. Great heavens, what appointment has been given her? [*To the* CHEVALIER.] Was the Queen satisfied?

CHEVALIER. Her Majesty's sensibility could not but respond to such great virtue. The Queen has commanded that the Innocent be released.

COMTESSE. I am overwhelmed with emotion. Is it permitted to pay one's respects to this lady?

BARON. [*To* MME. LEGROS.] Madame, I hear that you have achieved your most noble purpose. Allow me to present my felicitations. I beg that you will continue to hold me in your august favour.

[MME. LEGROS *looks at him in horror, and rushes from him downstage.*]

COMTESSE *and* ABBÉ. What has come over her?

CHEVALIER. I have ceased to understand her.

COMTESSE. What is to be her future rank?

CHEVALIER. None. And that you may believe or else think me a party to some new intrigue, as you will.

COMTESSE. An hour alone with the Queen—and no favour? Such simplicity cannot be. It must be virtue, I suppose.

CHEVALIER. I hope not. How much too difficult life would be if it were as beautiful as that.

COMTESSE. Why does she not look happy then?

ABBÉ. Vanity of the spirit—*that* is never satisfied.

MME. LEGROS. [*Downstage, alone.*] It has cost too much.

CURTAIN

ACT III

Scene.—Room adjoining the LEGROS' *shop, with window and door rear giving on to a side street. The interior of the house is visible left.* MONSIEUR LEGROS, *the* YOUNG RELATIVE, VIGNON, MADAME TOUCHE, *and* FANCHON *are present.*

MME. TOUCHE. I'll tell you what she is, M. Legros. Presently she'll be home after her triumph, and then I shall tell her myself. A saint, that's what she is.

M. LEGROS. I am forced to believe it.

MME. TOUCHE. If you had only seen her when she came into that hall with the domed roof where all the gentlemen of the Academy awaited her . . . ! They let *me* in, but not you, M. Vignon. Of course you have not a cousin a footman in the royal palace.

VIGNON. That is true. A gentleman of the Garde Française honours me with his friendship, however, and so I saw Mme. Legros as she left her carriage to enter the Academy. It was as though I had never known her—a grand lady.

MME. TOUCHE. My word is better—a saint. And the prize for virtue is said to amount to a thousand louis.

VIGNON. It was a solemn moment too when one looked upon the Innocent. He wore an embroidered coat. His beard was long and white. They had crowned him with flowers.

YOUNG RELATIVE. They say he's nothing but an old scamp, just the same.

M. LEGROS. You mind your tongue.

FANCHON. How happy Mme. Legros must be! I have always wished her that.

MME. TOUCHE. All of us have been on her side since the very beginning. The whole of Paris turned out to see her. Her name was on every tongue.

VIGNON. And every one was loud in her praise.

LEGROS. It does me great honour.

289

MME. TOUCHE. And to have your wife's virtue bring you in so much money.

VIGNON. It seems indeed that something of great moment has happened, and that Mme. Legros who is known to all of us has brought it about. How strange it is that so often we entertain angels unawares.

M. LEGROS. And when it all concerns one's own wife, one does not know what to think.

MME. TOUCHE. All sorts of things might have been thought before. But she has been so successful.

FANCHON. She has set the Innocent free. How dearly I love her!

VIGNON. Dangerous words were to be heard in the crowd, as might have been expected. Talk of other Innocents deserving freedom in the Bastille and out of it. This will be but a beginning.

MME. TOUCHE. There were many evil looking folk about the streets. Who can tell what may follow this? Very little respect was shown when certain gentlemen of high office made their appearance.

M. LEGROS. Mme. Legros and I have nothing but respect for those above us.

VIGNON. Mme. Legros had no other thought than good. But that did not prevent my friend of the "Garde" from entertaining grave misgivings.

[*The crowd assembles outside the window. The door is opened.*]

[MME. LEGROS *enters slowly, the people falling back for her. She wears a white veil; her face is turned upward. She smiles with beatitude.*]

VOICES. Long live Mme. Legros! She has set the Innocent free. The masters and the rich are not laughing this morning. They have seen an Innocent set free. We have still more to show them. Our lives will be happier now. Prices will go down. Mme. Legros is a saint. Look at her face, how it shines. The sun does not shine so in this lane of ours. Mme. Legros is from our lane and she is a saint. Hail the saint! Hail the holy one! [*Many kneel.*]

VIGNON. Mme. Legros, we are assembled here to express our admiration for what you have done.

A MAN. What is *he* after? Kneeling down!

ANOTHER. You didn't admire her a little while ago. You shouted name after her then. Kneeling down! We were weak, all of us.

MME. TOUCHE. [*Dropping hurriedly to her knees.*] I was the first to know about her.

    [M. LEGROS *casts a bewildered look about him, assumes an expression of piety and also kneels.*]

MME. LEGROS [*Makes a step forward hesitatingly and touches the head of the kneeling* FANCHON.] Who is this? Fanchon! Dear child, get up. [*She turns.*] And all of you. What are you kneeling for? Because the Innocent is free? You yourselves freed him. Do not give me that credit, for I have been nothing more than your unworthy mouthpiece. You are now absolved of the great wrong.

SOMEBODY. [*Rising.*] I feel as though I had escaped from the Bastille myself.

ANOTHER. I have not drunk a drop today but I feel like singing out loud.

MME. TOUCHE. It is Legros who will sing today. What do you say, Legros? Think of having a wife like this!

M. LEGROS. [*In their midst.*] It is too much for me. [*He bows awkwardly before* MME. LEGROS.]

MME. LEGROS. [*Gives him her hand.*] My dear husband . . . [*There is an embarrassed silence.*]

    [*Crowd applauds.*]

VIGNON. [*To* MME. TOUCHE.] I would not change places with Legros if they gave me the whole Academy for a gift.

MME. TOUCHE. Surely you cannot mean you would not like to have a saint for your wife!

VOICES. This way, children, come for the saint! This way. We shall have a glorious celebration.

    [*Children all dressed in white, make their way through the crowd that falls back to give them access to* MME. LEGROS. *They dance around her, entwining her as they do so in a long rope of flowers.*]

    [*A Teacher gives the children a signal to say their speech.*]

FIRST CHILD. We thank you, Mme. Legros, for this beautiful day.

SECOND CHILD. And for having taught us virtue.

THIRD CHILD. We shall never forget.

FOURTH CHILD. And when we grow up we shall follow your example.

MME. LEGROS. You dear children! [*She speaks over their heads to the crowd.*] Taught you virtue, do you say? I could not do that. Some day you may know it. It will come to you like a fearful secret and rob you of your peace. And afterwards you will come to doubt whether it was indeed virtue. But you must believe in it, do you hear me? Otherwise, how shall the Innocent be set free? . . . Ah, he is free already, and I am so tired.

FANCHON [*Supports her.*] Now you must rest, Mme. Legros. We all love you so much.

VOICES. Is she not coming?

MME. TOUCHE. A celebration has been arranged for you. You must not deny your neighbours that pleasure, or you will displease them greatly.

VOICES. Forward to Vignon's! With Mme. Legros in our midst.

VIGNON. Mme. Legros, there awaits you in my house a very modest meal. Will you do me the honour?

MME. LEGROS. I am exhausted, M. Vignon. Will you not excuse me? This has overspent my strength. You would not wish to have a sick woman at your meal.

MME. TOUCHE. Already we are not good enough for her, it seems.

FANCHON. Stop tormenting her.

VIGNON. Gentlemen, let us lead the way. Mme. Legros needs quiet. You must see that. She has done a great deal for all of us.

VOICES. We are not barbarians. The saint has deserved her rest. [*The people withdraw.*] Hail the saint!

M. LEGROS. [*To the* YOUNG RELATIVE.] Shut the door.

YOUNG RELATIVE. [*Whispering.*] Now what's to do?

MME. LEGROS. [*In an armchair, sits gazing before her. Suddenly she becomes aware of her surroundings.*] Is anyone here?

M. LEGROS. Only ourselves—Lisette and I. The others have all gone over to Vignon's. [*Timidly.*] Could we now eat something perhaps?

MME. LEGROS. Surely yes—dinner—and the shop. Customers are waiting. [*She makes a movement to rise.*]

M. LEGROS. There is nobody there. It is a long time now since we have had a customer waiting.

YOUNG RELATIVE. And I have nothing in the house to eat.

M. LEGROS. Why not? You lazy piece!

YOUNG RELATIVE. [*Impertinently.*] Well, hasn't the house been full of gaping crowds the whole morning? Nobody works at a fair.

M. LEGROS. Into the kitchen with you, at once!

YOUNG RELATIVE. Give me some money then. There'll be nothing to eat if you don't.

M. LEGROS. You've spent the household money on your finery again. You wait. [*He aims a blow at her.*]

YOUNG RELATIVE. Not so fast. I am not Mme. Legros. You have Mme. Legros back now. I turn the house over to her, blows included.

M. LEGROS. Out of here, I say!

YOUNG RELATIVE. Enjoy yourself with your saint. [*Exit.*]

MME. LEGROS. Why don't you give her money to buy food?

M. LEGROS. [*First hesitates, then says in a rush.*] Because I have none.

MME. LEGROS. You have none?

M. LEGROS. If it stops coming in, there comes a day when there is no more left. With the housewife gone, that day comes soon.

MME. LEGROS. [*Still confused in her mind, gets up.*] How long it is since I have seen to anything. Where are the laces from Alençon?

M. LEGROS. They have all been sold at a sacrifice.

MME. LEGROS. Does your apprentice not come to meals any more?

M. LEGROS. I sent him away. There was no work for him.

MME. LEGROS. Dear husband, then we have become poor.

M. LEGROS. Not you, Mme. Legros, certainly not you. Only I. You have earned much in this time. [*He takes a bag from the dresser, puts it on the table.*]

MME. LEGROS. What is that?

M. LEGROS. Your prize for virtue.

MME. LEGROS. [*Drops her eyes.*] You take this money, please.

M. LEGROS. I have never taken the money of others.

MME. LEGROS. [*At the table.*] What is mine is yours also.

M. LEGROS. At other times. Not this time.

MME. LEGROS. You are my lord and master.

M. LEGROS. That I have not been in this matter. Not I—the Innocent. Share the money with him. [*Puts the bag away where he took it from.*]

MME. LEGROS. I wanted to give it all to him, but his relatives refused it.

M. LEGROS. He finds himself all of a sudden with relatives?

MME. LEGROS. Only a little while ago some rich people appeared, noblemen too, saying they were his kinsmen. [LEGROS *bursts out laughing.*]

M. LEGROS. This thing is certainly turning out not at all badly for him.

MME. LEGROS. It was bad enough for him for many years.

M. LEGROS. And that is why he is being fed and pampered now. Not every one can boast of as much.

MME. LEGROS. I have made him rich, and you poor. You reproach me, and you are right. I ask your forgiveness.

M. LEGROS. I have nothing to forgive a saint.

MME. LEGROS. What I did, I had to do.

M. LEGROS. And everyone speaks your praises. I was wrong to try and prevent you.

MME. LEGROS. Now it is done. I must remember that it is all over and ended.

M. LEGROS. I do not believe that. A little of what you have done is bound to remain. Those people out there will still have certain rights over you.

MME. LEGROS. I have come back to you.

M. LEGROS. You went too far away. Your deed was too extraordinary. After such a career one does not become again the wife of the hosier Legros.

MME. LEGROS. But that is what I am.

M. LEGROS. They say I am to worship you—and I do.

MME. LEGROS. Be my husband as before.

M. LEGROS. I knelt to you.

MME. LEGROS. Shall I kneel now to you then? [*She attempts to do so.*] See how weak I am. It seems to me that all I did was in vain. I wanted to hear you speak to me again in your loud voice, and grasp me roughly as you used to. Forgive me, dear husband, forgive me for having freed an Innocent from the tower. [LEGROS *turns to the door.*] You will not? Do you not love me any more? Were you then glad in your heart that I was so much from home? Have I been supplanted?

M. LEGROS. Shall a saint prepare my soup? Selling stockings is no occupation for a saint. [*Exit.*]

MME. LEGROS. [*At the closed door.*] Have a care, Legros, or I will leave your house indeed.

YOUNG RELATIVE. [*Comes in.*] If you want to eat, Mme. Legros, you may come into the kitchen. There is nothing but potatoes.

MME. LEGROS. Indeed. I may come into the kitchen? And may I also lie down in my bed—unless I find it has been defiled in my absence?

YOUNG RELATIVE. I'm as clean as you are.

MME. LEGROS. Vermin, that's what you are. You came creeping into my house and tried to gnaw me out of it. Go!

YOUNG RELATIVE. If I am to be turned out of doors, only M. Legros can do that, and he will know better. He needs me.

MME. LEGROS. What for? Say it if you dare!

YOUNG RELATIVE. And why not? For everything that it is a woman's place to be in the household. You left M. Legros, so I have been taking care of him.

MME. LEGROS. Do you love him too?

YOUNG RELATIVE. What concern is that of yours?

MME. LEGROS. Because I—I loved him.

YOUNG RELATIVE. Until you lost your head over the Innocent.

MME. LEGROS. Viper! [*Throws herself upon the* YOUNG RELATIVE, *who puts the table between them.*]

YOUNG RELATIVE. It is the truth. That's why you have become a saint, while I who took care of M. Legros, get nothing but abuse.

MME. LEGROS. I will wring your neck.

YOUNG RELATIVE. A pretty saint! I shall tell M. Legros. He was saying the other day that he only wished he was rid of you. [*Exit.*]

MME. LEGROS. [*Half-fainting, leans against the wall.*] Rid of me! What will become of me? A pretty saint! All the shameful things done. Nothing too base. Not even—oh God—the promise of her body . . . Legros was right. No, it is not over. Somebody out there still has his rights over me. [*She draws herself up.*] What do I fear? Whom have I . . . ? It may be that he will come.

[CHEVALIER *stands in the doorway.*]

[MME. LEGROS *shrieks, throws out her hands.*]

CHEVALIER. Do not be afraid. I know that I have no place at this celebration. Yet I could not refrain from witnessing your triumph—the triumph of a saint. That is a thing not often to be seen in a lifetime. [*Looks about him.*] I thought to find more people here.

MME. LEGROS. They left me alone as you see. The celebration is not for me. They are all there. I am not missed.

CHEVALIER. But you are the reason for their festival.

MME. LEGROS. The Innocent is free. So for me everything is over and done with.

CHEVALIER. That has a note of regret.

MME. LEGROS. [*In a strong voice.*] No!

CHEVALIER. You have succeeded where everyone was certain you must fail. You could have turned your achievement to the profit of yourself and yours, and those who stood near you. But you disdained to do so. [*With a hint of irony.*] For that I cannot sufficiently admire you. You have had your reward in a few incomparable experiences and you are of course the talk of Paris. You are of those whom people have knelt before.

[MME. LEGROS *averts her head.*]

CHEVALIER. [*Uncertainly.*] It does not please you to hear that? You expected other words from me, no doubt. And it is true. I have come here on a different errand.

[MME. LEGROS *starts.*]

CHEVALIER. We have been at cross-purposes long enough, Mme. Legros, you and I. Your contempt begins to weary me. Even now, as you stand here listening, your eyes wear their look of martyrdom. This also has come to weary me. I came to tell you—it is so hard to find the words—but you are listening are you not?—Mme. Legros, you are the first human being I have ever stood before in shame. Young as I am, I have known that in despising those whom I have despised I did them no injustice. I have despised while I loved. And I have despised while I slew. It has been my pride to be without illusions. And since the beginning I have known in the depths of my heart who you are. But I did not wish to believe it. The penetrating insight which revealed all men's weaknesses to me had become a vice, and it fought against you. I longed to unmask you, so that I might not be driven to confess that there *was* something in very truth which everyone pretended he possessed and which I myself desired yet could not mention without a sneer—virtue, Mme. Legros. And with your unmasking I hoped I might be able to stifle this desire which arose in me again. [*He throws himself down before her, resting his brow on her hand.*]

MME. LEGROS. [*Bending over him.*] In this moment you have more virtue than I.

CHEVALIER. At first I believed that I loved you as one loves the enemy whom one defeats and humiliates. But it was you who raised me up and brought me to tenderness for mankind against my will. Shall I tell you what my great secret was? I wanted to follow you and at last to become annihilated in all those unknown multitudes for whose sake you set your Innocent free, and reinstated innocence on earth. [*He gets up.*] You may smile. And I will admit without your reminding me that I should not have been so overcome by you had you not been beautiful and had I not loved you already.

MME. LEGROS. And the love that overcame me was of a kind that I, too, had never known before. In a moment it had taken possession of me, when I picked up the letter that fluttered down from the tower.

CHEVALIER. You may believe mine to be a boy's infatuation or a man's highest passion, but I am not ashamed. Take me. [*He flings himself upon her breast.*]

MME. LEGROS. What am I to do with you, my child? What was to be done I have done.

CHEVALIER. Yes. A task accomplished lies behind you. So great a task, I can only guess how great it was. What can it matter to you after all, that one, out of all the people you have spoken to, has been transformed by you and raised beyond himself.

MME. LEGROS. The return is the hardest of all.

CHEVALIER. Yes, this is inconceivable, that you should stand here so passively, as though all that had not happened. Coming now into this house, those whom you conquered find the same woman who was here before it all began. Then what is there left to live for? I will go.

MME. LEGROS. No, not the same woman. You must know that too. I am not as strong as you say. I have been made even weaker than before by what I have done. Until now I could think of myself as far away with the one who wanted me. If only I might be for once under the will of another. I am so tired.

CHEVALIER. It is a sacred weariness.

MME. LEGROS. Nor do I wish you to thank me for I have betrayed you.

CHEVALIER. You, me? [*He laughs.*] That would be the end indeed. [*Reflecting.*] When? How? But I do not want to know. Make your confession to one more worthy than I. You will spare me that. I shall have faith in goodness now until I die. And this hour with you shall be the base on which it stands. It will travel a hard road, faith like that. I know. And life will lead you also towards other matters than the salvation of an Innocent.

CROWD. [*Passes the window with shrill whistles and beating drums. Their shouting becomes audible.*] Mme. Legros, Mme. Legros! On to the Bastille!

CHEVALIER. They have come for you already. But it is not they who will see you in doubt and despair—I alone in this great hour of my life have truly known you. Farewell, Mme. Legros. [*He is about to leave.*]

    [*Men with picks and axes block the doorway.*]

A MAN. Here is Mme. Legros! You must come with us! You are the people's friend!

ANOTHER. You have set the Innocent free!

ALL. Honour to the people's friend.

FIRST MAN. There are other Innocents in the Bastille.

SECOND MAN. And outside it too. Come with us, be our leader! [*Shouts.*]

ALL. To the Bastille! To the Bastille!

MME. LEGROS. Have mercy, Messieurs! What do you want of me?

FIRST MAN. We want you to lead us.

MME. LEGROS. But where must I lead you? I have done my task. The Innocent is free.

SECOND MAN. It's our task now. If we have you with us, Mme. Legros, we shall win. We shall have a victory.

MME. LEGROS. Over whom? The Innocent is free.

FIRST MAN. You must understand, there is still more to do. We are all oppressed.

MME. LEGROS. I have finished my task. The Innocent is free.

FIRST MAN. She will not come.

SECOND MAN. She is betraying us. [*Shouts.*] To the Bastille! To the Bastille! Drag her along.

MME. LEGROS. [*Is surrounded and seized.*] Dear people, spare me!

CHEVALIER. Away! [*He draws his sword.*]

SHOUTS. An aristocrat! Hang him on the lamp-post! Harlot! Betraying us with her aristocrat!

CHEVALIER. Away, I say!

A MAN. Away with *you!* [*Attacks him.*]

    [*Others join in the affray. The* CHEVALIER *is killed.* MME. LEGROS *shrieks.*]

MME. LEGROS. Murderers! Murderers!

    [*Shouts from the women.*]

WOMEN. Her, too! Kill her too!

MME. LEGROS. [*Her arms thrown wide.*] Dare to!

CROWD. [*Muttering.*] She set the Innocent free! [*They fall back.*]

MME. LEGROS. You have stopped the beating of a human heart at the moment when it beat highest for virtue, higher than yours, higher than mine. Ah, what was the use! Why did I set the Innocent free? [*She kneels beside the corpse.*]

CROWD. [*Withdrawing.*] To the Bastille!

[*Dusk falls.*]

M. LEGROS. [*Enters.*] Your friends have been here again. It is not to be denied that they are somewhat noisy. Ah, *nom de Dieu*, what is that? [*He points to the* CHEVALIER'S *body.*]

MME. LEGROS. Oh, Legros, help me! Is he dead? How terrible this is!

M. LEGROS. [*Examining the body.*] Yes, I believe all is over with him. A dead man in our doorway. There will be questions, and if I cannot answer— [*He describes a circle round his neck, with his forefinger.*] Well, Mme. Legros, this is what has come of your adventure. It has led us both to the gallows.

MME. LEGROS. I do not understand these things that are happening. Oh, dear husband, will you not take pity on me!

M. LEGROS. There. In the end it is your husband who must take care of everything. [*He stands listening, hurries toward the left, calls through the door, which stands slightly ajar.*] Get back into the kitchen, you, and don't stir out of it! [*He comes back.*] There's not a soul in the street. I'll take him and put him on the surgeon's doorstep. Then I'll knock at the door and be gone round the corner before he comes to open. What business is this of ours? Wash the step, Mme. Legros. And not a word, mind. [*He closes the door, as he goes out carrying the* CHEVALIER'S *corpse.*]

MME. LEGROS. [*Wanders distractedly about the room, with her hands pressed to her head, moaning. From time to time she regards the closed door with alarm. There is a knock. A cry escapes her. The knock is repeated.*] Come in.

[*A member of the Academy enters.*]

MEMBER OF ACADEMY. It is growing dark, Madame. I cannot see very distinctly whether it is indeed Mme. Legros before whom I have the honour to be standing.

MME. LEGROS. I am the wife of the hosier, Legros, monsieur.

MEMBER OF ACADEMY. Then you are the heroine whom the Academy today was privileged to crown. I should say rather that your presence amongst us was our coronation, not yours. The coronation of all our work. Will you allow me, Madame, to touch in reverence the hands that tore open the doors of an Innocent's dungeon?

[MME. LEGROS *draws her hand away.*]

MEMBER OF ACADEMY. I fear I am unwelcome. But I can understand that great deeds leave a great weariness in those who perform them.

MME. LEGROS. Monsieur, I ask your forgiveness. I am ill. [*She gives him her hand.*]

MEMBER OF ACADEMY. Your hand is too hot, and your face, Madame, bears a look of sorrow. When our speaker sought to glorify you by his words today, a sublime joy shone in your face. It is there no longer. Seeing you now, indeed I do not recognize the saviour of the prisoner Latude.

MME. LEGROS. Are you astonished, Monsieur? All that was far too much for the wife of the hosier Legros—the long travail of the soul, the struggle against all the world, and at last the crimes.

MEMBER OF ACADEMY. The crimes?

MME. LEGROS. Do you suppose that hands that opened the Bastille can still be clean?

MEMBER OF ACADEMY. These are the fantasies of fever, my child. Reason tells us that through good all things are one, and in the end all shall attain to happiness.

MME. LEGROS. [*Pacing the room rapidly.*] And the fear that is in me and the beating of my heart tell me that I have become a criminal. Listen to me, Monsieur, there was one man who believed in me, and him I betrayed. I caused his death. Have I not betrayed all the others too? Will not all their deaths be laid now at my door?

MEMBER OF ACADEMY. The Innocent lives and he is free.

MME. LEGROS. [*Pauses in her agitated walk and draws a breath of relief.*] Yes, *he* is free.

MEMBER OF ACADEMY. What if it were to do over again?

MME. LEGROS. Ah no, not I. I should never do it again. [*She collapses, sobbing wildly.*] I am worn out. I am destroyed.

MEMBER OF ACADEMY. Poor erstwhile heroine! Others after you then will have to do the deeds that reason demands.

[*Drums are heard in the distance, and shouts:* "To the Bastille!"]

MME. LEGROS. I will not hear them! I cannot bear it!

MEMBER OF ACADEMY. It is your song, Mme. Legros. You led that chorus. You have my deepest homage. And now I will leave you. [*He opens the door and his foot slips.*] What's that?

MME. LEGROS. You may stain the soles of your shoes on thresholds like this, Monsieur. It is slippery. Be careful.

MEMBER OF ACADEMY. We jump over them then and go on our way. [*He goes out.*]

[M. LEGROS *comes in through the open doorway.*]

MME. LEGROS. [*Runs to meet him.*] Save me!

M. LEGROS. What has happened? Who has been here?

MME. LEGROS. An enemy. They leave me no peace!

M. LEGROS. Indeed, it seems so. But you have your husband now. Now we shall see how much longer all these people will walk in and out of this house as if it were their own. Light the lights, Mme. Legros, while I put up the shutters. [*He goes out into the street, and puts up the shutters.*]

MME. LEGROS. [*Lights the candles.*] Oh hurry, husband, I am afraid! There is so much happening out there.

M. LEGROS. [*Comes in.*] The door too. Now we shall be left in peace. [*He whispers.*] No one saw me. I am sure of that. The corpse is sitting against the surgeon's door. It was not without risk that I got him there, but simple human respect kept me from leaving him to lie in the gutter.

[MME. LEGROS *sobs aloud.*]

M. LEGROS. You do not like to hear that? I only say it to show you how little we have to fear. I might say nothing at all. For many aristocrats have lost their lives in Paris tonight. Then who is likely to find out about ours?

MME. LEGROS. You speak as though we murdered him ourselves. His blood is not on my hands, not on mine.

M. LEGROS. Not on yours indeed. None of us can be called guilty of these murders so much as the aristocrats themselves.

MME. LEGROS. He was the best of all of them.

M. LEGROS. That is a question not asked anymore. All over Paris there is only one cry, that an Innocent spent three and forty years in the Bastille—what matter then that those who are being killed in his behalf are guilty or innocent? They say the Bastille is to fall. Things will become serious today or tomorrow. And it was Mme. Legros, they are saying, who gave them the signal.

MME. LEGROS. It is not true. I have been with you all the time, dear husband. You can bear witness to that. The entire day I have not been out of the house.

M. LEGROS. But what of all the days before? You have been little at home, Mme. Legros.

MME. LEGROS. Forgive me. I beg you to forgive me now. It was like destiny, leading me where it would. I could not but follow. It was not that I wanted to hurt you, dear husband.

M. LEGROS. How do you know, Mme. Legros, that you were not hurt also? If wrong has been done here, I have done my share too. I need your forgiveness as you need mine.

MME. LEGROS. Send her away, Legros.

M. LEGROS. I have already in my pocket her ticket for the stage coach tomorrow morning. Before daybreak I shall see her into it myself. And bon voyage. Let her go back to her village and spend the rest of her life prattling of what she has seen today.

MME. LEGROS. How good you are! Do you still love me?

M. LEGROS. You must feel that I do. It is not good for a wife to get beyond her husband's control.

MME. LEGROS. How strong you are. I will obey and serve only you all the rest of my life.

M. LEGROS. But this thing that you have done—although it puzzled me greatly I do not realise that it was something good.

MME. LEGROS. Was it truly good?

M. LEGROS. I am a burgher of Paris, and I know as well as any other that reason and virtue must govern our conduct. But we are apt to believe that it is always a stranger who teaches us this. This time it was my own wife, and it took me no longer to accustom myself to that idea than it would have taken any other man.

MME. LEGROS. Now everything is as it was before. You are my lord and master.

M. LEGROS. It is the same and yet not the same, for between us lies all this that you have done, and I shall not forget. The others will forget, do not doubt it. They may even turn against you for it, and persecute us both. There is no telling what these times will bring forth.

MME. LEGROS. But we will have each other.

M. LEGROS. And I will still revere you, dear wife, even while I make you do my bidding. [*They embrace.*] I have not talked at this length since our wedding day.

MME. LEGROS. There is work to do. I shall begin at once.

M. LEGROS. At this time of night?

MME. LEGROS. Look at that chest of drawers, covered with dust. Mlle. Palmyre's bonnet is still there. It is high time I sewed on the bows.

M. LEGROS. But this has been a tiring day for you. First, the crowning and the celebration—then something harder still to bear.

MME. LEGROS. I will sew the bows on now.

CURTAIN

A PLACE IN THE WORLD

A Comedy in Three Acts

by

CARL STERNHEIM

Authorized English Version

by

BARRETT H. CLARK

and

WINIFFRED KATZIN

CAST OF CHARACTERS

CHRISTIAN MASKE
COUNT PALEN (*about* 50)
VALET
THEOBALD MASKE, *Christian's father* (*about* 60)
LUISE MASKE, *Christian's mother* (*about* 55)
SYBIL (*about* 28)
MARIANNE, *Count Palen's daughter* (*about* 25)
MAID

ACTS I and II—A room in Christian Maske's apartment, in a large German city.

ACT III—A hotel drawing-room.

TIME: Just before the war.

A PLACE IN THE WORLD

ACT I

CHRISTIAN MASKE's *furnished rooms.*

CHRISTIAN [*Opening a letter.*] This is grotesque! [*At the door.*] Sybil!

SYBIL. [*Enters.*] What's up?

CHRISTIAN. At the age of sixty my father has brought off a bastard. He's up against it for funds. Listen to this: "So I must request you to lend me enough to cover what I have had to lay out for obstetrical services." How does that strike you, eh?

SYBIL. All right—only I wish you'd follow your parent's example and do as well by me.

CHRISTIAN. Don't talk like a fool! Absolutely preposterous—don't think I'm to be caught in that trap—or you'll find the consequences very different from what you expect. I've got to have a serious talk with you.

SYBIL. It's time I was going home.

CHRISTIAN. Yesterday closed a chapter in my life. You've been living with me four years and you've seen me getting nearer and nearer my goal, day by day, haven't you?

SYBIL. You've slaved for it.

CHRISTIAN. The African mines I helped to float are showing excellent returns. The Board of Directors met yesterday, and proposed me as President of the company. There is not the slightest doubt that the stockholders will second that.

SYBIL. A triumph for you!

CHRISTIAN. I own a fifth of the stock. Bought it when nobody else would touch it—no one knows, though. Now I'm on the way, there's no limit to the progress I'll be able to make in society— all that money, you understand.

SYBIL. Who was it that first discovered your gift for business and made you stop that dismal philosophy you were wasting your brains on?

307

CHRISTIAN. You pulled me out of a bog, Sybil—showed me how to wear my clothes decently, taught me manners, as far as you knew how——

SYBIL. If you could only have seen yourself in trousers too short for you and sleeves all frayed at the cuffs!

CHRISTIAN. In addition, you contributed yourself and sometimes money.

SYBIL. And all my life—last but not least, eh?

CHRISTIAN. I wish to have it understood by both of us—I am in your debt—profoundly——

SYBIL. Don't let's talk about that——

CHRISTIAN. More than grateful to you. I am about to make you an adequate return for it all, after which I wipe the whole thing out of my mind for ever.

SYBIL. Simple and painless.

CHRISRIAN. I could not think of entering upon a new epoch in my life, without first having liquidated all the obligations of the last one. To the best of my knowledge and belief, every expense you ever incurred for me has been entered in my book here. I now repay it—plus interest at five per cent.

SYBIL. Christian!

CHRISTIAN. Your association with me may possibly have caused you to miss other opportunities; I have computed these together with the rest. The total comes to 24,000 marks. You shall receive that amount today.

SYBIL. [After a pause.] Delicacy would be——

CHRISTIAN. You cured me of giving way to that sort of weakness where more important matters were at stake—swept it out of me with a wire broom. So today I make up our accounts and close our books. You will find they balance correctly. Our relationship has lasted until now because of my financial indebtedness to you. I can no longer countenance such a reason. If I am to have the faith in the reality of my altered station in life which I am bound to have, everything must alter accordingly. And you must either accept my perfectly reasonable decision——

SYBIL. Which is——?

CHRISTIAN. How shall I put it? Shall we say merely a greater distance between us for the future? It will be made feasible by means of the sum mentioned and a certain allowance, monthly.

SYBIL. You tear my feelings to shreds.

CHRISTIAN. I follow your own teachings. You will perceive that when applied to yourself they hurt. I am about to embark upon public life. I can't afford to make any false steps.

SYBIL. It's true the world allows you a paid——

CHRISTIAN. That will do——

SYBIL. Am I the only thing in your life that might embarrass you in the future? Is there no worse obstacle to your desire for a place in the world of society than my relations with you?

CHRISTIAN. You know as well as I do——

SYBIL. If you'll be sensible. . . .

CHRISTIAN. I make no bones about it. I can face the world as what I am, my appearance and my brains are all I need. But my parents, as you know, are low-class.

SYBIL. So if you're going to rise in the world, they must——?

CHRISTIAN. I do not require you to prompt me. You know I am able to think for myself. They're nobodies. My good mother especially.

SYBIL. They weren't able to teach you the most ordinary decent manners.

CHRISTIAN. The position I am making for myself is almost unheard of for a man of my class. It would be obviously a mistake to emphasise the abyss between my origin and my present status by dragging my progenitors into the limelight. In fact, it would be the utmost bad form to do so.

SYBIL. And as good form is what you now worship before all other gods——

CHRISTIAN. Sarcasm from you would be more telling if we were not aware of your own highly undesirable antecedents. Nobody even knew who *your* parents were. You got them out of the way quite simply by murdering them both. Perhaps your father was a jail-bird? Was his name really Hull? [*Laughing.*] Your charm is your fortune, however, and though you'd have that in either case, he must have had something about him too, to have been the author of a splendid creature like you. Now stop interrupting. I have elucidated the discrepancy between origin and attainments. Nevertheless the consciousness of being under obligation, even for my life, remains the weak spot in my armour. The world began with me—I am its source and centre. I may consider no one and nothing in my forward progress. My father and mother are in my way —therefore I stand in danger of them.

SYBIL. What do you propose? Bribing them to stay out of sight?

CHRISTIAN. My father is not shy; he demands it himself here.

SYBIL. Have you learned the value of money?

CHRISTIAN. I have learned all sorts of things.

SYBIL. You are so logical; nobody who loves you could help admitting you're right, no matter how much it costs them to say so. . . .

CHRISTIAN. I hope my parents will be equally understanding. Is our affair settled to your satisfaction then?

SYBIL. I am passing into the new régime already; a certain distance has come between us in these few minutes and already I feel faintly servile as I look at you!

CHRISTIAN. Things don't gain in truth by being talked about, only by being done.

SYBIL. But they gain in clearness.

CHRISTIAN. Wiseacre!

SYBIL. I love you, Christian. You are the one mistake in my ledger. I would give the whole twenty-four thousand to have you back again.

CHRISTIAN. Then you deserve to die in misery and want. Here, here's a kiss for nothing.—Now you've made a mess of my tie.

SYBIL. It looked like the deuce, anyway.

CHRISTIAN. Much as I have learned from you, that one thing I never have—I can *not* tie a tie. Show me again—for the hundredth time.

SYBIL. [*Tying the necktie around the neck of a large vase.*] A plain knot first—then one end through it—so—then the other one through —and there you are!

CHRISTIAN. There's a bit sticking out on the right.

SYBIL. Cut it off.

CHRISTIAN. And ruin as many as I tie?

SYBIL. So that those who know, may know that *you* know.

CHRISTIAN. Which is the purpose of everything.

SYBIL. Mr. President, your humble servant.

CHRISTIAN. It's nothing to laugh at!

SYBIL. I understand perfectly.

[SYBIL *goes out.*]

CHRISTIAN. On the whole, a very pleasant creature! [*At the desk— He writes.*] "Dear Count Palen, I accept with gratitude your kind invitation for the second of this month." With gratitude? Well . . . "Greetings to the Countess." Too familiar. Too humble, or the one hand and too jaunty on the other. He must by no means guess how glad I am to go. This paper's wrong. A Monambo Mine letterhead would be better. "Dear Count von Palen." Shoving in the "von"'s a good idea. More dignified.— As my first communication in writing to that circle, this letter must be absolutely correct and still carry an air of importance somehow or other. How does he write himself? "Dear Herr Maske, Will you come to dinner with us on the 26th? just ourselves. Yours." On ordinary cheap paper. Friendly, casual, unforced. "Dinner" is perfect! We shall be a shade more formal, but I'd like to put in one Latin word. Always lends a masculine touch. How to find four or five syllables that can make a man important for a minute or two to the real people? There's a puzzle if you like, but the answer's got to be found. Five syllables now, with lots of vowels and a good rolling start. Here goes! Dum-da-da-dum-da "Indisputable." To my ear the second syllable is longer than the first. Won't do.—Praenumerando—that's the right *sound*, but it doesn't make sense. Dum-da-da-dum-da. Hang it all!

THEOBALD MASKE. [*Enters.*] I thought I'd come up alone. Mother's downstairs waiting.

CHRISTIAN. Father!

THEOBALD. A bit of bad luck that was, Christian. I didn't want it. Can't stand fireworks, anyway. But women never know where to stop. Well, it's done now, and can't be undone, so there we are!

CHRISTIAN. Since you retired, you've had a little surprise like this for us every year.

THEOBALD. You should have let me go on with my job. You had me idle too soon. I've as much energy now as I ever had, only I've got nothing to do with it any more, so I have to use it up in multifarious pursuits. In the meantime the girl can't be left stranded.

CHRISTIAN. I'm going to call mother up to begin with——

THEOBALD. Let's settle our own business first.

CHRISTIAN. Not first, but with all the rest. It's all right—no one'll know but us two.

THEOBALD. How?

CHRISTIAN. A sum will be mentioned in our conversation.

THEOBALD. Conversation—what about? And how much?

CHRISTIAN. A sum, I tell you, one of many thousands. If we agree on the rest of the matters I'm going to discuss with you, you can add a thousand marks in your head to the sum mentioned, that will get you out of this mess you've got yourself into——

THEOBALD. You make conditions?

CHRISTIAN. I make conditions.

THEOBALD. I'm curious to hear them——

CHRISTIAN. [*At the window.*] There she is. [*He waves his hand.*] She saw me. She's coming up. How unspeakably that woman dresses! You used a word just now that gave me an idea.

THEOBALD. What was I talking about——

CHRISTIAN. It went to a different rhythm from the one I wanted, but it had a ring. Remind me of it later.

THEOBALD. A thousand?

CHRISTIAN. If we agree on the rest. [*He goes out.*]

THEOBALD. I wonder what he's up to!

[CHRISTIAN *and* LUISE MASKE *enter.*]

THEOBALD. Put your hat on straight, Luise. It's not a student's cap to be worn down over the nose. Well, Christian, we're thinking of moving to the city, I'll get something or other to keep me from dying of dry-rot. . . .

LUISE. It's a bee in his bonnet, Christel—you know Father!

CHRISTIAN. I must tell you both that as my attention is concentrated on the goal I'm working for, I wouldn't have a free moment to spend with you.

THEOBALD. We're used to that lately. It's little enough you've bothered about us. And what may this goal of yours be, if we may inquire?

CHRISTIAN. I have been offered the chance of being made President of the company I work for.

LUISE. President!

THEOBALD. President!

CHRISTIAN. If I am to carve out a really great career for myself, I must be your first consideration; which means—above all——

THEOBALD. Now you listen to me, my lad—we went without for twenty years so that you could have a good education and you've had one you need never be ashamed of. Many's the time you cost us our roast joint of a Sunday. They say that of all animals— human and otherwise—monkeys love their children most. Well, we loved you like monkeys——

LUISE. [*Softly to herself.*] President.

CHRISTIAN. [*Trying to recall the word.*] Dum-da-da . . .

THEOBALD. We kept in the background so as not to hinder you getting up in the world. But we've not been getting younger all these years and now it's this way: if we're going to have any good of you, it now or never.

CHRISTIAN. First of all I'd like to correct one important misstatement: I am unable to recollect any sacrifice you have made for my sake since my sixteenth year.

THEOBALD. Good God!

LUISE. Father!

CHRISTIAN. I remember you of old, Father—how you grabbed four-fifths of all the space in the house, and made yourself the pivot of the universe. I earned enough at tutoring while I was still a schoolboy to cost you nothing and paid my way through the university, living expenses included. Who was it that forced a boy of seventeen to eat his dinner in his father's presence, standing. . . .

THEOBALD. I loved you like a monkey. You were a dear little chap. Wasn't he, Mother?

LUISE. Such a little bit of a thing . . .

CHRISTIAN. You have been an utter egoist—you never bestowed a thought upon my life until recently. But lately you seem to have been received by a revelation—the widening scope of my life seems to have made an impression upon you at last.

THEOBALD. This is getting tiresome. Let's come to the point—what's this solemn conclave all about?

CHRISTIAN. You happened to turn up on the very day that I am closing the books of my past life. No false entries will be found in them.

LUISE. What does he mean?

THEOBALD. Wait a bit.

CHRISTIAN. I have entered in this book the actual expenses you have incurred for me—so far as I am able to remember them. Interest at the rate of five percent has been added to the amount.

THEOBALD. Is this for my benefit?

CHRISTIAN. It is.

THEOBALD. [Sitting down.] Let's see what you've put down here. [He puts on his glasses.]

LUISE. What do you mean, both of you?

CHRISTIAN. Have a little more patience, Mother.

THEOBALD. [Reading.] Maintenance from one year to sixteen years —six hundred marks per annum. If that includes the doctor and druggists, I'd call it a bit on the skimpy side.

CHRISTIAN. I was never ill.

THEOBALD. No? I remember the time we had you down with measles. And you were always catching cold—your nose was for ever running— Douches of catnip tea from year's end to year's end. . . .

LUISE. You had a temperature of a hundred and six once. I thought my heart had stopped beating.

CHRISTIAN. All my illnesses are amply covered by the sum I have entered.

LUISE. Rings as big as saucers all over his little body.

THEOBALD. Sixteen times six hundred makes nine thousand six hundred marks. See here. "Miscellaneous"—How can you pretend to remember all the odd items over sixteen years? There's no counting them. Your "Miscellaneous" is thoroughly unreliable from beginning to end.

CHRISTIAN. Certain amounts I've given you from time to time—lately in particular—have not been entered here against you.

THEOBALD. All right—all right——

CHRISTIAN. [To himself.] I'd give a lot to be able to remember that word. [He stares at the letter lying on the table.]

LUISE. [Shyly to CHRISTIAN.] And the ulcer on your neck, that time.

CHRISTIAN. Don't worry, Mother, I've remembered that too. . . .

THEOBALD. "Half a dozen shirts and collars, two pairs of shoes, to go to the University with—fifty marks. A gold ring—" So that's where my ring went—I call that pretty steep. And I turned everything upside down hunting for the blamed thing.

CHRISTIAN. It was Mother's; she gave it to me for my start in life.

LUISE. Do you still wear it?

CHRISTIAN. [Shows it on his finger.] Though it gets tighter every day.

THEOBALD. Absurd! But just like Luise. Grand total, eleven thousand. Hm! Plus interest, eleven thousand eight hundred marks.

CHRISTIAN. [With emphasis.] Eleven thousand eight hundred. [Clears his throat.]

THEOBALD. So—that's what you're paying me, is it?

CHRISTIAN. I am in your debt to that amount precisely.

THEOBALD. And the obligation is weighing on you?

CHRISTIAN. Not any more—it is being discharged now——

LUISE. [His hand in her hands.] It could be made larger.

THEOBALD. Well—you're a good boy, after all. You've handled the whole thing famously. [Embracing him.] I like to see things done with style— We appreciate it—So it's all settled, and everybody's satisfied.

CHRISTIAN. You expressed the intention of moving up to town. I can't allow that.

THEOBALD. Do you dare order me about?

CHRISTIAN. I have given you back all your money—one good turn deserves another.

THEOBALD. But I'd got it all arranged.

LUISE. The child must have his reasons, Father.

THEOBALD. That woman drives me mad! It's impossible to speak a sane word while she's about.

CHRISTIAN. [*Accompanies* LUISE *to the door*.] Mother, wouldn't you like to have a look round my house?

LUISE. Yes— And don't you be worrying, Christian—everything shall be as you say. [*She goes out.*]

CHRISTIAN. As I said before, if I had you to cope with here, I should not be able to devote my entire energy to the matter in hand. Which is what I must do.

THEOBALD. Is that the condition that goes with your eleven thousand eight hundred marks?

CHRISTIAN. To start off with——

THEOBALD. Well, let's consider it— Where do we come in? It's all very well to love you like monkeys, but even monkey-parents have to live; we've got to make sure of our income. How much does the eleven thousand bring in?

CHRISTIAN. Six hundred in industrial stocks.

THEOBALD. You're out of your mind! Stocks indeed. *My* money goes into the savings bank.

CHRISTIAN. Five hundred, then——

THEOBALD. That's nothing to get excited over. Eleven thousand sounded like something. Well, a poor man's got nothing but his freedom to call his own—and you want me to give up mine for a measly five hundred, do you? Think it over. No—if I give you my word as an honest man that your mother and I'll stay where we are . . .

CHRISTIAN No—that's not what I want.

THEOBALD. Oh, indeed!—You don't want this and you don't want that. Then for God's sake what *do* you want, your royal highness?

CHRISTIAN. This visitation of yours today shows me that I should never be safe from you, so long as you're within reach of me.

THEOBALD. What do you mean, visitation?

CHRISTIAN. What I said. My life is about to assume an entirely new aspect. For the present especially I must be free from any family business.

THEOBALD. Nothing like this has ever happened in the world before, for a son to do this to his mother and father, after they've eaten dry bread so that he could have everything. We sacrificed our lives for you, you can say what you like. All parents do. Doesn't every breath their brats draw, mean them giving up some pleasure or other? They get no sleep—they can't eat their meals in peace— nothing. Always something wrong, that's got to be put right and what it doesn't cost in money it costs in aggravation. And all the fool birthdays and christenings and what not that are nothing but a pest and an abominable nuisance. . . .

THEOBALD. [To CHRISTIAN, *who is sitting in an armchair, loudly.*] And this is the reward! Filial affection—[*hits the table with clenched fist.*] Yes! ! !—I *don't* think!

LUISE. [*Sticks her head through the partly opened door and unseen by* THEOBALD, *motions to* CHRISTIAN *to keep calm.*] I'm not disturbing anything, dear.

THEOBALD. What? [*As* CHRISTIAN *remains quiet, he throws himself into a chair at a distance from him and says calmly.*] If I had known what I know today, I'd have had you drowned in your first bath. [*Pause.*] Living more than a hundred miles away from you, as it is. Whoever talked about filial affection was talking through the back of his neck! [*He gives a laugh.*] Ha! And what about the practical side of the matter? Have you thought about that? We could only just make ends meet as we are with my pension *and* your five hundred. We can't be expected to go through all the fuss of moving away and settling in a new place, unless we're paid suitably for our trouble.

CHRISTIAN. No one does expect it.

THEOBALD. Considerably remunerated, too. And who's going to do it?

CHRISTIAN. Under certain conditions, I.

THEOBALD. The devil you say!

CHRISTIAN. There are a great many cities in Europe noted for charming scenery and economic advantages, that is, if you don't like the idea of America to begin with.

THEOBALD. What?

CHRISTIAN. Keep calm—keep calm. [*He has gotten out a large atlas and a Baedeker.*] Brussels, for instance. [*Reading from the book.*] Brussels, the capital of the kingdom of Belgium; population eight hundred thousand. The city is situated in a fertile region on the banks of the Senne, a tributary of the Scheldt. The upper city is the residental section occupied exclusively by the aristocracy and the *haut monde.*

THEOBALD. [*Who has been sitting comfortably and listening devoutly.*] Not bad, let's see. [*He reads aloud.*] "And the *haut monde.* Language and customs French." Can you see an honest-to-God German turning himself into a damned Frenchman, eh? can you? Idiotic!

CHRISTIAN. The place I favour most is Zurich. A perfectly ideal spot, a perfect little paradise in every respect. And the language is German.

THEOBALD. Let's hear about it——

CHRISTIAN. [*Reading from another volume.*] "Zurich, with approximately two hundred thousand inhabitants is the most important city in Switzerland. It is situated on Lake Zurich and the evergreen Limmat."

THEOBALD. That's pine forests! Evergreens, they call them!

CHRISTIAN. "Its west side is on the banks of Silil, which in spring becomes a rushing torrent."

THEOBALD. I could live without that. There's water enough already. What's the good of it, if you can't swim?

CHRISTIAN. "The city is magnificently situated, on the crystal lake, whose gently rising banks are dotted with tall houses, orchards and vineyards."

THEOBALD. Very pretty, I must say.

CHRISTIAN [*Reading.*] "In the background rise the snow-covered Alps, and to the extreme right we behold the mighty summit of the Glärnisch." [*Pointing to the atlas.*] This white spot here!

THEOBALD. I'll be shot!

CHRISTIAN. [*Reading.*] "The Zürichois's are good cooks. They are a simple and frugal people."

THEOBALD. Save the mark——

CHRISTIAN. "The enchanting surroundings invite the excursionist."

THEOBALD. The Promised Land!

CHRISTIAN. "Lucerne and Interlaken, in short the entire Alpine region will be at-hand whenever you wish to visit them—a private pleasure-ground, so to speak." Have you any conception of the meaning of the words, "Alpine glow"?

THEOBALD. None——

CHRISTIAN. I will tell you then. It is a phenomenon constituting a scenic drama of incredible magnificence. If you accept Zurich, also the condition that you leave me alone entirely for the next few years, I will add enough to the income from the 11,000 to make up a very satisfactory sum per year.

THEOBALD. [*After a pause.*] If I don't say "yes" at once, it's that I'm not devoid of feeling, and——

CHRISTIAN. Comment is superfluous——

THEOBALD. I prefer to discuss it.

CHRISTIAN. The life of a man like me is built on facts and performances. Conversation is a waste of time. One other important matter is still undecided. . . .

THEOBALD. Christian, I'm sixty years old today, your mother is nearly the same. We haven't had much happiness in our lives, and we've not much longer to be with you before we go. . . .

CHRISTIAN. Can't you realise that the other things in my life are so strong that an appeal to my feelings at this moment falls on stone-deaf ears? The day will come when we shall discuss these matters comfortably and in detail, you and I. But now I'm wasting golden chances every second . . . let's get this over. You shall have two thousand four hundred francs additional income from me each year. You can move in three weeks. Make haste, Father, and decide. I'm burning up with impatience to get on with my life. A man must race a legion for his place in the world. If I stop for an instant, there will be no passing them again.

THEOBALD. You've got me dizzy, Christian. Never saw anything like you in my life, I can't take in so many new things in one gulp. And when is all this going to benefit my soul? When is the spiritual income due?

CHRISTIAN. Immediately; I will give you five minutes.

THEOBALD. It's like offering a drowning man a rescue on conditions. . . .

CHRISTIAN. Trust me!

THEOBALD. It's the spiritual benefit I want to know about!

CHRISTIAN. Later on for that. Is it settled, Father?

THEOBALD. God's whiskers! You've turned my life upside down.

CHRISTIAN. Two thousand four hundred, that makes nineteen hundred marks.

THEOBALD. Plus five hundred—that will make close on five thousand six hundred, with what I've got already.

CHRISTIAN. Seven thousand francs. [*At the door.*] Mother!

THEOBALD. On the Limmat? My head's whizzing. . . .

CHRISTIAN. [*Handing him the atlas and guide books.*] Inform your-self——

LUISE. [*Enters, softly to* CHRISTIAN.] Everything will be as you want it, Christel. I'll see to that. . . . That's a handsome cover on your night table. I saw all those lace and batiste underclothes too— Oh, Christel, do be careful with the women. Everyone gets led away by their pleasures sometime or other, I know. But you'll have children of your own one day, Christel, and soon you'll be a presi-dent and then you'll be proud that you can take your oath that your mother was a right-living woman.

CHRISTIAN. Certainly, Mother. [*Embraces her.*]

LUISE. [*As she leaves.*] My dear child.

[LUISE, THEOBALD, CHRISTIAN *go out.* CHRISTIAN *quickly returns.*]

CHRISTIAN. Had it on the tip of my tongue that time—[*Looking at the letter.*] He was talking about his premature retirement; dissipate his strength in . . . in . . . what *could* it have been? . . . in multifarious, multifarious. . . . Eureka . . . I've got it at last. [*Writing.*] "Dear Count Palen, I regret the multifarious demands of business prevent my accepting your kind invitation." So it's turned into a refusal, but it may be better so—who knows? [*He has rung the bell. Goes out. Enters again immediately with* COUNT PALEN.]

COUNT. I have come for a final discussion with you over your im-pending presidency, Herr Maske. Before the board of directors can make a definite nomination they naturally require very detailed personal information. I greatly dislike talking business, so I asked Baron Rohrschach to deputise for me, but it was thought more suitable that I should settle the matter myself as I was already on quite intimate terms with you.

[CHRISTIAN *bows.*]

COUNT. The Monambo Mines are, as you know, an enterprise run by a small group of people whose views are essentially the same in all basic matters. Although business and social codes need not necessarily tally, the man at the head of a syndicate like this should be one of ourselves in every respect. [CHRISTIAN *bows.*] We con-sider that in you we have found a man in whom commercial ability is united with the far rarer gift of a knowledge of values where the niceties of life are concerned, which of course is indispensable in cases where the brutal candour of figures has to be met with extreme skill in adjustment. [CHRISTIAN *bows.*] In our chats about life in general, you have frequently expressed opinions which fall in perfectly with ours—indeed they have often shown greater perspicacity than our own. In the vernacular of the Liberal Party, I should call you an aristocrat-reactionary. [*He laughs.*] In fact, I have been most deeply impressed by the sincerity which I have always sensed beneath your words. Was I right?

CHRISTIAN. Quite right.

COUNT. Remarkable, really. And something to reflect upon. I need no further guarantee for you. Your social status is irreproachable. Your education is perfect even to your recognition of the fact that in view of our apartness as a class, it is important for us to resemble each other as closely as possible, as individuals. Inconspicuous uniformity is the thing—in gesture, in the tying of a tie, in everything. All we need now is something tangible that we can present to our shareholders with our nomination, as, so to speak, your statement of what you stand for.

CHRISTIAN. I understand.

COUNT. The case of Rohrschach is a little different; his title of "Baron" suffices—unless of course he should be discredited for any reason. Otherwise, certain assurances are desirable—many a man who has risen from the people, has behind him notable achievements of his ancestors. These may be accepted in lieu of . . .

CHRISTIAN. It is not so in my case.

COUNT. No reproach, my dear sir. Bourgeois families who enjoy high repute in their own spheres, stand upon the achievements of their sound and honourable qualities. I have not yet had the privilege of meeting your father, hm . . . your parents, in short . . .

CHRISTIAN. Dead. All of them—dead.

COUNT. May I say, then, that I am most gratified, to have met their representative descendant? I see you are moved?

CHRISTIAN. I am, Count. Because the time has come at last when I may give voice to the longing which has possessed me since my boyhood; it has been my unswerving ambition to resemble those whose titles are the outward and visible token of their ancestors' achievements; to be permitted to second their labours and impose the principles whose hereditary guardians they are, upon the world at large. It is not for me to tell what sacrifices I have made to this end, but here and now in your presence, I reiterate my vow to dedicate my future to that object as I once dedicated my past.

COUNT. You are a splendid fellow, Maske, a sterling chap, indeed. This talk has made assurance doubly sure. I thank you. And I think you may take your appointment on Wednesday for granted. May I smoke? Can you come, Friday?

CHRISTIAN. Well, I——

COUNT. What?

CHRISTIAN. Then I will—in spite of the multifarious demands of business——
.

COUNT. I know how busy you are. My daughter Marianne is of the kind to appreciate your type.

CHRISTIAN. I have often heard that the countess is uncommonly gifted——

COUNT. You shall judge for yourself, dear Maske——

CHRISTIAN. I am greatly obliged to you, Count Palen——

COUNT. Count Palen—sensitive to nuance too, I see!

CHRISTIAN. Otherwise inconspicuously uniform!

COUNT. Excellent, my dear Maske—witty! charming!
     [*Exit.*]

CHRISTIAN. [*Who has escorted him to the door, returns, looks hastily in the mirror and then begins to tie a necktie on a vase.*] First a plain knot. . . . Second, one end through . . . so. . . . Then pull the other end through. . . . And now the scissors. [*He cuts.*] If your left eye offend you, pluck it out! There, I've got it right at last! I have won!

CURTAIN

ACT TWO

Drawing room at CHRISTIAN MASKE'S.

COUNT. The servant says he'll be back any moment.

MARIANNE. We are ten minutes early. That's the Corot, over there.

COUNT. Which is what we came for, remember.

MARIANNE. Beautiful. How fortunate to be able to surround oneself with lovely things.

COUNT. You can, if you wish——

MARIANNE. As his wife? Do you mean that, Father?

COUNT. Mean it, Marianne. We have refrained from discussing it, but what else has occupied our minds these past weeks? And lately there has been no mistaking the man——

MARIANNE. Is he in love with me?

COUNT. Put it another way. Suppose he had none of this wealth, which could rescue us from our many difficulties—would you still consider him as a husband?

MARIANNE. That is a question I cannot answer. The first time you brought him to the house, I knew practically nothing about him or his circumstances. I had a perfectly unbiased impression of him and it has not changed. He seems to me a man whose will would drive everything before it, and that one would submit to him with joy as if to an elemental force.

COUNT. *Tiens!*

MARIANNE. That is Marianne's decision, father.

COUNT. I had taken it for granted that you would have a certain inward opposition to overcome.

MARIANNE. I have. We are on the most distant terms with each other! Our conversation has never been anything but small-talk. But the moment he came near me I was on the defensive—I felt I was being attacked. But I felt also that I had met in him the only man who would ever win me wholly.

COUNT. He gives me the creeps.

MARIANNE. Have you found him incorrect in any detail?

COUNT. None.

MARIANNE. Isn't he one of ourselves in every way?

COUNT. Absolutely. That's the very thing I resent. I have been watching him for two years, and the very thing I found most sympathetic in the beginning almost horrifies me now. If this bourgeois is really genuine and spontaneous in his conduct then where does our class distinction come in? I have always considered nobility a product of breeding that only centuries can achieve. It could never be acquired in a single generation. As the Duke of Devonshire said to a parvenu who was envying him the beauty of his lawns; All it needs to have these is to keep them well swept every morning for a few hundred years. *Voilá!* I have never attempted to accomplish anything in particular but have merely lived the life of a man of our class, remembering the qualities that separate us from others. If this man proves that without ancestors certain priceless values can be acquired, then I become nothing in my own esteem.

MARIANNE. Might not a highly exceptional mind analyse us, and accomplish the work of many generations by intensive work upon himself?

COUNT. Nothing becomes your true property except by virtue of long tenure. It either bears that stamp or it is borrowed, and sooner or later the test always comes. An accident,—some inadvertence, will reveal the fraud. I'm waiting for it to happen to Herr Maske.

MARIANNE. You are rather deeply involved in his career.

COUNT. Not to the extent of becoming his victim. Rather to discover the wound that will eventually kill him—and I would willingly be the one to strike it if the chance offered.

MARIANNE. Then fate might set me against you.

COUNT. God forbid!

MARIANNE. Not God, but you! That man stirred me for the first time in my life. And the excitement he aroused in me has not yet entirely calmed down. I still remember him with joy even while I am repulsing him. It is some obscure and secret emotion that will declare itself when the time comes, but cannot be forced.

COUNT. Shall we ever see him unmasked?

MARIANNE. On the contrary, he will become more and more inscrutable and unexpected. I am certain from the few signs I have seen that he is no ordinary personality and far beyond the scope of your predictions.

COUNT. Marianne!

MARIANNE. It is my honest feeling about him, Father! But you gave me a glorious youth, and I'll always be grateful to you for that.

COUNT. I've spoiled you——

MARIANNE. And will continue to do so.

COUNT. There are limits. . . .

MARIANNE. [*Tensely.*] The limits of love are not easily reached. . . .

CHRISTIAN. [*Enters in riding clothes.*] Ah! Countess, Count. Forgive me, I can at least blame this on the Colonial Minister; he kept me all this time giving him advice.

COUNT. He is forever singing your praises, and he's anxious to present you to the Kaiser.

CHRISTIAN. His questions would require more talent to answer than I possess. The enormous responsibility of having the welfare of the State to care for destroys the power of any human opinion that is not directly inspired by God.

COUNT. *Magnifique!* Good riding today?

CHRISTIAN. Yes, a colt by Charmant out of Miss Gorse.—Do you like the picture, Countess?

MARIANNE. I am not learned in these things. But I find it moving.

CHRISTIAN. It's not his masterpiece; but its values and tones are unique.

COUNT. How is it you are so positive in your judgments?

CHRISTIAN. I dare say I have seen a good two or three hundred Corot's in my life.

COUNT. Where do you find time for all these things?

CHRISTIAN. It is difficult. But the first one came to me in a flash. And my consciousness once alive to them, the others revealed themselves. [*To* MARIANNE.] That is how I take everything.

COUNT. We must go. [*To* MARIANNE.] You are due at the Friesen's at half past eleven.

CHRISTIAN. Are you accompanying the countess, or may I ask you to stay for a moment?

COUNT. [*To* MARIANNE.] Do you need me?

MARIANNE. No—stay.

CHRISTIAN. Let me take you to your car.

  [MARIANNE *and* CHRISTIAN *exeunt.*]

COUNT. [*Takes a book from table.*] Almanach de Gotha. Handbook of the Nobility. Investigation, eh? [*He turns the pages and reads.*] Palen. Old Westphalian nobility, appears in records for the first time 1220. . . . Augustus Aloysius to Elizabeth Countess of Fürstenbach, died at Ernegg July sixteen, 1901. . . . My good Elizabeth. Children: Frederick Mathia, the last of our male line and Marianne Josephs, who is about to marry a plain Herr Maske.

CHRISTIAN. [*Enters.*] The Countess will pick you up here, when she comes by about twelve o'clock. Count Augustus von Palen, I ask you for the hand of your daughter Marianne.

COUNT. You are very brief—you must have thought this over very carefully.

CHRISTIAN. As carefully as you and your daughter the answer, Count.

COUNT. You are mistaken. I have no idea what the countess' final decision would be.

CHRISTIAN. What is it tentatively then? But forgive me, I should like to have your views first.

COUNT. Personally I disapprove—profoundly. But that is merely a point of view, and has no real weight in the matter. Had you counted on my consent?

CHRISTIAN. I felt you were strongly opposed to the idea.

COUNT. Yes—in spite of my admiration for you, I find that the gulf between us does not diminish. To be quite truthful, however, you seem to have made an enormous impression upon my daughter.

CHRISTIAN. Would you like to have more detailed information as to my financial standing—and——

COUNT. I have watched your progress with my own eyes and am only too well aware of the financial and social successes your gifts have brought you. I am certain of a brilliant future for you.

CHRISTIAN. Is your objection based on anything undesirable in my character?

COUNT. There is nothing.

CHRISTIAN. Then might I question?

COUNT. I will be frank—it is class prejudice, pure and simple.

CHRISTIAN. Thank you. That was inevitable. The quality I have always honoured most in your class, is your fundamental inaccessibility. If your objection had been directed towards me as Christian Maske instead of as *Herr* Christian Maske, I should have minded very much.

COUNT. How can you both honour a principle and try to exterminate it?

CHRISTIAN. I love your daughter.

COUNT. And if she were not the Countess Palen, would you still wish to marry her?

CHRISTIAN. That I cannot say—I have not analysed the component elements of her charm for me.

COUNT. Assuming the countess's consent——

[CHRISTIAN *makes an involuntary movement which betrays his agitation.*]

COUNT. I thought I knew you. But now that I have to face the possibility of a closer association, I realise that you are still the stranger in our midst.

CHRISTIAN. In our class we have no books to tell us where our pedigree began. We are left groping in our past——

COUNT. Yes indeed—it is rarely that a bourgeois name is anything but a label on anonymity. You have no records, you are not observed; you may do as you please. We, whose record is in this book, live and die under the eyes of our class. We renounce the joy of freedom, which is the people's compensation for their obscurity, and in return for our sacrifice, we are given the right to see our services chronicled and rewarded.

CHRISTIAN. Undoubtedly. But a community such as yours should have a place for any man who is strong enough to hold the same views and stand by them.

COUNT. That is a strength which only time and many generations can prove.

CHRISTIAN. A bourgeois can have ancestors, too.

COUNT. Who are your parents, and theirs?

CHRISTIAN. Officials. They were devoted to the service of the State— though as petty officials merely—my father. . . .

COUNT. The individual's accomplishments shine all the brighter against a lowly background, as our illustrious master lately taught us, when he chose a man of your own rank to be the Minister of Posts & Telegraphs.

CHRISTIAN. And figuratively, the footmen will write "Tradesmen's Entrance" over the portes-cochère. [*Laughing aloud.*] The procession of poor but tidy parents approaches from all sides. . . .

COUNT. They do, indeed. Soon they will be seen in all our drawing-rooms. [*Laughs.*] Well, once more, we have managed to understand each other. The decision isn't ours to make, anyhow . . . we can only wait. There is just one thing more that I must mention: My daughter has no dowry. While your fortune has been coming up, ours has been going down, and we have had to practice the most rigid economies so as not to curtail my son's allowance, which would have left him very awkwardly off in his regiment.

CHRISTIAN. [*Bows.*] This is a matter we need not discuss.

THE SERVANT. [*Enters.*] The countess's car. [*Hands a card to* CHRIS-
TIAN, *who takes it and pantomimes that the caller should wait until
the* COUNT *goes.*]

COUNT. [*Exit.*] I shall let you know.

　　　　[CHRISTIAN *looks out of the window and turns to Servant.*
　　　CHRISTIAN *paces to and fro. Writes wire, gives to* SERVANT, *who
　　　takes it out.*]

CHRISTIAN. Show the lady up the other stairs.

　　　　[SYBIL *enters.*]

CHRISTIAN. Child, I'm glad to see you.

SYBIL. Yes, when I'm not in the way, I believe you are.

CHRISTIAN. My career still claims me. I have been thinking lately of
something that will surprise you. Who do you think is coming here?

SYBIL. Your people!

CHRISTIAN. Who told you?

SYBIL. You are not subtle.

CHRISTIAN. The Count von Palen was leaving as you came in. I might
have told him they were coming down from Zürich; he's poor—
I'd have seen to it that he sponsored their social début. But I let
that opportunity slip. No matter though—I shall make another. In
any case I've nothing to wait for. They must come, at once. How
delighted they'll be!

SYBIL. And you think they'll pass muster amongst all your fine
friends. . . .

CHRISTIAN. Mother shall take her holster to bed with her too. I think
of her lying in bed looking back on the days when we used to dream
about my future together—she will feel she has not lived in vain,
when she sees how immensely reality has surpassed the dream. We'll
soon cure her of her worst roughnesses, and dressmakers and mil-
liners will do the rest. But how did you know?

SYBIL. Quite simple to guess. They were becoming necessary to you.
You've missed them and missed them badly. I haven't spent many
nights with you these two years but enough still to know what you're
thinking about as you drop off to sleep. And it was always about
them. . . . I've known what was behind the flash in your eyes,
when you talked of your big profits. Since you've had them at such
a safe distance, you've been quite desperately keen on your old people;
at least as keen as you can be. You talked of nothing without referring to them by some roundabout inference. Oh, not directly, of
course.

CHRISTIAN. I have missed them very much.

SYBIL. Made yourself believe you did.

CHRISTIAN. Mother and I were real affinities. She did not exist except in me. I was a little god to her and she never doubted that the great career she prophesied for me would come to pass. We had ceased even to talk about it—a look and a smile said it all. And father was the bass-accompaniment.

SYBIL. Was my faith in your future any less than hers?

CHRISTIAN. You insisted on being thanked for yours. But *there* was a person who asked no thanks—I was all the happiness she demanded.

SYBIL. On the other hand, your father has behaved disgracefully. He knew he could scare you to death by threatening to turn up—and a very effective lever he made of it——

CHRISTIAN. Which he didn't use to any great extent—what does a couple of thousand matter one way or the other?

SYBIL. If he'd had the least idea of the style you're living in now, he'd have played the same game to better purpose. He'll take good care of himself.

CHRISTIAN. Let him. I ask nothing better— That is the fiendish thing about families whose roots lie just beneath the surface of the ground. They have no feeling of unity—they don't understand what it means to derive life and vital impetus from a single source. With us, one gorges while the other starves. But if we were to generate in ourselves the idea that we were each but the branch of a common trunk, bound to it by every vein and fibre and dependent upon its well-being for our own, then the happiness of each of us would be the concern of all of us.

SYBIL. A frightfully ancient idea—*our* generation never inspired that.

CHRISTIAN. How dare you take that position, my girl? Do you set your knowledge of the social changes of our time above mine? You are merely echoing the catchwords that socialists have drummed into your ears, about the lowest beggars being entitled to rights in the world.

SYBIL. I see what is, not what might be—and I see the countless masses of those who will have bread, no matter whom they trample underfoot to get it.

CHRISTIAN. The struggle for existence—I know. I've been through it. But I dug myself out in another way than theirs—my urge came from within, made me dash right through the middle way of bourgeois comfort—because I knew that real life only began on the other side. And you saw me reach it, tearing the mean rags off my back and changing the flapping ribbon at my neck into a decent and well-knotted tie, and gaining, little by little, the knowledge of social usage which a man of superior standing requires.

SYBIL. There is no end to that struggle, Christian. At the topmost step you will still find the one stronger than you waiting for you—there is always the unrelenting enemy whom you will have to overcome or be destroyed in the attempt.

CHRISTIAN. Typical proletariat theory. You are generations short of appreciating the real truth.

SYBIL. To think it was I who taught him——

CHRISTIAN. Not to eat fish with his knife, and not to pick his teeth! You never went beyond the superficial things. Outwardly you are a woman of the world, Sybil, but inwardly I wonder how much like one you have made yourself.

SYBIL. That was not my ambition.

CHRISTIAN. And the grapes are very sour.

SYBIL. And just because you've at last made up your mind to bring back your parents. . . .

CHRISTIAN. Whom I hold in the deepest affection. . . .

SYBIL. Yes, ever since humble origin has become the fashion——

CHRISTIAN. Adoration, even.

SYBIL. Yes—I understand parents are being shown this season! If you really cared for them, you couldn't tolerate——

CHRISTIAN. Be silent!

SYBIL. You couldn't tolerate the idea of your mother's Sunday straw bonnet and your Father's shoes providing entertainment for all those new high and mighty friends of yours. Your first idea, which saved them from ridicule and you from humiliation, was the greatest kindness you could have done them. And it was clever too—naturally —and served its purpose to perfection.

CHRISTIAN. I have become a rich man—I have satisfied all the more serious exigencies. I have at last earned the right to repose myself and contemplate the amenities of life. The first luxury a man of fortune may offer himself is surely his family.

SYBIL. Your father and mother are not "luxuries" that you can "afford" or "not afford." If you honestly love them, and feel like worshiping at the shrine of the household—do so, but don't parade it. Don't make them the victims of your passion for good form. Marry your countess if you want to, but you would not be wise to give her your people to judge you by. With her, your best safeguard is your mystery, and the remoteness of your caste from hers. You have so much that others have not—you're not obliged to have parents too.

CHRISTIAN. But I'm dead keen on the idea. I mean I've absolutely set my heart on having them. I have done the utmost to get an appointment for Father—took every bit of influence I could bring to bear. Don't try to talk me out of it—I have made up my mind. There are certain feelings you are not qualified to pass judgment on, since you yourself are nothing but the accidental product of an accidental union, and your entire career since has been a mere succession of accidents.

SYBIL. You are trying to create an impassable gulf between ūs.

CHRISTIAN. It was there long before today. We are utter strangers. You'd better go.

SYBIL. Such *utter* strangers as all that, boy? I seem to remember the same utter stranger borrowing 20 mark pieces from me—not so very long ago.

CHRISTIAN. You have a vivid imagination. Your services were for sale. I hired them. You have been paid—in full. You are now dismissed. No comments—please.

SYBIL. I have none to make. There is no word in any language for anything so contemptible as you! I'd give my life to know it if there were!

CHRISTIAN. Go home and look up your dictionaries. If you believe I am what yoū have just said, you will be creating a false likeness of me to yourself, and so ruin your memories of the great love of your life. However, that is your own affair. But if you attempt to take the world into your confidence about me, I shall see that the law deals with you without consideration.

[SYBIL *stands looking at him as though unable to believe her ears, then dashes out.*]

So much for that. Another boat burned, at last. [*Practises fencing exercises with a rapier.*]

[*The bell rings insistently.*]

Who's there? [*He goes to the door.*]

[*A moment later, his voice is heard outside in a cry.*]

Mother!" [*He returns with* THEOBALD *in deep mourning.*]

THEOBALD. [*After a pause, during which* CHRISTIAN *leans against the door sobbing.*] There's no arguing with fate, Christian. All you can do is to take what you get and go through with it. If it hadn't come on me like a thunderbolt, I could have let you down easier. But your mother was full of surprises all her life; we might have known the last thing she did would be a surprise too.

CHRISTIAN. We must bring her here and see that she is buried with all due honour. . . .

THEOBALD. She was—yesterday.

CHRISTIAN. And I was never sent for.

THEOBALD. I thought, why put you to all the trouble. Besides, how was I to know you could arrange to leave? The thing came over her all of a sudden. she knew she'd come to the end. She pulled me down to her and said—I could hardly hear her then,—"And don't you let my Christel know." Her wishes, so— What is it? Are you cold?

[CHRISTIAN *goes out.*]

THEOBALD. It's bowled him over——

CHRISTIAN. [*Returns with a black suit over his arm. He changes his clothes partially concealed by a screen.*] Now you can tell me all about it.

THEOBALD. There's very little to tell. She was sitting drinking her coffee—you know how she always did, with the lump of sugar on her tongue. She said she was feeling hot, and just fell all in a heap——

CHRISTIAN. [*Sobbing spasmodically.*] No illness before, no pain?

THEOBALD. Nothing.

CHRISTIAN. What were her last days like? Was she happy?

THEOBALD. She always made you think she was. That was my old Luise all over again.

CHRISTIAN. How did things stand between you after that last—regrettable event?

THEOBALD. I was very discreet after that. Only every now and then, at stated intervals, so she never found out.

CHRISTIAN. Do you mean to say you didn't break with that person then and there?

THEOBALD. No—she was a queer one, so I thought I'd better put off the split. But I kept it well in hand; no more fireworks. I was very considerate of your mother, Christian—her last days were quite happy, with nothing to bother her.

CHRISTIAN. I shall call in an architect and a sculptor at once—she shall have the monument *my mother* deserved. I could never tell any human soul how much she was to me. Perhaps an artist will be able to interpret my feelings to the world.

THEOBALD. Perhaps. [*Pause.* CHRISTIAN *is evidently grief-stricken. He puts the finishing touches to his mourning garments.*]

CHRISTIAN. How tragically our plans turn out. A telegram is at your house now, asking you both to come here because I had glorious news for you.

THEOBALD. You *wired* for us to come?

CHRISTIAN. I was counting the hours.

THEOBALD. What on earth can have happened?

CHRISTIAN. If you had arrived a few hours later, you would have found yourself a prospective father-in-law.

THEOBALD. Well, well! Is she pretty?

CHRISTIAN. She is a——countess.

THEOBALD. Christian! I don't know where you find the pluck to do these things——

CHRISTIAN. Pluck? . . .

THEOBALD. Well, it's your own funeral, of course—but it looks to me like you're making it mine, too. These wild leaps of yours!

CHRISTIAN. They've taken us a long way, Father.

THEOBALD. What are you doing about the other girl?

CHRISTIAN. So this is all you have to say?

THEOBALD. Well, it seems like fireworks to me——

CHRISTIAN. It is the logical outcome of a perfectly natural chain of circumstances.

THEOBALD. With a petty official for a father and a tailor's daughter for a mother—I'd call it highway robbery. And her father a count and all her relations—you've lost your mind, my boy—that's what's happened to you.

CHRISTIAN. What is this nonsense you're talking?

THEOBALD. It's crazier than all the farces in the whole world. You're making guys of us, that's all. You don't seem to have a vestige of consideration for us left. Why, I've never even set eyes on a count. Every time I come near you, you turn us all upside down. Why can't you let me be! You can't seem able to remember that your father is nothing but a petty official on the retired list. Tommyrot!

CHRISTIAN. You're talking rubbish.

THEOBALD. How dare you do this to me! You're making me a laughingstock and a by-word!

CHRISTIAN. But . . .

THEOBALD. It's the Seyfferts in you. Your mother had a screw loose too. I'll go daft over this. It's worse than when you sent us away—it's worse than your mother's death, even.

CHRISTIAN. But, Father . . .

THEOBALD. [*With increasing excitement.*] Trying to mate a mouse with a giraffe are you? Tight rope tricks—going in for the abnormal now—you've exhausted everything else! Sixty years old and your mother goes and dies on my hands. It was a blow, I'd got used to her. Still it was a natural thing to happen. But the Maskes—Theobald Maske that everyone knows what he is—what'll I be doing with a family of counts? You will make me as crazy as you are yourself.

[CHRISTIAN *has picked up the rapier with an air of resignation.* THEOBALD *is beside himself.*]

Going to murder me now, are you? I'd do a lot better dying right here as a decent civil-servant in his right mind which I am than die of ridicule. Don't you remember what you began as at all any more? Have you forgotten the little room and the canary, and the walks we used to take together? You had to be extra respectful to the chief clerk in those days. And now a count——

CHRISTIAN. [*Anxiously.*] Please listen though. . . .

THEOBALD. How far have we got up the ladder? Oh, I'm going daft with it all!

CHRISTIAN. I fail to understand this outburst. . . .

THEOBALD. And the consequences? Have you overlooked the absolutely fatal consequences? But they're as plain as a pikestaff whether you see 'em or not. When you got rid of me and your mother and sent us to live amongst strangers in our old age, I fairly frothed with rage. But Luise helped me over it and I even ended up by seeing a reason in it, a cruel one but still a reason. The spiritual uplift was there for you, if not for me. You saw that we wanted for nothing, so—you know—live and let live—and gradually I calmed down altogether. [*He jumps up.*] And now you've got the impudence to——

CHRISTIAN. Let me speak. Before I had any idea of this marriage, I began to be obsessed by something that had been gripping me tighter and tighter since the moment I parted with you. I wanted to live in close touch with you and Mother again—now that my fate has willed it otherwise, and I can't have both of you, I want you by yourself—to live here with me—in this house.

THEOBALD. [*Drops into a chair.*] Well, if that doesn't beat the cock fighting!

CHRISTIAN. Father! ! . . .

THEOBALD. You're joking. . . .

CHRISTIAN. Far from it. I could not know you would oppose the idea with such violence.

THEOBALD. You actually *mean* it?

CHRISTIAN. I don't understand you.

THEOBALD. [*Going towards him.*] What?

CHRISTIAN. [*Involuntarily steps back.*] Indeed I do not.

THEOBALD. Not now either, eh?

CHRISTIAN. I mean, I heard what you said, but your scruples seem to me far-fetched—at least most of them.

THEOBALD. Far-fetched?

CHRISTIAN. On the other hand. . . .

THEOBALD. Far-fetched?

CHRISTIAN. [*Timorously.*] Of course on the other hand—if you really . . . then, of course. But good Lord—doesn't it cost a man something to give up the dearest wish of his heart? However, I'll accept no excuse for your absence from my wedding.

THEOBALD. The answer to that is: Either you make this suggestion in sheer thoughtlessness, in which case I say that it is thoroughly low and caddish to make a circus-clown of your old father—a fine joke for you, I must say, me, in my get-up, walking the plank down the church-aisle with a countess on my arm—and at the reception afterwards, sitting there like a scarecrow out of a ditch, in the midst of all the nobility. . . .

CHRISTIAN. Father!

THEOBALD. Either that's your idea, or else you're trying to take it out of me in this rotten way to pay me for the way I made you feel I was your father when you were a boy—so now you want to demean me before all those people— Or perhaps you think you can lay this invitation on me like a poultice for the pain of mother's death. No, Christian, you could spare me this. Go on doing what you've been doing for me; I've been well satisfied with that. And if you should want to do more, don't do it like this with no thought for what it'll lead to. Let me stay in your life as someone that has nothing to do with all this—but won't interfere with you the least bit, either —not under any circumstances. That's why I came up the back stairs just now. I don't want anything but a few new clothes—that's all——

CHRISTIAN. Certainly—my tailor, my haberdashers. . . .

THEOBALD. Not for my style; I know where to get mine from. I'm taking the train back home tonight. [*He takes his hat and stick.*]

CHRISTIAN. [*Anxiously.*] Oh, but you can stay a day or two—surely.

THEOBALD. No such thing! And you stop that nonsense now— What's all this new-fangled way of talking to me? Nobody saw me come and nobody'll see me disappear again—no need for you to come with me. I'll get a bite at the next best inn. If you'd like to drop by some day to visit her grave, I'll be glad to see you. Anything else is all rubbish—you're a good sort, Christel—but live and let live is what I say.

SERVANT. [*Enters.*] Count Palen!

COUNT. [*Follows immediately.*] Marianne's first impulse—which showed her fine feeling—was to come herself with your answer, my dear Maske—she is exceedingly happy—very deeply so, I assure you. [*Theobald has been trying to disappear.*] Won't you introduce me?

CHRISTIAN. [*In the utmost confusion.*] My father . . .

COUNT. Tiens! Now this is—ah—a delightful surprise indeed. Most happy, my dear sir! [*He extends both hands to* THEOBALD.] And I'd always had the impression—how was that I wonder?—that our friend here was an orphan—! [*Laughs.*] I honestly did. So much the happier surprise! Ah, splendid!

CHRISTIAN. Zurich has been my father's home for some time. He came today to tell me my mother died suddenly. I have won Marianne when I need her most. [*He sinks on the* COUNT'S *breast.*]

COUNT. My sincere sympathy! [*To* THEOBALD.] With you too, my dear sir.

THEOBALD. [*Bowing.*] Thank you, your excellency.

COUNT. The best consolation I can offer is for you to go and find your fiancée at once. We two old gentlemen can entertain each other. [*To* THEOBALD.] Have you had lunch? Not yet? Let's get along then. I can't replace your wife with a fiancée for you, but what a decent meal will do, I . . .

CHRISTIAN. My father had planned to return to Zurich immediately.

COUNT. Oh—out of the question—I won't hear of it.

THEOBALD. In either case, one must have lunch.

COUNT. My prerogative. We'll get our condolences and congratulations over as soon as possible, and then— Your son has kept you under lock and key too long. We'll have a bottle of claret and sniff each other over!

THEOBALD. Sniff—is good.

COUNT. Not right?

THEOBALD. [*Laughing.*] I'd say it was a capital word, your excellency.

CHRISTIAN. [*In* THEOBALD'S *ear fiercely.*] Count! [*To the* COUNT.] My father insists upon taking the midday train.

COUNT. [*Energetically.*] Let us alone, do! The old gentlemen are going to eat a good lunch first of all. The rest will take care of itself. Come on!

[COUNT *and* THEOBALD *exeunt.*]

CHRISTIAN. What was that sudden tone he took with me? Have I made a mistake? [*At the window.*] He's making him get into the car first! Is my face red? Am I pale? [*He runs to the mirror.*] I'm shaking like an aspen leaf! [*He jumps on a chair at the window.*] He's taking a cigar. And they're laughing—roaring— Oh my God—it must be at me— What a mistake—what a mistake! [*He rings.* SERVANT *enters.*] Prepare the guest rooms. My father has come. See that he is well looked after.

[SERVANT *goes out, followed to the door by* CHRISTIAN. *Left alone,* CHRISTIAN *gives way to the most violent agitation. Growing somewhat calmer, he goes to the inner room and reappears with two handkerchiefs, one white and one bordered with black. He tries the effect of these alternately before the mirror as the curtain falls.*]

CURTAIN

ACT THREE

Drawing room of a hotel suite. Flowers everywhere. At rear, a wide curtain screening entrance to bedroom.
[*Enter* CHRISTIAN *in evening clothes and cape, wearing many decorations, and* MARIANNE *in bridal dress and cloak.*]

CHRISTIAN. A breath of air and peace—at last.

MARIANNE. What flowers! [*Looking at bouquet.*] From Father! [*She picks up a card and reads.*] For my lost angel, Marianne! And these divine orchids! [*Reading.*] From an unknown.

CHRISTIAN. Romantic! What could those two have kept up that continuous chatter about? Did you hear them?

MARIANNE. Who?

CHRISTIAN. You surely must have noticed our fathers. They absolutely ignored their partners. The stout countess . . .

MARIANNE. Aunt Ursula's almost stone-deaf, anyhow. She had to eat most of her dinner out of her lap—she always drops her food.

CHRISTIAN. Who was that Knight of St. John, two away from you to the right?

MARIANNE. Mother's cousin, Albert Thüngen.

CHRISTIAN. The fellow stared at me as if I'd been a ghost. He forgot to eat.

MARIANNE. We call him Frog-face—he looks it, doesn't he?

CHRISTIAN. There were some orders there that one rarely sees. . . . You and the princess seemed to be very intimate.

MARIANNE. We were together for seven years—when we were little.

CHRISTIAN. For seven years. . . . You call each other by your christian names then?

MARIANNE. Good heavens—we had the same great-grandmother!

CHRISTIAN. The archduchess you mean?

MAID. [*Enters.*] Are you ready for me, your ladyship?

MARIANNE. I'm only madam, now, Anna.

MAID. Very well, your ladyship.

MARIANNE. Stop your "ladyship" and your nonsense. I insist on being obeyed.

MAID. [*Sobbing.*] Yes, madame.

MARIANNE. What's the matter?

MAID. [*Bending over* MARIANNE's *hand.*] It's so sad, madame—you don't belong to us any more.

MARIANNE. I don't belong to myself any more. That's the fate of girls. Yours too. [*Both exit through the curtain.*]

[CHRISTIAN *rushes over to listen to what goes on behind the curtain.*]

Pantomime: Suspicion of ANNA *and resentment.*

MAID'S VOICE. . . . Looked heavenly. The pastor was crying. . . .

MARIANNE. . . . Old Jansen. . . . Rubbish!

MAID'S VOICE. . . . Genuine Brussels . . . flounces of Brussels—so wide . . . Rosebuds . . .

MARIANNE'S VOICE. . . . Ilse Zeitlow in light blue satin to set off her blond hair. . . .

MAID'S VOICE. . . . so décolleté . . . on purpose . . .

MARIANNE'S VOICE. Really, Anna! . . . [*Giggling, then whispering.*]

[CHRISTIAN *leans closer to overhear dialogue—appropriate pantomime.*]

[*Laughter from time to time comes through curtain.*]

MAID'S VOICE. . . . pointed moustache.

[CHRISTIAN. *pantomime.*]

MAID'S VOICE. . . . rather silly-looking, *I* thought.

MARIANNE'S VOICE. Be quiet!

CHRISTIAN. [*Mutters.*] I heard that, Marianne. [*More laughter.*]

[CHRISTIAN *pantomime: Increasing anger.*]

MAID'S VOICE. Killing!

CHRISTIAN. [*It is quiet behind the curtain. Listens with intentness and alarm. Kneels down and tries to look through the curtain.*] You won't step over the threshold of my name, woman, unless that name inspires respect and emotion in you.

MAID. [*Enters.*] May I go to Madame's trunk? [*She takes several things out of the trunk with* CHRISTIAN *looking fiercely on. Then disappears behind the curtain.*]

[CHRISTIAN: *he rivets his eyes on the trunk, suddenly resolved. Picks up Bible out of the trunk. Regards it with contempt and continues rummaging.*]

[THEOBALD *in evening clothes pokes his head round the door.*]

CHRISTIAN. What the devil——

THEOBALD. Just a minute.

CHRISTIAN. What do you want?

THEOBALD. Your loving father——

CHRISTIAN. You're drunk.

THEOBALD. A bit. Loving father all the same. Tried to blow a kiss to you, all evening; couldn't catch you though. Don't argue with me, boy. You're a wizard, you are; I'm proud of you; out and out proud of you, I am. You've dragged all my old notions off of me like so many tissue paper shirts. Principles—opinions—tramped all over 'em; you've done wonderful. All my life I lived by proverbs; Cobbler, stick to your last and all the rest. But not you—you made your own proverbs. The way you treated those people today, as if they weren't your equals, even. You absolutely patronised them. And the way they looked at you, with the greatest respect. You're a marvel. And now here you are with a nice little bit of the nobility to go to bed with!! [*Embraces him.*]

CHRISTIAN. Be quiet, can't you? She's in there! Are you drunk or not?

THEOBALD. A bit. But I know what I'm talking about. I sat at the table and looked at all those toffs with their decorations—and you sitting there too, like a king. . . .

CHRISTIAN. Father!

THEOBALD. Like a king, my darling boy. Our mother ought to have seen you. I had a feeling as if I was looking at a sunrise—a sunrise—no joke— Extraordinary, wasn't it?

CHRISTIAN. Do you mean it?

THEOBALD. You've let out the belt of the Maske family—oh, several holes, my boy. All of me that matters is in you. . . . No—don't say anything. I've got to the confession at last—a question of dignity, not a thing fathers say to their sons: Well here goes: I'm in the way here—I'm going to do the disappearing stunt. So far as the world goes—the best of Theobald Maske is Christian Maske. You've been wanting to get rid of me—you've thought of it before, but it looked a bit brutal, as if you were my enemy. But it's all plain sailing now—we'll both be everlastingly grateful to each other. [*In a sing-song.*] "Adieu—adieu—Hamlet remember me"— Zurich, Grosse Hauptgasse No. 16. There resides Maske, retired civil servant, watching his son with—with rapture from afar!

CHRISTIAN. Someone's coming.

THEOBALD. Let 'em come! Go on as you've begun and don't put your foot in it. They distrust you and despise you and hate you and so on, but they've enormous respect for you. The unknown quantity, eh what?

CHRISTIAN. How do you know?

THEOBALD. The tighter the man, the looser the tongue. They were all blind drunk, but I was only a bit. Get to the point where you don't know the Eagle of Hohenzollern from the Iron Cross and you'll let anybody see down to the middle of your insides.

CHRISTIAN. What about the old man? Has he ever said anything about that awful day he came and found I wasn't an orphan after all?

THEOBALD. Oh, he'd suspected it before—maybe he still remembers. But at the reception when I was absolutely basking in your glory I could see he'd caught it too. Besides his heart had been softened in advance by your little dove in there. As a father, his resistance broke down altogether.

CHRISTIAN. So *they're* licked!

THEOBALD. Done for. Now keep tight hold and don't let go. As a matter of fact I've always believed our stock stood for something, but I could only pass on the idea to the ones nearest me—had no wider influence.

CHRISTIAN. To me, you mean?

THEOBALD. Yes—and you shot us further along——

CHRISTIAN. I've bent the bow! The string is vibrating under my hand.

THEOBALD. Then let the first arrow be for her and see that it strikes home.

CHRISTIAN. We're going to weave ourselves into this fabric now.

THEOBALD. Yes—part of its texture and design!

CHRISTIAN. I hold the trump and I'll play it for all it's worth!

[THEOBALD *goes to curtain looks back and winks. They laugh. Both chuckle and then laugh heartily together.*]

CHRISTIAN. Hurrah for the Maskes!

THEOBALD. I'm on to you, boy—or words to that effect! What's bred in the bone— [*He trots to the door, turns to throw a kiss to* CHRISTIAN *and goes out.*]

[CHRISTIAN *strides pompously about the room.*]

MARIANNE. [*Enters in negligé.*] How do I look?

CHRISTIAN. [*In a preoccupied manner.*] Very nice. . . .

MARIANNE. This lace has associations. On the same night in *her* life my mother wore it.

CHRISTIAN. There's no such thing as "the same."

MARIANNE. No? Is there no other woman in your past that I remind you of—at this moment? You must tell me everything about your life—you must have no secrets from me now. What number am I on the list, and which of the others meant a great deal to you? Have you come to me with memories of any of them still in your mind?

CHRISTIAN. You mustn't talk like this. I've got to keep my thoughts in order.

MARIANNE. [*Her arms around his neck.*] I was in love with an ensign once. I was only sixteen then. A pink and white boy with a little blond moustache. That was all I ever knew about him.

CHRISTIAN. What do you know about me?

MARIANNE. I see you when I shut my eyes; you are tall and dark, and very thick set, and you roll from side to side when you walk.

CHRISTIAN. Do I? [*He goes to the mirror and takes a few steps.*] A slight swaying movement, perhaps. Rather rhythmical—certainly nothing worse.

MARIANNE. [*Gives a clear laugh.*] And how do *I* walk? [*Raises her skirt and trips along.*]

CHRISTIAN. What else do you know about me?

MARIANNE. Your business.

CHRISTIAN. Well?

MARIANNE. Banker. Does it matter?

CHRISTIAN. At the age of thirty-six years I am president of the greatest commercial enterprise in the empire. Controls one-fifth of the national wealth.

MARIANNE. *Tiens!*

CHRISTIAN. Your father's pet word! Has he discussed my affairs with you?

MARIANNE. Sort of——

CHRISTIAN. That means he has done so—in full detail.

MARIANNE. I'm tired.

CHRISTIAN. Not yet. Am I not after all still a stranger to you, since your father never spoke seriously to you about me. Are you sure he never did—think! Didn't he come home one day in a state of wild excitement? Didn't he? Try and remember.

MARIANNE. I've never seen him wildly excited in my life.

CHRISTIAN. I suppose he wasn't then. But at any rate it's an achievement isn't it, for a man to be in such a position at my age? It's like becoming a general at thirty-six.

MARIANNE. Only a prince can be that. [*She sits on his lap.*]

CHRISTIAN. Or?

MARIANNE. Or who?

CHRISTIAN. Think!

MARIANNE. I don't know.

CHRISTIAN. Or a genius. In the course of this past year they tried to make forty-one companies issue new stock to a total of about three quarters of a billion marks. I said that I was opposed to the idea for the following reasons: That for those seven hundred and fifty millions the public would not be given actual goods, but merely the hypothetical product of the labour of some half a million potential workers which the land will be encouraged to produce. The stock capital of manufacturing concerns consists entirely in the mass of people and their output. Do you follow me?

MARIANNE. [*Still on his lap.*] I'm trying to——

CHRISTIAN. Pay attention! If there's no work, the masses choke the producing machine. The minute a new chimney-stack goes up, a new ventilator is opened. So we leaders stand—I told them—at the valve controlling the source of population; it is therefore our charge to see the capital is not disproportionate to the natural increase of population. Do you understand?

MARIANNE. I think so.

CHRISTIAN. We should do better to slow up production and thereby improve quality. So there you have a slight idea of Political Economy as I practice it. [*Lost in his theme he dumps her off his lap and marches around the room.*] Eh? That's what I mean by a distinguished idea, as Helmholtz would have said. [*He seizes* MARIANNE *by a button on her gown and shakes her gently backwards and forwards, looking piercingly at her as he speaks.*] I could tell you another of my marvellous utterances on the question of the reduction of rates for steerage passengers on our steamship lines. The vast majority of people are short-sighted, so that the economic destiny of millions lies in the hands of us few.

MARIANNE. Are you so very rich?

CHRISTIAN. That is a shopkeeper's word; I have power to achieve everything that my blood gives me strength and stamina to achieve. You've seen my father a few times. Personality, isn't he? The dominant traits of our family are strongly marked in him. Nothing superfluous, nothing without a purpose. Did you notice at the reception, how impressively he made himself felt? A pity you never knew my grandfather. A gay dog—but— So you see what my ancestors planted in me. I am the late but inevitable efflorescence of their qualities.

MAID. [*Enters.*] Madame—your diamonds. You would rather have them with you here—these hotels—you never know. Or, you, sir?

[CHRISTIAN *takes the coronet.*]

Good-night, madame. . . . Good-night, sir. [*Exit.*]

CHRISTIAN. What an odd shape.

MARIANNE. The coronet of a marquise. A great-aunt of my mother's, the Marquise d'Urfes, left it to all the women of our family to wear on their wedding day.

CHRISTIAN. *Bon.* What was I saying?—Never mind, I've a surprise for you.

MARIANNE. [*Clapping her hands.*] Oh, do let me see.

CHRISTIAN. Turn round a minute while I unwrap it and set it up for you.

MARIANNE. [*Her back turned.*] One, two, three——

CHRISTIAN. [*Uncovers a picture which has been leaning against the wall, and stands it up in front of him, his legs supporting it. It is the portrait of a woman.*] You may look now.

[MARIANNE *looks at it.*]

My mother, Marianne, she also wants to see you face to face to-day. She loved her boy very dearly.

MARIANNE. What a striking face!

CHRISTIAN. Isn't it? It's a Renoir.

MARIANNE. [*Flies to* CHRISTIAN'S *arms. To the portrait.*] I shall love your son better than myself. *My* Christian!

CHRISTIAN. Careful. It's a great work of art; you mustn't hurt it. [*He has stood the picture against a table.*]

MARIANNE. Such lovely thick brown hair. You have her coloring. Exquisite skin.

CHRISTIAN. She came of a peasant family many centuries old. Rumours of Viking ancestry. See those substantial jewels—heirlooms, of course, that red coral ear-ring— A remote forbear had some official post at Delaro in the Swedish straits. There's a tradition of how he once met Charles XII.

MARIANNE. I never saw such marvelous hair!

CHRISTIAN. It came down to her knees. Renoir saw her in the Bois de Boulogne one day. It was decision at first sight—at all costs he must paint her.

MARIANNE. I don't wonder.

CHRISTIAN. But hear the way it happened. That's the best part of the story. Undo your ears for the prettiest calamity you ever heard. She and Father were walking in the Bois after one of those ceremonious luncheons at the Cascades. Complete with Burgundy. All of a sudden she becomes rooted to the ground. Absolutely refuses to budge. Father, with his grey top hat at a slightly too festive angle— he's told the story a thousand times—called her and coaxed her and begged her. But there she stood.

MARIANNE. What was the matter?

[CHRISTIAN *whispers in her ear.*]

[*With a peal of gay laughter.*] Oh, charming! Perfect!

CHRISTIAN. [*Laughing unrestrainedly.*] And that Renoir! You can well imagine, he loved to tell me the story too. Roaring—literally roaring with laughter. The creature's lovely embarrassment. A sight for the gods.

MARIANNE. And of course she couldn't dare to pick them up! So she had to go on standing there against the sun! Oh, delightful! [*Laughs.*]

CHRISTIAN. To make a long story short—he contrives admittance to the honeymoon retreat, taking with him a French vicomte, who was also present at the scene.

MARIANNE. How long ago was that?

CHRISTIAN. About a year before I was born.

MARIANNE. Isn't it odd how the stories of people's lives bridge the distances between them. I feel I know her so much better now. But it must have been a most unpleasant predicament for your father.

CHRISTIAN. He was even then the *bon garçon* he is today—a piquant comedy like that caught him too. He adored his bride, and in her delicious confusion she was more adorable still!

MARIANNE. She knew how to dress.

CHRISTIAN. A past-mistress.

MARIANNE. How lovely those old fashions were with the ruffled capes! It is sad to think that all the exquisite women who wore them that way are dead and gone.

CHRISTIAN. I'm having a monument put up in Buchow to her memory. [*He hangs the picture on the wall.*]

MARIANNE. Have you bought it?

CHRISTIAN. I'm going to. It's a fine estate. Especially for the monument. She was in every way so much a sort of superwoman that the most imposing monument is no more than she deserves.

MARIANNE. I have misjudged your family dreadfully—I realise it now. But I begin to correct my idea of them. When you talk of people, you have the gift of making them come so vividly alive.

CHRISTIAN. Put it better and say I am capable of ideas. Most people are capable only of words and words and more words.

MARIANNE. I want Anne.

CHRISTIAN. Not that wretched girl again!

MARIANNE. I can't undo this thing in the back.

CHRISTIAN. Come here. [*He begins to look for hooks and eyes.*] Words by which no two minds understand the same thing and which are therefore, useless in bringing any two people to complete understanding.

[MARIANNE *yawns.*]

Pure reason assembles groups of similar visual or mental concepts into a single expression which determines the concept in its essence and is called the *idea*.

[MARIANNE *yawning loudly.*]

It is the conquest of multiplicity. The slip too?

MARIANNE. Please.

CHRISTIAN. Now let me have your attention, Marianne. Every accomplishment of the human mind is directed to a single end, namely, to taking its bearings in the infinity of the world about it—thus achieving its victory over multiplicity. Hence, the words beech and oak, and so forth, names which have been forced to contain their own multiplicity, become simply "woods." [*He has come to the last hook.*]

MARIANNE. Thank you. [*She puts her foot on a chair and unbuttons her shoes.*]

CHRISTIAN. Only stupidity and ignorance can make the joke "He can't see the woods for the trees."

[MARIANNE *goes behind the curtain into the bedroom.*]

Where are you going? What they mean is of course: "He can no longer see the trees for the woods." [*He follows her and stands at the curtain.*] To master this principle is to have the entire theory of knowledge in your pocket. [*He comes toward the front and says loudly over his shoulder.*] At any rate, there's an inkling for you into the way a brain like mine works. Eh? [*Rubbing his hands, to himself.*] Ça marche. [*Remains standing in front of the picture, deeply moved.*] Dear Mother! [*Loud.*] As a young girl she went with friends on a visit to the United States, returning via the South Sea Islands and Asia. In Honolulu King Kalakaüa fell madly in love with her.

[*Someone is heard going to bed behind the curtain.*]
That was in eighteen-eighty or eighty-one.

[*He has taken off his shoes; and only now removes his coat, so that he stands revealed in the full magnificence of his decorations. He raises his arms and looks round expectantly.*]

MARIANNE'S VOICE. What became of the vicomte?

CHRISTIAN. What vicomte?

MARIANNE'S VOICE. The one who was with Renoir in the Bois that day, and went with him to your people's house afterwards.

CHRISTIAN. Ah, the vicomte! Yes, of course—why, he——

MARIANNE'S VOICE. What became of him?

CHRISTIAN. [*With immense triumph as the inspiration strikes him.*] My God—I've got it! [*He strides across the room past the mirror.*]

MARIANNE'S VOICE. Is it a secret?

CHRISTIAN. [*To himself.*] Ah, my little countess—you're for it this time.

CHRISTIAN. [*He goes to the curtains and whispers through.*] Marianne!

MARIANNE. [*Agitated.*] I'm coming—what's the matter? [*She enters in peignoir hastily donned.*]

CHRISTIAN. That question of yours—it was predestined—I knew it instantly.

MARIANNE. What did I say? I don't understand.

CHRISTIAN. The vicomte; what happened to him.

MARIANNE. Well?

CHRISTIAN. The truth would never have passed my lips if——

MARIANNE. Christian! What *is* it?

CHRISTIAN. No—No! I cannot tell you.

MARIANNE. Christian! I am your wife—it is my right . . . !

CHRISTIAN. I am a son too.

MARIANNE. Your duty is to me.

CHRISTIAN. There is also a son's respect for his mother—and his own self-respect.

MARIANNE. You mean——

CHRISTIAN. Not a word from me, Marianne.

MARIANNE. So they—the vicomte . . . ?

CHRISTIAN. [*Sternly.*] Marianne, I forbid you ever—so long as we live—to broach this subject again. Nobody, not even I, must ever so much as guess what you imagine or suspect. My name is Maske, and that's an end of the matter.

MARIANNE. Good Heavens above! I promise you all that. But what you are to me, now that I know this—that is my own affair! [*Softly.*] Ah, my Christian, the last barrier between us has fallen now. I am all yours, from this day forward, yours utterly! [*With outstretched arms before the picture.*] Blessed Adulteress! Mother! [*Sinking into* CHRISTIAN's *arms.*] And my dearest husband, lord and master!

[CHRISTIAN *smiles and makes his vast and sweeping gesture.*]

THE END

UNCLE'S BEEN DREAMING

An Old-fashioned Comedy

by

KARL VOLLMOELLER

After a story by Fyodor Dostoievsky

CAST OF CHARACTERS

MARIA ALEXANDROVNA
AFANASSIJ MATVEITCH, her husband
SINAIDA, *her daughter*
PAUL ALEXANDROVITCH MOSGLIAKOFF, *a young man of good family*
THE PRINCE
NASTASIA
SOFIA PETROVNA, *the Colonel's lady*
ANNA NIKOLAIEVNA, *the wife of the Public Prosecutor*
NATALYA DMITRIEVNA ⎫
FELISSATA MIKAILOVNA ⎬ *Ladies of the haute volée of Mordassoff*
KATERINA PETROVNA ⎭
GLAFIRA, *a servant*
GRISCHKA, *Afanassij's valet*
THE OLD WOMAN IN BLACK

The action takes place in a small provincial city.

UNCLE'S BEEN DREAMING

ACT I

The big drawing-room in the house of MARIA ALEXANDROVNA. *Faded red silk hangings, old-fashioned plush furniture, white door. On the whole, a good-sized, not over-comfortable apartment, furnished with provincial elegance. In the centre of the rear wall, a fireplace with a large baroque mirrored overmantle, and in front of it a porcelain clock in very bad taste. On either side of the fireplace a door. A third door in the wall, left. On the right, a grand piano. A few comfortable chairs in picturesque disorder about the fireplace. In the centre of the room, a round table covered with a cloth of dazzling whiteness, on which stand a silver samovar and a handsome tea service.*

The MAID *and* NASTASIA *are setting up the samovar.* SINAIDA *is sitting in the foreground apathetically, gazing with sombre eyes, into space.* NASTASIA PETROVNA *is a widow, scarcely thirty years old, dark and fresh-complexioned, with dark, bright eyes. She is a really pretty creature and gay by nature. She laughs readily, has a shrewd head on her shoulders, and is a born gossip. She has two children and would gladly marry again. She is somewhat independent in manner. Her husband was an officer in the army.*

SINAIDA *is one of those visions of womanhood whose entrance into any company always arouses universal delight. She is tall, slender and dark, with marvellous, almost jet-black eyes and the bosom of a goddess. Her arms and shoulders are of statuesque beauty, her little feet ravishing. She walks like a queen. Today she is a trifle pale. Between her exquisitely chiselled lips, the small, even teeth are seen like two rows of pearls. She moves with haughty nonchalance. She is dressed very simply, in white—white becomes her to perfection. Now she goes listlessly to the piano, and turns over the leaves of an old almanac. Glafira, a blond, stout, elderlyish peasant-woman, watches her furtively, trying to catch her eye.*

Evidently, she has something to tell her which NASTASIA *is not to hear, and her thoughts are only half on her work.*

NASTASIA. Well, I never did! Such surprises! What do you think of it, Sina? Two at a time! [*To the* SERVANT.] Do be careful, Glafira! That's the second cup you've knocked over. [*To* SINAIDA.] I thought Paul was not to be here for another week yet, and here he comes already bringing another surprise with him in the shape of the Prince. . . . [*To the* SERVANT *who is still busy with the samovar.*] Hurry up, Glafira. The gentlemen will be here for their breakfast any minute now! [*To* SINAIDA.] Oh Sina, just think of it! Actually! Why, it's five years since the Prince has been seen in Mordassoff! Sinotschka? [SINAIDA *shrugs her shoulders indifferently.*] I asked the Prince's valet what he took for breakfast. White bread toast and orange marmalade. That shows how long he's been abroad. [*To the* SERVANT.] Hurry up, Glafira! [*Turns and goes busily towards the door on the left of the fireplace.*] I'll see to his marmalade myself. [*She goes out.*]

    [GLAFIRA, *as soon as* NASTASIA *has left the room, leaves her work and looks stealthily at* SINAIDA.]

SINAIDA. [*Coolly, in a low voice.*] Here is the letter—take it back! Haven't I forbidden you once and for all to accept letters for me. . . . Has that mother of his been here again? [GLAFIRA *nods.*] After I have forbidden you a dozen times to have her in the kitchen.

GLAFIRA. [*Sighing.*] Oh Sinaida Afanassjevna, if you only knew! If you could only have seen her! Such a poor little old woman in her black silk dress! She'd been standing outside the kitchen door for hours, shivering all over and peering in until I come along. The little old shrivelled-up thing! How could any of us have the heart to turn her away?

SINAIDA. Take her letter back to her. I've had her told a hundred times that I don't wish to hear another word about him.

GLAFIRA. These last few days she's been taking on so, Nastasia got suspicious. I always say she's a godmother of mine that's down on her luck. She was here before six this morning . . . she's downstairs now, sitting there at a corner of the kitchen table, crying over her Vasja.

SINAIDA. [*Winces for the first time.*] That will do, Glafira.

GLAFIRA. Oh, Sinaida Afanassjevna, how can you hear her without your heart bleeding for her! First thing this morning, when she came, she said: "For the love of God go to your mistress and tell

her that my poor Vasja can't live and can't die. Say he calls down
the blessing of God and the Saints on her, and he begs her pardon
on his bended knees . . . and say . . . "

SINAIDA. Take the letter back. Take it, I say.

GLAFIRA. She said: "For the blessed Virgin's sake, ask your mistress
if she won't send one word of forgiveness to my Vasja—he can't
live and he can't die," she said . . . "before it is too late, tell her
. . . before it pleases God to take him to Himself . . . her only
son . . . and . . . and . . ." [SINAIDA *gazes at her with dark
intensity. Encouraged by* SINAIDA's *silence, goes on.*] And she won't
leave this place, dead or alive, till she . . . till she has talked with
you herself, Sinaida Afanassjevna.

SINAIDA. [*Is about to fly into anger, but controls herself, and relapses
into her thoughtful mood. Pause.*] Is he worse again?

GLAFIRA. The fever is on him day and night, she says.

SINAIDA. [*Suddenly.*] That's enough. Let her wait. I shall see what
is to be done. Go now.

[VOICES *outside.* GLAFIRA *escapes in haste through the door
in the rear through which* NASTASIA *had left, and does not re-
appear.* SINAIDA *goes back to the almanac, and turns over the
leaves.*]

[MARIA ALEXANDROVNA *and* PAUL ALEXANDROVITCH MOS-
GLIAKOFF *come in from the left.* NASTASIA *brings up the rear.*
MARIA ALEXANDROVNA *is stately and dark, well-preserved, with
the utmost assurance of manner, obviously born to command. She
loves the dignified and ceremonious; well-turned phrases are a
delight to her. She is incontestably the first lady of Mardassoff,
and does not for a moment forget it. On this occasion, she has
arrayed herself most miraculously, and is radiant.* MOSGLIAKOFF
*is blond, well-groomed and twenty-six. He is of sprightly humour,
a confirmed raconteur, and is inclined to swift enthusiasms.
Secretly,* MARIA ALEXANDROVNA *considers him feather-headed,
but for the moment she is at her most agreeable towards him.*]

MARIA. [*To* PAUL.] I hope you'll admit now, Paul, that we have
accommodated the prince in a manner befitting his rank. We have
arranged for him to have the small drawing-room, the yellow bedroom and the front room next to this one for his dressing-room.
[*She points to the small door to the left.*] At first I thought he
might have the guest room on the first floor, but this will be more
comfortable for him, the dear, delightful prince! [*To* SINAIDA,

standing by the piano, idle and indifferent.] Sinotschka, what do *you* say to all these surprises? [SINAIDA *gives her a forced smile, and goes on turning over the leaves of the almanac.*] I am so very happy, Paul; I could shout it from the housetops! Quite apart from the delicious surprise of your own coming, two weeks before you told Sinaida and me to expect you . . . that is something by itself. But I am really quite overcome with joy at your bringing the prince with you. Do you know what we were to each other, once upon a time, he and I? That must be about six years ago, quite. . . . You remember, Sina, surely? Oh but of course not— I am forgetting. You were at your aunt's then. . . . You may not believe me, Paul, but I was a friend, a sister, a mother to him then! That is why he held *my* house in such grateful recollection, *ce pauvre prince!* And all these six long years I have been filled with anxiety about him. They say that dreadful woman he's been living with in Duchanovo has positively ruined his life. However, thank God you have delivered him from *that* captivity at last! Do please tell us once more how you succeeded in your ruse.

PAUL. [*Flattered.*] I have already gone over it once, Maria Alexandrovna. It was this way: I had been travelling all night—without a wink of sleep, naturally—[*With a hesitating glance at* SINAIDA.]—I need not say what eager haste I was in to get here. Well, it was about six o'clock when we pulled into the last station, which was Igischevo, and called for horses. They told me there that a prince had just left the station, after spending the night there. He had said he was on his way to his estate. About nine versts out of the town, I come upon an ancient coach overturned in a ditch, with the coachman and two servants standing by, doing nothing. Heartrending groans and shrieks from within! I investigate—good God, who should it be but himself—Prince Gavrila! What an encounter! I yell at him: "Prince! Uncle!" He not only doesn't budge—he hardly recognises me, even. The last time we'd seen each other was at St. Petersburg seven years before. I wasn't much more than a child then. I introduce myself. He is overjoyed. He throws his arms round my neck, still trembling with fright, and bursts into tears—yes, actually—into tears. I make him take a seat in my carriage, and tell him I insist on his coming with me to Mordassoff for one day at least, to recuperate. He says that Stepanida . . .

MARIA. Stepanida. . . . Do you hear that, Sina? That's that un-

speakable woman who has been keeping the poor dear prince a
prisoner on his own estate for six years.

PAUL. She it is! Last year she chased me out of Duchanovo herself, at the end of a broom! Well, it seems that Stepanida had
just had a letter from Moscow to say that someone—her father,
or one of his other daughters, was dying—I don't know who
exactly. But the long and short of it was that she had decided to
part from her prince for ten days and adorn the capital with her
presence. He was quite wretched without his Stepanida, apparently,
so on the next day but one after she'd gone, he ordered his carriage
and said he would drive over to the monastery at Swjetosersk. They
capsized, however, swinging round a curve, and I became their
rescuer. I suggested the house of our mutual and honoured friend,
Maria Alexandrovna, as an alternative destination. And immediately he said that you were the most delightful woman he'd ever
known. And here we are.

MARIA. There's a charming raconteur for you, Sina! But do tell me,
Paul, just how *are* you related to the prince. You call him uncle,
don't you?

PAUL. Lord, I honestly don't know where the connection does come
in. I call him uncle, and he calls me nephew. That's about all
there is to it, up to the present at any rate.

MARIA. And I repeat, Paul, that your bringing him straight to me
was a direct intervention of Providence! I tremble to think of
what would have become of the poor creature in any other house.
They'd have fallen upon him tooth and nail and devoured him
like harpies. You've no conception what an ill-bred, ravening lot
of people they are here!

NASTASIA. Whom else could he have taken him to, I'd like to know!
Not to the Public Prosecutor's wife, I should hope! That Anna
Nikolaievna, indeed!

MARIA. He's a long time making his appearance—isn't that rather
strange?

PAUL. Uncle, you mean? Oh, he'll be a good five hours more making
his toilette! Besides, he's got absolutely no memory left, so it's more
than likely he's completely forgotten he's staying in your house.
He's a marvellous old gentleman!

MARIA. Oh, but you really must not talk like that.

PAUL. Well it's true, Maria Alexandrovna. He's not really a *person*
at all, as you might say, but a sort of "general effect." Half a corpse

that has escaped being buried, due to an oversight. He's got artificial eyes and false teeth; his legs are made of wood and cork and go by machinery; he also talks by clockwork.

MARIA. Good Heavens! How can I hear you saying such things! Young man, aren't you ashamed to speak so of so venerable a gentleman, and you his nephew? Quite apart from his unparalleled kindness of heart, and his chivalrous generosity. But I must at least ask you to remember that he is what we may call the flower of a fast-fading aristocracy. I understand that you, my friend, with the modern ideas which are constantly upon your tongue, can turn such things to ridicule; but I have lived longer in the world than you, and seen more of it. And believe me, *mon cher* Paul, a prince is still a prince, though he wear a peasant's smock. . . . But here I am, wasting my time in chatter instead of going to find out whether the prince has everything he needs. He may be wanting something, and I can assure you that *my* servants . . . [*She goes out.*]

NASTASIA. Maria Alexandrovna is very happy, if you ask me, that the prince didn't install himself at the Public Prosecutor's; that wife of his is such a flirt! And she's always hinted that she's related to the prince in some way. [*Receiving no answer, she looks round at* PAUL *and* SINA, *at once surmises the truth and leaves the room as though she has business elsewhere in the house.*]

PAUL. [*Looking shyly at* SINA.] Sina, are you angry with me?

SINAIDA. [*With a trace of confusion.*] Angry? Why?

PAUL. Because of my premature return. But I had no patience to wait two whole weeks. I must know at once, now, what my fate is to be. You look so gloomy. . . . Are you very angry, Sina?

SINAIDA. I expected you to bring that up again. You want your answer. My answer to you is the same as it has always been: wait. If it will set you more at rest, I will add that you need not consider this a definite rejection. But I wish to be left absolutely free to make up my mind, and if I decide not to accept you in the end, you will not be able to reproach me with having raised false hopes. Now you know my whole mind on the subject.

PAUL. But what do I know? Do you mean to hold out hope for me? Does all this mean that you allow me to hope, Sina?

SINAIDA. Remember carefully what I said, and interpret it as you choose. Exactly as you choose. I can only repeat: wait! And there's

still this much more to say, Paul Alexandrovitch. By coming back
sooner than we arranged, . . .

[*At this moment* MARIA *reappears, closely followed by* NA-
STASIA.]

MARIA. He'll be here directly, Sina. Quick, Nastasia, fresh tea!

NASTASIA. The District Attorney's wife has lost no time spying on us.
She's just sent her maid over to our kitchen for something. She'll
be up to some intrigue pretty soon. . . .

MARIA. What is that to me? Really, Nastasia, it astonishes me to find
you continually referring to me as an enemy of that poor Anna
Nikolaievna's. She is young, and she hasn't a thought in her head
apart from dressing up. Still, I firmly believe that it is better to
have even clothes as an interest rather than certain other things,
like Natalya, for example, with her . . . well, I can't mention
what . . . Or is it perhaps that poor Anna can't endure staying
at home for an hour? It's not her fault, poor thing—she's merely
one of those coquettish women who make eyes at every imbecile
that passes her in the street. I admit she dances rather too much.
But then, *why* does everybody tell her she's such a ravishing dancer?
Her hats are utterly impossible. But is it *her* fault that God denied
her the gift of good taste? She's a gossip, but so is everybody else
in this part of the country. Who isn't, tell me? And of course
there's no denying that that Colonel Suchiloff, with his dyed side-
whiskers haunts her house from morning till night—and perhaps
from night till morning, who knows? But after all, what is the poor
woman to do with herself, when her husband sits playing cards
till five o'clock in the morning? No; I always have defended
Anna and always shall. . . . Oh, great heavens—here is the prince.
Mon prince—is it really you! [*Hastens towards the* PRINCE *who
has just entered.*]

[*At the first rapid glance, the* PRINCE *is almost youthful. It
is not until one looks at him at closer range and more attentively
that one realises that he is a kind of corpse on springs. Every
device of artifice has been employed to give this mummy the
appearance of a young man. He is dressed in the height of fashion,
as though he has been cut out of a magazine of modes for men.
Gloves, waistcoat, linen are of dazzling whiteness and in exquisite taste. He has a slight limp, but manages it so cleverly that
he creates the impression of having cultivated it for a fashionable*

fad. He wears a monocle, but over his glass eye. He is heavily perfumed, and when he speaks, is apt to falter somewhat, either on account of his feeble old age, or because all his teeth are false, or because he has affected that peculiarity of diction. His memory is not what it was, and at any moment is liable to leave him wandering. A conversation with him requires great skill.]

MARIA. [*In a flutter.*] Dear prince—you haven't changed a bit! Not the very least! [*She seizes both his hands and leads him to an armchair.*] Sit down, prince!—It is six years—six whole years, since we last saw each other! Oh, I assure you I've been exceedingly angry with you, *mon cher* prince! But where is the tea? Tea, Nastasia—tea . . . what are you thinking of?

PRINCE. Thank you—thank you so much! And think of it—last year I thought I couldn't stay away from Mordassoff a moment longer, but they frightened me into not coming. They told me the cholera was raging here.

MARIA. No such thing, prince! There was never even a rumour of cholera—it was hoof and mouth disease.

PRINCE. Oh well, hoof and mouth disease—I remember it was something or other of the kind. At any rate, it kept me at home. But tell me, what is your husband doing now, Anna Nikolaievna? Is he still the Public Prosecutor?

MARIA. No indeed, prince. My husband never was Public Prosecutor.

PAUL. Uncle's shooting wide again—he thinks you're Anna Nikolaievna.

PRINCE. Why, of course . . . of course . . . you're Anna Nikolaievna—how foolish of me! I begin to forget things, I'm afraid!

MARIA. [*With a wry smile.*] No, prince; I assure you I am not Anna Nikolaievna. I am your old friend, Maria Alexandrovna. Don't you remember?

PRINCE. Maria Alexandrovna! What do you think of that! *C'est délicieux!* And all the time, my boy, I thought you were taking me to that Anna Matveievna's. This sort of thing happens pretty often to me . . . I come so rarely to Mordassoff. I don't mind what happens—I enjoy it whatever it is. So you're not Nastasia Vassilievna! That's very interesting. . . .

MARIA. Maria Alexandrovna, prince, Maria Alexandrovna! It is not at all nice of you to forget your best friend!

PRINCE. Why, of course—my best friend! . . . A thousand pardons! [*He looks at* SINAIDA.]

MARIA. This is my daughter, prince!

PRINCE. Your daughter? Oh, charming—charming! Most beautiful!

MARIA. [*Creating a diversion.*] Tea, prince? . . . We heard of your dreadful mishap. I assure you, the very thought of it made me quite mad with horror! Are you sure you weren't hurt? You ought really to be less rash!

PRINCE. [*Taking his tea.*] Capsized—capsized! The coachman capsized me. I thought the end of the world had come. That coachman of mine, that Theophile—it was all his fault. I'm convinced it was a wilful attempt on my life . . . his head's full of modern ideas . . . imagine it! He repudiates everything. In fact, he's a Nihilist.

MARIA. You would never credit what I have to endure with my stupid, worthless servants.

PRINCE. Oh quite—oh quite! But frankly, I prefer them stupid. Take that Terenti of mine, for instance—you remember him, don't you, nephew? The moment I saw him, I saw right through him: "Porter!" I said to myself. He's a perfect miracle of stupidity. He stands all day at the door, like a sheep gazing into the water. But a manner . . .

MARIA. [*Laughs aloud in delighted admiration, and claps her hands.* PAUL *does likewise.* NASTASIA *laughs with them, and even* SINA *smiles.*] What a sense of humour you have, prince! A true wit! You have a marvellous gift for catching what is essentially funny in these things! And with that gift you shut yourself up for five long years! You should most certainly write, you know, prince!

PRINCE. Oh quite—oh quite! In my younger days I used to be rather clever that way—oh, remarkably so! I even went so far as to compose a vaudeville piece that had some ravishing couplets in it. Naturally, the thing's gone completely out of my mind now. But I do recall two or three puns that were in it . . . and such puns . . . ! [*Kissing his fingertips with a flourish.*] As a matter of fact, I always created a sensation whenever I travelled. I remember Lord Byron . . . a wonderful dancer he was. . . .

PAUL. Lord Byron, uncle? What in God's name are you talking about?

PRINCE. Oh quite—quite . . . certainly Lord Byron! As a matter of fact, perhaps it wasn't Lord Byron . . . someone else, perhaps. That's right—it wasn't Lord Byron; it was some Pole. Yes, it's all clear in my mind now. A most amazing person, that Pole.

Posed as a count, would you believe it, and then it came out that he was nothing but a hairdresser! But he danced the Krakowiak marvellously, and broke his leg in the end! I remember putting the incident into verse at the time:

> All the Polish men,
> Dance La Cracovienne!

and so on. . . . I don't remember how it went on. As a matter of fact, I find I'm forgetting a great many things. I'm so busy these days.

MARIA. But, prince, I do wish you would tell me what you have been doing with yourself, all these years in solitude?

PRINCE. Doing? Oh, I have a great many things to attend to, one way and another. Part of the time I merely repose my mind, and part of the time my imagination is kept busy with all sorts of matters. Now and then I put a thought down on paper.

MARIA. You must have a most powerful imagination, prince!

PRINCE. Most powerful! I am often positively astounded when I think in retrospect of the things my imagination has conjured up. When I was in Kaluga . . . [*To* PAUL.] By the way, you were Vice-Governor of Kaluga, were you not?

PAUL. Good God, uncle—what next!

PRINCE. Just think of that, my dear boy! Somehow I always thought you were the Vice-Governor, but I kept saying to myself: How odd—he seems to have an entirely different face now! He was an extraordinarily clever-looking man, you know . . . the Vice-Governor, you know. . . .

MARIA. Really, prince, these five years have been your undoing. Another year, and it will be all over with you, prince!

PRINCE. [*Terrified.*] All over with me? What do you mean? Do you really mean that?

MARIA. I do most solemnly. I speak to you as a friend, as though I were your sister. You must change your way of life from the very foundation, or you will surely fall mortally ill and wither and die.

PRINCE. [*Thoroughly terrified.*] Die! Oh my God! Do you really mean that I am near to dying? So soon? Did you hear that, Paul? What have you to say? . . . Of course—quite—I know what it is. I think too much. Yes; I think far too much. For a long time now I have been having dreadful pains! No, dear friend, not headaches . . . [*in a stage whisper*] haemorrhoids! I'll tell you exactly. In the first place . . .

PAUL. Some other time, uncle. Later on.

PRINCE. Very well—some other time. But remind me, my dear boy. I'll describe my case to you fully tonight.

MARIA. But you must certainly take a cure, prince. You must go abroad . . .

PRINCE. Abroad. . . . Yes, of course! When I was abroad before— I was in my twenties then—I had a most extraordinarily gay time! I very nearly got myself married to a French viscountess. But she took somebody else at the last moment. A German baron. He'd just come out of a lunatic asylum, and he went back afterwards for a time. . . . Abroad; yes, by all means. But now . . . [*He seems very restless, and keeps looking at the door.*]

MARIA. Be that as it may, *cher prince*—you had better take your state of health into serious consideration. First and foremost, you should leave Duchanovo immediately. . . .

PRINCE. Certainly! Get away! Get away! I will. I confess you have alarmed me exceedingly . . . with all this talk of illness and dying . . . I'm sure I feel most unwell this very moment . . . I am afraid I must. . . . Indeed, I am completely upset. . . . Besides . . . I'll be back directly. . . . [*Makes a hasty exit, left.*]
    [PAUL *roars with laughter.*]

MARIA. I fail to understand what you are laughing at. [*In great excitement.*] Is it because he doesn't recognise the people he sees, or because he talks nonsense now and then? Is that it? Well, that is a natural result of the frightful life he has been leading these five years, locked up, with that fiend of a woman standing guard over him. He didn't even recognise me—you were witness of that yourselves, all of you! It is imperative to save him! I will convince him that he must go abroad at once; anything, so that he may be rid of that woman.

PAUL. [*Laughs.*] I'll tell you what—he ought to get married.

MARIA. [*Sternly.*] Are you quite incorrigible, Paul?

PAUL. Not at all. I'm perfectly serious this time. Why shouldn't he? Suppose he could find some girl, or still better, some good and charming and clever and gentle—and most particularly, poor— widow, who'd look after him like a daughter. She'd have to be pretty, of course. My uncle still has one eye. Did you happen to notice how he kept staring at Sina?

NASTASIA. [*Provocatively.*] And how do you expect to find such a treasure at short notice?

PAUL. How about yourself? And why, may I ask, shouldn't you be his bride? One, you're pretty; two, a widow; three, of noble family; four, poor; five, you're clever. And you could have him to love and nurse; you'd chase that terrible woman away from him and take him abroad, feed him with pap and sweets until his last moment arrives and he leaves this wicked world—which will be due in about a year; probably less, even in two or three months maybe. You are then a princess, a widow, and wealthy; and as a prize for your virtue and self-sacrifice you'll get a marquis or a high military official for your next husband. *C'est joli, n'est-ce pas?*

NASTASIA. Why, good heavens, yes! I feel I could fall genuinely in love with the blessed little man! If only out of sheer gratitude, to begin with. . . . But it's all nonsense, anyway.

PAUL. Nonsense? You just treat me nicely, and if I don't get you betrothed to him this very day, you can cut off my hand. Nothing easier than to put ideas—any ideas—into my uncle's head, and convince him they're his own. You know him: "Oh, quite . . . quite!" We'll get him married so that he won't even know it's being done. So hold yourself in readiness, Nastasia.

NASTASIA. [*Confused.*] I'm certainly looking an untidy fright now. [*She gets up, her eyes shining.*]

MARIA. [*During all this, has remained immobile, thinking profoundly, her face set.*] *Mon cher* Paul, you have been talking the most arrant rubbish. And what is more, this kind of thing is in the worst possible taste.

PAUL. But why, in heaven's name? What's the matter with it?

MARIA. Because you are a guest in my house, and so is the prince. I must insist upon your respecting this fact. Do not forget it again, please. Thank goodness, here's the prince come back. [*Enter* PRINCE.]

PRINCE. I feel better now that that thought's off my mind! You know, my dear boy, it is extraordinary what a crowd of thoughts I have today—at other times, none at all.

PAUL. It's falling into the ditch this morning that's done it, uncle! It upset your nerves.

PRINCE. Most likely. Most likely. At any rate, I feel greatly relieved now. I've decided to let Theophile off this once. Do you know,

I am rather inclined to think that perhaps he had no real designs on my life this time . . . none at all, probably. What do you think about him?

PAUL. I think it's time we started to pay our morning calls, uncle.

PRINCE. Oh, quite . . . quite!

MARIA. I hope you don't mean to call on anyone but the Governor, prince. You're ours for today, you know. I have no wish to criticise the so-called "society" of nowadays. But I should like to remind you that *I* am your hostess, sister and nurse for the moment, and I confess that I fear for you, prince. You don't know the people hereabouts!

PAUL. Put your faith in me, Maria Alexandrovna.

MARIA. I do, Paul. I shall expect you for luncheon, prince. We have it rather early, I'm afraid. I am deeply sorry my husband happens to be out on the estate this morning. He would have been overjoyed to see you—he admires you enormously and always talks of you with the utmost affection.

PRINCE. Your husband? Oh, have you a husband?

MARIA. Oh prince—you drive me to despair! Surely you remember my husband, Afanassij Moskaleff?

PRINCE. Afanassij Moskaleff? Imagine that—isn't it too droll! You have a husband then! Most odd! As good as a farce—you know the way it goes—husband at door, wife . . . Oh, a thousand pardons, I've quite forgotten what we were talking about. . . . I've got it now—yes; we were going visiting, my dear boy, were we not? Madame, au revoir! Adieu, *ma charmante demoiselle!* [*He goes out with* PAUL.]

MARIA. [*Calling after him.*] Don't be late for luncheon, prince—try not to forget that! [*To* NASTASIA.] You might just see what's going on in the kitchen, Nastasia Petrovna. I've a premonition that that utterly impossible Nikita of ours is going to ruin the food today. . . .

[NASTASIA *goes, casting a look full of distrust at* MARIA *as she goes towards the door.*]

[*When she is gone,* MARIA *looks meaningly at* SINA, *and surveys the scene with the keen eye of a general observing the field of an impending battle. She goes cautiously to the door and listens for* NASTASIA'S *footsteps going in the direction of the kitchen.* SINA *watches these manœuvres with an expression half of mockery, half of torment.*]

SINAIDA. You may be perfectly certain she's eavesdropping at one of the doors, mamma.

MARIA. I'm afraid so too, dear. We shall have to talk very softly. [*There is a pause.* MARIA *sits down, facing her daughter.*] Sina!

SINAIDA. [*With perfect calm.*] Well, mamma?

MARIA. Sina, I have something highly important to ask you. It is this: What are your present feelings towards that Paul Mosgliakov?

SINAIDA. You have known for a long time what my feelings are towards him.

MARIA. Of course I have, *ma chère enfant!* But I have the impression that he has been rather more urgent latterly.

SINAIDA. He persists in being in love with me—that covers all sins, doesn't it?

MARIA. This is very curious! You have never been so forgiving towards him before.

SINAIDA. This is very curious! Until now you have always taken up cudgels for him.

MARIA. Sina, I am not going to deny that I once hoped very deeply that you would become Paul's wife. When I used to look at you, so sad and dejected, I was filled with distress for you. We are not rich—we can't afford to travel as other people do. And all the imbeciles of the district find amusement in pointing you out as a girl of twenty-three unable to find a husband. But what prospect is there for you in this place? Paul is a brainless fellow, I grant you—still he is by far the best of them all hereabouts. That is why I considered him for you. But I swear to you, Sina—I never liked him personally at all—not really. How fortunate it is that you have held him off. . . . [*Uncertainly.*] You made him no promises today, did you? Did you, Sina?

SINAIDA. Is there any need for all this hypocrisy, mother?

MARIA. Hypocrisy, Sina? What do you mean by using such a word to your mother?

SINAIDA. Don't, mother! We need not quibble over words. You want to marry me to the prince, and that is the long and short of the matter.

MARIA. I said no such thing, Sina. But I will not pretend that a marriage with Prince Gavrila would not be a very lucky thing for you.

SINAIDA. [*Angrily.*] What nonsense, mother! The trouble with you is that you have far too much of a romantic imagination. You are forever making up all kinds of schemes, and the fact that they are foolish and fantastic never seems to hinder you in the very least. I expected you to come to me with this idea. All the time that idiot Paul kept insisting the old man ought to be married, I could read your thoughts on your face as though you'd spoken them aloud. I don't wish to hear one more word about it now—do you hear me, mamma? Not one single word!

MARIA. You're a child, Sina! You're a spoiled, sick little child! Not another mother on earth could bear what you make me go through for you every day of my life. But I know you suffer too, and I am a mother! I must bear everything patiently, and forgive everything you do to me. [*She pauses.*] As I see it, Paul showed great shrewdness and good sense when he said the prince ought to marry. Not that hussy of a Nastasia, of course!

SINAIDA. Please mamma—you might at least not shout! You may be sure she is listening at one of these keyholes.

MARIA. Now tell me, Sina, why should this be all nonsense?

SINAIDA. [*Stamps her foot.*] You ask me! Well, according to my ideas, taking advantage of an old man's dotage to deceive him and marry him and take his money away from him, is not merely nonsense; it is such a foul thing, such a loathsome, sordid, unspeakable thing, that I . . .

MARIA. Sina, do you ever recall a certain thing that happened two years ago?

SINAIDA. Mamma, you gave me your faithful word of honour that . . .

MARIA. I know I did, Sina. And you don't know how terrible it has been for me to keep silence so long. It can't go on, my child—I implore you on my knees to let me talk about it now! Listen, Sina— your mother is begging you . . . and I swear solemnly that this shall be the last time I shall mention it.

SINAIDA. [*Nerving herself for a desperate ordeal.*] Very well . . . you may!

MARIA. I thank you, Sina. Well, two years ago a tutor came to this house for our little Mitja, God rest him.

SINAIDA. Don't be so ominous, mamma! The eloquence and the details don't seem particularly necessary . . .

MARIA. They are, my child. Because I have to justify myself in your eyes. I am your mother, child. Don't for a moment think I wish to play fast and loose with you. No, Sina. But just this once, I want to tell you everything, right from the very beginning, so that you may know my heart. Otherwise I prefer to say nothing . . .

SINAIDA. I am listening. . . .

MARIA. This tutor, hardly more than a boy himself, made an inexplicable impression upon you, Sina. I found I had placed too much confidence in your intelligence and pride and in his insignificance—especially that. And one day you came to me, suddenly and without warning, and announced that you wished to marry him. That was a knife-thrust into my heart, my child. Only think of it. . . . A youth, the son of a choir-singer, worth nothing but the twelve roubles a month he earned teaching your brother, good for nothing but to concoct his bad poetry, utterly ignorant of everything but talking about his ridiculous Shakespeare! And that you wanted for a husband! That was to be the husband of Sinaida Moskalevna! I send him about his business, but you continue to see him, and worst of all, you start a correspondence. The whole town is full of rumours about you already; then one day you quarrel with him for some reason or other, and break it off. And he proves himself the cad I knew he would be. He threatened to distribute your letters all over the town—do you remember that? And at that you lost control of yourself and struck him across the face. Yes, Sina—think! Then this unspeakable person actually did show one of your letters about, and within an hour it had fallen into the hands of Natalya Dmitrievna, my mortal enemy. By that time he had repented, and was almost out of his mind with remorse, and tried to poison himself the same night. An atrocious scandal, with you the central figure in it. And I held myself in check, my child. I did not go off into a faint. Instead, I summoned every ounce of strength I possessed, and . . . Ah, Sina—you will never know the torture I went through then, and all because of you! Then that shameless Nastasia came to me and offered to get the letters back, if I would pay her 200 roubles. 200 roubles at a moment's notice—for me to find! I took my jewels that your grandmother left me, Sina, and rushed out in the snow in my thin house shoes, to the Jew Bimstein. I pawned them. In two hours, the letter was in my hands. Nastasia had stolen it. Your honour was saved—that letter was the only proof. What did I not suffer that awful day—all for your sake! The next morning I looked in the glass and saw my first grey hairs. Sina, you have known for two years now that that boy is not worth even thinking about—but still you torture yourself on his account, my angel, and refuse to marry anyone because he is still furiously and insanely jealous. I know his mother must have come spying for him when Paul's proposal began to be talked of. You are simply trying to spare him, my child. I can see through you, clearly. But only God sees the bitter tears I weep into my pillow . . .

SINAIDA. [*Coldly.*] Never mind that, mamma. Your pillow has nothing to do with the matter. But you can't ever resist your oratory and complications . . .

MARIA. Don't look at me like that, Sina, as though I were your enemy. I have wept over this every day for two long years. Nothing will convince me that you have the slightest feeling for that unspeakable boy; it is your own lost happiness that is preying on your mind, your high ideal of him. I too have loved in my time—I have also had high ideals of men. And where is the mother who would condemn me now for seeing, in a marriage with the prince, something to your immense advantage?

SINAIDA. So you seriously wish to mate me with this prince! Truly mamma, I cannot understand you.

MARIA. I am surprised that you should not understand this very easily indeed, *mon ange.* First of all, you will be able to leave this repulsive provincial hole for ever! You could start travelling at once, this summer—Italy, Switzerland, Spain! Spain, Sina, where the Alhambra is, and the Guadalquivir—not this insignificant stream of ours with such a common name.

SINAIDA. Just a moment, mamma. You're talking as though the prince had already proposed to me.

MARIA. Leave that to me, my angel! About the second matter now: I know how you will recoil before giving your hand to that Mosgliakoff . . .

SINAIDA. I have no intention of becoming his wife!

MARIA. Dear child, I perfectly understand his striking you as repulsive in the extreme. It is terrible to belong to someone one despises! Nothing is more appalling than to have to pretend all one's life long. I have borne it myself for five and twenty years! Your father ruined my life . . .

SINAIDA. Please let us leave Father out of this.

MARIA. I know, you always side with him. Oh, Sina—the prince won't cause you any trouble in that respect, my child. That is quite obvious —you will not need to bother about loving him. . . .

SINAIDA. Good heavens, mamma, what nonsense! I'm not going to marry him at all! Remember that once and for all—*I am not going to marry him*, and there is no more to say about it.

MARIA. For pity's sake, don't excite yourself, dear heart, before you have heard me out. The prince has only one more year to live—two at the outside. To my mind, it is better to be a young widow than an old maid. Listen, you angel of kindness, the next time your thoughts go out to that poor boy, remember that your marrying the prince will not arouse his jealousy—on the contrary, it will please him. He will say you married wisely, and because you had to marry somebody, and . . . in fact, you will be free to marry again after the prince dies.

SINAIDA. In fact, what you mean to say is this: "First marry the prince, then rob him; that is to say, gamble on his dying, so that your lover may succeed him!" Very clever! I understand you perfectly! You can't resist your tendency to parade the noblest sentiments, however shady the matter is in itself, can you, mamma? Wouldn't it be more decent to come straight out with it and say: "Sina, we've a bad and rotten business on hand, but we can turn it to your advantage, so you'll follow me when I explain it to you."

MARIA. My dear child, look at yourself in the mirror! A beauty like you is worth a king's ransom! Yet you are willing to sacrifice your best years to an old man. Are his money and his title worth more than your person?

SINAIDA. Deceiving is deceiving, mamma.

MARIA. Nothing of the kind, child—nothing of the kind! Consider the question from a Christian point of view. You told me yourself once that you would like to become a sister of mercy. Very well—that old man is suffering. He is unhappy—he is being persecuted. Be a friend to him—a sister. Cheer his last days—what you do for him you will be doing for God. There lies healing for your own wounded soul—a loftier calling; a school of self-abnegation! Where is the selfishness in that? What is there bad, or rotten, or shady in it? . . . I see you don't believe me. [*She changes her tactics.*] The element that pains you most in this, I see, is the money. Very well, let the money go. Keep only what you need for the barest necessities, and give the rest to the poor! Help that poor wretched boy on his death-bed, for example.

SINAIDA. [*Very low, as if to herself.*] He refuses help.

MARIA. He does, but his mother does not. She accepts it in secret. I know. You have sold your ear-rings which your aunt gave you . . . you did that about six months ago, I know all about it . . . to be able to help him . . .

SINAIDA. He will be beyond all help soon.

MARIA. [*Sighing.*] I know. They say he has consumption and can't last very long. I spoke to the doctor about him a few days ago, and he told me he was certain now that it was not consumption, but some other trouble with his lungs. He assured me he would stand a good chance of getting over it under different conditions, especially if he could have a change of climate in a new place that would take him out of himself. The doctor told me of some remarkable island in Spain, Sina—Malaga, I believe—it sounded like the name of some wine, at any rate—where the climate worked miracles, not only for people with lung trouble, but for consumptives as well. People go there for that purpose. You realise of course, that only the most high society, or else the richest of the merchant classes can afford it. But the enchanted Alhambra by itself, with its myrtles and lemons—and those Spaniards riding about on mules you know— all that would make a deep impression on a poetic nature! Are you afraid he would refuse your money if you offered it to him for that chance? Deceive him, then. Let him hope. Say you will marry him when you become a widow. You may say anything—anything—so long as your motives are lofty! Your mother would not prompt you to do anything base, Sina. Then he would begin of his own accord to be careful of his health; he would want to get better, so he would obey the doctor's orders. Then he would recover, but there would be no question of your marrying him . . . still, he would have his health back, and it would be you who saved his life. Of course I know he should inspire pity rather than blame, and it is possible that his tribulations have improved him greatly. For my part, you might even marry him—when you become a widow. You will be rich and independent—you might procure some position in society for him—you might make him a career. What has either of you to expect, if you persist in your present folly? You'll be looked down on, you'll be poor, you'll spend the rest of your lives in this desert of Mordassoff—and his inevitable and early death hanging over you, into the bargain. But by taking my advice, you give him fresh hope and set his heart at peace because you have forgiven him. If the worst came to the worst then, he would at least die happy, and in your arms, absolved, certain of your love and pardon, under the myrtle and lemon branches, under the exotic, azure sky! Don't you see, my child—it is all within your grasp. You have everything to gain. And all will be yours, for the mere marrying of the prince!

[*A long silence falls between them.* SINA *has listened to her mother's last oration with blushing cheeks, breathing painfully. She makes up her mind.*]

SINAIDA. Listen, mamma! [*She breaks off.*] Listen, mamma!

[*A medley of noises now comes from the front room, and a shrill, sharp voice is heard demanding* MARIA. *She springs up.*]

MARIA. Merciful heavens—it's the colonel's wife! What in the name of all that's hateful brings that scarecrow back here? It's not two weeks ago since I practically showed her the door! [*In desperation.*] Well . . . it's impossible not to receive her now, quite impossible, of course! Probably she has some errand here—I can't see how she could have dared to come otherwise. [SOFIA PETROVNA *now enters, and* MARIA *hastens effusively towards her.*] How charming of you to call, Sofia Petrovna—thank you so very much for this most delightful surprise! How exceedingly sweet of you to have remembered me, my dear!

[SINA *has made her escape.* MARIA, *with her most honeyed smile, invites her guest to sit down. The colonel's wife is a little lady of fifty, with small, sharp eyes and freckles and yellow spots all over her face. Her small and dessicated body which is supported by a pair of feet as thin as the claws of a sparrow, is enclosed in a gown of black silk which creates a ceaseless rustle in the room, for she is never still a minute. She is a malicious and vindictive gossip. In addition to which, she takes two or three little glasses of schnapps every morning, and as many every night.*]

SOFIA. I've only run in for a moment, *mon ange.* I've no time to sit down. The whole town has come out of its shell to gaze at the prince. *Ces intrigantes, vous comprenez!* They're all trying to bait him into their houses with offers of champagne! Quite incredible! Why did you ever let him escape? Do you know, he's at Natalya Dmitrievna's at this moment?

MARIA. [*Almost leaping out of her chair.*] At Natalya Dmitrievna's? He left here intending to visit only the Governor, and perhaps Anna Nikolaievna—certainly no one else.

SOFIA. Well there you are! You'll have all your work cut out to get him back again! The Governor wasn't at home, as it happens. So from there he drove to Anna Nikolaievna's. There Natalya caught him and dragged him over to her house, so as to dance attendance upon him a little before luncheon. There's your prince for you!

MARIA. But what about Paul? He promised me that he . . .

SOFIA. [*Scornfully*.] Paul! Paul's there too, of course. Put him down at a card-table and he is not to be moved. He'll lose everything he owns again, as he did last year, and of course they've hoodwinked the prince into joining them. And the stories Natalya can tell! She's been shouting it from the housetops that you've set out to capture the prince—oh for the most obvious reason, *vous comprenez!* But Natalya presents her little Sonka to off-set you . . . conceive of that if you can—a fifteen year old schoolgirl, with her skirts hardly down to her knees! Did you ever hear of such a thing! . . . Then she sends for the little Maschka—another one—another schoolgirl in dresses that hardly come to her knees! And they put a red cap with feathers on her head—I've no idea what that signified—and had the two of them dance the Kasatschka for him. Well, you know his weakness—he was utterly carried away. "What figures! What figures! What figures they have!" He kept on saying that over and over again, staring at them through his lorgnette. They rose to the occasion in great style, you may be sure, and twisted and turned, and lifted their little skirts higher and higher—a regular orgy! Trallala! [*She laughs*.] Revolting! I blushed for them. I got scarlet in the face! I couldn't stand such a spectacle!

MARIA. But . . . were you at Natalya's yourself? I understood she . . .

SOFIA. She did, *ma chère*—she most certainly insulted me last week. But I did so want to catch just a glimpse of the prince, so I went! Imagine it! Champagne was handed to everybody in that room except me. And the whole time I was there, she scarcely addressed a syllable to me. . . . Excuse me *mon ange*, I really must go now—I can't stay another minute. I must run over to Akalina Pamphilovna's presently and tell her. . . . But you might just as well say good-bye to your prince now, for they'll never let him come back to you! They're all afraid that you . . . *vous comprenez* . . . on Sina's account. . . . Frightful people! Well, as I told you, the whole town's full of it! The Public Prosecutor's wife will keep him for lunch, by hook or crook. That is the trick *she's* up to, *mon ange!* Hurry up, if you want to get him back! He's your guest, isn't he? And that wily one is having a good laugh up her sleeve in the meantime—*intrigante* that she is—the low-down creature! Well, *adieu mon ange!* My sleigh's waiting for me downstairs; otherwise I should go with you. There's not a minute to lose! [*She goes.*]

MARIA. [*Looks after her, with arms crossed and knitted brows. The situation demands decisive action. She goes to the door and calls.*] Glafira! Have the sleigh brought round at once. Do you hear? The sleigh, at once!

SINAIDA. [*Comes in again, right, and stands contemplating her mother with a cynical smile.*] Listen, mamma. Your beautiful speeches have been absolutely thrown away. Please don't try any more to gloss over the beastliness of this affair by talking of noble purposes or any such thing. It is all just being jesuitical, and it doesn't take me in for a single moment. I want you to understand that very clearly.

MARIA. But *mon ange!*

SINAIDA. Don't, mamma. Please listen to me now, and have patience. . . . And this is what I want to say: I know that every word you said was utterly jesuitical, and I'm entirely convinced that your scheme is the very reverse of noble . . . but I accept it unconditionally. Do you understand? Unconditionally! I am prepared to marry the prince. I am even prepared to abet you in your tricks to get him. You want to know my reason? You need not. It is enough that I am willing to go through with everything. On the other hand, I will go through with the sequel too—he shall not regret having married me. I ask you only one thing, and you must tell me that quite candidly: just how are you going to set about accomplishing this? I can't go into it blindfold.

MARIA. [*Stands for a long moment, too thunderstruck to move. She gazes at her daughter with shining eyes, triumphant.*] Sina, Sina! My little dove! My darling, own little daughter! [*Makes for her with outstretched arms.*]

SINAIDA. [*Repulsing her.*] My God, mother—I don't want your embraces! Keep them! It is an answer I want—that's all.

MARIA. But Sina, my darling! I love you dearly—I adore you, my child. And you push me away. Believe me, your happiness is all I care about in the world. [*She turns tear-filled eyes on* SINAIDA.]

SINAIDA. Don't be angry, mamma. There is so much on my heart that I'm not in my right mind any more.

MARIA. I am not angry with you, my angel. Very well, I will be frank with you, absolutely frank and open. I must tell you to begin with, that I have no complete plan laid out yet—in detail, that is. Nor would that be possible—your clever little head will tell you why. There are even certain set-backs which I can foresee. . . . That horrible Sofia Petrovna has been saying all sorts of things! . . . Oh heavens, I must hurry! But I promise you, Sina, I swear to you that I will put this through for you. Of course I count to a certain extent upon the prince's—peculiarities. But leave everything in my hands and trust me. The principal thing is that they should not be allowed to spoil him for me, which is what those stupid imbeciles are trying to do. [*Her eyes flash; she brings her hand down violently upon the table.*] I must act at once—that is the chief thing. The main question must be settled this very day . . .

SINAIDA. Very well, mamma. I have made up my mind to connive at this swindle. But the moment I find the details of your scheme too disgusting and unspeakable, I give you fair warning that I will drop the whole thing. And there will be no going back on that.

MARIA. But, Sina! Why do you always look for hatefulness, mon ange? After all, it's merely a matter of getting you decently married.

SINAIDA. For pity's sake, mamma, allow me to call the thing by its proper name, please. [*She smiles bitterly.*] Perhaps that is now—my only consolation.

[MARIA *goes solicitously towards her and looks at her deeply.*]

SINAIDA. If only I could know how you mean to set it going. I'm certain it is bound to come to a bad end.

MARIA. If that is all that is troubling you, my angel, set your mind at rest now. You have no idea what situations I have managed to get out of, without even singeing my fingers! However, the most important thing is to bring the prince definitely to the point as soon as possible. On that all the rest depends—I realise that perfectly, though I know it will lead to open war in Mordassoff. But I confess. . . . It's that Paul who worries me; I know I can deal with the others.

SINAIDA. [*Disdainfully.*] Paul?

MARIA. Yes, Paul—unfortunately. But have no fear, Sinotchka. He shall even help us. You don't know your mother yet, my child! . . . Ah, my dear heart, this thought flashed through my mind the moment I heard of the prince's coming. It was as though suddenly everything became clear to me. Not in a thousand years will such a chance occur again, my little angel! What is there dishonourable in your marrying an old man? It is no marriage in one sense at all;

merely a family contract, as it were. And the charming old dotard
has nothing to lose and everything to gain. . . . How beautiful you
look today again, Sina. You're a wonderfully lovely girl! If I
were a man, I should lay half an empire at your feet! [*She kisses
her daughter's hand with passionate maternal fervour.*] My own
flesh and blood—and I have to use force to get her married, the
little goose! What a life opens before us now, Sina! Doesn't it,
darling? You won't part with me, Sinotchka, will you? When you
become the prince's happy wife, you won't chase your mother away,
will you? . . . We may have quarrelled often, my little angel, but
in spite of that you have never had a friend like me.

SINAIDA. Mamma, it must be time for you to begin . . .

MARIA. [*Collecting herself.*] You're right, my little dove! Here have
I been chattering, while they're using all the tricks they know to
keep the prince for themselves. I shall drive there at once, and have
a word with that imbecile of a Paul. . . . I'll get him out of there
by force, if necessary. Adieu, my angel! Don't be angry with your
mother. And whatever you do, don't be discouraged. Everything
will turn out perfectly, and will be done in the most dignified manner. The thing that most concerns me is, from which angle to . . .
well, never mind that now. Adieu, my love, adieu! [*She blesses her
daughter in parting with the sign of the cross, and hurries out of
the room.*]

SINAIDA. [*Walks agitatedly to and fro, then stands with arms folded
across her bosom. But her pale face betrays all the martyrdom she is
suffering. She speaks, in a very low voice.*] Yes . . . there is still
time . . . there is still time. [*She listens, and seems to hear the
sound of sleigh-bells announcing that her mother has already left.
She smiles bitterly.*]

[*The door at the left opens furtively, and* GLAFIRA'S *round
face appears. She looks at* SINAIDA *in dumb inquiry. There is a
pause.*

Very well.

[GLAFIRA *vanishes.* SINA *stands immobile, looking expectantly
at the door, which opens soon, very cautiously.* THE OLD WOMAN
IN BLACK *comes in, very frightened and hesitating—closes the
door behind her, remains standing irresolutely, making no attempt
to approach* SINA. *She sinks down on her knees where she stand
at the threshold and clasps her hands.*]

THE OLD WOMAN. Forgive my Vassja! . . . One word of forgiveness for my poor boy, in the name of God's pity for us all.

SINAIDA. [*Slowly approaches her, and gazes at her for a long time, silently and lost in thought. Then she whispers, scarcely audible, and as though the words are meant for herself.*] So you are his mother. . . .

CURTAIN

ACT II

The same scene. Four o'clock in the afternoon.

The dining-room door is open, and through it the PRINCE, NASTASIA, MARIA *and* PAUL *are seen at dessert. Their faces are flushed and animated; they are evidently in brilliant spirits. One chair stands empty.* MARIA *betrays a certain uneasiness, and casts frequent glances towards the drawing-room. Finally she leaves her place and approaches the door, just as* SINAIDA *enters through the other door into the drawing-room. The girl sinks dejectedly into an armchair by the fireplace, and twists her handkerchief agitatedly with nervous fingers. She has been crying.* MARIA *catches sight of her and hastens towards her, in high excitement.*]

MARIA. [*Sotto voce.*] For the love of God, child, where have you been? They all noticed it. How could you run away from the table like that! Just as everything was turning out so beautifully! Oh, Sina—the dear old gentleman is completely bewitched by you. He has been asking for you with the utmost impatience. . . . You've been crying. Sinotschka, my child, tell me—have you been crying?

SINAIDA. [*Her handkerchief twisted now into a string.*] I can't go on, mother!

MARIA. [*Casting her eyes despairingly upward.*] Not go on! Sina, my angel, look at your mother. Look at her, sacrificing herself for you, fighting for you like a tigress. . . . Not go on? Think of all I have been through for you. Only for you, Sina, all for you! How much courage and cleverness did it not need to capture this absent-minded, fascinating prince again, and his imbecile of a nephew! And what do you think I did? On Anna Nikolaievna's very door-step, I took them prisoner—yes actually, took them prisoner! In the open street! Under the very nose of my mortal enemies! . . . I can do all that, and *you* say you can't go on! . . . Sina, where is the promise you gave me? Think of Spain and the Guadalquivir! Think of that poor . . .

[SINAIDA *springs up, throws her head back and interrupts her mother's speech with a gesture.*]

MARIA. Yes; I've done everything a human being could do. And so far everything has succeeded. God Himself has taken me by the hand and shown me the way, my child. And everything will continue to go perfectly, if only you don't leave me in the lurch at the last moment, Sina.

SINAIDA. I am ready. Only for pity's sake, mother, keep quiet—keep quiet!

MARIA. [*Kissing her on the brow.*] *Mon ange!* I have nothing more to worry me—I *know* everything will go smoothly now until the end. Only that Paul is still in my way, the pestiferous creature. I catch him exchanging looks with that graceless Nastasia all the while. Oh, if only God would send me an inspiration how to get him out of the way. . . .

[*Enter PAUL, rear.*]

MARIA. [*In her most honeyed voice.*] Why, my dear boy, wherever are you going? Were you furious that Sina disappeared from the table? [*To SINAIDA.*] Then go back, child—don't keep them waiting. Let Nastasia serve the coffee . . . [SINA *goes out, rear. To* PAUL.] Surely you don't mean to leave us now, *cher* Paul? You can't possibly think of depriving us of your delightful conversation! Why, you've only managed two glasses of champagne—you certainly don't wish to let yourself be outdone by that dear delightful uncle of yours! Come, *mon ami!*

PAUL. [*Embarrassed.*] Maria Alexandrovna, I . . . I find myself in a most peculiar situation all of a sudden. . . . I don't quite know how to explain it. But please—please advise me what to do.

MARIA. Well, what is it?

PAUL. It's like this. Today I ran across my godfather . . . Borudoiev . . . you know—Borudoiev, the merchant. And the old man accused me of behaving as though he wasn't good enough for me. He said he knew this was the third time I'd been in Mordassoff, and I'd never once set foot inside his house. "You're to come to tea today," he said. It's four o'clock already, and it's a time-honoured custom in his household to have tea the moment he wakes from his afternoon sleep, which is at five. What am I to do? Don't think too badly of me, Maria Alexandrovna. He saved my father from ruin after he'd been tampering with government money—that was how he became my godfather, the old fellow. I've not much to marry Sina on now. But he's worth a million at the very least. And no children. He's practically certain to leave me a hundred thousand—even two hundred thousand. And he's seventy. Think of that!

MARIA. My good Paul, why talk so much? What on earth are you standing here for? Drive to your godfather's at once—and hurry! This is not a matter to trifle with! I noticed at luncheon how restless you were. Go along, *mon ami*, and be as quick as you can. You ought to have called on him this morning, simply as a mark of ordinary, decent respect towards an old man, and your godfather. Ah, you young people; you young people.

PAUL. But you have always disapproved of my associating with him. You've always said he was nothing but a peasant, and a boor of a Tartar, and that he kept company with a lot of riff-raff tavern-keepers and crooked lawyers.

MARIA. Oh, as though one doesn't say all manner of things thoughtlessly! I can be mistaken sometimes, like everybody else. I'm not a holy saint! But don't hesitate another moment, Paul. Spend the evening with him. And mention me to him, will you? Say I respect and honour him! Everything will come right—I know it. I should have made you go there long before this.

PAUL. Maria Alexandrova, you save my life! I swear I'll come to you for advice about everything now for the rest of my life—and follow it, too. Good-bye; I'm off at once!

MARIA. And my blessing goes with you, *mon ami!* Don't forget to mention me to your godfather. He's a very charming old man really —and I've always liked him very much, though I may not have said so. He's the old-fashioned, full-flavoured Russian type we don't see so often any more. Au revoir!

[NASTASIA *comes into full view, wearing a dress of pale green, a pink ribbon in her hair. She minces and simpers.*]

[MARIA, *on her way back to the dining-room, comes face to face with her, and calls back over her shoulder with the most engaging sweetness.*]

MARIA. Darling, don't keep us waiting any longer for our coffee, will you? And do help our dear Paul on with his overcoat—he's going out. . . . [*To* PAUL.] Aū revoir, *cher ami!* [*Aside.*] Imbecile! Even the devil is helping me in this! [*She passes into the dining-room.*]

NASTASIA. [*At the other door, now beckons to* PAUL. *He looks at her in astonishment, but obeys.*] So you let yourself be routed, do you?

PAUL. [*Unsuspicious—somewhat amused.*] Routed? I'm going over

to Borudoiev's. He's my godfather you know, and he's most frightfully rich. I must be careful to keep in the old fellow's good
books. . . .

NASTASIA. Borudoiev? Is that where you're going? Well, you had
better bid a long farewell to your betrothed before you leave.

PAUL. What?

NASTASIA. I suppose you think you have her in your pocket? Well,
they're giving her to the prince, if you must know. I heard all about
it with my own ears.

PAUL. Giving her to the prince? That will do, Nastasia.

NASTASIA. Very well, do you want to hear and see it all for yourself?
Come with me then . . . into the next room. [*She indicates the
door to the left.*]

PAUL. Good heavens, Nastasia—what in the world is all this?

NASTASIA. You'll soon find out. The prince's dressing-room gives you
the best view. Most likely the performance will begin at once.
That's why she sent me out of the room.

PAUL. What performance?

NASTASIA. Ssh! Not so loud! Well, it begins this way: You're done for
—you're out! When you were out with the prince, paying calls,
Maria Alexandrovna took Sina in hand for one hour, persuading her
to marry the prince. She said nothing could be easier than to bring
him to the point, and the horrible intrigue she planned made me truly
ill to listen to. I heard the whole thing from behind that door there.
Sina accepted. And you should have heard how they talked about you.
You're an "imbecile." And I am a "hussy."

PAUL. But it is impossible to conceive of anything so vile!

NASTASIA. Very well—all you have to do is to listen at that door.
You'll hear what you'll hear.

PAUL. Nastasia . . . I . . . I am not in the habit of eavesdropping.
. . . I couldn't. . . .

NASTASIA. Very well, if you feel you can't . . . just leave things as
they stand, and slink away to your godfather's by all means. What
do I care? I'm certainly not going to wait here all night for you to
make up your mind. Go along in there—hurry up! [*With trembling
knees* PAUL *goes into the next room.*] Ha-ha-ha-ha! [*She makes a
gesture of scorn towards the dining-room.*] I'll show you who's a
hussy! [*Exit.*]

[MARIA ALEXANDROVNA, SINA *and the* PRINCE *come into the
drawing-room. The old soul is considerably weak after six*

glasses of champagne, and can hardly stand on his feet. He babbles
unceasingly. MARIA *is fully aware that his high spirits can't last,*
and that sleep is likely to overwhelm him at any moment. She
notices with gratification, that the old man casts exceedingly amor-
ous glances at SINA, *and her maternal heart leaps with joy.*]

PRINCE. Extraordinarily charming! Extraordinarily charming! I
assure you, an incomparable creature, that Natalya, incomparable!

MARIA. [*To whom this praise of her rival is like a stab through the*
heart.] Oh prince—have a little pity! If that Natalya is an incomparable woman, then I know nothing any more. . . . You
don't know what society is, nowadays! Nothing but veneer, prince
—gilded veneer! Take that away, and you disclose an utter hell
underneath the flowers—a wasp's nest.

PRINCE. A wasp's nest? Indeed? Most remarkable! Most remarkable!
A wasp's nest?

MARIA. Yes. . . . Believe me, it is! Sina, I must tell the prince about
that absurd and sordid thing which happened with Natalya last
week! You remember, don't you? . . . Yes, prince—this very
Natalya whose praises you sing so loudly. And I swear to you, I
am no slanderer! Well, about a fortnight ago, she called on us.
Coffee was served, and I happened to go out of the room for a
moment, leaving her alone. I knew exactly how many lumps of
sugar there were in the sugar basin. It was quite full. When I
came back, there were only three lumps left. And as you know,
she lives in a veritable palace on the principal street of the town,
and she has a perfectly fabulous amount of money. It was ridiculous
to the last degree, of course—but there you are. And that is a
fair sample of present-day "society."

PRINCE. A wasp's nest! . . . Incredible! Do you suppose she ate all
that sugar herself?

MARIA. Quite incomparable, prince, is she not?

PRINCE. Ah, well. . . . But you know [*he outlines in the air the*
lines of Natalya's voluptuous form] *si belle femme!*

MARIA. What? *Belle femme?* Really, prince! Why, she is like a
barrel! . . . What can you be thinking of? . . . You disappoint
me—I had expected better taste from you!

PRINCE. Well, a barrel, if you say so . . . quite, oh quite! Still, very
voluptuous, don't you think? And that girl who danced . . . very
voluptuous too.

MARIA. Sonka? Why, she's only a child . . . she's scarcely fourteen.

PRINCE. Oh, quite—quite! But very knowing, and such a form, even at her age! Pretty little thing! And that other one who danced with her.

MARIA. Yes, that poor orphan girl! She's often at their house.

PRINCE. An orphan, is she? Inclined to be dirty—I wish she'd washed her hands! Very nice otherwise, though . . . [*With increasing interest he regards* SINA *through his lorgnette. He is now only half-audible.*] *Mais quelle charmante personne!*

MARIA. Play something for us, Sina . . . no, sing rather! . . . She is such a singer, prince! It would not be too much to call her a real artist! If you only knew . . . [*Sotto voce, as* SINA *goes to the piano, outwardly, as ever, calm and serene.*] if you only knew what a daughter she has always been to me! . . . so considerate . . . such a loving heart . . .

PRINCE. Oh quite! . . . Considerate—I understand! But do you know, I've known only one woman who could compare with her for beauty. That was the late Countess Kainska—she died about thirty years ago. A most delightful woman! Words could not describe her beauty! She finally married her chef!

MARIA. Her chef? Prince!

PRINCE. Yes, her chef . . . a Frenchman. Abroad of course. She went abroad with him and got him a title of some kind—count, I believe. He was a very handsome man, and extraordinarily cultivated. He used to wear one of those little moustaches, you know. . . .

MARIA. And . . . and . . . how did it work out, prince? Did they get on together?

PRINCE. Oh, perfectly! They separated after a while. He stole some money from her and decamped. They'd quarrelled over a sauce! . . . Then she married my cousin Kudachev, and went on the stage . . . oh no—that was someone else. . . .

SINAIDA. What am I to play, mamma?

MARIA. No, don't play, Sina—sing to us instead! She has such a lovely voice, prince! Do you care for music?

PRINCE. Oh yes. . . . *Charmant, charmant!* I'm very fond of music. I used to spend a great deal of my time with Beethoven when I was abroad. . . .

MARIA. Beethoven? Sina, think of it—the prince knew Beethoven! Did you really, prince? How wonderful! Beethoven!

PRINCE. Oh, we were quite friends! He always had his nose full of snuff!

MARIA. Beethoven!

PRINCE. Yes, quite! Or perhaps it wasn't Beethoven, after all—it may have been some other German! There are so many Germans abroad, and they're nearly all conductors! But you know—I often get things mixed up. . . . For instance, I can never tell the difference between . . .

SINAIDA. What shall I sing, mamma?

MARIA. Oh, Sina, sing one of those romances—you know—where the châtelaine comes in, and her minstrel! . . . Oh prince—I do so love those things; those castles—all that life of the Middle Ages, with the troubadours and heralds and tournaments! I'll play for you, Sina. Come and sit down over here, prince, a little closer to the piano. Ah, those castles!

PRINCE. Oh, quite! Castles! I'm very fond of castles too. [*His eyes are riveted upon* SINA.] But . . . oh dear me, yes—these old romances! I know them! That's to say, I heard of them once—that's very long ago though. This reminds me so much of . . . oh dear me, yes . . .

[SINA *sings an old French romance. She does sing beautifully. Her clear, true contralto goes straight to the heart. Her lovely face, her wonderful eyes, her delicate fingers that turn the pages, her rich, shining black hair, her breast that rises and falls as she sings, her whole proud and glorious body, all enchant the poor old man. By the time she has finished her song, he is almost in tears.*]

Oh, *ma charmante enfant!* [*He kisses her finger-tips.*] You enchant me! . . . I've just remembered at last . . . at last . . . but . . . Oh, bewitching, bewitching! [*He can go no further.*] . . .

MARIA. Yes, prince, why do you bury yourself? A person so sensitive to the beautiful things of life? A man who enjoys life as you do? It is unforgivable in you, prince! Come back to life—begin again. Take your place in the society you belong to—don't cut yourself off any longer! Go abroad to Italy, to Spain. . . . To Spain, prince! Do you feel the need for a loving heart to guide you and be with you? You have friends . . . you have only to call, and they will crowd round you. I should be the first to leave everything behind, to come to you. Ah, if only I were young and beautiful . . . like my daughter there. What would give me greater happiness than to be the companion of your travels, your friend, your wife, . . .

PRINCE. Beautiful? Yes, I am certain you have been *une très charmante personne* in your day! Beautiful? . . . I thank you, dear friend. . . . Beautiful . . . yes, that was very long ago. . . . [*He wipes away a tear, casting a furtive glance at* SINA.]

MARIA. We live again in the happiness of our children, prince! Look at Sina! She is my guardian angel, my closest friend, the companion of my soul. She has already refused seven offers of marriage, because she would not be parted from me.

PRINCE. [*Suddenly very wide awake and covetous.*] Oh quite, quite! She could come with us when you accompany me abroad. I shall certainly go if she will come with us. Abroad, by all means! The thought of Baden-Baden makes me feel young again already! . . . But can I flatter myself that there is hope for me? She is so enchanting! Ah, *ma charmante enfant!* [*He kisses* SINA's *hands and is about to fall on his knees before her.*]

MARIA. But, prince, how can you ask such a question? Indeed you are very strange! Do you think you are already past the time of life when women pay attention to a man? Youth is not the only charm. You surely do not forget that you are a flower of our aristocracy! Yes, you—the prototype of all that is finest and noblest and most knightly in sentiment and conduct. Did not Maria of old love the aged Mazeppa? I once read that Lauzun, that fascinating marquis of the court of Louis I can't remember the how-many-th, even as a very old man won the hand of one of the reigning beauties there. Besides, who says you are old? Can people like you be said ever to age? With your great riches of sentiment and intellect, your spiritual youthfulness, your brilliant personality! You would only need to appear anywhere in Europe, in Baden, if that be your choice, or in Aix—accompanied by a young and beautiful woman . . . a young beauty like my daughter here, for example —for your presence to create a furore. You, my dear prince, the representative of our highest nobility; your wife the loveliest of the lovely. You enter with the utmost dignity into the society of your equals there, she upon your arm; she sings, and for your own part, you dazzle the guests of the Kursaal with your sparkling wit. All Europe, all the newspapers and magazines will be full of you. Prince, prince—and you ask whether you may flatter yourself that there is hope!

PRINCE. Magazines! Oh quite—oh quite! [*To* SINA.] My child, if you are not fatigued, would you sing that song again for me?

MARIA. Oh prince, she knows others, even better than that one. Do you remember *L'Hirondelle?*

PRINCE. Yes, I remember that . . . oh no, I have forgotten it. Please, the other one, never mind about *L'Hirondelle*—I want to hear the other again. [SINA *repeats it. The* PRINCE *is beside himself. He falls on his knees.*] Oh, *ma belle châtelaine!* My ravishing lady! You wake so many memories in me of that time so long ago . . . I used to think that everything became better as the years went on. I used to sing duets with a marquise in those days . . . this very ballad! I would kiss the tips of her fingers and her arm . . . so! But now . . . I don't know what . . .

MARIA. Be careful, prince—I shall soon believe you are falling in love with my Sina.

PRINCE. [*Attempting to kiss* SINA's *arm.*] Oh quite, oh quite! I think I am going mad with love of her. [*He is still on his knees, trembling with joy.*] I lay my life at her feet, and if I only dared to hope . . . if I only dared to offer her my heart . . . then I . . . then she could sing her ballads to me every day, and I could go on gazing at her for ever . . . gazing at her for ever. . . . Oh dear me, dear me! . . . Ballads for ever . . . from morning until night . . . ah, the marquise!

MARIA. [*Hastily interposing.*] Prince, prince, are you trying to rob me of my treasure, my Sina, my angel? My dearest Sina! But no —I shall never leave you, my child. Who will dare to snatch you from your mother's arms! [*Falls on* SINA's *neck and clasps her close, in spite of the girl's obvious resistance.*] Nine offers of marriage she has already refused, because she would not be parted from her mother! But this time there is a premonition of parting in my heart! I noticed how she looked at you. You have captured her, prince, you have cast a spell upon her by the subtle, insidious means only you great aristocrats know how to use. . . . You are about to separate us, alas. I feel it!

PRINCE. I adore her! I worship her!

MARIA. So you really want to leave your mother at last, Sina?

[*She falls once more upon her daughter's neck.* SINA *is stirred to rapid action in order to put an end to the torturing scene. She holds out her beautiful hand to the* PRINCE, *and even forces a smile. The* PRINCE *seizes the hand and covers it with kisses.*]

PRINCE. [*Sobbing with ecstasy.*] Only now I begin to live!

MARIA. Sina! [*With great solemnity.*] Behold in this man before you the finest nobleman I have ever known; a knight of the Middle Ages!

PRINCE. [*Sobbing.*] Oh quite . . . quite! The Middle Ages . . . quite!

MARIA. She knows it all too well, to my sorrow! Oh, why did you come here? I am sacrificing to you the sunshine of my life, my angel! Guard her well, prince. You have torn my heart into shreds. What mother would condemn me for my grief?

SINAIDA. [*Whispering.*] Mamma, this is enough!

MARIA. [*Paying no attention.*] You shall defend her against insult and harm—you will flash your sword before the eyes of all who would harm her by word or deed.

SINAIDA. No more, mamma, or I . . .

PRINCE. Oh quite, oh quite! . . . Only now do I begin to live. I want to have the wedding immediately—tomorrow—this very moment . . . flash, did you say? I . . . I wish to send to Duchanovo . . . I have some diamonds there. I want to lay them at her feet . . . flash . . . sparkle . . .

MARIA. And you, capable of such ardour, such noble sentiments—you could bury yourself for years in the depths of Duchanovo, prince. I become quite desperate to think that . . .

PRINCE. [*Looking about him fearfully.*] Oh dear me, dear me! Whatever shall I do? They tried to put me into a lunatic asylum, you know.

MARIA. What? Oh, how terrible! How can people be so contemptible and base . . . the most cowardly of all things to do. . . . I know about it, prince—I heard. But what made them do such a thing?

PRINCE. I've no idea . . . [*Sinks wearily into a chair.*] It was at a ball—I told a story there; this was how it went: There were two people on a train, and one . . . well, you say you know it already . . . however, it didn't please them, and they concocted the whole affair out of that.

MARIA. Really, prince?

PRINCE. Oh quite—quite! And later on, I was playing cards with Prince Peter Dementiisch, and got into rather a fix. I had two kings and three queens, or rather three queens and two kings . . . no, one king, and I distinctly remember something about some queens too . . .

MARIA. Inhuman! Fiendish! But I shall be near you in future, prince. I will never part from Sina. We'll see now who will dare to . . . Don't you see, prince—your marriage will amaze them all, and put them all to shame. They will realise that a beauty like Sina does not marry an insane husband. Henceforth you may hold your head up proudly, and face them all. . . .

PRINCE. [*Collapses utterly at last. His eyes closed.*] Oh quite—quite! Face them all . . . two queens and an ace.

SINAIDA. This will do, mamma! You're simply throwing your words away!

MARIA. You have let yourself get over-excited, prince. You must rest now. [*In a mothering tone.*] May I take you to your room?

PRINCE. Well, I should like to rest a little while . . . flash, did you say? . . . We'll have the wedding in a quarter of an hour. Just give me a minute or two and I'll be as right as rain again. . . . Oh, enchanting!

MARIA. Calm yourself, prince. I'll take you straight to your bed. . . . Why do you gaze so at that picture?

PRINCE. *Charmante, charmante!* She wears her hair exactly as the marquise used to.

MARIA. That is a portrait of my mother, prince. She was an angel. Oh, why is she not with us now? She was a saint, prince. A saint —I can think of no other way to describe her.

PRINCE. Well, that is a very good way. A saint—*c'est joli, ça!* I had a mother too . . . the princess! Imagine it—she was one of the fattest women I ever saw! Extraordinary! Immense! But I didn't mean to talk about that. . . . I think I'm rather tired. [*To* SINA.] *Adieu, ma charmante enfant!* . . . with what joy I shall . . . today . . . tomorrow . . . oh immediately! Au revoir! Au revoir! [*Tries to blow her a kiss, but stumbles over the door-sill and very nearly falls.*]

MARIA. Be careful, prince! Take my arm!

PRINCE. *Charmante! Charmante!* [*Going.*] Only now I begin to live. [*They both go out, left.*]

[SINA *is left alone. Her only emotion is one of profound disgust; she despises herself. Her cheeks burn. With crossed arms, her teeth tightly clenched and her head bowed, she stands motionless, while tears of shame flow from her eyes. The door opens, and* PAUL *comes in, beside himself with rage, and deathly pale.*]

PAUL. [*Panting—his voice coming with difficulty.*] At last I know what you are!

SINAIDA. What I am? [*At first she looks at him vacantly, as though she had gone mad, then her eyes blaze with fury. She steps up to him.*] How dare you speak to me like that?

PAUL. [*Falling back.*] I heard it all.

SINAIDA. [*Contemptuously.*] You have been eavesdropping, then?

PAUL. Yes; I have been eavesdropping. I descended to that. But I found out what a . . . I can't find words for it . . . what I am to expect of you from now on. . . . [*His embarrassment increasing with every word.*]

SINAIDA. What crime are you reproaching me with? What has given you the right to talk so insolently to me?

PAUL. What gives me the right? You are trying to marry that old fool behind my back, and I have no right to say anything to you? After you have given me your word . .

SINAIDA. When did I do that?

PAUL. What do you mean, when?

SINAIDA. This morning when you tried to force an answer from me, I told you I could say nothing definite.

PAUL. Naturally! You wouldn't refuse me, because you wanted to have something to fall back on!

[*SINA's face contracts with pain, as though something has stabbed her with a thrust that penetrates to the depths of her being. But she controls herself.*]

SINAIDA. [*Very clearly and deliberately, though her voice trembles slightly.*] You have only to thank my pity for you that I did not turn you out altogether this morning. You yourself came begging me to delay, so that you might not hear me say "no" just yet. And now you dare to insinuate that I have been leading you on with false hopes? You could see, and did, that your coming back here today offended me deeply. Is that what you call wanting you "to fall back on"? You are a fool; and a spiteful fool into the bargain. Good-bye! [*She turns from him and goes slowly to the door.*]

PAUL. [*Gnashes his teeth in his rage.*] Very well, I am a fool! Splendid! Good-bye, by all means! But before I leave this town, everyone in it shall know how you and your mother caught the poor old prince napping. You shall know whom you have to reckon with in me!

[*SINA starts, and seems about to remain in order to argue*

with him. After a moment's thought, however, she shrugs her shoulders contemptuously and goes out, slamming the door behind her.]

[MARIA *appears from the left. She has heard* PAUL's *last outburst and instantly guessed its meaning. She experiences a moment's panic.* PAUL *is preparing to give her away to the* PRINCE *and to the whole town at large! But a plan to circumvent him comes immediately to her mind, and she loses no time in putting it into action.*]

MARIA. [*Goes towards him with her hand outstretched, at her most cordial.*] Why, *mon ami*—whatever is the matter?

PAUL. *Mon ami!* [*Furiously.*] You trick me right and left, but I am still "*mon ami*" as usual! Do you think you can go on leading me by the nose for ever?

MARIA. I regret extremely to see you in such a state of mind, Paul. That is not the way one speaks to a lady!

PAUL. A lady! You! . . . You may be anything else on the face of the earth, but a lady you are certainly not!

MARIA. [*Gently.*] Sit down, Paul. [*She indicates the chair which the* PRINCE *occupied during the preceding scene.*]

PAUL. Listen, Maria Alexandrovna! You look at me as though you were the picture of innocence, and as though you expected an apology from me instead! This is really more than human patience can endure!

MARIA. [*Looking at him reproachfully.*] Were you listening?

PAUL. [*Roughly.*] I was! And why not? You've simply been making a fool of me, that's all! Well at last, I've found you out—I heard it all.

MARIA. After the way you have been brought up, Paul—with your family code—*you* would stoop to such methods? I should never have believed it possible!

PAUL. [*Leaping out of his chair.*] Maria Alexandrovna—this is outrageous!

MARIA. Only one question remains—who induced you to do it? Who is the spy in this house? That is a thing I should dearly like to know!

PAUL. You will excuse me if I do not tell you!

MARIA. As you please—but I shall find out, of course. I have told you already, Paul, that I reproach myself greatly on your account. But if you will take everything into consideration, I think you will realise that I only tried my best to do what was best for you in every way.

PAUL. Best for me! For me? I like that! I assure you, Maria Alexandrovna, you have made a fool of me for the last time! . . . [*Wheels round on his chair.*]

MARIA. Try and restrain your excitement, my dear boy, if that is possible. Listen to me carefully. To begin with I shall say that you would have heard all this from me, at the proper time, without having to find it out by eavesdropping. Secondly, and this above all, my daughter is to blame for nothing—remember that. She loves you with her whole heart, and I had infinite trouble to bring her to accepting the prince's proposal.

PAUL. [*Sarcastically.*] She has just given me proof of how she loves me with her whole heart!

MARIA. You may think so. But how did you talk to her? Like a gentleman? Hardly, I dare say.

PAUL. We need not discuss gentlemen or ladies just now, Maria Alexandrovna! This noon, while I was driving with the prince, you put me so to shame that I . . . Well, I know all about everything now!

MARIA. From the same vile source, no doubt. [*Portentously.*] I painted you blacker than you are, Paul. Yes, I did that. But I had to diminish you somehow in Sina's eyes, or I could never have made her promise to give you up. You must have seen for yourself that Sina has never encouraged the prince's advances by so much as a word or a gesture. She hardly spoke a single word throughout the entire time, as you know. I am certain that the moment we left her alone, she wept. When you found her here, did you not notice that she had been crying?

PAUL. [*Begins to reflect.*] What is all this driving at, Maria Alexandrovna?

MARIA. If you had come to me in the beginning, in a sensible way, and asked me the meaning of it all, you would have been answered long ago. I will tell you now. First of all, it is for Sina's happiness. The prince is wealthy and distinguished, a brilliant match for Sina. He dies; Sina is left a young widow, a princess, and wealthy too. She is then at liberty to marry whom she pleases. Naturally she then bestows her hand upon the man she loves.

PAUL. [*Thoughtfully examining his shoes.*] Hm!

MARIA. In the second place, I wish to see the prince married to Sina for his own sake. He is now in the clutches of that unspeakable housekeeper of his, who is driving him into an untimely grave. God will be my witness that the only argument with which I was able to persuade Sina to accept this marriage, was by showing her how holy a deed of self-sacrifice she would be doing.

PAUL. [*Mockingly.*] Indeed! So the whole scheme was really devised for the benefit of the prince? Hm!

MARIA. My dear Paul, it occurs to you perhaps that I have made a somewhat jesuitical combination of the prince's welfare and my own advantage. That I will not altogether deny; it is possible that some such thought did flash through my mind for a moment. But Sina is as innocent as a dove. She is incapable of calculation and scheming. All she knows is loving. If the element of bargain in this affair occurred to anyone, it was to me only. But where could the advantage lie for me? Frankly, I do not know. My life is almost over—what more can I need at my age? No, Paul—if I schemed, it was for her, for my child, my angel Sina. And what mother would blame me for it?

[*Tears glisten in* MARIA's *eyes.* PAUL *hears this candid confession with the utmost astonishment. He lowers his eyes.*]

PAUL. What mother indeed! You are extremely plausible, of course. but . . . but, you made me a certain promise, you may remember. You raised my hopes. . . .

MARIA. And you do not understand even yet, that I might have had you in mind too, in these so-called schemes of mine? I assure you, *mon cher* Paul, your interests have been by no means ignored.

PAUL. *My* interests?

MARIA. [*Raising her hand to heaven.*] My God, is it possible for anybody to be so naïve and so blind? Ah, youth, youth! Do you truly not understand, Paul? Well, let me explain then. Sina loves you—that is true beyond a shadow of doubt. But let me impress this upon you, too: in spite of her love for you, she feels that you are not wholly to be depended on. That is why she is deliberately cold to you sometimes. Have you really never noticed that?

PAUL. Yes, I have certainly noticed it. But I still don't follow you.

MARIA. It seems to me that she still has a doubt as to whether her feeling for you is a permanent one. I am a mother—I ought to know my daughter's heart! If, instead of coming in like a whirlwind, full of reproaches and epithets which could only lacerate that proud

and innocent girl—if instead, you had taken the matter calmly
and in a generous spirit, with tears of regret, even with despair . . .

PAUL. Hm!

MARIA. If you had come to her and said: "Sinaida, I love you better
than life itself, but circumstances more important than either of us
seem to hold us apart. I understand them, and know that your
happiness will be the outcome, so I will not stand in your way. I
forgive you, Sinaida. Be happy if you can!" And if you had looked
at her with sadness instead of glaring at her full of rage, and said:
"Good-bye, Sinaida . . ."—you would have left a very different
impression upon her heart, believe me.

PAUL. Very well. Suppose I had acted according to your programme,
what then? I remain the loser.

MARIA. No, no, no, my dear boy! Don't interrupt! I will tell you the
rest—in detail. Then, later on, you meet her again—say at a great
society ball, with all the brilliant illumination and the ravishing
music and exquisite women—you can imagine the scene. And in
the midst of the merry-making, you stand leaning against a pillar,
pale and melancholy. But plainly visible to her, as she whirls in the
dance! She does not see you at once, however; she is aware only
of the incomparable Strauss waltz and of the gaiety and *éclat* of
the company. Then she catches sight of you at your pillar, pale
with the turmoil of your love for her. What takes place at that
moment in Sina's heart? She thinks: "And that is the man I doubted!
He, who has dedicated his life to me, and whose heart bleeds to
death for my sake!" The old love revives within her, invincible
at last! [*She pauses for breath, and rises.* PAUL *turns in his chair
with such violence that it creaks ominously.*] For the prince's health,
Sina travels. They go to Italy, to Spain! To Spain! Where the
myrtle grows and the lemon—and where the Guadalquivir flows
under a sky eternally blue—the land of love. Where without love,
one cannot live! And you follow them. You resign from the army,
you abandon your family and friends—you leave everything behind you! Of course there will be certain malicious gossips who
will insist that your reasons for following your uncle round the
world have nothing to do with sympathy for his state of health. But
I tell you that a love like yours for Sina, can only be pure and
sacred. I am a mother, Paul—I could not give you evil counsel.
. . . And at last the good old man passes away, blessing her for
the happiness of his declining days! And who should marry Sina

then, if not you, my dear boy? Through her, you instantly receive an important government appointment, and take your place in the highest society. You have now but a mere hundred thousand roubles to your name—then, you would be able to dispose of millions! The prince's will will be as it should be—I shall make that my concern. And last, though not least, Sina will worship you as a martyr to self-abnegating love. . . . And then you ask me *how* I have safeguarded your interests! Paul!

PAUL. [*Leaps out of his chair and clutches his head with both hands.*] Maria Alexandrovna, I have behaved like a cad!

MARIA. No—it is chiefly thoughtlessness in you, Paul—chiefly thoughtlessness!

PAUL. Oh, what a fool—what a brainless fool I am! I've thrown away the happiness of a lifetime because my love for her drives me mad, and I can't think.

MARIA. All may not yet be lost!

PAUL. If I could only think so! Help me, Maria Alexandrovna! Save me! [*He bursts into tears.*]

MARIA. My dear boy! [*Holds out her hand with a pitying smile.*] You were desperate—I know. You lost your head. Sina will understand!

PAUL. I am out of my mind with love of her, Maria Alexandrovna! I will make any sacrifice to win her—gladly, more than gladly!

MARIA. I will intercede for you, Paul.

[*Paul is speechless with gratitude.*]

MARIA. Yes—we shall go to her together, and tell her everything we have just said.

PAUL. You are an angel from heaven, Maria Alexandrovna! . . . Could we . . . couldn't we go at once?

MARIA. God forbid! This only shows how little you know about women, my dear boy! Sina is far too proud for that! She would take it for a fresh insult. No—impossible! But tomorrow, I shall see that everything is made right for you. Go quietly now to your godfather's. . . . For my part, you may come back here tonight if you wish, but I shouldn't advise it.

PAUL. I'll go at once! At once! Ah God—you have given me back my life! But there's one thing more I want to ask you—suppose the prince is a very long time dying?

MARIA. What a child you are, Paul! So far from wishing him harm, we must pray to God to keep him in good health! With all our hearts, we must wish the dear, good, old gentleman a long, long life! Though alas—I fear his condition is not very hopeful! But at all events, he will have to present himself at court, to introduce Sina to society. Though that, unless I am happily mistaken, may prove too much for him! We can only pray, my dear Paul, and hope for the best for him! The rest is in God's hands! . . . But go now! And my blessing goes with you, *mon ami!* Don't give up hope—be brave and patient! Above all, brave! I have never doubted the nobility of your heart. [*She presses his hand warmly, and* PAUL *goes out on tip-toe.*]

MARIA. Well at least, I've brought that imbecile to his right mind! [*The door opens and* SINA *comes in. She is even paler than usual, but her eyes are blazing.*]

SINAIDA. Make a quick end of this, mamma, or I'll not be able to go through with it. I wish I could run away from this house and everything in it, it is all so frightful and degrading.

MARIA. Sina! What on earth ails you, my angel? Have you also been eavesdropping?

SINAIDA. Yes! Are you going to rebuke me now, as you did that poor fool? Now listen to me, mother—if you go on torturing me any longer, and force me to keep on playing this miserable part in this comedy of yours, I'll throw up the whole thing and make an end of it. I know I said I would be a party to it—great swindle though I knew it was. But I am suffocating—it is choking me! [*She collapses on the piano-bench.*]

MARIA. [*Hastily glancing at her.*] *Pauvre enfant!* . . . Now indeed, there is no time to be lost! Quick, quick! If the pack is after us, and goes spreading the affair all through the town, everything will be ruined! I must get the prince away from here, onto the estate— I'll go myself and fetch that stupid father of yours! Let him be good for something, once in his life! [*She rings.* GLAFIRA *appears.*] Is the sleigh at the door?

GLAFIRA. [*With a hasty glance at* SINA.] It's been waiting a long time already, Maria Alexandrovna!

MARIA. [*Goes to* SINA, *who is still sobbing noiselessly.*] Sina—my angel! Sina?

[SINA *does not even raise her head. She is dissolved in tears. Her long, beautiful hair has come unbound. From time to time a shudder passes over her as though an icy shaft had pierced her through.* MARIA *stands looking at her, in the greatest anxiety.*

She doubts the wisdom of leaving SINA *alone in such a state.*
But time is flying, and the horses waiting to go.]

MARIA. Sina, Sinotschka, my little dove! Control yourself, my sweet
angel! We're going to leave town tonight. And the good prince
will go with us. I'll only be gone half an hour, darling—just to
fetch papa! For the look of the thing, you know. Once we are
out of this place, everything will be all right. And in the morning
we'll have the village priest, and you will be married in the house.
Then let the whole city of Mordassoff get up and shriek holy murder
if it wants to—much good may it do them! But first of all, that
useless clod of a father of ours will have to come here and invite
the prince formally to visit the estate. He can be of that much
assistance, at any rate. . . . Imagine it, sweetheart—just like an
elopement! A secret wedding on the country estate! With a couple
of the village girls for bridesmaids, in their pretty best dresses, and
the old village priest. Nobody else . . . Sina, please answer me
. . . Sina . . . [SINA *sobs more audibly, but does not raise her
head.*] But I must go, child. I'll fly, and be back almost at once.
Go and lie down for a little while, my dove! I'll soon be back.
[*Presses a kiss on* SINA's *head, gives her one more look of deep
anxiety, and is gone. The moment she is out of the room,* SINA
utters a low moan.]

[GLAFIRA *waits ominously at the door, and crosses herself.*
SINA *suddenly becomes aware that she is not alone, and turns
with a cry.* GLAFIRA *says nothing, neither does she move. They
look at each other in silence.*]

SINAIDA. [*In mortal fear.*] Is she here again?

[GLAFIRA *nods her head.*]

SINAIDA. No, no, no! I cannot see her again! No more! [*Pause.*] I am
frightened. . . .

[GLAFIRA *again crosses herself.*]

SINAIDA. Send her away! Send her away! What is the use? It has all
been settled now! [*Pause.*] What does she say about him? Is he
worse?

GLAFIRA. She said before that you'd have to hurry if you wanted to
see him alive. Now she doesn't say anything any more. Nothing.
She sits at my kitchen table and cries. I can't look at her. . . .

SINAIDA. [*Arranges her hair again, and remains for a long time standing, deep in thought.*] Not now, Glafira . . . not yet. . . . But
tonight. [*A long pause.*] Glafira . . . tell her I will come!

ACT III

The drawing room, as before. Six o'clock in the evening.

MARIA, *her husband,* AFANASSIJ, *the valet* GRISCHKA *and* GLAFIRA *enter from the rear.* GLAFIRA *takes their fur coats.*]

MARIA. Quick! Quick! [*To* GLAFIRA.] Take the suitcase upstairs and lay out the master's clothes. [*To* GRISCHKA.] Do the master's hair. Quick, do you hear? [*Takes off* AFANASSIJ'S *cap.*] Why do you roll your eyes so, sleepyhead? Why haven't you had your hair cut? [*To* GRISCHKA.] Why didn't you see that the master's hair was cut, Grischka? I told you about that a week ago.

GRISCHKA. The master wouldn't let me do it—that's why. I've gone to him with the scissors ten times already and said: "The mistress'll come on us sudden one of these days, and then what shall we do if your hair isn't cut?" But the master kept on saying: "Let's chance it for another day."

[MARIA *annihilates him with a look. He vanishes with* GLA-FIRA.]

AFANASSIJ. [*Dejectedly.*] But, mamma . . . but you might at least explain. . . .

MARIA. Don't call me mamma! How often have I told you not to call me that, stupidhead? I'm not a peasant. . . .

AFANASSIJ. Oh dear . . . I'm sorry . . . Maria, then! Still, you are my wife, after all, legally and all that, so . . .

MARIA. Scarecrow—what nonsense are you talking! Are you trying to make excuses for yourself? How dare you talk about my being your wife, legal or otherwise? Don't I try hard enough to forget it now and then? Dolt! . . . [*Feels his hair.*] What? Wet, too? How can I let you be seen in this condition? Just look at your hair!

AFANASSIJ. But, mamma . . . I'd just come out of my bath when you pounced on . . .

MARIA. Be quiet! Let me hear you call me mamma once again, and you'll have no tea for a month!

AFANASSIJ. Oh dear . . . I'm sorry . . . I meant, mam. . . .

395

Maria Alexandrovna I mean, I'm sure I caught cold, rushing out of doors straight from the bathroom like that . . . What do you want with me now, please?

MARIA. Listen to him, that's all—the useless goat! He has the impertinence to ask what *I* want with him! Why, you've never had gumption enough to get yourself a single decoration! What sort of a figure do you think you'll cut in society with your dress coat bare?

AFANASSIJ. [*Making a feeble effort to smarten himself up.*] The Czar gives decorations as he sees fit, and I'm not a useless goat; I'm a first class State Counsellor.

MARIA. Be quiet, and pay attention to me! Prince Gavrila is here on a visit. Do you remember him?

AFANASSIJ. Yes, mamma—I remember him. What is he doing here?

MARIA. Be quiet—and mind your own business! You're his host—you are to invite him to accompany us to the estate tonight do you hear? And you're to be extremely cordial about it. That is what I've brought you to town for. We're to drive back again this evening. And if you dare to say one word beyond what I've told you to say, either this evening, or tomorrow, or the day after, or at any other time so long as you live, I'll make you mind geese for a year! Not a word now! You know what you are to do—do it!

AFANASSIJ. But suppose they talk to me?

MARIA. That makes no difference! You keep your mouth shut!

AFANASSIJ. But I can't keep my mouth shut for the rest of my life, mam. . . . Maria Alexandrovna!

MARIA. Then just make sounds. Say "hm!" or something like that—monosyllables. That will give them the impression that you're very clever and think a long time before you answer. Understand me now, once for all: I brought you here so that you might tell the prince you had heard of his arrival and had rushed to town immediately to welcome him and pay your respects, and invite him out to the estate! Is that clear?

AFANASSIJ. Hm!

MARIA. You needn't begin with your "hm!" just yet, blockhead! Answer me!

AFANASSIJ. All right, mamma—everything shall be as you wish. But why am I to invite this prince?

MARIA. What? You dare to ask me reasons? What business is it of yours, I'd like to know!

AFANASSIJ. But, Maria Alexandrovna, if you'll only tell me how I'm to invite him if I've got to keep quiet all the time?

MARIA. I'll do the talking—all you have to do is to bow at the right moments, do you hear? Just bow—that's all! You hold your *chapeau claque* in your hand, understand?

AFANASSIJ. Yes, yes—I understand ma. . . . Maria Alexandrovna.

MARIA. The prince is a great wit! Whenever he speaks, even if it is to somebody else, you're to smile politely, do you hear?

AFANASSIJ. Hm!

MARIA. There you go again! You needn't say "Hm!" to me, I told you. Tell me straight now—do you thoroughly understand?

AFANASSIJ. Certainly I understand, Maria Alexandrovna! How could I fail to? I'm only saying "Hm!" now to practice it, nothing else, mamma! It's this way, isn't it—when the prince talks to me, I'm to look at him and smile. Very good. But what about if he should ask me a question?

MARIA. Simpleton! I have told you already to just keep still. I'll answer for you—you are to do nothing but look at him and smile.

AFANASSIJ. Then he'll think I'm dumb!

MARIA. What if he does? Let him! It's at least a way of not showing him what an imbecile you are!

AFANASSIJ. And what if anyone besides the prince should ask me something?

MARIA. Nobody will! Because nobody will be there. But if, by accident, which God forbid, anyone else should be there and ask you a question, you're to smile sarcastically! Do you know what a sarcastic smile is?

AFANASSIJ. Hm!

MARIA. Go upstairs now and change your clothes—be as quick as you can! And don't forget to look into the mirror before you come down. . . . Now mind what I've told you. If you make a mistake tonight, I'll . . . I don't know what I'll do with you! [*Exit* AFANASSIJ.] Now I've that blockhead to cope with! It might have been better to leave him out altogether. [*To* GLAFIRA *who enters.*] Where is that Nastasia? As if I hadn't enough to do! Is the table set inside? Let us have the buffet in here.

GLAFIRA. Nobody's seen Nastasia Petrovna for the last hour! [*Whispering.*] She sent for the hairdresser, Karagin—she's dressing up. . . .

MARIA. [*Under her breath.*] Dressing up—that hussy! [*Aloud.*] Put the champagne glasses on a tray and bring it in here. I am going now to change my dress—I'll be down directly. Is the prince still asleep? Has he rung since I've been gone? No? Well, I'm going up now. You are not to let anyone in. Do you understand? If callers come, no one is at home. No one, mind. No one. [*Exit.*]

[GLAFIRA, *sets out plates and glasses. After a moment,* SINA *comes out of the dining room.*]

GLAFIRA. Maria Alexandrovna has just come back with Afanassij Mattweitsch. [SINA *nods.*] The hors-d'œuvres are to be set out here. [*Whispering.*] Sinaida Afanassievna . . .

SINAIDA. [*Whispering, but without looking at her.*] Was she to come again this evening?

GLAFIRA. She hasn't come yet. She was crying with happiness this afternoon when she went away. She said she'd be back at six to fetch you. . . .

SINAIDA. Yes.

GLAFIRA. I wanted to give her something to eat. But she couldn't wait to get home and tell him.

SINAIDA. Is it far?

GLAFIRA. They live at Gerber's—outside Novgorod. You cross a wooden bridge. . . . She said she'd be sure to come because you'd never find your way alone.

SINAIDA. Did you take my coat and overshoes into the kitchen for me?

GLAFIRA. Yes, Sinaida Afanassievna! And one of my woolen kerchiefs for your head. She was shaking so with joy, Sinaida Afanassievna, she nearly fell down the steps to the back gate—she was in such a hurry to tell him. . . . [*Pause.*] She'll be back a few minutes past six.

SINAIDA. When she comes, give me some sign. Bring in a plate and drop it. No . . . [*Reflecting.*] just bring me my orangeade—that would be the best way. Say: "Here's your orangeade" . . . anything. . . . I'll understand.

GLAFIRA. Yes, Sinaida Afanassievna!

SINAIDA. When I've gone, tell them I wasn't feeling well, so I'm locked in my room upstairs . . . [*Almost to herself.*] . . . they'll have to know in the end. Tant pis . . . [*In the doorway.*] Mind you don't forget anything Glafira. Oh, there's one thing more . . .

[*Voices are heard outside.*]

[GLAFIRA *pulls* SINAIDA *into the dining-room.* PAUL *and* NASTASIA *enter from outside.*]

NASTASIA. [*Sotto voce.*] Paul Alexandrovitch, I tell you you're simply making yourself ridiculous with all this . . . you've been talking utter nonsense.

PAUL. What do you mean? What is there nonsense about it?

NASTASIA. All that high-falutin chatter—the romantic rubbish you've been babbling—simply repeating the words of that unmitigated matchmaker, who's as cunning as a fox if you only knew it. "Spain . . . the Guadalquivir . . . the good old dying prince who joins your hand and Sina's on his deathbed and gives you his blessing as he goes." And the ball-room scene: "Alone—pale—leaning against a pillar, trying to catch her eye . . . heroic sacrifice, rewarded in the end by a brilliant marriage!"

PAUL. Nastasia, I must beg you to stop talking, please. Your poisonous tongue has already . . .

NASTASIA. I have already opened your eyes for you once, Paul Alexandrovitch, and insults are all the thanks I get for it. I'm beginning to believe you're nothing but a child. The moment she finds you alone, that unscrupulous wretch grabs hold of you and winds you up in her sentimental speeches, and you're lost. Is it possible that you don't realise that all that surface-noble talk is an out-and-out swindle—don't you see that it's a way of playing for time while she lands the haul? . . . What they're going to do actually, is take away your bride and get her hitched at breakneck speed to that dandified mummy of a prince—and gag you with false promises while they do it.

PAUL. [*Thinking it over.*] Do you honestly believe this, Nastasia Petrovna?

NASTASIA. They were willing to have you as the bridegroom of their beauty so long as no one better had come along, but the moment he does, out you go! Maria's latest *coup* is the talk of all Mordassoff, and you will of course be made to pay the usual social penalty of having been jilted practically at the altar. I only hope I shall live to hear the roar of laughter that will go up at your expense, Paul Alexandrovitch. And you'll be able to tell them all about your marvellous self-sacrifice, and your heroic powers of resignation. Complete with the story about the ball and you leaning against the pillar, and Spain and the Guadalquivir. . . .

PAUL. [*Shuts his ears with his hands.*] Stop, Nastasia Petrovna—you're driving me mad. . . .

NASTASIA. Well, do as you please—it's all one to me. I've done my duty by you, and I've no wish to waste any more time on your affairs. Once a fool, always a fool. By all means let that chattering *intrigante* flatter you into unconsciousness while the beauty marries her mouldering mummy—I don't care. So far as I'm concerned, I've had enough of this madhouse. And what's more, I could tell you very different stories about this young lady with her pale face—the châtelaine whose worshipping troubadour you are! Come back to your senses if you can, and use a little judgment. I have other things to bother about, Paul Alexandrovitch. [*She goes off, rear.*]

PAUL. [*About to run after her.*] What was that? What was that? What did you say? Nastasia; wait a minute!

[*The door shuts.* PAUL *gazes at the closed door, undecided whether to go after* NASTASIA *or not. He strides frantically up and down the room.*]

PAUL. My head's spinning! . . . To the devil with their high-mindedness! To hell with their damned self-sacrifice and their Guadalquivir! [*He spits with rage and contempt, and sits down thinking deeply, looking up every now and then with vacant eyes that look at nothing.*] Suppose it *is* another trap—all this hero twaddle? . . . Oh, I don't know what I'd do! [*Leaps up in a fury. Knocks at the door, left.*] Uncle! Uncle! It's I! Paul! May I come in? I've got to talk to you . . . just for a minute. But now!

[*The door opens. The* PRINCE'S *valet appears with a wig in one hand and a comb in the other.*]

THE PRINCE'S VOICE. No—of course you can't come in—certainly not. I'm not dressed!

PAUL. [*Raging.*] That doesn't matter, uncle! I'll help you!

[*Forgetting, the* PRINCE *pokes his hairless head out of the door; then recoils inside again with a shriek.*]

PRINCE. Oh dear, my secret—you've discovered it now! Give me your word of honour at once—your sacred word of honour, mind, that you'll never tell a living soul about my wig! Swear!

PAUL. Great heavens, uncle—do you really think I could do a low-down thing like that!

PRINCE. Oh quite—oh quite! Of course you're as honest as the day! The idea of your giving me away! I need have no secrets from you! Tell me—what do you think of my moustache, dear boy?

PAUL. It's wonderful, uncle! Truly remarkable! However have you managed to keep it so long?

PRINCE. False, dear boy—oh yes, false!

PAUL. Not possible! I can hardly credit it! But what about the side-whiskers? Now come on, confess they're dyed!

PRINCE. Dyed? Not a bit of it! Why, they're false too—all false!

PAUL. Artificial, you mean? Now really, uncle, there are limits to what you can make me believe! You're trying to make a fool of me!

PRINCE. Sober truth, my dear nephew! Imagine it—they take everybody in; absolutely everybody! Even Stepanida doesn't believe they're false, though she puts them on for me herself sometimes! But of course, I can rely on you, thoroughly—you'll never give me away, will you? Word of honour?

PAUL. Word of honour, uncle! I say again: surely you don't think me quite so low?

PRINCE. Oh, my dear boy—I've had such a terrible day! Theophile threw me out of my carriage again!

PAUL. What? When?

PRINCE. When we were on our way to the monastery.

PAUL. Well I know all about that—that was early this morning.

PRINCE. No—not that time! This was no more than two hours ago! I was on my way to the monastery, and he capsized me deliberately into the ditch. I was terrified! . . . My heart is still palpitating!

PAUL. But uncle— haven't you been asleep?

PRINCE. Yes—I slept for a while—then I went out driving, as I say. Oh, but . . . perhaps . . . well, dear me —how odd. . . .

PAUL. You dreamt it, uncle—take it from me! You've been sleeping here quietly ever since luncheon.

PRINCE. Have I really? Oh well, perhaps I did dream it! First I saw a terrifying bull with huge horns, and then I saw a Public Prosecutor with horns also!

PAUL. Antipoff, most likely! Anna Nikolaievna's husband, of course!

PRINCE. Yes, yes—it must have been! Next I saw Napoleon Bonaparte! You know, everybody tells me I resemble Napoleon Bonaparte to a most extraordinary degree; and in profile, I resemble one of the late popes almost as remarkably! What should you say, my dear boy—do I look like any of the popes you know of?

PAUL. I think you look more like Napoleon, uncle!

PRINCE. Well, d'en face, I am inclined to agree with you. You know Paul, I'm very fond of you, my dear boy! I was on an island, and there he was, all of a sudden, standing in front of me—as

odd and talkative a specimen as you ever could imagine! I found
him most extraordinarily amusing!

PAUL. [*Distracted.*] Napoleon, do you mean, Uncle? [*An inspiration
is beginning to come to him.*]

PRINCE. Oh quite—Napoleon! I discussed philosophy with him. You
know, my boy, I'm genuinely sorry he was so harshly treated.
Those English! Of course if they hadn't put him in chains, he'd
certainly have descended on the world again. He was a rabid
fellow, if ever there was one! Still it does seem a shame! I'd not
have handled the matter that way at all—I'd have been content
to have him on a desert island.

PAUL. But why a desert island?

PRINCE. Well, an inhabited island, for my part! But superior inhabitants! I'd have had amusements arranged for him—plays,
music, ballets, all at the state's expense! I'd have permitted him to
be at large, under guard naturally, or he'd certainly have got away.
He was excessively fond of pie! Well, I'd have had pie baked
for him every day.

[PAUL *listens absently to the old man's babbling, biting his
fingernails.*]

PRINCE. Oh, *mon ami*, I had almost forgotten to tell you! Imagine
it—I made a proposal of marriage today.

PAUL. A proposal of marriage, uncle?

PRINCE. Quite—oh yes indeed! [*To his valet.*] What's that, Pacho-
mitch, you're ready to go? Very well, you may. . . . [*To* PAUL.]
A ravishing creature, Paul, but . . . but . . . I must confess, it
seems to me now that I might have been somewhat rash! Oh yes,
I realise it now! Good God!

PAUL. But excuse me, uncle—when did it happen?

PRINCE. Oh dear, oh dear! I really don't exactly remember. I wonder
whether I didn't perhaps dream that too? It's very strange—all
very strange indeed!

[PAUL *is overjoyed. He stands up. The new thought has taken
definite shape in his mind.*]

PAUL. But whom, for Heaven's sake, did you propose to, uncle?

PRINCE. Our hostess's daughter, my dear boy. *Cette belle personne!*
I've quite forgotten her name for the moment! But don't you
see, dear boy, it's utterly out of the question for me to marry!
What on earth am I going to do about it?

PAUL. Of course, marriage will be the ruin of you—there's no question about that. But let me ask you something, are you absolutely positive that you actually did make this proposal?

PRINCE. Oh quite—quite! Absolutely certain!

PAUL. What if you only dreamt it, uncle? Like being capsized again in your carriage.

PRINCE. My God, do you think that's possible? Really? I'm all at sea now! How am I ever going to get it straight now? I'd better use all the tact in the world and find out whether I proposed or not. What would you do in my place?

PAUL. I'll tell you what, uncle. I don't think you need worry about getting it straight.

PRINCE. Why?

PAUL. Because I'm perfectly convinced you only dreamt it.

PRINCE. I quite agree, my dear boy. I have so many dreams of that sort, that I know this was more than likely one of them.

PAUL. You see, uncle, you'd been drinking considerably even at breakfast. Then you had a good deal more at luncheon, and after that. . . .

PRINCE. Yes, my dear boy, it could easily have been that. . . .

PAUL. And it's absolutely impossible that you should have ever made such a proposal actually. I know you well enough to know that you're always most careful. . . .

PRINCE. Quite—oh, quite . . .

PAUL. Imagine what will happen if this should get to your family's ears. You're in hot water enough with them as it is. . . . What do you think would be the consequence of a thing like this?

PRINCE. Oh dear—oh dear. Yes, what *would* the consequences be?

PAUL. They'd shout all over the place that you weren't of sound mind when it happened. They'd say you're insane . . . and they'd put you under guard. It's most likely of all, that they'd have you safely locked up somewhere for the rest of your life, out of harm's way.

PRINCE. Oh my God—you don't mean that, do you?

PAUL. I do. Think it over, uncle! But just consider for a moment first: could you possibly have done anything so rash? It is really hardly possible—now isn't it? I assure you, you dreamt the whole business.

PRINCE. Certainly I did! Imagine my thinking for a moment that it could have happened in reality! A dream, of course, of course! You *are* a clever fellow, Paul! I thank you for this! You've certainly taken a terrible load off my mind this time!

PAUL. I'm extremely happy to have been here to save you from yourself. If you'd been left alone, imagine what you'd have gone through with the thought in your mind that you had engaged yourself to be married! Think of the consequences!

PRINCE. Oh quite—quite—the consequences would have been frightful!

PAUL. Just glance the situation over, my dear uncle! Here's a young lady, already twenty-three years old and on the shelf, when all of a sudden a rich and distinguished suitor appears! Do you suppose she wouldn't hold you to your delusion until you honestly believed you'd become her fiancée and marry you by force if it came to a pinch! Well, it would be the end of you, that's all!

PRINCE. But would it—do you really think so? Should I die soon after? Am I going to die soon, anyway?

PAUL. Not at all. But a man of your powers need not go about picking up the first thing that comes along!

PRINCE. Oh well, "my powers!"

PAUL. Certainly, your powers! And your wit and charm!

PRINCE. Yes "wit," I grant you.

PAUL. And a prince into the bargain! Don't you suppose you could make a better match than this, if you ever do want to marry? Just give a thought, while you're at it, to what your family would have to say if you made an alliance of this kind!

PRINCE. I know—they'd eat me alive, dear boy! I've had nothing but spitefulness and ill-will from them as it is! Why, do you know . . . I'm firmly convinced they even tried once to have me put in an lunatic asylum! Have you ever heard anything like it? Why, in God's name, why *me* in a lunatic asylum? What for?

PAUL. Yes—I know they're like that. I could believe anything of them. That's why I mean to stand by you now. There's a tea-party here this evening, I believe . . .

PRINCE. A party? Oh, my God!

PAUL. Don't be afraid, uncle! I shan't leave you.

PRINCE. Words can't express my gratitude to you, my dear boy! You've saved my life! I'll tell you what—I'll go away from here this very minute, er . . . What is your name? I've forgotten.

PAUL. Paul Alexandrovitch, uncle—your nephew! Yes, we'll go away tomorrow morning at seven. And when you see these people this evening, say good-bye to them all, and say you're leaving first thing in the morning.

PRINCE. I most certainly am! . . . But suppose they stick to this engagement business—oh, *mon ami*, whatever shall I do?

PAUL. You've nothing to be afraid of—I'm here. You have only one thing to concentrate on—let them say what they like, in whatever way they like—you dreamt the whole thing from beginning to end. Do you understand? Besides, it's the truth! Isn't it?

PRINCE. Oh quite—quite! Of course I dreamt it! But you know, my dear boy—it was a delightful dream! Extraordinarily lovely girl! And a figure . . .

PAUL. Well good-bye, for a little while, uncle! I'm just going upstairs for a moment!

PRINCE. What? You're leaving me alone?

PAUL. No, I'm not! Don't be afraid of anything! We're leaving to-morrow morning.

PRINCE. Yes—early. Oh, but *charmante! Charmante!* Really, my dear boy, an amazingly beautiful girl! What a figure! . . . And it I were to marry, I could do worse—believe me!

PAUL. God forbid, uncle!

PRINCE. Oh quite—God forbid! . . . I'll follow you presently. Oh, by the way, I've been meaning to ask you for a long time—did you ever read Casanova's memoirs? And that reminds me—I've got a thought to write down this morning. . . .

PAUL. Yes, I've read them. Why?

PRINCE. Oh dear—I've forgotten now what I was going to say about them. . . .

PAUL. Never mind! It'll come back to you later on. Au revoir!

PRINCE. Au revoir, my dear boy! But a delightful dream! Oh, delightful! Such a figure . . . !

[*The* PRINCE *disappears.* PAUL *is about to close the door behind him when the sound of voices is heard outside the room. The door in the rear opens suddenly.* PAUL *vanishes into the* PRINCE's *dressing-room.*]

[MARIA *propels her husband and* SINA *into the drawing-room, and stands in the doorway with* GLAFIRA, *scolding mightily.*]

MARIA. Run, I tell you! We are not at home! None of us! Nobody! Say we have left for the country! Say we all fell ill and died! Say anything, but WE ARE NOT AT HOME!

GLAFIRA. I told the ladies that already, Maria Alexandrovna. They don't believe me. I called Nastasia Petrovna to help me send them away. They came in three sleighs. One after the other. There's

Natalya Dmitrievna and the Public Prosecutor's wife and Katerina Petrovna, and . . .

[*The voices grow louder.*]

MARIA. [*Looking out.*] May the cholera take that Nastasia—she's actually taking them upstairs! [*Bangs the door.*] We are lost! This is the end of everything! In another fifteen minutes, the whole of Mordassoff will be here! [*Strides desperately back and forth. To her husband.*] Everything is lost—do you hear, blockhead? What are you standing there for like a graven image? Don't you hear me? Everything is lost!

AFANASSIJ. [*All at sea.*] But, mamma . . .

MARIA. It's all Nastasia's doing—she's driving them on at me like a pack of wolves. What have you to say to that? Your Nastasia—your relation! And I've cherished her in my house like a sister! Fool—imbecile—why don't you say something! Do you suppose these horrible, low-class women would dare . . .

[*The door opens. With a polite smile,* NASTASIA *ushers in the wife of the* PUBLIC PROSECUTOR *and* NATALYA.]

MARIA. [*Rushing towards them.*] You dear people! I am overjoyed to see you; so unexpectedly too! *Mais quelle charmante surprise!*

ANNA NIKOLAIEVNA. We're all coming! All of us! Louisa Karlovna, and Praskovia Ilischna, and . . . [*To* NASTASIA.] You'd better run and see that the front door's open, my angel—they'll be here any moment now. . . .

[*A long and venomous look passes between* NASTASIA *and* MARIA. NASTASIA *disappears.*]

NATALYA. [*Looks inquisitively about her, as though she expected to find* SINA *and the* PRINCE *together in a corner.*] Katerina Petrovna's coming too. So is Felissata Mikailovna, I believe—she said she was.

[FELISSATA *is the lady of colossal dimensions whose figure so delighted the* PRINCE. *She is addicted to tiny hats, usually of some pinkish colour. For the past three weeks, she has been* ANNA NIKOLAIEVNA'S *mortal enemy.*]

MARIA. I really cannot express how delighted I am to see you both in my house this evening—in spite of the lateness of the hour! But tell me please, what miracle of Providence brought you here just today . . .

NATALYA. [*Sweetly.*] No miracle, dearest Maria Alexandrovna. . . .

ANNA. [*Hastily interrupting.*] *Mais, ma charmante!* It is high time we had everything arranged for the theatricals! We happened to be all together tonight—for once—all four of us. So we thought— let's go over to Maria Alexandrovna's and get things settled once and for all. Natalya told the others; they'll all be here presently. I suppose you think it's dreadful of us to squabble over such silly things, don't you, *mon ange?* [*Kissing* MARIA.] But we'll have a final meeting now, and after that everything will go smoothly. . . . Heavens—there's Sinaida! Child, you grow more beautiful every day! [*Makes for* SINA, *evidently to embrace her effusively.*]

NATALYA. She might just as well do that—she does nothing else!

MARIA. [*To herself.*] May the devil take her! I'd forgotten all about the theatricals! They're clever, these vipers!

ANNA. [*Undeterred.*] The dear prince being here with you gave us a reason the more. Did you know there was a theatre on his estate in the former owner's time? We made inquiries, and it seems that there's all kinds of scenery there still, and curtains and costumes and so forth. . . . We'd like to discuss the performance with the prince, if he will. If you would use your influence, we're sure he would be glad to send us whatever we want from there—it's of no use to him. There's no chance of getting scenery in Mordassoff. And if he won't do that—he ought certainly to give us a donation —it's for charity, after all. Perhaps he'd even be willing to be in it. He is so delightful. His being in it would surely give us an enormous success!

NATALYA. [*With guileful emphasis.*] Certainly he shall take part in it! I hear he's easily persuaded.

ANNA. Did you hear that, you lovely Sina? You'll take part in it too, won't you? Have you chosen which rôle you would like best?

NATALYA. I don't think Sina ought to play in the play itself. She should sing, rather.

ANNA. A French ballad, *mon ange!* Oh yes—please!

NATALYA. Yes—one of those châtelaine-and-troubadour things!

SINAIDA. [*With a gesture of contempt.*] I'm not going to sing.

MARIA. [*Trying to head them off.*] The poor child doesn't feel very well today. . . . [*Turns towards the door, where the rest of the guests are beginning appear.*]

ANNA. Indeed? How strange! We heard she was in marvellous voice today! [*She and* NATALYA *swoop down upon the master of the house.*]

[*Enter* KATERINA, FELISSATA *and two more ladies,* NASTASIA *is with them.*]

MARIA. [*To herself.*] The entire plague of Mordassoff! [*To* SINA.] Disappear, my angel, if you can. They're out to finish us off this time! [*She hastens towards the newcomers with her most radiant smile.*] My ravishing Katerina Petrovna—this is indeed wonderful! And Felissata Mikailovna, you too have deigned to remember my humble home at last!

FELISSATA. Well, we were discūssing the theatricals this afternoon, and it suddenly occurred to us that . . .

MARIA. Yes, I know. . . . I know. . . . [*Loudly, to* NASTASIA.] The ladies will have tea, Nastasia. [*In an undertone.*] It's you who have foisted them onto me; I shan't forget it.

NASTASIA. [*At the top of her voice.*] I hope you'll have good cause to remember me, Maria Alexandrovna. I'll teach you to talk about hussies. . . .

[MARIA *turns her back upon* NASTASIA, *and surveys the field of battle with alarm.*]

NATALYA. [*To* SINA.] But, Sina—where is the darling prince hiding himself?

FELISSATA. You surely don't mean to say you're holding this party tonight without your most ardent admirer?

MARIA. [*Interposing.*] Our dear Paul is at his godfather's this evening. . . . Borudoiev, the merchant . . . you know him . . .

ANNA. Oh, Maria—do come over here, please! We can't get a word out of this husband of yours! Come and tell him he should be a little more gallant to his lady guests!

MARIA. [*Going over to the group about the fireplace.*] I can't make out what is the matter with him today! He's been just as silent with me! Why don't yoū talk, *mon cher?* Tell me what they've been asking you!

AFANASSIJ. [*Timorously.*] Bŭt . . . but, mamma, you said I . . .

[*He is leaning against the mantlepiece, one hand thrust into his waistcoat and a glass of tea in the other, sipping very slowly in this picturesque attitude. As he begins to excuse himself to his wife, he encounters such a deadly glare, that he almost drops the glass in terror. He can think of nothing to do to cover his* faux pas, *but take a great gulp of the tea, though it is boiling hot. He burns his tongue and overturns the glass. The tea goes*

down the wrong way, and he is overcome with a spasm of cough-
ing; altogether he is in a pitiable plight, poor man.]

FELISSATA. [*To* MARIA.] But where is the delightful prince?

KATERINA. Yes; we simply can't go without seeing our dear old friend
once more.

NATALYA. You're not hiding him from us, I hope.

MARIA. *Mon ange*—how can you be so absurd! As a matter of fact,
my dears, he's lying down. He was so tired after dinner.

ANNA. Really—was he? The dear prince . . .

[PAUL *enters from the left, and stands for a moment un-*
noticed, contemplating the company with a supercilious smile.]

ALL. Look—there's Paul Alexandrovitch!

FELISSATA. So he is! You said he was at Borudoiev's, didn't you?

NATALYA. They told us you'd run away from us to Borudoiev's, Paul
Alexandrovitch!

PAUL. [*With a meaningful look at* MARIA.] I beg your pardon,
Natalya Dmitrievna—I never run away from anything; nor have
I anything to run away from!

ANNA. Tell me, Paul, is it true you have been given your congé?
. . . From the civil service, of course, I mean. . . .

[FELISSATA *giggles and pokes* KATERINA *in the ribs.*]

PAUL. [*Stupidly.*] Congé? How do you mean? Oh yes—I happen to
be after another position in St. Petersburg at the moment.

NATALYA. Well, good luck to you! We understood you were after
one in Mordassoff. Though there's never anything much going here,
heaven knows!

ANNA. No—the best you'd be likely to get would be a job as teacher
in a district school. Now and then there is an opening there. . . .
Or a tutorship . . .

[NATALYA *finds these allusions alarmingly obvious, and prods*
her poison-tongued friend with her foot, secretly.]

FELISSATA. Do you really suppose our handsome Paul would accept
such a wretched position as that?

[PAUL *doesn't know what to say. He turns and collides with*
AFANASSIJ *who holds out his hand.* PAUL *ignores the gesture,*
and makes him a deep and mocking bow. Very much agitated
now, he crosses to SINA, *looks into her eyes with an expression*
full of hatred, and whispers.]

PAUL. You wait; tonight you shall see whether I'm a fool or not. . . .

SINAIDA. [*Aloud, as her eyes travel slowly and with loathing over him, from head to foot.*] Why wait? They know already what you are! [PAUL *turns away from her, afraid.*]

MARIA. [*To* PAUL.] Have you just come back from your godfather's, *mon cher* Paul?

PAUL. No—from my uncle!

MARIA. Your uncle? Oh dear . . . then . . . is the prince up? Is he awake at last?

NATALYA. [*Venomous.*] We understood he was fast asleep!

PAUL. [*Spitefully.*] Don't you worry about the prince, Natalya! He is wide awake, and in his right mind again, thank God! He'd been drinking too much, first at your house, then here—it always goes to his head! And his head being what it is, it's easy to see what that means! But now, I'm glad to say, I've brought him back to his senses. He's quite lucid, even clever. He'll be here in a moment to say good-bye to you, Maria Alexandrovna, and to thank you for your hospitality. We're leaving at daybreak tomorrow. I shall take him myself to Duchanovo, to prevent this sort of thing from occurring again. Stepanida will be there to receive him, and once he's safely back in her hands, he won't be let out again in a hurry! I promise you that!

[MARIA *sits down under this onslaught, dumbfounded. Perhaps for the first time in her life, she experiences a tremor of cowardice.*]

NATALYA. [*To* MARIA.] Leaving at daybreak tomorrow? What can be the meaning of that?

OTHER LADIES. [*Innocently.*] What's that? . . . But we heard that . . . Too astonishing! . . . Most extraordinary! . . . Did you ever! . . .

[*The hostess is at a loss. . . . While she is considering what to do, there comes suddenly from the front room, a strange noise, followed by high-pitched shouts, and without warning* SOFIA PETROVNA KARPUCHIN, *the colonel's wife, bursts into the drawing-room. It is clear that she has already had three or four drinks, and she is in an extremely independent mood.*]

SOFIA. Ha! So this is how you treat me, Maria Alexandrovna! Very nice, I must say! Oh don't disturb yourself, please! I'm not going to stay more than a minute. I shouldn't dream of sitting down! Don't be afraid! All I've come here for is to find out whether what they're saying is true! I hear you're giving dances and banquets

and soirées and engagement parties at your house, while Sofia
Petrovna stays at home darning stockings—not asked! You invite
the whole town, but not Sofia Petrovna! And this afternoon it was
still *"mon ange,"* and *"my dear,"* when I was kind enough to
come and tell you how Natalya was carrying on with the prince.
Natalya indeed! Whom you called every name under the sun this
afternoon, as she did you! But here she sits as large as life at your
party! Keep your seat, Natalya Dmitrievna! I don't need any of
your *chocolat à santé* at ten kopeks a cup! I've got all I want to
drink in my own home, thank you—and more than you have!
[*She utters a snort of illimitable rage and contempt.*]

NATALYA. Dear Sofia Petrovna, that is perfectly obvious!

MARIA. But what on earth is the matter with you, Sofia Petrovna?
Do be sensible.

SOFIA. Don't you worry about me, Maria Alexandrovna. I know
what I know. [*To the guests at large, who take no pains to hide
their glee at this unlooked-for scene.*] And I know everything!
Your darling Nastasia came and told me the whole story—from
beginning to end! You made the prince drunk and then made him
propose to your daughter! Your Sina—that not a man in the town
will have anything to do with! [*She snorts again.*] Don't think
I mind not being invited to the lovely engagement party—I don't!
I spit on it! I've my own circle, thank you, and it's a very different
one from yours, thank God! I go to dinner at Countess Salich-
watska's; Colonel Kuroschin has been flirting with me for years!
I don't need your invitations! [*She makes inarticulate noises of fury
as she pauses for breath.*]

MARIA. [*Trembling with rage.*] Sofia Petrovna, this is no way to
break into a respectable house! Relieve us of your presence this
moment, or I shall see to it that you are assisted to do so.

SOFIA. Certainly! You want to have me thrown out by your servants!
But don't bother yourself! I'll find my way out alone! Good-bye!
Marry your darling Sina to whomever you choose! Don't you laugh
at me, you Natalya Dmitrievna! I spit on your chocolate! They
may not have invited me to their party, but I didn't dance the
Kasatchka for the prince—in skirts above my knees! You needn't
laugh either, Anna Nikolaievna—your friend Suchiloff broke his
leg tonight! He's just been brought home from the train. [*She
snorts.*] And as for you, Felissata Mikailovna, you stop having
your barefooted servant Matroschka chase the cows right under my

windows, so that they bellow until I can't hear myself speak—see that she stops that or I'll break her neck! I beg your pardon, Maria Alexandrovna! I hope you'll have a long and happy life!

[*With a last snort,* SOFIA PETROVNA *disappears. The guests laugh.* MARIA ALEXANDROVNA *is terribly embarrassed.*]

NATALYA. [*Sweetly.*] I'm sure she was drunk!

ANNA. The impertinence! *Quelle abominable femme.*

FELISSATA. What was all that nonsense about an engagement?

MARIA. Frightful person! It is through just such monsters as she that the most insane rumours are spread about! Are you not astonished that ladies of that kind are admitted into our society here? It is still more astonishing to me that anyone should listen to them and believe what they say!

[*The door on the left opens.*]

ALL. The prince! The prince!

NATALYA. Good Heavens, at last! *Le voilà, notre cher prince!*

FELISSATA. Thank goodness he has come—now we shall know what's what. . . .

[*Smiling sweetly, the* PRINCE *comes into the room. The ladies stampede towards him with shrill cries of joy.* MARIA ALEXANDROVNA *gazes at him with fearsome intentness, as though trying to read something in his face. It is now evident to her that* PAUL *has set some catastrophe afoot, but the* PRINCE's *face is inscrutable.*]

SOME OF THE LADIES. Oh prince! Dearest prince! How impatiently we have been waiting to see you! Ah, dear prince—here at last!

OTHERS. We could hardly bear to wait another minute! Hardly another minute, dear prince!

PRINCE. Flattering! Extraordinarily flattering, I'm sure.

[*He sits down at the table where the samovar is boiling. Immediately the ladies make a circle round him. Only* ANNA *and* NATALYA *remain near* MARIA ALEXANDROVNA. AFANASSIJ *grins and bows.* PAUL *smiles, and glances provocatively at* SINA. *She, however, behaves as though she is not conscious of his existence, and goes over to her father at the fireplace. They sit down side by side.*]

FELISSATA. Dear prince, is it true that you are on the point of leaving us?

PRINCE. Quite, mesdames. I am going abroad very soon.

ALL. Abroad? Abroad? We didn't know you were planning to go abroad, prince!

PRINCE. Yes. For the sake of modern ideas—that is why I am going.

FELISSATA. How do you mean, prince? What have modern ideas to do with going abroad? [*Looking at* SINA.]

PRINCE. Modern ideas—certainly! [*Very solemnly, and gaining conviction as he goes along.*] You see, the trend of everything nowadays is towards new ideas. I want to get some too.

PAUL. Hadn't you thought of becoming a freemason also, uncle?

PRINCE. Well, you probably won't remember, but in my early days, I was a freemason. I belonged to some lodge abroad. It was extremely uplifting to the mind! So much so that I decided I must do something for the enlightenment of the world. To begin with, I thought I would free my valet, Ivan, when we got to Frankfort. But to my surprise, he forestalled me and ran away himself! Extraordinary person, Ivan! Then one day, all of a sudden, I ran across him in Paris walking with a mademoiselle along the boulevard, dressed to kill! He nodded to me as I passed. That mademoiselle was certainly a bright-eyed, ravishing . . .

PAUL. [*Laughing.*] How about freeing all your serfs when you go this time, eh uncle?

PRINCE. You've guessed it exactly, my dear boy. That is what I intend to do. Give them all their liberty.

FELISSATA. But good gracious, prince—they'd all run away, and who would pay you your rents and taxes?

ANNA. Certainly! They'd be off before you could say knife!

PRINCE. Oh dear, would they really?

NATALYA. No question about it! And you'll be all alone.

PRINCE. Oh dear, oh dear—that would never do! Then I can't free them, that's all. Besides, it was only a thought.

PAUL. So much the better, uncle!

[*During all this,* MARIA *has set listening and observing, not saying a word. The* PRINCE *seems to have forgotten her altogether.*]

MARIA. [*In a loud and ceremonious tone.*] Prince, allow me to present my husband, Afanassij Matveitch. He came over from the estate especially, as soon as he heard you had come to stay with us for a few days.

[AFANASSIJ *smiles.*]

PRINCE. Delighted! Afanassij Matveitch—I must make a note of that!

Ah well, I'll remember. He's the one who was on the estate when
I arrived. *Charmante!* Delighted to make your acquaintance, indeed!
[*Shaking the smiling* AFANASSIJ'*s hand.*] How are you?

MARIA. He's very well, thank you, prince!

PRINCE. That is obvious! So you spend your time on your estate?
Splendid! What red cheeks he has! Look at him, how he laughs all
the time!

[AFANASSIJ *smiles, bows, and even essays a clumsy curtsy. At
the* PRINCE'*s last words, however, he can control himself no
longer and bursts into shrieks of foolish laughter. Everyone joins
in. The ladies titter, and can hardly contain their relish of the
situation.* SINA *flies into a white rage and looks at her mother with
blazing eyes.*]

MARIA. [*Creating a diversion.*] Did you sleep well, prince? [*Flings
a warning look at her husband to pull himself together.*]

PRINCE. Very well indeed! And I had a most delightful dream.

FELISSATA. A dream! I adore hearing people tell their dreams!

NATALYA. So do I! There's nothing I love better!

PRINCE. Oh, a delicious dream! But alas—it is a deep secret!

ANNA. What do you mean, prince? You're not going to tell us? But it
must have been something quite extraordinary, if that's the case!

PRINCE. [*Delighting in the ladies' curiosity.*] Oh quite—quite! A deep
secret!

SEVERAL LADIES. It must be something perfectly enthralling!

FELISSATA. I'll wager it was all about the prince getting down on his
knees before some beauty, and making her a declaration! Come,
prince, own up! Dear prince—you might just as well confess!

ALL. Confess! Confess!

PRINCE. [*Flattered.*] Though I insist upon keeping my dream a profound secret, I must confess, dear ladies, that you have very nearly
guessed it.

FELISSATA. Have we? Then, you could go a little step further and
tell us who your divinity was.

ALL. [*In a tumult.*] We must know that! Was she from here or somewhere else? Dear prince, please, please tell us!

PRINCE. Mesdames, I'm afraid your insisting will do you no good
this time! All I can tell you is that the lady was most ravishing!
. . . oh, indeed—a beauty not of this earth! . . . A celestial
maiden!

THE LADIES. Maiden! Celestial! Dear me! Was she from here, prince? And if so, who on earth . . . [*They exchange significant nods.*]

NATALYA. Who could it be but the reigning beauty of Mordassoff, of course? [*Looks at* SINA *with cossack's eyes. The others also stare.*]

FELISSATA. Now really, prince, since your fascination for us poor women is so great, why don't you seriously consider marrying? [*Looks meaningly round the circle.*]

KATERINA. There are such admirable opportunities in Mordassoff!

ANNA. Dear prince—do, please, get married!

ALL. Yes, do! Do! Why shouldn't you?

PRINCE. Oh quite—why not?

PAUL. Uncle!

PRINCE. Oh quite—I understand, my dear boy! Ladies, I must tell you that I can no longer contemplate the idea, alas! In fact . . . in fact . . . [*He falters.* PAUL *prompts him.*] And at the end of this delightful evening with our fascinating hostess, I shall say good-bye, and tomorrow I shall pay my visit to the monastery. Immediately after that I shall start on my travels, which will bring me back into touch with European culture . . .

[SINA *turns pale and looks at her mother with a disgust beyond words. But* MARIA *has decided that the many-headed hydra must be annihilated at a single blow. Solemnly and with great dignity, therefore, she rises and walks steadily towards the table, her proud gaze passing over the heads of her infinitesimal foes. A noble passion flames in her eyes.*]

MARIA. [*Solemnly.*] Mesdames, I have listened with pleasure to your vivacious conversation, and your gay and brilliant remarks, and I believe it is now time for me to contribute a word. This gathering tonight was of course unpremeditated and accidental, and I am very happy it occurred. . . . Under other circumstances, I could never have dreamt of giving away our family secret so soon, and now I must ask our dear guest's pardon for doing so. But it seems to me that his words have implied that a formal and solemn announcement of that secret would not only not distress him, but would, on the contrary, fall in with his own wishes. Is this not so, prince? Tell me, please, if I am mistaken.

PRINCE. Far from it—I am indeed very, very happy . . .

[MARIA *draws a deep breath, and surveys the entire company. The guests hang on her words with avid and impatient curiosity.*

PAUL *is frightened.* SINA *blushes and rises.* AFANASSIJ *clears his throat noisily, expecting something out of the common, whatever it is.*]

MARIA. Yes, mesdames—it is with rejoicing that I place in your safe keeping our family secret. [*Tears tremble in her voice.*] Today, after dinner, the prince, enchanted by the beauty and character of my daughter, honoured her with a proposal of marriage! Prince—dear, dear Prince; you will surely not be angry with me! Only the deepest happiness of my family in this alliance could have drawn this secret out of my heart before the proper time. And where is the mother who would condemn me in this?

[*They are all numb with amazement. The spiteful gossips are completely taken aback by this forthright method. A vague murmur arises, rapidly changing into shrill shouts of joy.* NATALYA *is the first to rush into* MARIA's *arms; then* ANNA *follows; then* FELISSATA. *They all leap from their chairs almost at the same instant. Some of the ladies are pale with fury. Congratulations overwhelm the bewildered* SINA, *and* AFANASSIJ *as well.* MARIA *stretches out her arms in an attitude and sweeps her daughter, almost forcibly, into her embrace. Only the* PRINCE *is left, contemplating the scene in quiet wonder, the smile still on his face. At the embrace of mother and daughter, he produces his handkerchief and wipes a tear from his eye. He too, naturally, is deluged with congratulations.*]

ALL. We wish you joy! Now live happily ever after! So you *are* marrying, after all! Congratulations! Congratulations! Dear prince—well you have come to it at last!

PRINCE. Oh quite—quite! Your kindness touches me deeply—I shall never forget it! *Charmante! Charmante!* I am moved to tears!

FELISSATA. [*Loudly.*] Kiss me, prince!

PRINCE. What most amazes me is how our hostess guessed my dream with such extraordinary accuracy! She's marvellous—she might have been there! Extraordinary! Most unusual!

ANNA. But, prince, are you still talking about a dream?

ALL. You'll have to tell us now, prince! Come, be candid! Confess!

MARIA. [*Sternly.*] Yes, prince, tell them whatever they wish to hear. The time for secrets is over now. It may all be told! I interpreted your beautiful allegory rightly, prince, and through it the exquisite delicacy with which you conveyed your desire to have the engagement made public. Yes, mesdames, this thing happened in reality, not in a dream: today the prince fell upon his knees before Sina and made her a solemn proposal of marriage! In reality, I say, not in a dream!

PRINCE. Oh quite—quite! I could have sworn it was real! Oh quite! And the circumstances were identical! Marvellous! [*To* SINA.] Mademoiselle, mademoiselle—if others had not done so before me, I should never have dared to mention your name. I will ask you to believe that. But I am happy to have been given this opportunity to tell you. *Charmante! Charmante!* How exquisite a dream can be! And as real as reality itself! Enchanting beauty!

ANNA. [*In a whisper to* MARIA.] What on earth is he talking about now? Is he still on that dream of his?

SEVERAL LADIES TOGETHER. What's this? [*They look at one another and whisper.*]

MARIA. Your pardon, prince . . . [*Forcing a smile.*] . . . but I confess you surprise me! What is this strange idea of continuing to talk about a dream? I understood your graceful pleasantry before, but if you persist in it as a pleasantry, then I can only say that it is a very poor one! . . . I attribute it, of course, to your notorious absentmindedness.

NATALYA. Yes, it's his absentmindedness—that's all!

PRINCE. Oh quite—quite! It must be that! Which reminds me of an anecdote—I must tell it now, before we go on to anything else! I was invited one day to a funeral—in St. Petersburg—middle-class people, you know, but very respectable. And I got it into my absent-minded head that it was a birthday party! There had been one in the same family; but a week earlier! . . . At any rate, I took the lady a bunch of camellias. When I got to the house, what did I see but a good, substantial business-man lying in his coffin! I was terribly upset, and couldn't tell how in the world to get rid of the bunch of camellias!

MARIA. Prince, I am afraid this is not the moment for anecdotes. Fortunately, my daughter has no need to pursue any suitor, whoever he may be. But the fact remains that a few hours ago, you proposed to her, over there at the piano. . . . Your visit here was spontaneous on your part; I had not invited you. I might even say that it surprised me greatly. I have a good idea that certain people have been working on your mind until you are almost driven crazy, and I have a very strong suspicion who those people are. But this is your chance to vindicate yourself, prince. Explain yourself now, please, and at once. Such jests as this, if it is one, cannot be tolerated in a respectable home.

PRINCE. [*Nervous.*] Oh quite—quite! By all means not! One certainly does not jest in a respectable home—I should think not indeed!

MARIA. That is no answer, prince. I ask you to confirm, in the presence of all here, your proposal of marriage to my daughter.

PRINCE. Certainly I confirm it! I did that long ago. The moment Felissata Jacobovna guessed my dream, I admitted the whole thing!

MARIA. I am not discussing dreams, prince! [*Furiously.*] Why do you persist in talking about your dream? It was all real, prince! Real—do you hear?

PRINCE. [*Getting up.*] Real? [*To* PAUL.] It's turned out as you said it would. [*To* MARIA.] Maria Alexandrovna, my dear and honoured hostess, you are mistaken, I assure you. I *know* it was nothing but a dream. Was it, Paul? . . . You be my witness! A dream—a dream—a dream!

MARIA. [*Desperate.*] Oh God in heaven, have mercy on me!

NATALYA. Don't excite yourself, Maria Alexandrovna; it may have merely slipped his mind for the moment! You know how he is!

MARIA. [*In an outburst.*] Natalya Dmitrievna, you astonish me! How can a thing like that be forgotten! Prince, don't mock us any longer, I beg of you! It ill becomes your years, and I assure you you will achieve nothing by it. My daughter is no French marquise! But a few hours ago, she sang for you here, on this very spot, and you fell upon your knees, bewitched by her singing, and made her a proposal of marriage. Am I dreaming? Am I asleep? Tell me, prince, am I asleep or am I not?

PRINCE. [*Floundering.*] Dear me—dear me! As to that . . . ah . . . perhaps, and then again perhaps not. I mean to say that now . . . I don't believe I'm asleep now any more. . . . It was this way, you see. . . . I did sleep, but before that I had a dream. . . . And in the dream I saw . . .

MARIA. [*Herself touched by his confusion.*] Nonsense, prince! What on earth are you trying to say? Dreaming, not dreaming—not sleeping, sleeping—what does it all mean? God only knows—or the devil perhaps. You are not well, prince—you have a touch of fever, haven't you?

PRINCE. [*Looks about him anxiously.*] Well, perhaps the devil does know. . . . It seems to me, though . . . oh dear, oh dear—I'm all confused now . . .

MARIA. [*More calmly.*] Try and think, prince! How could I possibly have told you your own dream so accurately, before you had told it to anyone?

NATALYA. Perhaps he had told it.

FELISSATA. [*Whispering.*] What kind of a performance do you call this?

MARIA. Oh God! Is it not enough to drive one raving mad? [*She wrings her hands.*] She sang a ballad for you, prince! Did you hear that too in your dream?

PRINCE. Oh quite—yes indeed! I have a distinct recollection of having heard her sing a ballad for me . . . [*Recollection comes back suddenly. His face lights up. To* PAUL . . .] Yes, my dear boy—I quite forgot to tell you about the French romance that was sung in my dream. There were castles in it—oh, a great many castles! And a troubadour! Oh dear, I remember it all now—even that I cried as I listened. . . . Now I really do doubt whether it could have been a dream—surely it was reality?

PAUL. But uncle . . . [*His voice is unsteady.*] I should think this could all be very simply explained. Most likely you did hear a song—really. Sinaida sings most beautifully. They brought you in here after dinner and Sinaida sang her romance for you. I was not present, of course, but I dare say you were deeply moved by it, and it must have brought back recollections of the past. You may have been reminded of that marquise you used to sing duets with—the one you were telling us about this morning. So when you slept afterwards, the pleasant emotions the song had awakened in you translated themselves into the dream of falling in love with Sina and proposing to her.

MARIA. [*Dumbfounded.*] Insolence!

PRINCE. My dear boy, that must be what happened! Thank you! Thank you! I remember that song very well. And after it, of course I thought of marrying—but by that time I was dreaming. The marquise was there too. . . . Ah, my dear Paul, what a clever fellow you are, to be sure! Well, I'm convinced at last that I dreamt it all! Maria Vassilievna, I do assure you that you are mistaken—it was all a dream. Do you imagine I should have dared otherwise to trifle with your noble feelings?

MARIA. At last I see whom I am to thank for this! [*To* PAUL, *beside herself.*] You, sir! You are responsible for it, you unspeakable person! To revenge yourself upon my daughter for rejecting you, you

have played upon this poor old fool's mind, and made him do your
will. But you shall suffer for it, you contemptible fellow——I shall
see to that!

PAUL. [*In an equal rage.*] Maria Alexandrovna! You speak as . . .
as no——I don't know how to say it——as no lady could ever speak.
You were on the point of kidnapping my relative——I am here to
protect him.

PRINCE. Oh quite——kidnap——that's it! [*He tries to hide behind* PAUL.]

MARIA. [*Completely losing control.*] Afanassij Matveitch, can't you
hear that you're being insulted by these people? Or are you nothing
but a block of wood? What are you sitting there gaping for? Any
other man would have wiped out such insults with blood——long
before it came to this pass. Is your family honour nothing to
you?

AFANASSIJ. But . . . mam . . . mamma . . . mightn't you have
been mistaken, after all? Couldn't it really have been a dream?
You know you have a way of . . .

[*Until now, the guests have remained undecided which side to
be on. But at* AFANASSIJ'S *words, their reserve breaks loose, and a
great outburst of wild laughter shakes the room.* MARIA, *throwing her dignity to the winds, lunges at her husband as though to
tear his eyes out, and is only restrained by force.* NATALYA *makes
the most of the occasion to pour in another drop of venom.*]

NATALYA. Of course that's what it was, Maria Alexandrovna! There's
nothing to get excited about!

MARIA. What do you mean? What do you mean?

NATALYA. I mean what your husband means, *chére amie!* It is a common occurrence . . .

MARIA. What is? Are you trying to tear my nerves to pieces?

ANNA. [*Sweetly.*] Perhaps it was you who dreamt it all.

MARIA. I? I dreamt? And you dare to tell me this to my face?

FELISSATA. Well, who knows? Anything is possible!

PRINCE. [*Muttering to himself.*] Anything is possible!

MARIA. He too——he too! Oh God! Oh, dear God!

ANNA. [*With unction.*] But, *mon ange,* don't get so wrought-up——
please! Dreams come from God, remember! No one can go against
His will; He rules over everything, waking and sleeping! We may
not rebel against His holy purposes!

PRINCE. Oh quite——quite! We may not rebel!

MARIA. [*Fighting for breath.*] So you're all trying to make me out insane—is that it? [*She rushes to a chair, and faints.*]
    [*Consternation.*]

NATALYA. [*Sotto voce, to Anna.*] She certainly has a talent for doing the right thing! There was positively nothing left for her but to faint! [*There is a moment of anxious and painful silence.*]
    [GLAFIRA *stands in the doorway with a tray.*]

GLAFIRA. The orangeade for Sinaida Afanassievna.

SINAIDA. [*Who until this moment has remained seated motionless and silent at the fireplace, now rises slowly.*] Very well, Glafira. Don't go away. I want you.
    [*Pale, with determination in her eyes, yet trembling with emotion; incredibly lovely in her agitation, she moves towards the company. She includes them all in a long, challenging gaze, then turns towards her mother who, at the first word, emerges from her faint and opens her eyes.*]
    Why go on with this sham, mamma? Why should we all stoop to lying? It has all been so unspeakably base already, that there is no reason why anything should be concealed any longer.

MARIA. [*Terror-stricken, leaps up.*] Sina! Sina! What ails you, child? Are you in your right mind?

SINAIDA. I told you long before this, mamma, that things had gone far enough! Need we degrade ourselves any further? I take it all upon myself; the greatest guilt is mine. This hideous plot would never have been possible, had I not consented to it. It was your love for me, mamma—I know. To the best of your understanding, and in your own way, you believed you were acting for my happiness . . .

MARIA. Sina, you are surely not going to tell how . . . Oh God—you stab me to the heart!

SINAIDA. Yes, mamma. I am going to tell it all. We have shame enough upon our heads as it is . . .

MARIA. You exaggerate, Sina. You're so terribly excited that you don't know what you are saying. What have you to tell? I can prove to everyone that we have done nothing to be ashamed of.

SINAIDA. Mamma, let me speak! [*Her voice now begins to tremble with anger.*] I do not wish to remain silent any longer before these people. I have nothing but contempt for their opinion; their only purpose in coming here tonight was to laugh at us. There is not one who should dare to throw a stone at us, for not one of them would hesitate to do things a hundred times worse than you or I would do—and for half the reason.

THE LADIES. This is wonderful! Sh! Listen! What is it all about? She's insulting us now!

NATALYA. Yes. I've not the vaguest idea what she is talking about, have you?

> [SINA *pauses, then turns to the* PRINCE. *So impressive is she in this moment, that he rises involuntarily to his feet and remains standing, in an attitude full of respect.*]

Prince, forgive me . . . forgive us! We have deceived you. We have treated you shamefully.

MARIA. [*Furious.*] Sina, hold your tongue!

PRINCE. [*In utter confusion.*] Ladies and gentlemen!

SINAIDA. Prince, we have both deceived you. Mamma, by trying to force you into a marriage with me; I, because I allowed it. You were made to drink too much, and I then, unasked, sang to you—and flirted with you. We caught this poor, defenceless old gentleman in our net, as Mosgliakoff has told you, because he was wealthy and a prince. There are no words for such baseness. I am sorry. I have only one thing to say to you, prince, and that I swear on my word of honour: I had a motive in doing this wicked thing, and the motive was not wicked. I wished to . . . wished . . . but—it does not matter. Nothing can excuse me.

> [*Her voice fails her. The petrified guests listen with staring eyes. The* PRINCE *is moved to tears, though he has not understood half of what she said.*]

PRINCE. [*Tearfully.*] But of course I am going to marry you, *ma belle enfant;* whenever you wish! I should consider it an immense honour! Still, it was all a dream, I assure you. . . . Why is everybody so excited? [*To* PAUL.] It seems to me more and more, my dear boy, that I have really understood very little about this. I should like you to explain it to me. . . .

SINAIDA. You are right, prince. There is no need for excitement. I thank you. You are a good man. The only good person in this room. You do not need to have anything explained now. You need not marry me. I have other plans—I have had them for a long time.

> [*Turns toward* GLAFIRA, *and gives her a sign.*]

NATALYA. "Her plans"—a brilliant stroke!

ANNA. "I thank you!" . . . sweet angel!

FELISSATA. Ssh! It's getting thrilling now!

SINAIDA. [*To* GLAFIRA, *so that all may hear.*] Did you bring my coat and overshoes down to the kitchen for me, Glafira? Please go and get them. You've had them hidden there all day.

[*The ladies put their heads together, and a loud whispering arises.* GLAFIRA *shudders and crosses herself. Casts a furtive and terrified glance at her mistress.*]

SINAIDA. Yes—let them hear it all now. You've had them hidden there all day, I said. Go.

[GLAFIRA *goes, reluctantly.*]

MARIA. Sina! What is this? My poor child—she is out of her mind!

ANNA. [*Sweetly.*] Be calm, *chère amie!* You heard her say she doesn't need the prince to marry her. God, in His great goodness, may have vouchsafed her a better match!

FELISSATA. "Coat and overshoes!" . . . the plot thickens!

[GLAFIRA *comes back with the coat and a kerchief for* SINA's *head.*]

MARIA. Sina! My little dove! What are you doing? Where are you going? [SINA *puts her mother aside, and gets into her coat.*] Don't leave me, Sina! I am your mother—I am your friend . . . [SINA *turns away from her, and goes to* PAUL.]

SINAIDA. And as for you, Paul Alexandrovitch, whom I once looked upon as my future husband—you plotted with these creatures to bring insult and shame on me. And yet you used to say you loved me! Very well—it is not my place to judge you, when my own faults are greater than yours. I did you wrong by allowing you to go on hoping! All my promises to you were lies. I never loved you! And if I had brought myself to marry you in the end, it would have been only to escape from here, out of this paltry little place—this hateful, wretched place! But I swear to you that if I had married you, I would have made you a good and faithful wife. You have been terribly revenged . . . and if it flatters your pride . . .

PAUL. [*Moved.*] Sina!

SINAIDA. If you still bear rancour against me . . .

PAUL. Sinaida!

SINAIDA. If you once [*Forcing back the tears.*] if you ever loved me . . .

PAUL. Sina!

MARIA. [*Moaning.*] Sina, Sina! My child!

PAUL. Sinaida, I am a despicable brute! I have been a cad!

[*Murmurs among the ladies, astonished and disapproving.*]

Oh, what have I done! [*Bursts into sobs, and falls to his knees.*]
I've been mad, Sinaida! No—I've been a thousand times worse than
mad! But I shall show you, Sinaida, that I am not without decency
altogether . . . [*To the* PRINCE.] I fooled you, uncle! It wasn't
a dream! You did propose to her, but I talked you into believing you
had only dreamt it!

NATALYA. [*Sotto voce to* ANNA.] Some very interesting things are
coming to light!

PRINCE. My dear boy, keep your head! You really frighten me to see
you crying like this. You're quite wrong, believe me. If I must
marry, I am quite prepared to do so—only for pity's sake don't try
and make me say again that it was not a dream.

PAUL. Oh, how shall I be able to convince him now? [*To* MARIA.]
How shall I convince him? You tell me! . . . Oh uncle—uncle!
This is a serious matter, uncle; it may lead to something dreadful
if you don't try and think hard, and remember that it wasn't a
dream at all!

PRINCE. Very well, my dear boy, I'll think hard if you say so. But wait
—just give me time. Let me go back to the beginning. First I saw
my driver, Theophile . . .

PAUL. This is nothing to do with Theophile, uncle!

PRINCE. No, of course it isn't. Let's see now—there was Napoleon;
then we had tea, and a lady came and ate up all the sugar . . .

PAUL. You didn't dream that, uncle. It is what our hostess told you
this afternoon about Natalya Dmitrievna—I heard it through the
door.

NATALYA. What's that, Maria Alexandrovna? You told the prince that
lie? That I stole sugar out of your sugar-bowl? So! I come to your
house to steal sugar, do I?

MARIA. [*Violently.*] Get out of my house! Get out, I say!

NATALYA. Not for the world, Maria Alexandrovna! You dare to say
such things about me! Steal your sugar, do I? I've known for a
long time that you go about with such low stories about me. Sofia
Petrovna has told me often about something of the sort! So I steal
your sugar!

PRINCE. But, mesdames! It was only my dream! How can it matter
what I dreamt?

MARIA. [*Sotto voce.*] The damned cow!

NATALYA. What was that? You dare to call me that? And what are you? At least I have a husband who's right in his head—yours is a congenital idiot!

MARIA. Afanassij! Do you hear her?

PRINCE. [*Mutters—only half-conscious now of what he is talking about.*] Quite! There was a cow in my dream too . . . no, a camel, I think . . . however, I do remember that it had horns!

NATALYA. [*To the* PRINCE.] Are you trying to insult me too? Prince—what do you mean? If I'm a cow, you're an old simpleton—with a wooden leg into the bargain!

PRINCE. What? A wooden leg? I?

NATALYA. Yes! Two most likely—wood or cork! And false teeth too!

MARIA. Yes—and a glass eye!

NATALYA. And corsets instead of ribs!

MARIA. And not a real hair on his head! The old fool even has to stick his mustache on with glue!

PRINCE. [*Vastly astonished.*] Leave me my nose, Maria Stepanova—please let my nose be real! [*To* PAUL.] My dear boy, you did betray me then! You even told them I wore a wig!

PAUL. Uncle!

PRINCE. No, my friend—I really can't stay here any longer! Please take me away. Anywhere! Oh, *quelle société!* How could you bring me to such a place! My God!

MARIA. Idiot! Doddering old fool!

PRINCE. [*With tears in his eyes.*] Oh God! I have quite forgotten why I am here— It'll come back to me in a moment, though! Come, little brother—let's go away, quick! They'll tear me to pieces in another minute. Come—but first I must put down a thought.

MARIA. Get out!

PRINCE. Oh quite—quite! Let's go to a hotel! [*To* SINA.] Adieu, my *charmante enfant.* . . . Only you—only you are good here. Only you. Come, my dear boy! Oh, my God!

[*As the* PRINCE, *leaning on* PAUL'S *arm, moves towards the door,* MARIA *seems to go raving mad. She rages through the room and seems about to assault the company with her fists. Her voice rises to a bellow.*]

MARIA. Get out! Get out! The whole pack of you! Get out!

[SINA *remains motionless in the midst of the tumult. It is as though only the shell of her stood there, as she stands seeming to listen to a sound inaudible to the rest. The door from the out-*

side is suddenly wrenched open. A short conversation is heard, and wild sobbing. Silence falls upon the company in the drawing-room. Even MARIA *stops for an instant in her insane career.* THE OLD WOMAN IN BLACK *appears in the doorway; crying loudly into her handkerchief.* GLAFIRA *is beside her, attempting to hold her back, but* THE OLD WOMAN *pushes her aside and storms into the room.*]

THE OLD WOMAN. My boy! My Vassja! My only child! [*She looks about her, searching for someone.* SINA *has made a step towards her, and signs to the others to stand back.* THE OLD WOMAN *now sees* SINA, *and advances to within an inch of her face. Then she says in a loud voice:*] Murderess!

CURTAIN